Age of Deception

A VOLUME IN THE SERIES

Cornell Studies in Security Affairs

Edited by Austin Carson, Alexander B. Downes, Elizabeth N. Saunders, Paul Staniland, and Caitlin Talmadge

Founding editors: Robert J. Art, Robert Jervis, and Stephen M. Walt

A list of titles in this series is available at cornellpress.cornell.edu.

Age of Deception

Cybersecurity as Secret Statecraft

JON R. LINDSAY

Cornell University Press

Ithaca and London

This book is made available in Open Access with generous support
from the Georgia Institute of Technology.

First published 2025 by Cornell University Press

Librarians: A CIP catalog record for this book is available from the
Library of Congress.

ISBN 978150178321-0 (hardcover)
ISBN 978150178347-0 (paperback)
ISBN 978150178322-7 (pdf)
ISBN 978150178323-4 (epub)

GPSR EU contact: Sam Thornton, Mare Nostrum Group B.V.,
Mauritskade 21D, 1091 GC, Amsterdam, NL, gpsr@mare-nostrum.co.uk.

Contents

Acknowledgments

M. C. Escher's *Eye* is a self-portrait that depicts a skull staring back from the artist's pupil. The effect is unsettling. The viewer stands in the same viewpoint as the artist, who has long since passed away, viewing a precise drawing of a mirror image of the organ of vision, which reflects a shadowy symbol of death. At the center of an infinite regress of reflection and substitution we find our own mortality. It is a fitting cover for a book that reflects on technologies of representation and the dangers they contain. The contest of deception in cyberspace is a mirrored regress of our own devising.

Years ago, before the plague, I had the hubris to tell my wife that this book would not take as long to write as had *Information Technology and Military Power*. I told her I would just tease out the cyber implications of information practice, the subject of my previous book with Cornell University Press. I told her I would just revise a few of my articles about cybersecurity, write some transitions, and staple it all together. But then I ended up rethinking everything, researching new cases, writing a brand-new book, and rewriting it several times. I dedicate this book to Heather, who has loved me through all my self-deception.

Many people helped to make this a better book. Austin Carson and Erica Lonergan provided extensive feedback on manuscripts that were not as mature as I had thought. John Ferris, Jenna Jordan, Nadiya Kostyuk, Michael Poznansky, Joshua Rovner, Rebecca Slayton, and Rachel Whitlark offered generous advice at a book workshop at Georgia Tech. Constructive comments on early drafts of chapters were also provided by Deborah Avant, Gil Baram, Charles Freilich, Milton Mueller, Mark Raymond, and Gavin Wilde. I received able research assistance and feedback from Zuoqi

Dong, Jinhui Jiao, Valerie Kindarji, Kangkyu Lee, Steven Loleski, and Lennart Maschmeyer. Students in my seminar on cybersecurity at Georgia Tech provided an invaluable sounding board. This book also draws on conversations with and inspiration from Emanuel Adler, Michael Bailey, Dennis Broeders, Myriam Dunn Cavelty, Carmen Cheung, Ron Deibert, Florian Egloff, Stacie Goddard, Avi Goldfarb, Emily Goldman, Juan-Andres Guerrero-Saade, Richard Harknett, Jason Healey, Robert Jervis, Lucas Kello, Monica Kello, Austin Long, Ryder McKeown, Ryan Shandler, Max Smeets, Janice Stein, Peter Swire, Brandon Valeriano, Jelena Vicic, Michael Warner, and J. D. Work. I would especially like to thank the staff at Cornell University Press—Jacqulyn Teoh, Katlyn Bond, Susan Specter, Eric Levy, Karen Hwa, and others—who guided this book to completion. Enid Zafran completed the index. Any flaws that remain are either my fault or a complicated ruse.

Anticipations of this book are scattered throughout a decade of publications on cybersecurity. Chapter 3 contains faint vestiges of Jon R. Lindsay, "Restrained by Design: The Political Economy of Cybersecurity," *Digital Policy, Regulation and Governance* 19, no. 6 (2017): 493–514. Portions of chapter 4 appeared in Jon R. Lindsay, "Abducted by Hackers: Using the Case of Bletchley Park to Construct a Theory of Intelligence Performance That Generalizes to Cybersecurity," *Journal of Peace Research* 61, no. 1 (2024): 87–102. Chapter 5 radically reconsiders Jon R. Lindsay, "Stuxnet and the Limits of Cyber Warfare," *Security Studies* 22, no. 3 (2013): 365–404. Ideas about deterrence in this book are developed more fully in Erik Gartzke and Jon R. Lindsay, *Elements of Deterrence: Strategy, Technology, and Complexity in Global Politics* (Oxford University Press, 2024).

Finally, I thank family and friends for supporting the odyssey of this book (beset by monsters and crying for home). I am deeply grateful to Heather, Lily, and Ellie (waiting for me to finish a quest) for far more than I can express. I'll take the infinite regress of love over cyberspace any day. I promise that the next book will not take as long . . .

Introduction

Intelligence Now

On December 8, 2020, the chief executive officer of the cybersecurity firm Mandiant announced, "We were attacked by a highly sophisticated threat actor, one whose discipline, operational security, and techniques lead us to believe it was a state-sponsored attack."[1] Five days later, Mandiant and Microsoft released coordinated reports on an espionage campaign targeting SolarWinds, a company that provided network management services to Mandiant and many other organizations.[2] SolarWinds disclosed that eighteen thousand customers were exposed to the threat.[3] Over a hundred of them—including the US Departments of Defense, State, Justice, Energy, Commerce, and Treasury—experienced follow-on intrusions. The president of Microsoft called the breach "the largest and most sophisticated attack the world has ever seen" and estimated that it required "more than 1,000" engineers.[4]

About a month later, the US government publicly declared that the intrusion was "likely Russian in origin."[5] Politicians quickly seized on military language to describe it. Senator Mitt Romney said that "a cyber-hack of this nature is really the modern equivalent of almost Russian bombers reportedly flying undetected over the entire country."[6] Senator Dick Durbin called it "virtually a declaration of war," and Senator Marco Rubio demanded that "America must retaliate, and not just with sanctions."[7] President-elect Joseph Biden even declared, "I will not stand idly by in the face of cyberassaults on our nation."[8] His administration later accused the Russian Foreign Intelligence Service (SVR), "also known as APT29, Cozy Bear, and The Dukes," of hacking SolarWinds and five other software vendors.[9]

But Biden responded with economic and diplomatic sanctions, not military retaliation.[10] The SVR was an intelligence agency, not a military unit. Its goal was data, not destruction. Commercial firms, rather than the US military, played a leading role in incident response. Spying is hardly unusual in politics, of course, but the scope and scale of the SolarWinds breach were discomfiting. According to the chief of cybersecurity at the National Security Agency (NSA), "We observed, absolutely, espionage. . . . But what is concerning is from that platform, from the broad scale of availability of the access they achieved, there's the opportunity to do other things, and that's something we can't tolerate."[11]

Cyberspace raises hard questions about national security. How dangerous are cyber threats? Does cyberspace transform war? Do hackers shift the balance of power? Why are critical systems so insecure in the first place? Has commercial industry become the front line of national defense? And how should governments respond to the mounting threat? Answers to such questions vary depending on whether we interpret network intrusions as warfare or as something else. This book reconsiders cybersecurity through the lens of *secret statecraft*.

The Reinvention of Secret Statecraft

Secret statecraft is the use of organized deception for strategic advantage. It is logically distinct from the organized violence of military statecraft or the organized commerce of economic statecraft, even as they are often mixed in practice. While statecraft in general is the art of using what you have to get what you want, secret statecraft is the art of using what *others* have to get what you want. Political actors may use military or diplomatic means to pursue their goals directly, or they may use intelligence or covert action to pursue them indirectly. Secret statecraft enables actors to gather information about threats and opportunities, advance political interests without provoking a fight, or fight more efficiently if they must.

Secret statecraft is not new. Ancient strategists like China's Sunzi and India's Kautilya commend the use of espionage, subversion, and counterintelligence. The strategy of deception is even older if we consider animal mimicry and disguise. But deceit is flourishing today as never before. Secret agents have never been able to steal so much data. Con artists have never been able to fool so many marks. Commercial firms have never encountered so many threats. Digital networks enable spies to steal sensitive data, saboteurs to disrupt critical systems, and disinformation to flood the internet, all at unprecedented scale. In this sense, the information age is also the age of deception.

But we should not deceive ourselves. The discourse of cybersecurity is full of hyperbole and confusion, as seen in the responses to SolarWinds. Pundits regularly warn of cyberwar, but the reality is more complicated. In the empirical record we see little evidence of catastrophic digital disruption. There is instead a profusion of intrusion—mostly cybercrime, espionage, and disinformation. The existential threats of cyberwar are exaggerated, but nevertheless, governments and companies are still worried about cybersecurity, and rightly so. Digital technologies are vital for economic and military power, after all.

This situation is uncomfortably ambiguous. Network intrusions are at once a normal feature of global politics and an enduring source of dread, threatening yet tolerated, provocative yet restrained, alluring yet frustrating, neither peaceful nor warlike. I argue that this ambiguity is inevitable. Secret statecraft is a form of competition that exploits cooperation. Spies take advantage of trusting colleagues, and spyware masquerades as trusted software. If we want more social trust, then we invite more abuses of trust. The common protocols and shared systems of cyberspace embody a remarkable degree of cooperation, so cyberspace in turn enables a remarkable degree of deception.

Cyberspace dramatically expands the scope and scale of secret statecraft, but this has countervailing implications. Cooperation-enabled competition is a double-edged sword. Threats have more places to hide in complex systems, but they can make more mistakes. Intruders can connect to more targets at lower risk, but intrusions depend on the willing assistance of unwitting victims. Saboteurs can inflict damage by remote control, but secrecy and anonymity undermine the credibility of political signals. Deception can provide benefits at reduced cost, but overreliance on deception risks losing benefits completely. These trade-offs have important implications for understanding the impact of cyber operations on international security. In short, cyberspace expands not only the opportunities of secret statecraft but also its liabilities.

Intelligence Performance at the Operational Level

It is tempting to assume that technology transforms politics. It is widely believed, for example, that it is easy for hackers to exploit critical systems—cheaply, rapidly, remotely, and effectively. As a result, offense is getting easier while defense is getting harder. Offense dominance in turn creates asymmetric advantages for terrorists, rogue states, and weaker actors. Hacking thus provides an efficient offset to military power, with dramatic implications for world politics. These technological arguments are plausible, but they are incomplete.

The political impact of technology usually depends on social context, which is complex, contingent, and changeable. The overarching theme of this book, accordingly, is that institutions both enable and constrain secret statecraft. Institutions are the social and technical means for improving information, lowering transaction costs, and solving collective action problems. Governments, cultures, organizations, and software systems are all sociotechnical institutions in this sense. Secret statecraft in turn works by exploiting or subverting cooperative institutions for competitive gain.

Secret statecraft is not simply deception, moreover, but *organized* deception. Effective intelligence and covert action depend on spy agencies, counterintelligence units, criminal networks, and security companies. All such deception specialists are organizational institutions that exploit collective institutions. I describe the working practice of deception specialists as *intelligence performance*, which is the operational implementation of secret statecraft.

The operational level of intelligence is analogous to the operational level of war. Scholars have studied military effectiveness at this level extensively, but the literature on intelligence performance is less developed. Just as military campaigns plan and direct tactical engagements to achieve strategic objectives in a war, intelligence campaigns cultivate and employ sensitive sources and methods to advance strategic interests, in peacetime or war. In intelligence as in war, the operational level shapes, but does not determine, strategic outcomes. Militaries can win battles while governments lose wars. Yet militaries that fail on the battlefield make it harder for leaders to achieve their objectives. Leaders can likewise misunderstand or misuse the secrets that spy services steal. Yet spies that fail to gain access to valuable targets make it harder for states to gain an information advantage.

The SolarWinds hackers ran a successful intelligence campaign for most of 2020. They subverted a software supply chain to create and maintain a backdoor into over a hundred organizations. They used this secret channel to collect a lot of data, and in principle they might have used the same channel to inject data or disrupt functionality. But the Russian operation was not perfect. As we shall see, a few missteps compromised the whole campaign. It is entirely possible, even likely, that the data that Russia did collect from sprawling US bureaucracies yielded little intelligence of value. Russian policymakers, furthermore, may not have received or acted on any of it. Yet at the same time, Moscow would have a hard time learning about the internals of a dozen US agencies without some sort of intelligence access.

While intelligence can be used, misinterpreted, or ignored, secret access to targets is a necessary first step to advantage. By gaining and maintaining persistent information channels, deception specialists can extract or inject information. They also must prevent competing specialists from doing the same. Information advantages derived thereby may help leaders to identify threats, create opportunities, target resources, finesse trade-offs, and generally make better decisions. Intelligence performance may not be sufficient for strategic advantage, but it is necessary for organized deception.

This book develops an institutional theory of intelligence performance and applies it to prominent cyber campaigns. After chapter 1 defines the concept of secret statecraft, chapter 2 argues that its operational implementation depends on two conditions: *vulnerable institutions* and *clandestine organization*. The former refers to institutions shared between the intruder and its target, while the latter refers to institutions that the intruder can control by itself. These conditions matter in any historical era, but they are becoming more complex in cyberspace. They also apply not only to intelligence collection but also to covert action. A general implication is that offensive advantage and strategic stability in cyberspace are contingent on institutional context.

A Century of Russian Spies

To convey the basic intuitions of this theory, let's consider two cases of Russian espionage nearly a century apart. The Russian SVR, responsible for the SolarWinds operation, is a historical descendent of the Soviet Committee for State Security (KGB). It may be helpful to compare the SVR's most famous hack with the KGB's most famous spy: Kim Philby.

The Soviets recruited H. A. R. Philby—who went by the nickname "Kim" after Kipling's famous operative—in the mid-1930s. Philby and four other Cambridge graduates known as the "Cambridge Five" were recruited by a savvy "illegal" in London; he appealed to the young men's Communist sympathies and promised them adventure.[12] Philby went on to join the British Secret Intelligence Service (SIS, a.k.a. MI6) in World War II, head the British intelligence mission in the United States, and gain the confidence of the Central Intelligence Agency (CIA). He was even considered for the role of chief of SIS, but he was a KGB agent the entire time.

The cases of Philby and SolarWinds share several similarities. Philby was a mole in SIS, an organization designed to enhance national security. The SVR exploited a backdoor in Orion, a network service trusted to install cybersecurity patches. The KGB used Philby to learn what Western agencies knew about Russian activities. The SVR accessed Mandiant's red-teaming and network-monitoring tools that were designed to counter Russian threats.[13] Both were, in effect, counter-counterintelligence operations. These cases also contrast in important ways, which I will discuss later. First I will focus on two common conditions for intelligence performance.

VULNERABLE INSTITUTIONS

The basic condition for the possibility of deception is *vulnerable institutions*. This refers to the operating environment for intelligence operations. Institutions are most vulnerable to exploitation when they are well connected and their monitoring and enforcement functions are flawed. Flawed monitoring enables threats to hide. Flawed enforcement provides access to targets.

Deception works by exploiting the willing but unwitting assistance of the deceived. The Cambridge Five took advantage of the collegial culture of Western intelligence. The SolarWinds campaign took advantage of widespread trust in software supply chains. Both Philby's confidence games and the SVR's social engineering relied on gullible human personnel and lax security procedures. The SVR further exploited technical design flaws and software features that SolarWinds and Microsoft developers had created of their own free will.

Both operations were long cons. The KGB infiltrated agents into British agencies, and the SVR infiltrated tainted code into SolarWinds' customers. Over a period of many years, the Soviets recruited the Cambridge Five and encouraged them to advance through the ranks of British intelligence. Philby's status in the British establishment and his background in wartime service gave him impeccable bona fides. He even served as a British counterintelligence officer targeting Russian spies, providing perfect cover for meeting Russian handlers.[14] Philby knew what his opponents were looking for, so he could produce credible signals of trustworthiness. His colleagues unwittingly helped by overlooking suspicious behavior, rationalizing numerous red flags, and even vouching for Philby's character as suspicions arose.

The Russians first gained access to the SolarWinds software development environment as early as January 2019, via a compromised VPN account.[15] They spent a year studying the Orion network management service and running test builds. Then in February 2020, they dropped in a malware file (labeled "Sunspot" by CrowdStrike) that hijacked the build process to inject a subtly modified library file (.dll) to create a backdoor in Orion ("Sunburst"); according to a CrowdStrike analysis, the "developers invested a lot of effort to ensure the code was properly inserted and remained undetected."[16] This backdoored component was digitally signed with a SolarWinds certificate, so it appeared completely legitimate to customers who received Orion updates. Sunburst remained dormant on victim networks for two weeks or more as a security precaution, and then it established communication to the SVR via remote command-and-control servers and performed network reconnaissance.[17] The SVR selected a subset of victims to install another backdoor ("Teardrop" or "Raindrop"), which in turn installed a popular penetration testing tool ("Cobalt Strike").

While the KGB and SVR used radically different tradecraft, there are some familiar echoes. Much as Philby was left in place for a while to increase his credibility, the SVR was patient in developing and deploying its exploits. Much as the KGB communicated indirectly with Philby through cutouts and dead drops to protect their most valuable agent, the SVR worked through a staged operation that insulated their most sensitive exploit (Sunburst) from discovery. Much as Philby subverted organizational resources in SIS, Russian hackers evaded security features on victim networks and leveraged legitimate administrative functionality (i.e., "living off the land").

CLANDESTINE ORGANIZATION

The second condition for intelligence performance is *clandestine organization*. Professional spy services provide a platform for planning and managing sensitive intrusions while mitigating counterintelligence risks. They must have the capacity to balance administration and adaptation while exercising discretion to protect their operation.

Organizational deception specialists like the KGB and SVR are repositories of operational expertise and administrative capacity. KGB handlers provided training, guidance, and assistance to the Cambridge Five, although there was often friction between Philby and Soviet residents.[18] The SVR likewise drew on deep expertise and ample resources in its Solar-Winds campaign. Both organizations had analytical capacity and (occasionally strained) relationships with Russian leadership. Such clandestine infrastructure is valuable yet fragile. Compromise to hostile counterintelligence can result in the loss of sensitive sources and methods, or accesses and exploits. Compromise can also invite retaliation, so it is useful to have the protection of a powerful state, as the KGB and SVR did.

Deception specialists have incentives to practice operational security and exercise restraint. Weak administration or overexuberant operations can undermine intelligence performance. Operators must be careful because accidents and indiscretions are often the beginning of the end. Philby and the SVR each took elaborate security measures to throw off suspicion. And it worked in each case, for a while. Despite the skill of Russian spy agencies, however, Philby's treachery and the Sunburst backdoor were eventually compromised. That's why we can talk about them today. In each case, small mistakes triggered an investigation that eventually unraveled the conspiracy.

Philby's luck ran out when the NSA started decrypting KGB traffic because of Soviet misuse of one-time pad procedures.[19] The Venona trove of KGB agent-handling communications drew attention to the indiscreet behavior of two members of the Cambridge Five. But Philby had access to Venona as well, so he was able to warn Donald Maclean and Guy Burgess to defect to the Soviet Union in 1951. As suspicion settled on Philby too, SIS terminated his access to classified material, and he endured serious investigations before being exonerated by the British prime minister. After the Venona break, Philby and his Soviet handlers became so preoccupied with playing defense that he was effectively useless as a collection asset. As more incriminating evidence accumulated, Philby finally defected in 1963 to the Soviet Union, where he spent the rest of his life as a consultant and propaganda tool for the KGB.[20]

The SVR was also spooked by emails from the US Department of Justice during the internal evaluation of Orion.[21] The SVR removed the Sunburst backdoor from the Orion build server on June 4, 2020, likely as a security precaution. While the Russians could not, therefore, install Sunburst on any new victims, they could keep exploiting those who had it. But then on November 10, a routine security alert piqued the interest of a security analyst at Mandiant. An employee had enrolled a new Samsung phone into his VPN account from Florida, but his old iPhone was still logged in from another state. This anomaly triggered an investigation that led to the discovery of a disk image at SolarWinds containing the altered .dll (Sunburst); such files were normally deleted during the build process, but an automatic cleanup process had terminated abnormally.[22] By December, an ad hoc coalition of security firms and government agencies had attributed responsibility for the SolarWinds intrusion to the SVR and started remediating victim networks.

The offensive advantages of stealth and subterfuge are fragile. The KGB tempted fate by running a spy in the heart of British intelligence, and the SVR hacked one of the world's leading commercial threat-intelligence companies (Mandiant). It was only a matter of time until someone got suspicious. A small compromise and accidents in each case led to an accumulation of clues, an unraveling of operations, attribution of culpability to the Russians, and implementation of countermeasures. As counterintelligence organizations were alerted and energized, the advantage in the intelligence contest shifted from offense to defense. Clandestine organization became more visible, collective institutions became less vulnerable, and persistent intelligence access became less feasible.

COMPLEXITY AND COUNTERINTELLIGENCE

There are important contrasts between these cases. The KGB used good old-fashioned espionage tradecraft to run an agent in a rival spy agency. The SVR relied on advanced technical methods to corrupt a global software supply chain used by both public and private organizations. Philby had to get up close and personal with the victims he betrayed, which limited his access to only a few intelligence agencies. Philby also faced interrogation, incarceration, or worse if he was caught. SVR hackers, by contrast, were able to access and exploit manifold more organizations without putting any human operators in danger. A single upload from a Cobalt Strike infection on a compromised network could exfiltrate more data than the Cambridge Five smuggled out in a decade.

More potential for intelligence exploitation, however, entails more counterintelligence exposure. Russia leveraged commercial software to access thousands of targets, potentially, but it took only one of them (Mandiant) to doom the entire campaign. Evidence of Russian compromise drew threat intelligence firms and the US intelligence community to SolarWinds like antibodies to an infection. Companies like Microsoft quickly provided detailed mitigation advice (and advertised their security products in the process).[23] While Orion and Office software provided a common vector to access customers downstream, the same infrastructure enabled patching and remediation. Common threats, once discovered, became easier to mitigate for everyone. Digital connectivity expanded the opportunities of exploitation at scale, but a wider conspiracy made it more likely that attackers would make mistakes, leave clues, alert defenders, and be countered at scale.

Greater scope and scale also tend to shorten operational timelines. This is a blessing and a curse. While the SVR had access to more victims through Sunburst than the KGB did through Philby, its technical access was short-lived. The KGB was able to exploit social vulnerabilities in SIS for years on end. Philby betrayed his friends for decades, but the Sunburst backdoor in Orion was viable for just two months. Even after the Venona break, Philby weathered the storm for a dozen years before defecting. In order to control reputational damage, the British government did not publicly acknowledge Philby's treachery until he defected in 1963.[24] This tacit collusion between rivals enabled the KGB to keep Philby in place for twelve years after suspicions first emerged, even though he was useless as a collection asset. British agencies took years to cobble together a coherent response to the embarrassing incident.

By contrast, defenders noted issues with Orion within weeks or months of the corrupted release. The SVR remained hidden in Mandiant's network resources ("living off the land") for only a few months. Mandiant went public a month after receiving clear indications of Russian penetration. The US government, as declared in a statement by the FBI, quickly "formed a Cyber Unified Coordination Group (UCG) to coordinate a whole-of-government response."[25] There were processes and relationships in place to coordinate public and private defenses that did not exist in the early 2010s, and certainly not during the early Cold War.

The SolarWinds incident also had a major commercial dimension that was wholly absent in the Philby case. Business entities like Mandiant, Microsoft, CrowdStrike, and Symantec played a leading role in detecting, investigating, and responding to a state intelligence campaign targeting a commercial supply chain to infiltrate multiple state and nonstate organizations. Many years of Russian and Chinese cyber intrusions into government and corporate networks, moreover, had encouraged greater coordination between the US intelligence community and the multibillion-dollar global cybersecurity industry.

Chapter 3 explores the ambiguous complexity of cyberspace in detail. I explain how historical design choices in the early internet era improved collective institutions for both legitimate users and malicious threats.

Efficient packet-switching networks were administratively and commercially attractive because they improved communication and computation at scale. This supercharged the global economy. Unfortunately, vendors often neglected security in the race to capture lucrative network effects. The internet connected millions of gullible minds and vulnerable machines, and it also enabled hackers to hide their tracks. But this complex data infrastructure was not an unmitigated boon for the offense. Software dependencies and organizational frictions also became liabilities for operational security and control. The vulnerable institutions of cyberspace became more pervasive but more complicated. Clandestine organizations became more capable but more exposed.

POLITICS AND PERFORMANCE

The conditions that enable intelligence performance can change, even when technology remains the same. The KGB and SVR were able to conduct successful intelligence operations only as long as both conditions were met. Even then, intelligence performance had only an indirect impact on politics. When conditions changed, intelligence performance degraded.

The SVR's technical tradecraft was more sophisticated, but Philby's achievements are more infamous. I expect that we will still be talking about Philby decades from now, long after SolarWinds is forgotten in the noise of countless other cyber incidents. The institutional conditions for intelligence performance were permissive for a much longer time for Philby than in SolarWinds. If the SVR was an advanced persistent threat (APT), then Philby was less advanced but more persistent.

Much about the SolarWinds episode remains shrouded in secrecy, of course. But there is no public evidence that the SVR found anything of value in all the data it vacuumed up. If valuable intelligence was collected, and if analysts understood what they found, it is far from certain that Russian decision-makers acted on any of it. A Mandiant executive went so far as to describe the operation as "a hell of an expensive operation for very little yield."[26] SolarWinds is famous for demonstrating the vulnerability of supply chains, not the political utility of intelligence. The ensuing policy panic was relatively short-lived.

Philby's treachery, by contrast, led to the capture and execution of hundreds of Western agents.[27] He may have contributed to the failure of CIA operations in Ukraine and Albania, although the Soviets already knew about Albania from other sources.[28] Philby undermined Western intelligence operations, harmed Anglo-American intelligence collaboration, and heightened paranoia. Philby's betrayal was an especially bitter blow to James Jesus Angleton, the CIA counterintelligence chief who had personally vouched for Philby's trustworthiness. Angleton spent the rest of his career searching for moles in a "wilderness of mirrors," imposing onerous counterintelligence controls on the CIA.[29] Unlike SolarWinds, however, Philby did not spark general panic about Russian sabotage. Russian spies may even have had a stabilizing effect, ironically enough, by enabling the superpowers to quietly compete without destroying the world.

The campaign studies in this book illustrate different configurations of the intelligence performance conditions. Chapter 4 examines another famous example of intelligence collection: Bletchley Park, the British code-breaking agency in World War II. For years on end, the institutions of German operational security were vulnerable, and Bletchley Park was a sophisticated organization. This lucky combination provided an indirect information advantage for Allied military operations. Signals intelligence (SIGINT) from Bletchley Park made it possible, for example, to validate the credibility of British double agents (offensive counterintelligence), who in turn provided disinformation to German leadership (covert action) about the location of Allied landings on D-Day (military support). Intelligence thus improved both operational efficiency (economy and precision of force) and strategic effectiveness (gaining lodgment on the Continent). And yet, Bletchley Park's phenomenal success still made only an indirect contribution to military outcomes in World War II.

Not only is Bletchley Park an intrinsically important case in intelligence history, but it also anticipated many features of cybersecurity. Civilian academics and engineers at Bletchley Park invented some of the world's first electronic computing machines, and they pioneered SIGINT at scale. They developed a new approach to intercepting, deciphering, and analyzing German radio traffic (intelligence collection) that was encrypted with machines like Enigma (defensive counterintelligence). The case of Bletchley Park is also better documented than most modern cyber campaigns, which remain cloaked in secrecy. This makes it useful for revealing the working details of intelligence performance, and for understanding why things are even more complicated in cyberspace. Even in the best possible case of intelligence success, nonetheless, we still find that strategic advantage is highly contingent.

Covert Action

The cases of SolarWinds, Kim Philby, and Bletchley Park are all examples of espionage. Yet the same secret channels that can be used for gathering information may also be used for influence or disruption. Much of the hype around cyberwar turns on this possibility. Just as a spy can become a saboteur, spyware can inject malicious instructions. But the point often lost in worries about cyber warfare is that the same institutional complexities that bedevil espionage also complicate covert action in cyberspace.

Because covert action shares a similar operational foundation with collection, the same theory of intelligence performance can be used to explain it. I argue that the same two conditions that enable espionage (vulnerable institutions and clandestine organization) matter for sabotage and subversion as well. While chapter 4 (on espionage) demonstrates the beneficial effects of meeting both conditions, chapters 5 (on sabotage) and 6 (on subversion) show what happens when either condition is not met. Another contribution of this book, therefore, is to provide a common framework for interpreting both intelligence and covert action, by any means and in any era.

SABOTAGE AT SCALE

There are two main types of covert action. The first is *sabotage*—the use of deception to disrupt or destroy equipment or functionality. The second is *subversion*—the use of deception to influence or manipulate human beliefs and behavior. Traditional examples of sabotage, broadly construed, include CIA efforts to arm resistance movements in Ukraine and Albania, which Philby disclosed to the KGB. The latent possibility of sabotage at scale was what made SolarWinds seem so alarming. The SVR's goal was espionage, not sabotage, but the Russian Main Intelligence Directorate (GRU) has been more active in this space, as I discuss in this book's conclusion.[30]

Chapter 5 revisits the most famous case of cyber-enabled sabotage to date. The Stuxnet attack on Iran's nuclear program has been extensively studied, but it is worth revisiting in light of new evidence and interpretation. Well over a decade later, there are still not many serious cyber-physical attacks in the historical record, so it is helpful to understand why Stuxnet is an outlier in this regard. Indeed, the most famous case of cyber warfare to date is not really a case of warfare at all; Stuxnet is better understood as a case of covert action.

It is well known that Stuxnet was designed to subtly disrupt centrifuge operations. Its architects exercised discretion to protect their exquisite capabilities, and its sabotage effects were limited by design. Stuxnet was accidentally compromised nonetheless. In the end, cyber sabotage caused only minor, temporary disruption. Worse, Iranian enrichment increased significantly after Stuxnet. From this perspective, Stuxnet was not very successful.

But we now know that the forensic timeline of Stuxnet-relevant artifacts spans two decades. This complicated pattern of interlinked clandestine operations, conducted by and targeting many different actors, is suggestive of a chronic covert contest between the United States, Israel, Iran, and others. Stuxnet, moreover, was a means not only of sabotage but also of secret diplomacy. The United States used collaboration on Stuxnet to help dissuade Israel from starting a preventive war. Stuxnet's strategic target was not just an adversary but also a headstrong ally. Stuxnet also bought time for nuclear diplomacy with Iran, which ultimately curtailed enrichment more effectively than cyber sabotage. Instead of a reckless escalation on the road to war, Stuxnet was a quiet intervention that helped to avoid a war.

For the theory of intelligence performance, Stuxnet showcases the implications of mixed conditions. The United States and Israel had to negotiate physical and logical barriers to access the vulnerable institutions of their target. They drew on extensive clandestine organization to do so, yet divergent goals in the coalition ultimately undermined the operation. Iran kept on enriching, but Israel did not launch a preventive war. Mixed conditions led to mixed results.

SUBVERSION AT SCALE

While sabotage hacks machines, subversion hacks minds. Russia practiced subversion with mixed effects throughout the Cold War. For example, the KGB fabricated news stories and grassroots organizations throughout the Cold War to try to manipulate Western public opinion. Cyberspace today is awash with disinformation, forgeries, deepfakes, astroturfing, and other forms of digital manipulation.

Chapter 6 turns to the most extensively investigated cyber campaign to date: Russia's interference in the 2016 US presidential election. This episode transformed the cybersecurity debate. While security professionals previously focused just on technical threats, the US media ecosystem was wide open to foreign influence. The condition of vulnerable institutions was easily met in this case. The condition of clandestine organization, however, was not met to the same degree. The extent of Russian meddling was discovered and publicly disclosed in the summer of 2016. More importantly, the scale of foreign content was dwarfed by similar messaging from the Republican campaign and other domestic sources. Russia was messaging a receptive and to some extent complicit audience.

Russia may or may not have altered the outcome of the election (there is still no scholarly consensus on this question), but it certainly became a lightning rod in US politics. The Russian campaign also poses a puzzle for any theory of deception: How does secret statecraft work when organized deception becomes an open secret? This question takes us back to the fundamental importance of social institutions. While technology can supply misleading content at scale, the political demand for disinformation is often more important. In this case, if the Russians achieved their goal of electing Donald Trump, they do not necessarily deserve the credit. The political demand for disinformation trumped the technical supply. The domestic drivers of disinformation became even more apparent in the 2020 and 2024 elections, which were even more polarized.

The 2016 election showcases a different mixture of conditions for the theory of intelligence performance. Whereas Stuxnet is a case of sophisticated organizational capacity in a complicated institutional environment, 2016 features a more dependent organization and wide-open institutions. In the former mixture, persistent intrusions are still possible, but operations become much more complex. In the latter mixture, successful outcomes are also possible, but clandestine organizations are more likely to lose control of their operation.

Strategic Competition

Great-power politics in the twenty-first century is characterized by dangerous security competition amid deep economic interdependence. This pattern is most pronounced in the relationship between the United States and China, which are both military rivals and major trading partners. Leading theories of war and peace point in opposite directions in this case, suggesting that growing military challenges should be destabilizing while economic ties should be stabilizing. These same conditions—competition amid cooperation—are also ideal for secret statecraft. No wonder that cybersecurity is so fraught in US-China relations.

The concept of *cyber power* refers to the use of information technology in different facets of national strategy. Chinese cyber power works by repurposing US cyber power, in effect using liberal technologies to build illiberal applications. While chapter 3 shows how the US created the internet, chapter 7 shows how the United States' leading rival took advantage of it. Beijing has embraced cyber espionage abroad as a tool of economic development. Chinese strategists also see cyber warfare as a key to victory in future war. Systematic censorship and surveillance at home bolsters the regime's control over its own population. Chapter 7 thus revisits the themes of cybersecurity (chapter 3), espionage (chapter 4), sabotage (chapter 5), and subversion (chapter 6) in a different national context.

There are several articles of conventional wisdom about Chinese cyber power: (1) alternative Chinese standards and authoritarian governance will undermine the functionality of the internet, (2) rampant Chinese cyber espionage provides a significant unfair advantage in economic competition, (3) cyber warfare provides the Chinese military with a dangerous asymmetric advantage over the US military, and (4) internet censorship and surveillance have locked down Chinese society. There are grains of truth in all four claims, but the reality is complicated by the institutional nature of secret statecraft.

Institutional changes at both the international and domestic levels are affecting China's vulnerable institutions and clandestine organizations. Attention to institutional context thus suggests some alternative interpretations about Chinese cyber power: (1) the Western-dominated internet ecosystem of technical protocols and governance institutions is resilient; (2) rampant cyber espionage does not translate directly into competitive advantage; (3) cyber warfare depends on a dynamic offense-defense balance that does not necessarily favor the Chinese military over the United States; (4) Chinese censorship is porous by design, which, when combined with regime security forces, enhances political control. In short, contingent institutional context conditions cyber power.

China has been able to use information technology to gain some advantages in areas where it has made complementary institutional investments to support cyber operations. But China still struggles in areas where enabling institutions are missing or dysfunctional. The Chinese military aspires to exploit cyberspace in war, but precisely because institutions are most fraught in war, the challenges of information friction and cross-domain coordination loom large. The US military has underappreciated institutional advantages in this respect. The conclusion of this book will return to these themes.

Demystifying Cybersecurity

This book pushes back on the hype about cyber warfare, but I do not minimize the importance of cyberspace in global politics. Students of cybersecurity must chart a middle way between the Scylla of exaggeration and the Charybdis of complacency. I do so by viewing cybersecurity, to paraphrase Clausewitz, as secret statecraft by other means. This perspective has implications for the way we think about advantage, intelligence, and institutions in international relations (IR). This section summarizes some contributions of this book in these areas.

THE CONTINGENCY OF ADVANTAGE

The five years between the SolarWinds breach and this book's publication is an eternity in cyber time. If technology alone determines advantages in cyberspace, then this book will be of little use. But if cyber advantage depends on enduring institutional factors as well, then read on. Because the conditions of intelligence performance were relevant long before the internet (e.g., for Kim Philby and Bletchley Park), I expect them to be relevant long after the quantum internet (should that ever be built). This book is about the enduring institutional dynamics of cybersecurity in any era.

An institutional perspective on cybersecurity calls into question a number of popular assumptions about it. We often hear that cyberspace enables anonymous hackers to inflict great harm at large scale with little cost or risk. Offense is said to dominate defense when it is relatively less costly to attack than to defend. Information technology seems to reduce the costs of projecting power through cyberspace while raising the costs of mitigating threats. Digitally dependent democracies have an especially large attack surface. Cyberspace seems like a disaster in this regard.

But the Philby and SolarWinds comparison shows that a greater quantity of technical operations does not simply translate into a greater quality of intelligence. Public and private cyber defenses create access barriers and counterintelligence capacity that complicate offensive cyber operations. Threat actors must deal with many challenges to conduct controlled infiltrations into hostile organizations to achieve specific strategic objectives, all while protecting costly investments in sensitive sources and methods from professional deception detectors such as SIS or Mandiant.

The organizational requirements for managing complex operations with complex risks create barriers to entry. Offensive cyber operations require more than a hacker in a hoodie in the basement. This implies that assumptions about asymmetric advantage in cyberspace are backward. Intelligence agencies are most likely to conduct the best intelligence operations. State spy services such as the SVR and NSA have important advantages over relatively less capable targets, especially the civil society actors they exploit.

In short, technology does not determine advantage by itself. The institutional conditions of secret statecraft are both socially and technically constructed. They have a path-dependent history, and they change as attackers and defenders make different choices. Institutional contingency is especially salient in cybersecurity because the institutions that enable deception are incredibly complex. Precisely because offensive advantage in cyberspace is so contingent, threat actors must be more sophisticated in order to manage contingencies.

THE REINVENTION OF INTELLIGENCE

Cybersecurity is better understood as an evolution in intelligence affairs than as a revolution in military affairs. This in no way minimizes the importance of cyber competition. On the contrary, it reveals an underappreciated dimension of international politics. There are important logical differences between warcraft and spycraft. Soldiers break down enemy doors, but spies trick victims into opening them. Unfortunately, the IR field has long neglected the study of intelligence. Fortunately, IR scholars are now paying more attention to the dark arts. This book contributes to a growing literature on political secrecy by using cybersecurity to theorize intelligence in general.

Intelligence and counterintelligence are ancient practices, but cyberspace makes them more feasible, prevalent, visible, and complicated. Global information infrastructure embodies a high degree of overt cooperation, and this in turn enables a lot more covert competition. Intelligence contests leverage more technical tradecraft, at unprecedented scale, with greater involvement of private actors.

Commercial vendors and network operators build and maintain the vulnerable institutions that host digital intrusions. Nation-state spy agencies like the SVR and NSA target commercial firms like SolarWinds and Microsoft, while commercial intelligence firms like Mandiant and NSOGroup have capabilities that rival those of some government agencies. The cybersecurity industry now acts as first responder to many foreign intrusions. At the same time, some security companies weaken human security by marketing exploits and spy services to authoritarian regimes to target dissidents and journalists. Civil society bears the brunt of cyber exploitation by spy agencies, mercenaries, and criminals alike. Deception has become democratized, for better and worse.

Reinterpreting cybersecurity as intelligence may provoke an allergic reaction in some quarters. Many national security practitioners make strong distinctions between military and intelligence activities. In the United States, for instance, the NSA may be authorized to conduct SIGINT under Title 50 of the US Code, while US Cyber Command is authorized to conduct military reconnaissance in cyberspace under Title 10. Nevertheless, both organizations share the same commander, as of this writing, and they rely on similar capabilities. Military cyber units conduct technical reconnaissance and influence operations that, functionally, are very similar to the collection and covert-action activities of spy agencies. They just conduct them under different legal authorities and in different circumstances.

Something similar can be said about cybersecurity on corporate networks and information assurance on defense networks. They reinvent classic counterintelligence practice. This statement is also likely to provoke an allergic reaction. Practitioners may have good policy reasons to distinguish defensive cyber operations from law enforcement investigations, but from a functional perspective, these activities are all providing protection by deceiving deceivers.

Bureaucratic or legal distinctions between intelligence and cyber warfare, or between counterintelligence and cybersecurity, ultimately tell us more about the historical implementation of institutions than about the enduring essence of strategy. As an IR scholar, my focus is on understanding the underlying political phenomenon. This book is thus about the common functions of various deception specialists and the common strategic logic underlying cybersecurity and intelligence. I affirm the importance of contingent policy distinctions in the implementation of cyber strategy, if only because these distinctions provide resources for deceivers and counterdeceivers in practice. Distinctions in the United States between intelligence and war, moreover, are not as bright as they are for actors elsewhere, such as the Russian SVR and GRU. Clear distinctions are also tricky to maintain in modern war, insofar as battlefield effectiveness and civilian information practice have become more intertwined in the twenty-first century.[31] It is only fitting that practices of deception appear in many guises.

THE SUBVERSION OF LIBERAL ORDER

The theoretical problems of cybersecurity are bigger than cyberspace. If the rise of cybersecurity encourages renewed focus on secret statecraft, then secret statecraft turns classic ideas about institutions upside down. In the liberal tradition of IR, institutions improve cooperation and decrease the risk of war. Collective governance mitigates the dangers of anarchy, commercial trade increases the value of peace, and democratic norms decrease the legitimacy of war. In the world of secret statecraft, however, institutions enable conflict.

As institutions improve cooperation and collective action, they also provide the operating environment for espionage and subversion. The same historical trends that make economic interdependence more attractive to major powers, and that lower the attractiveness of major-power war, are correlated with a burgeoning of espionage and subversion in cyberspace. More complex economic practices enable more complex patterns of deception. Secret statecraft flourishes in the digital infrastructure of globalization; conversely, weakening of liberal order complicates secret statecraft. Put bluntly, institutional peace is the root cause of cyber conflict. This book thus joins a growing body of work on the downsides of liberal international order.

An ironic corollary is that *instability* in cyberspace may also support strategic *stability* in international politics. Threat activity can help security professionals to discover and correct institutional weaknesses. New options for covert action can provide off-ramps on the road to war. Offensive and defensive cyber campaigns become a form of maintenance to preserve the international system. In the shadows of secret statecraft, cooperation leads to conflict, and uncertainty leads to information. Better mutual information about capabilities and interests, in turn, improves strategic stability.

If cybersecurity is good news for *international* security, however, it may be bad news for *human* security. Strong states gain advantages, while weak individuals become more exposed. If cyber insecurity is most likely wherever institutions are most robust, then it should become more salient in domestic politics than in international anarchy. Technical surveillance and counterintelligence become attractive complements to internal security forces. International connectivity enables authoritarian regimes to export domestic control over dissidents abroad.

The reason, in a word, is institutions. Cyber warfare may thus be less relevant for conflict *between* societies, where institutions are weaker, than for conflict *within* them, where institutions are stronger. This is why cyber exploitation is such a scourge for civil society, even as its impact on international politics should not be exaggerated.

Plan of the Book

The overarching theme of this book is that contingent institutional context determines the quality of secret statecraft. I develop arguments and test them across eight chapters divided into two parts. The first part presents the conceptual framework in three chapters. Chapter 1 reviews the literature on cybersecurity and political secrecy and clarifies the distinctive strategic nature of secret statecraft. Chapter 2 moves to the operational level and develops a theory of intelligence performance. Chapter 3 provides an empirical segue by describing the institutional evolution of cybersecurity and its ambiguous implications for intelligence performance.

The second part presents detailed campaign studies of espionage, sabotage, and subversion. The chapters in this part showcase variation in explanatory conditions. Chapter 4 uses the case of Bletchley Park to show how a common institutional environment and a disciplined intelligence agency enabled successful SIGINT throughout World War II. Chapter 5 revisits the seminal case of Stuxnet to show how mixed conditions produced mixed outcomes: A robust organization in a problematic environment was less effective in sabotage but more effective in secret diplomacy. Chapter 6 uses Russia's intervention in the 2016 US election to examine the opposite configuration of mixed conditions: A compromised organization in an open but uncontrollable environment is associated with an inconclusive outcome. Note that the fourth logical combination of conditions—degraded organization in a complicated environment—is illustrated by the counterintelligence compromise of Philby and Solar-Winds described above.

The final two chapters open the aperture to explore cross-cutting themes rather than individual campaigns. Chapter 7 examines Chinese information technology policy, digital espionage, cyber warfare, and internet control. The conclusion brings us up to the end of the Biden administration, which witnessed several major Chinese, Russian, and Israeli cyber campaigns. Many of these events occurred after most of this book was written, which offers a useful test of the concepts in it. I find that ongoing military operations in Lebanon and Ukraine, and preparations for war elsewhere, provide further evidence of the complicated complementarity of deception and warfare, which are based on two very different political logics. The book thus concludes with a synthesis of empirical findings and a discussion of policy implications.

These are boom times for deception. Intelligence threats emerge in the seams between systems, organizations, policies, and jurisdictions. The SVR snuck into the Department of Defense through a commercial software supply chain, and Philby snuck into British intelligence in its haste to expand for the war. The study of cybersecurity falls between the seams of disciplines too. There is much to learn from technical reporting about threat activity, the IR subfields of security studies and political economy, and the interdisciplinary fields of intelligence studies and science and technology studies. Yet none of them are sufficient alone for understanding cybersecurity in global politics. Key insights have yet to be integrated into an accessible synthesis, which is what this book provides.

PART I. THE POLITICAL LOGIC OF DECEPTION

CHAPTER 1

Defining Secret Statecraft

There are two important questions to ask about any technology in international security. First, why do actors expect it to provide political benefits at acceptable costs? Second, how can actors use it in actual operational conditions? These are questions about strategy and operations, respectively.[1] The answers are usually complicated.

Too often, technologists focus only on questions of how, and then only narrowly on technical feasibility. One might assume that a new weapon will revolutionize war, but why do belligerents go to war in the first place? Just because it is scientifically possible to inflict harm under some idealized conditions does not mean that political actors will be willing and able to cause harm in practice. Strategic outcomes depend on political interests, and usable technologies depend on social institutions.

In an earlier era, for example, the theory of strategic bombing did not work out as well as its advocates hoped. Air operations required extensive infrastructure for logistics, training, and planning. Daytime raids were exposed to withering enemy defenses, and nighttime raids could not hit their targets. The enemy populations and industries that were bombed also proved to be more resilient or resolved than expected. Coercion by aerial punishment turned out to be hard to implement and ineffective when feasible. Air power was more useful for other things, such as enabling land warfare.[2]

In cyber warfare, likewise, it may be hard to control remote intrusions in complex environments, and anonymous disruption may not be politically useful. Not every organization that uses vulnerable computers is an easy target. Not every hacker capable of cybercrime is capable of cyber warfare. States that do have the ability to inflict death and destruction through cyberspace, moreover, are usually not motivated to do so. Cyberspace is more useful for other things, such as intelligence. Cyber operations further depend on institutional cooperation in a fundamental way that strategic bombing does not. While it is technically possible to break things and kill people by remote control, it is premature to focus on *how* to conduct cyber warfare without first understanding *why* it makes sense to do so, or not. This chapter thus focuses on strategy, leaving operations and technology for the following chapters.

I use "secret statecraft" as a general covering concept for things like cyber exploitation and traditional espionage. The underlying similarity of these phenomena is at once obvious and underappreciated. Hackers reinvent classic spycraft by exploiting shared protocols and common connections to steal and manipulate data. The scale of exploitation may be unprecedented, but the underlying logic is ancient. To adapt an axiom of strategic studies, the nature of secret statecraft does not change, but its conduct changes constantly. The first step to understanding the role of cybersecurity in politics, therefore, is to understand the general political logic of deception.

This chapter uses classic ideas from political theory to clarify the nature of secret statecraft. I begin with a high-level overview of the book's conceptual framework. Then I review the international relations (IR) literature on cybersecurity and political secrecy. Next I introduce a typology of political strategy to clarify the distinctiveness of secret statecraft. I conclude by describing four different types of secret statecraft: espionage, sabotage, subversion, and counterintelligence.

Conceptual Overview

Figure 1.1 provides an arrow diagram of the basic elements of the theory developed in part 1 of this book. This chapter focuses on the level of strategy, linking interests to institutions. The next chapter focuses on the level of operations, linking institutions to intrusions. These concepts are relevant in any era of technology, which is an indirect factor that makes institutions more complex but does not determine strategic outcomes directly. Chapter 3 turns to the specific challenges of cyberspace, which tends to increase the complexity of secret statecraft.

All kinds of political actors (states, organizations, movements, etc.) have various interests (security, resources, prestige, prerogatives, etc.). The sources of interests are manifold and largely external to this framework. I simply assume that interests, whatever their source, inform decisions to cooperate or compete. Actors with cooperative interests are more likely to embrace win-win strategies such as governance or commerce. These usually entail collective action problems, which actors typically solve with institutions such as legal regimes or technical standards. Actors with highly competitive interests, by contrast, are more likely to embrace zero-sum strategies such as warfare or compellence.[3] But there is an intermediate option too. Actors can compete by feigning cooperative interests via secret statecraft, the use of organized deception for strategic advantage.

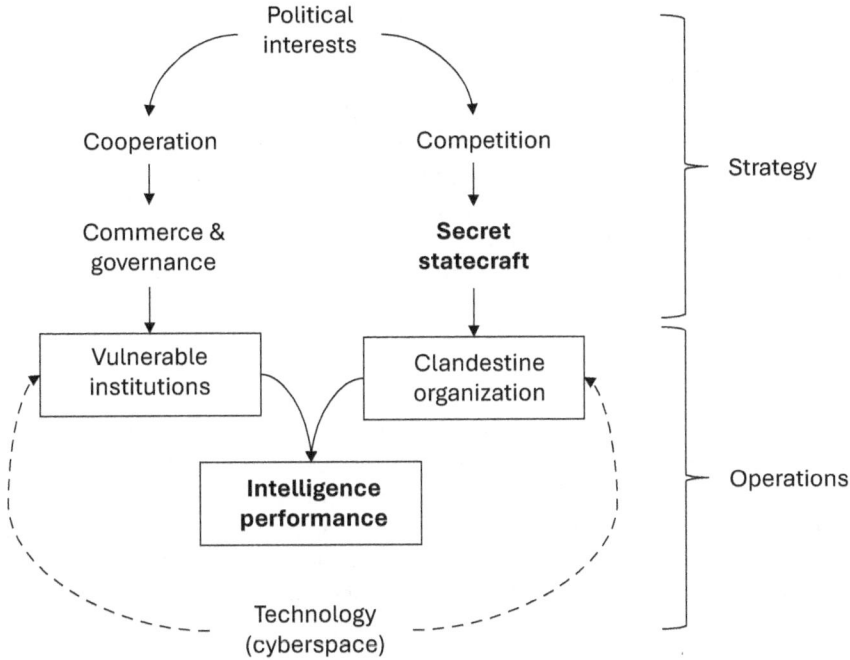

Figure 1.1. Conceptual framework of the book

The constitutive tension between cooperation and competition at the strategic level complicates the implementation of secret statecraft at the operational level. All four types of secret statecraft depend on two institutional conditions: (1) cooperative interests encourage the creation of *vulnerable institutions* that make deception possible, and (2) competitive interests encourage the creation of *clandestine organization* to operationalize deception. The former describes institutional resources shared across intelligence competitors, and the latter describes resources that those competitors autonomously control. These "independent variables" determine the "dependent variable" of *intelligence performance*, the maintenance of secret information channels and the subject of chapter 2. Note that "independence" is an analytical convenience; the empirical chapters discuss problems of complexity, nuance, and endogeneity in detail.

Cybersecurity and Political Secrecy

Spies have been stealing secrets, passing disinformation, and sabotaging things for millennia. But today there are more data to steal, more media to manipulate, and more systems to disrupt. Change in the conduct of intelligence has been so significant in recent decades that it is easy to mistake it for a new form of warfare.

Narratives about "cyberwar" are evergreen among pundits and policymakers. IR scholars who study cybersecurity have generally been more skeptical.[4] Meanwhile, IR scholarship on political secrecy is burgeoning.[5] But these strands of literature have not intermingled much. Cyber scholars tend to focus on recent technical cases, while secrecy scholars mine archives on historical cases. One community is interested in emerging technology, while the other is interested in eternal politics. They have much to learn from each other.

The cyberwar narrative has been a fixture in national security discourse for decades. Winn Schwartau testified before Congress in 1991 that computer insecurity was "an electronic Pearl Harbor waiting to occur."[6] Three decades later, a retired director of the NSA warned, "We will all be faced with a 9/11-scale threat in cyberspace: The question is simply when."[7] Analogies to traumatic historical events such as the Japanese attack on Pearl Harbor on December 7, 1941, or the terrorist attacks of September 11, 2001, are a staple of threat inflation.

While the technical details change, a few basic themes recur again and again: Offense is getting easier, defense is getting harder, asymmetric dangers are growing, China has the advantage, and digital catastrophe is inevitable.[8] Critical infrastructure—a catchall term for energy grids, industrial factories, transportation systems, food supplies, military command and control, and so on—appears to be increasingly vulnerable to anonymous attackers. Open democracies seem especially vulnerable. Artificial intelligence (AI) makes all this even worse by speeding up operations and outthinking human beings. Militaries thus face a technological imperative to contest "virtual territory" in cyberspace, which is construed as a "warfighting domain" like the physical environments of land, sea, air, and space.[9] While the Chinese and US militaries may agree on little, they both agree that the future of war belongs to information technology.

The cyberwar narrative is a variant of the "technology theory of victory" that I criticized in *Information Technology and Military Power*. Both views hold that technology makes it possible to do more with less, achieving dramatic effects without much (or any) military force. The difference is that the technology theory of victory emphasizes the military advantages of networked sensors and shooters, while the cyberwar narrative emphasizes the societal vulnerabilities and asymmetric threats of cyberspace. The fact that similar technological developments give rise to opposite expectations— decisive fighting or catastrophic disaster—suggests that there is something other than technology at work here.

The cyberwar narrative is a story about the future, but cyberspace has been around for at least half a century. The internet emerged in the 1970s, and the World Wide Web took off in the 1990s. This means that empirical studies of cyber conflict can draw on decades of data. Scholars find little evidence of dramatic digital disruption or escalation.[10] Instead there is a lot of espionage, cybercrime, hacktivism, and disinformation. Threat activity is highly skewed toward the lower end of the conflict spectrum. All cybersecurity data are plagued by missingness, of course, but this works against the cyberwar narrative.[11] Destructive incidents are less likely to escape notice, while the long tail of low-intensity activity is probably even longer and lower than observed. It is reasonable to conclude that the reason we do not see catastrophic attacks is that they are not there. (The mass sabotage of Hezbollah pagers by Israel in September 2024, which resulted in thousands of casualties, seems like a major outlier in this trend, but there are several important caveats that I will discuss in this book's conclusion.)

IR scholars of every theoretical persuasion also find conceptual reasons to be skeptical of cyberwar. Realists object that secret or nonlethal cyber weapons are poor instruments of coercion, challenging the idea that cyberspace revolutionizes war.[12] Institutionalists point to significant organizational requirements for offensive cyber operations, challenging the idea that cyberspace is offense dominant.[13] Constructivists highlight ulterior motives for threat inflation, such as commercial marketing or bureaucratic empire-building, challenging the idea that cyberwar is nigh.[14]

It would be a mistake, however, to dismiss all threat narratives as cynical politics, commercial marketing, or benighted thinking. Data breaches have economic consequences.[15] Victims of digital abuse experience psychological trauma.[16] One study finds that ransomware attacks on US hospitals between 2016 and 2021 contributed to the deaths of as many as seventy-five Medicare patients.[17] The scourge of cybercrime supports a multibillion-dollar cybersecurity industry to combat it.[18] Military units have also gained extensive experience with cyber operations in wartime, peacetime, and the gray zone in between.[19] Digital danger clearly does not have to be cyberwar to matter, politically or economically. But if it is not war, what is it?

THE INTELLIGENCE ANALOGY

Computer security expert Matthew Monte describes "computer network exploitation" as "the latest reincarnation of espionage."[20] Political scientist Joshua Rovner likewise describes "cyberspace competition" as "an intelligence contest in a technologically novel domain. . . . Because it is not a test of overt military power, traditional strategic theories about force and war may not be our best guide."[21] From this perspective, cybersecurity is more of an evolution in intelligence affairs than a revolution in military affairs.[22] Thus we see a growing literature on digital espionage,[23] cyber-enabled covert action,[24] proxy conflict and subversion in cyberspace,[25] internet censorship and surveillance,[26] digital propaganda and disinformation,[27] and cyber threat attribution.[28]

The intelligence analogy is compelling, but it is also contested.[29] Potential disanalogies include the scale and disruptive potential of cyber operations, and the prominent role of civilian entities. One alternative framing is "cyber persistence theory." This view holds that cyberspace creates a new structural condition of "constant contact" between geopolitical competitors that encourages "persistence" and "agreed competition" below the threshold of armed conflict. Adversaries use "faits accomplis" to create "cumulative gains over time" through large-scale intellectual property theft, influence and information campaigns, and offensive counter–cyber operations.[30] This view informs the more proactive "defend forward" strategy that US Cyber Command adopted in 2018 as an alternative to relying on deterrence or static defense.[31]

Cyber persistence theory is right to insist that cyberspace competition differs from combat and deterrence. But so does intelligence. Indeed, Kim Philby was "persistently engaged" in the organizational culture of SIS and was in "constant contact" with his victims. The discovery of the Cambridge Five revealed a "fait accompli" of stolen secrets, but this alarming discovery did not trigger military escalation. Indeed, the KGB and CIA continued their "agreed competition" throughout the Cold War. Intelligence contests have long been technology-intensive, long-term competitions for "cumulative advantage."[32] Civilian innovation in communications, transportation, and science throughout the twentieth century has dramatically increased the variety of technical intelligence disciplines and the volume of data they collect (as discussed further below). Many counterintelligence units act proactively below the threshold of armed conflict to discourage hostile exploitation. From this perspective, the emergence of cyber warfare units reflects a broader historical trend of increasing military dependence on information technology and intelligence.[33]

Another reason to be skeptical about cyber persistence theory is that there are clear bureaucratic incentives for new military communities to articulate new doctrines to differentiate themselves from existing services. The US Air Force, for example, came up with the idea of strategic bombing in part to justify its divorce from the US Army. It makes sense that US Cyber Command would also try to differentiate itself from the NSA, even as they share the same building and commander (as of this writing). Intelligence agencies have a bias for quiet restraint, in order to protect sensitive sources, while military units have a bias for decisive action, sometimes described as "the cult of the offensive."[34] Doctrines of cyber warfare thus serve a dual purpose: They justify separation from intelligence agencies, and they make cyber more intelligible to military communities. While this is undoubtedly useful for military coordination, it obscures the political nature of cybersecurity as secret statecraft.[35]

THE RENAISSANCE OF DECEPTION THEORY

A deeper problem is that intelligence is undertheorized in IR. It is confusing to debate whether cyber is like intelligence if we do not understand what intelligence is and why it matters. As Robert Jervis wrote in the 1980s, "For all its glamour, intelligence has also been a stepchild to academics."[36] IR scholars traditionally focused more on war, peace, and deterrence. While there is a cottage industry on "intelligence theory" in the intelligence studies field, its descriptive and evaluative ideas are not well integrated with mainstream IR theory.[37] In the absence of clear explanatory theories about intelligence and statecraft, it was perhaps inevitable that cyber persistence theory, or something like it, would emerge to fill the gap.

Change is afoot. As Allison Carnegie points out, "Scholarship on the politics of secrecy in international relations and foreign policy has experienced tremendous growth in recent years."[38] One reason is more data: Newly open archives provide rich evidence about historical operations. Another reason is more activity: Reporting from open-source intelligence and commercial threat-intelligence sources provides more evidence about recent operations. An emerging IR literature thus illuminates what Austin Carson calls the "backstage" of international politics.[39] While traditional IR focuses more on the front stage, the backstage helps to manage the illusion of political theater. Secrecy enables political actors to manage their relationships out of view of foreign and domestic audiences.

The upshot is a renaissance of scholarship on political secrecy. In seeking to understand the role of cybersecurity in international affairs, therefore, we can now draw on a growing literature on secret wars,[40] covert regime change,[41] election interference,[42] clandestine signaling,[43] mendacious elites,[44] underground resistance,[45] subterranean diplomacy,[46] political subversion,[47] disinformation campaigns,[48] government surveillance,[49] military intelligence,[50] surprise attack,[51] and intelligence-policy relations.[52] I refer to this body of work as "deception theory" for lack of a better name. This "theory" is a loose community of practice encompassing a diverse set of methodological approaches and substantive claims, much like "deterrence theory" before it.[53]

Deception theory is as relevant for the twenty-first century as deterrence theory was for the twentieth. In each case, technological innovation drove demand for new ideas. The nuclear revolution inspired the development of deterrence theory: Nuclear weapons made war prohibitive and thus deterrence essential. The information revolution, I would argue, likewise inspires the development of deception theory. As I discuss further below, cyberspace makes commerce and coordination more efficient, which in turn makes deception more pervasive. If nuclear weapons supersize the means of war, so to speak, then cyberspace supersizes the means of peace. Indeed, these theories are paradoxical in opposite ways. Deterrence theory deals with the paradoxes of using military threats to negotiate mutual deals. Deception theory deals with the paradoxes of exploiting peaceful institutions for competitive advantages. Glibly put, deterrence uses the means of war for the ends of peace, while deception uses the means of peace for the ends of war. This suggests that specialized means of deception (like cyber operations) may not play well with specialized means of deterrence (like nuclear weapons).[54]

Deception theorists find that subterfuge has ambiguous implications, appropriately enough. Secrecy can be stabilizing or destabilizing in different circumstances. Intelligence can provide reassuring knowledge, or it can create dangerous information asymmetries. Silence can cover devastating surprise attacks like Pearl Harbor and 9/11, or it can be used to save face and mitigate tensions. Covert action can provocatively upset politics, or it can provide a pressure release for strategic competition. Underground diplomacy can undermine norms by flouting them, or it can reinforce them by feigning compliance. The appeal, viability, and effectiveness of backstage operations are highly contingent on political circumstances. This is a vital insight for cybersecurity.

Most of the scholarship on political secrecy to date has focused on historical cases. Scholarship on cybersecurity, meanwhile, has not fully engaged with the new IR literature on intelligence and covert action. Deception theory and cyber studies have been artificially separated by technology, yet technology makes deception more prevalent than ever.

What Is Secret Statecraft?

A fresh concept helps to sidestep all the confusion around cybersecurity and intelligence and to take advantage of the renaissance in deception theory. This section develops the notion of secret statecraft to describe the common political essence of traditional espionage and modern cybersecurity.

Morton Kaplan describes statecraft in general as "the construction of strategies for securing the national interest in the international arena, as well as the execution of these strategies by diplomats."[55] Kaplan focuses on national governments, but the idea is more general. Terrorists like al-Qaeda or criminals like Cosa Nostra can cultivate alliances, manipulate perceptions, use coercive force, and engage in commerce. Any actor with a degree of political autonomy can execute strategies to secure its interests, although not all can do it as well or to the same extent. Governments with large tax bases, capable security forces, and political legitimacy have real advantages in statecraft. Many nonstate actors seek advantage in the shadows, likewise, even as states are past masters in intelligence and covert action.

David Baldwin's notion of statecraft emphasizes the choice of "instruments used by policymakers in their attempts to exercise power, i.e., to get others to do what they would not otherwise do."[56] Baldwin describes four types of statecraft: (1) negotiation and diplomatic statecraft, (2) propaganda and cultural statecraft, (3) coercive diplomacy and military statecraft, and (4) trade policy and economic statecraft.[57] War colleges use the mnemonic "DIME" for these diplomatic, informational, military, and economic instruments of national power.[58] Baldwin observes that "each category can be subdivided" via "such distinctions as . . . covert versus overt operations."[59] This suggests that secret statecraft is merely an accent on more fundamental types of statecraft.

But if different types of statecraft are defined by their instrumentalities, then secret statecraft is interestingly distinct. All forms of statecraft rely on some characteristic means. Military statecraft relies on specialized armed services to employ instrumental violence. Economic statecraft relies on specialized regulators to influence commercial transactions. Secret statecraft, likewise, relies on specialized agencies to collect intelligence, sabotage competitors, subvert societies, and perform counterintelligence. Secret statecraft is not just deception but *organized* deception.

THE ESSENCE OF DECEPTION

I use "deception" as a general term describing any form of simulation or dissimulation, including both active manipulation and passive concealment.[60] Secrecy is a form of deception in this general sense. Organized deception specialists employ camouflage, disguise, concealment, confidence games, or covert manipulation. Organizations that specialize in these activities include intelligence services, reconnaissance units, counterintelligence agencies, private investigators, commercial threat-intelligence firms, and criminal conspiracies. Secret statecraft is not limited to state spy agencies, therefore, even though no one does it better.

The key political feature of deception is that it exploits the willing but unwitting cooperation of the deceived. As Niccolo Machiavelli famously observes, "Princes who have done great things have held good faith of little account, and have known how to circumvent the intellect of men by craft, and in the end have overcome those who have relied on their word."[61] The prince's dupes are complicit: "Men are so simple, and so subject to present necessities, that he who seeks to deceive will always find someone who will allow himself to be deceived."[62] Overconfident enemies walk into ambushes, solicitous friends ignore our indiscretions, and gullible marks hand over savings to con men. Deception offers cooperation in bad faith.

Machiavelli uses zoological imagery to distinguish covert deception from overt confrontation and coercion: "The lion cannot defend himself against snares and the fox cannot defend himself against wolves. Therefore, it is necessary to be a fox to discover the snares and a lion to terrify the wolves."[63] In the Florentine menagerie, wolves are military rivals who conquer and pillage, while lions are coercive threats that keep wolves at bay. The fox, by contrast, lurks in the shadows to lure prey into a false sense of security. Foxes rely on cunning more than strength or resolve. While warriors fight their enemies, and diplomats deter them, deceivers fool opponents into acting like friends. Foxes lie, cheat, and steal to gain an unfair advantage under false pretenses. Spies and hackers are inherently foxy.

POLITICAL STRATEGY

Strategy of any kind is a relationship between ends and means.[64] Figure 1.2 plots different configurations of ends and means to distinguish secret statecraft from more intuitive forms of politics. The x-axis (political ends) describes the degree of competition between goal-seeking actors. Near the origin, interests are more aligned, so there are win-win opportunities to work together. Further away, interests are less compatible, so competition becomes more zero-sum. The y-axis (institutional means) describes the degree of institutionalization of the resources used by actors. The origin is absolute anarchy, so actors help themselves with autonomous means such as military power. Further away, actors rely on shared institutional means that regulate social interactions, such as governments.

My focus here is on secret statecraft, so I will only sketch the other strategies for the sake of triangulation. The top-left and bottom-right corners of figure 1.2 (governance and warfare, respectively) embody the eternal debate between the liberal and realist traditions of IR.[65] At the risk of caricature, liberalism is about cooperation via institutions, while realism is about

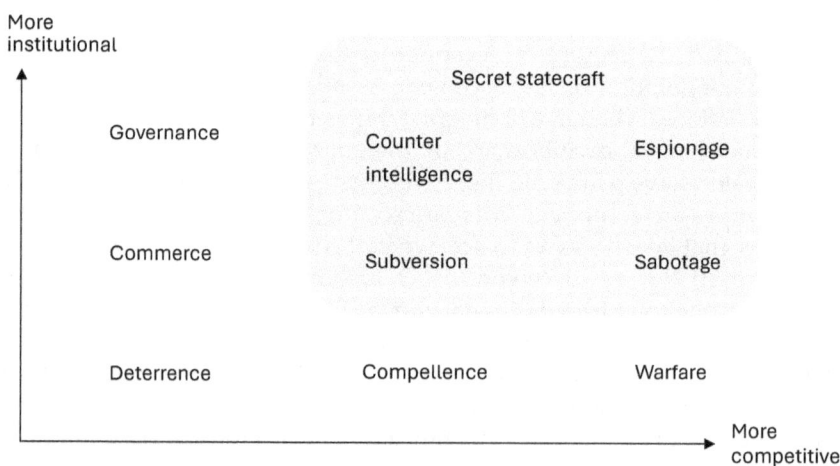

More institutional

		Secret statecraft	
	Governance	Counter intelligence	Espionage
	Commerce	Subversion	Sabotage
	Deterrence	Compellence	Warfare

More competitive

Figure 1.2. Typology of strategies differentiated by institutional means and competitive ends

competition in anarchy.[66] But the world is full of interesting exceptions. Realists can be optimists, and liberals can be pessimists.[67] Revisionists can be networked, and interdependence can be weaponized.[68] My typology sidesteps the eternal debate by disaggregating means and ends and treating them as continuous dimensions.[69]

Coercion is a hybrid strategy that uses the means of warfare (armed forces) to negotiate the ends of governance (mutual cooperation). The IR concept of coercion encompasses deterrence to preserve the status quo and compellence to revise it. These are all anarchic strategies like warfare (at the bottom of the y-axis) but are somewhat less competitive than it. Thomas Schelling emphasizes that coercion "requires that our interests and our opponent's not be absolutely opposed. . . . Coercion requires finding a bargain, arranging for him to be better off doing what we want—worse off not doing what we want—when he takes the threatened penalty into account."[70] In warfare, by contrast, "brute force can only accomplish what requires no collaboration."[71] In practice, coercion often uses force to compel cooperation, so I depict revisionist compellence as midway on the x-axis between zero-sum warfare and status-quo deterrence.

Commerce is another important hybrid. Markets are obviously competitive, but voluntary exchange ideally leaves all parties better off (i.e., efficient markets are Pareto improving). I thus plot commerce on the cooperative side of the x-axis. Efficient cooperation, moreover, depends on institutional coordination via government regulation, common currencies, and shared technical standards and protocols. Otherwise commerce becomes vulnerable to subversion and other market failures. Economic statecraft, furthermore, may threaten sanctions and trade barriers to exclude actors from common markets. Thus I plot commerce as midway on the y-axis between institutionalized governance and deterrence in anarchy. This visual depiction shows how the political and economic institutions of governance and commerce may be exploited by secret statecraft as interests become more competitive. Chapter 3 discusses the complex interaction of governance and commerce in cyberspace, which provides the modern operating environment for secret statecraft.

Secret statecraft is yet a different hybrid. Note the complementary (opposite) configuration in figure 1.2 of coercion (bottom left) and secret statecraft (top right). Just as there is a basic tension between peace and war (top left vs. bottom right), there is a basic tension between deception and deterrence (top right vs. bottom left). As mentioned above, deterrence theory (the means of war for the ends of peace) is the converse of deception theory (the means of peace for the ends of war). Bluffing undermines coercive credibility, while secret capabilities are hard to brandish.[72] Interactions between nuclear weapons and cyber operations exacerbate this fundamental tension to a high degree, with dangerous implications for strategic stability.[73]

Figure 1.2 is just a simple heuristic. Political reality is staggeringly complex, obviously, with different patterns of institutionalization and cooperation appearing in various domains and at different levels of analysis. At the unit level, for instance, we may find a high level of governance within a military organization, which is a common institution that enables friendly troops to cooperate; but at the system level, this same organization may enable a high level of warfare with enemy troops, precisely because competing militaries do not share their institutions (as discussed further in chapter 2). Variants of the basic strategies in figure 1.2, often known by different names, as well as complex mixtures of these strategies, may be found in all sorts of political systems, ranging from a small group of people to the entire international community. But for the same reasons, there will often be inconsistencies across domains and levels in practice. As we shall see, these frictions and complexities both enable and constrain secret statecraft. The aim of this heuristic is to raise questions about what the relevant actors want and how they work together in any given case study, which must be carefully scoped to make the analysis tractable.

COMPETITIVE ENDS

This section fleshes out the x-axis. All political actors want things: Some desire safety and security, some pursue wealth and power, some crave status and prerogatives. Thucydides thus highlights the core motives of fear, interest, and honor.[74]

"Intentionality" is a general term for the ends, goals, objectives, interests, purposes, meanings, references, values, and beliefs that direct human action.[75] Assessing intentions in any given historical case is always hard.[76] In part this is because actors—especially collective actors such as organizations and governments—usually have many different intentions. It is also because the sources of intentionality are many and varied: psychology, personality, identity, ideology, bureaucracy, regime, culture, geography, experience, threats, and so on. Here I bracket all this complexity and focus simply on whether the intentions of political actors are compatible or not.

I assume that actors with incompatible intentions are more likely to compete. Competition will be most intense when one actor's gain is another's loss. One side of a dispute wins territory, resources, or prestige at the other's expense. The difference between winners and losers is most pronounced in the strategies on the right side of figure 1.2 (warfare, sabotage, espionage), while the strategies in the middle (compellence, subversion, counterintelligence) are slightly less agonistic.

Actors are more likely to cooperate, by contrast, when they have compatible objectives. The strategies on the left side of figure 1.2 (governance, commerce, deterrence) are motivated by more common interests. Compatible intentionality encourages actors to seek mutually beneficial solutions for common problems, such as airline safety, stable exchange rates, and arms control.

Mutual interest is often insufficient, however, for providing collective goods. Jean-Jacques Rousseau provides the classic metaphor for collective action: "If a deer was to be taken, every one saw that, in order to succeed, he must abide faithfully by his post: but if a hare happened to come within the reach of any one of them, it is not to be doubted that he pursued it without scruple, and, having seized his prey, cared very little, if by so doing he caused his companions to miss theirs." Rousseau's solution to the stag-hunt dilemma is "a contract by which [all] parties bind themselves to observe the laws therein expressed, which form the ties of their union."[77] When the hunters share common values such as honor and solidarity, or they all worship Artemis at the same temple, or the game warden requires them to swear an oath on pain of expulsion, or drones provide mutual surveillance, then they will be more likely to work together to hunt the stag.

INSTITUTIONAL MEANS

This section fleshes out the y-axis. Institutions evolve to improve collective action.[78] "Social contracts" such as governments, organizations, norms, rules, laws, standards, templates, customs, and practices are the "cement of society" that holds communities together.[79] Nobel laureate Douglass North defines institutions formally as "the rules of the game in a society or . . . the humanly devised constraints that shape human interaction."[80] Constraints that limit behavior, ironically enough, enable people to do even more things.

John Locke explains how constraints can improve liberty. In an unconstrained state of nature (anarchy), people are free to cultivate, invent, and trade, but they are also free to rob, conquer, and enslave. These dangers should lead enlightened communities to willingly give up some freedom in order to form a commonwealth. This, according to Locke, provides "an established, settled, known law, received and allowed by common consent to be the standard of right and wrong, and the common measure to decide all controversies between them."[81] These constraints improve life, liberty, and property. To take a whimsical example, patrons of Legoland pay the entry fee to the park (a universal tax), and they willingly renounce the freedom to break and melt Lego bricks (the rule of law), but in return they get to use a large stock of modular building blocks (economic commerce) to build anything they can imagine (political liberty). In this way, constraints can be enabling.

In chapter 3, I will develop the argument that cyberspace is essentially an institution in this sense.[82] Norms and artifacts—rules and tools—are just different types of "humanly devised constraint" that people can adopt to enact collective goals. Colonial entrepreneurs thus deployed both warships and bureaucracy in a process that John Law calls "heterogeneous engineering."[83] Just as speed limits can be enforced by traffic-calming devices or police citations, Lawrence Lessig famously argues that governance can be enforced by software or statute: "Code is Law."[84] Anticipating Lessig by two decades, Langdon Winner writes that "technology in a true sense is *legislation* . . . . New technologies are institutional structures within an evolving constitution that give shape to a new polity, the technopolis in which we do increasingly live."[85] Winner also points out that reliance on tools tends to encourage more rules: "An ever-increasing array of rules, regulations, and administrative personnel is needed to maximize the benefits of technological practice while limiting its unwanted maladies."[86] Institutions can thus be embodied in either tools or rules, mutually constraining and enabling human interaction. Software systems, moreover, are quite literally tools that are rules, encoding programs and protocols to automate bureaucracy and improve information processing.

Institutionalization—however implemented—can vary in scope and scale. Different aspects of the international system range from imperial hierarchy to ungovernable anarchy.[87] Most states in an ostensibly anarchic international system still rely on bureaucratic agencies and transnational organizations, and conversely, many managed firms typically rely on decentralized work practices and informal exchange. Militaries themselves are autonomous institutions that enable strategies at the bottom of the y-axis (warfare, compellence, and deterrence), while more collective institutions enable strategies at the top (espionage, counterintelligence, governance). Each set of strategies is further differentiated by the degree of cooperation along the x-axis. Governance, for example, is the collective regulation of a cooperative society, while coercion (and deterrence) threatens autonomous violence or institutional exit to impose (or preserve) cooperation. War, in contrast to them all, is the autonomous use of force for competition *between* societies. Espionage and counterintelligence, meanwhile, compete covertly *within* a society. Institutionalization is not an absolute feature but rather is relative to the degree of common constraint among any set of actors, at whatever scale.

USURPING EFFICIENCY

The great economic virtue of institutions is that they improve efficiency. Institutions lower the transaction costs of information processing and collective action. But secret statecraft turns the tables around. The efficiency advantages of cooperation accrue to a competitor instead.

Sunzi tells us that deception enables a commander to "subdue the enemy's troops without ever engaging them on the battlefield."[88] This is efficient indeed! Secret intelligence provides a "decision advantage" that enables actors to quickly, precisely, and efficiently tailor policies to the expected behavior of others.[89] Well-informed policymakers and commanders can optimize resources and targeting.[90] Stealing intellectual property, likewise, enables corporate rivals to economize on research and development costs. As intelligence practitioner and historian Michael Herman writes, "The general effect [of intelligence] is to optimize national strength and international influence in peacetime and promote the effective use of force in war and other conflict."[91] Intelligence thus enables "national governments to behave better, in international security terms, than they would without it."[92]

Secret statecraft is a subtle form of defection by which actors exploit institutional efficiency to gain a competitive advantage. Organizational deception specialists defect from the cooperative intent of collective institutions without actually leaving them. To mix metaphors from Machiavelli and Rousseau, the fox grabs the hare while pretending to be a hunter. Covert defection hijacks institutional functionality without necessarily undermining it. Deception specialists may even seek to preserve the institutions that provide them with unfair advantages, which enables them to occasionally play fair or keep on cheating in the future. Foxes cheat at the margins of a collective arrangement that everyone—foxes and hunters alike—continues to maintain.

The risk of institutional exploitation is not lost on liberal thinkers. Locke describes usurpation as "a change only of persons, but not of the forms and rules of the government." The usurper exploits the common means of governance for uncommon ends. Locke was worried about tyrants and venal bureaucrats usurping public resources for private gain, but we can also describe spies, hackers, and other Machiavellian foxes as usurpers "where one is got into the possession of what another has right to."[93] If cyberspace is an institution that improves the efficiency of global communication and coordination at scale (as I will argue in chapter 3), then cyber-threat actors usurp it by getting into systems that another has right to.

Most institutions are designed with features to detect and discourage abuse. This is part of the formal justification for having an institution in the first place. As North points out, "We devote substantial resources and efforts to the measurement, enforcement, and policing of agreements."[94] In Rousseau's stag hunt, for instance, hunters who make a social contract will want to know if their fellows are about to grab a hare and sanction any who do. Monitoring and enforcement practices can discourage defection, and these functions can be improved through security controls (such as surveillance cameras and police patrols, or network logging and access protocols in cyberspace).

But monitoring and enforcement functions are themselves institutional features, and no institution is perfect. As Rousseau writes, "The flaws which make social institutions necessary are the same as make the abuse of them unavoidable." Political struggles result in flawed institutions that perpetuate patterns of abuse. Rousseau arrives at the dismal conclusion that, despite all the benefits of collective institutions, "we have nothing to show for ourselves but a frivolous and deceitful appearance, honor without virtue, reason without wisdom, and pleasure without happiness."[95] This is not a bad description of large swaths of cyberspace.

North stresses that institutions are "determined by the relative bargaining power of the participants."[96] Echoing Rousseau, he notes that institutions often reflect "unequal access to resources, capital, and information and hence produced very uneven results for the players."[97] The historical features of institutions then become reinforced over time: "Once a development path is set on a particular course, the network externalities, the learning process of organizations, and the historically derived subjective modeling of the issues reinforce the course."[98]

It is tempting to attribute inefficient or unjust institutional designs to human stupidity. Political economists like to point out, however, that actors with the power to change a system often have interests in perpetuating it. As Paul DiMaggio and Walter Powell write, "Institutions arise and persist when they confer benefits greater than the transaction costs (that is, the costs of negotiation, execution, and enforcement) incurred in creating and sustaining them."[99] The path-dependent development of institutions tends to lock in inefficient practices of monitoring and enforcement. This inefficiency opens the door to deception. I will discuss institutional vulnerability in more detail in chapter 2.

Varieties of Secret Statecraft

Secret statecraft usurps institutional efficiency in different ways, through espionage, sabotage, subversion, and counterintelligence (table 1.1). These distinctions are blurry and often mixed in practice. For example, during the Cold War, the CIA worked with the West German Federal Intelligence Service to sell backdoored encryption machines in over a hundred countries;[100] thus a subversive conspiracy to sabotage equipment enabled espionage at scale. These logical distinctions are illuminating, nevertheless, because they vary along the same dimensions of means and ends that distinguish secret statecraft from other overt strategies in figure 1.2. Counterintelligence and subversion are marginally more cooperative than espionage and sabotage. Subversion and sabotage degrade institutions more than counterintelligence and espionage. This variation creates strategic constraints and opportunities for different types of secret statecraft.

Table 1.1. Ideal types of secret statecraft

Type	Description
Espionage	Secretly extract data while preserving institutional access (i.e., clandestine intelligence for information advantage)
Sabotage	Secretly infiltrate systems to degrade institutional functionality (i.e., covert action targeting technology)
Subversion	Conspire to disrupt institutions by influencing beliefs or behavior (i.e., covert action targeting society)
Counterintelligence	Cooperate to defend institutions by exploiting hostile deceivers (i.e., deceiving deceivers)

ESPIONAGE

Espionage is the purest form of secret statecraft, as suggested by its location in the top-rightmost corner of figure 1.2. The perfect spy quietly extracts data without altering the institutional environment that makes this possible. Sabotage and subversion, by contrast, reshape the institutions they target. Espionage, as the most exemplary form of secret statecraft, also happens to be the most prevalent type of threat activity in cyberspace. This is not surprising.

I use the term "espionage" to underscore the importance of secrecy in collecting information.[101] The term "intelligence" is often used more broadly to refer to any kind of useful information or its collection, such as marketing research or journalism. Open-source intelligence (OSINT) via websites, newspapers, conferences, and so on, is a gray area because an actor may want to hide the motivations or discoveries of OSINT. Correlation or "all-source fusion" of a mass of unclassified data may reveal a target's secrets, which also may be useful for counterintelligence.[102] My litmus test for espionage is that sources are degraded when collection is revealed. Since secret collection can provide a competitive advantage (under conditions discussed in the next chapter), rivals have incentives to prevent hostile collection.

Some use the word "espionage" to refer only to human intelligence (HUMINT), but I use it to encompass all forms of technical intelligence (TECHINT) as well. The diversity of collection disciplines today is a direct reflection of the increasing technological complexity of the human-built world.[103]

- HUMINT includes running agents and interrogations. This is the most ancient form of espionage, but it can also support or be supported by TECHINT. This is why James Bond and Q work together.
- Signals intelligence (SIGINT) includes communications intelligence (COMINT) from radios, phones, and digital networks and electronic intelligence (ELINT) from radars and other emissions.

- Geospatial intelligence (GEOINT) combines imagery intelligence (IMINT) from satellites and aircraft with cartographic analysis.
- Measurement and signature intelligence (MASINT) is an esoteric catchall category for the scientific analysis of acoustic, geophysical, chemical, biological, radiological, nuclear, and electromagnetic signals.
- Cyberspace intelligence (CYBINT) can refer to SIGINT through cyberspace or intelligence about cyber operations. Related terms include computer network exploitation (CNE), electronic surveillance, tailored access, and technical reconnaissance.
- There are OSINT analogues to most of these disciplines thanks to innovation in journalism, telecommunications, social media, commercial satellites, civilian science, and the cybersecurity industry. Indeed, OSINT is an engine of the global economy in the form of data analytics and surveillance capitalism.[104]

The common denominator in all forms of espionage is the pursuit of competitive efficiency advantage, gained by exploiting some form of collective trust, to collect information. I would also include computer fraud, digital piracy, intellectual property theft, and identity theft in this category. While criminal espionage mainly provides an economic advantage, ill-gotten gains may also be converted into political advantage. North Korea, for example, uses digital bank heists to fund its nuclear program.

SABOTAGE

Some secret methods of espionage can be employed to disrupt or manipulate targets. While espionage extracts information, covert action injects it. Covert action ranges from intelligence sharing and subterranean diplomacy to assassinating scientists and overthrowing governments. I distinguish two general types of covert action. *Sabotage* degrades capabilities, while *subversion* shapes ideas. The former hacks machines, while the latter hacks minds. This distinction is often blurry in practice: For instance, a secret program to arm guerrillas who blow up railways to intimidate a government mixes sabotage and subversion. But it is analytically helpful to distinguish them because sabotage is somewhat more competitive than subversion (along the x-axis of figure 1.2).

Joshua Rovner describes sabotage as "the weaponization of friction."[105] Friction refers to material breakdowns and malfunctions, physical and psychological stress, bad or confusing information, and other unpredictable obstacles.[106] The saboteur creates friction by altering, disrupting, or destroying equipment, capabilities, or infrastructure, which undermines the efficiency of the target organization or society. Friction eats away at efficiency.

Both espionage and sabotage create a competitive advantage, but in different ways. The former hijacks the efficiency of collective institutions while preserving them. The latter degrades institutional functionality by creating friction. Whereas espionage makes the collector smarter or more competent, sabotage makes the target more confused or less capable. This is why sabotage appears between espionage and warfare on the y-axis of figure 1.2. Indeed, sabotage is often employed as an adjunct to warfare. For example, Israel may have used cyber warfare in 2007 to blind Syrian radars and create a window of opportunity for an air strike.[107] Israel also caused Hezbollah's communication devices to explode prior to air and ground operations in Lebanon in 2024.[108] If sabotage reduces the effectiveness of enemy defenses, then a military attack can employ a more efficient force package.

The cyberwar narrative emphasizes the potential of sabotage at scale (and downplays the problems). Cyber analogues of sabotage have been described as offensive cyber operations (OCO), cyber-physical disruption, computer network attack (CNA), distributed denial of service (DDoS) attacks, data wipers, and industrial control system (ICS/SCADA) attacks. Electronic attacks on the electromagnetic spectrum (jamming) may be considered closer to warfare than sabotage to the degree that secrecy may not be required for them to work, but the fact that many electronic warfare techniques are classified is telling.[109]

Espionage generally relies on "clandestine" sources and methods that disguise the activity. By contrast, "covert" action disguises agency or attribution. While it may be hard to hide a factory explosion (sabotage), and a disinformation campaign (subversion) must be visible to its audience, it may still be possible to maintain "plausible deniability" about who is responsible or why.[110] It is possible for covert action to be clandestine, too, if the interventions are very subtle (e.g., the backdoored encryption machines mentioned above, or Stuxnet in chapter 5).

An important political implication is that reliance on secrecy complicates signaling. One challenge is the indistinguishability of intelligence and attack. Preparation for wartime sabotage often requires peacetime preparation, using the methods of espionage to gain access to targets.[111] Should the peacetime discovery of a clandestine intrusion be interpreted as ongoing espionage or preparation for sabotage? This problem is an intelligence variant of the classic strategic problem of offense-defense indistinguishability, which is thought to exacerbate security dilemmas and risks of escalation.[112] In practice, counterintelligence analysts can usually find additional indicators that make it possible to tell the difference (e.g., reverse engineering malware and assessing the political context based on other sources of intelligence). Escalation is empirically rare in cyber competition.[113]

Another signaling challenge is whether to conceal or reveal clandestine capability. Deterrence and compellence depend on communicating a willingness and ability to fight or punish. But what if the very act of communication undermines the ability to inflict harm? For example, Japan could not overtly commit to attacking Pearl Harbor in 1941 without alerting the US Navy's defenses in the process. Japan thus opted to conduct a surprise attack (warfare) rather than threatening one (compellence). A similar "cyber commitment problem" arises when sensitive accesses and exploits in cyberspace can be mitigated by patching or reconfiguring systems.[114] Vague threats are cheap talk, but specific threats can be disarmed, which means that a threatener cannot credibly commit itself to using capabilities that it cannot communicate. In practice it may be possible to reveal clandestine capabilities if countermeasures are hard to implement or the capability is not unique.[115] Extortion by ransomware or kidnapping, furthermore, may bypass the commitment problem somewhat by inflicting harm first and offering relief later, but anonymous extortionists still have credibility problems.[116]

To summarize the signaling challenges of sabotage, building clandestine capability is hard,[117] revealing it undermines both capability and commitment,[118] and covert deniability erodes both intelligibility and credibility.[119] Therefore, sabotage is generally better used or held in reserve than brandished for coercion. This is why, in figure 1.2, sabotage is closer to warfare than to deterrence.

An important exception is that covert action can be used to deescalate a crisis. For example, when Iran attacked civilian oil tankers in 2019, the United States considered but rejected military retaliation, opting instead for a cyber attack on Islamic Revolutionary Guard Corps computer systems.[120] The same features that make cyber attacks poor tools of escalation, ironically enough, can also make them useful tools for accommodation![121] When it is hard to go up the escalation ladder, it may be desirable to create more ways to climb down. In cyberspace, there is lots of room at the bottom. Minor, ambiguous, reversible sabotage can communicate an interest in avoiding escalation and resolving a crisis. Doing so, however, assumes an alignment of interests between actors. This moves us left in figure 1.2, from sabotage to subversion.

SUBVERSION

Sabotage and subversion—the two faces of covert action—both tend to weaken the institutions they target, but they do so in different ways. Subversion targets human beliefs and cohesion rather than material infrastructure and functionality. Lennart Maschmeyer describes subversion as "reverse structural power" that undermines the benefits of institutional structures.[122]

Classic subversion works through proxies, provocateurs, vandalism, forgeries, disinformation, or "active measures" (the Russian term of art).[123] Modern techniques include hacktivism, trolling, doxing, astroturfing, sockpuppetry, deepfakes, and search engine optimization (SEO). Related doctrinal concepts include information operations (IO), military deception (MILDEC), and psychological operations (PSYOPS). Subversion has been receiving more attention from IR scholars during the 2020s, which is suggestive of its growing importance in cyberspace.[124]

In cyberspace, disinformation is generally more prevalent than disruption. This can be explained in part by the relative positions of subversion and sabotage on the x-axis of figure 1.2. Cyberspace is a cooperative institution that improves economic commerce. Subversion is closer to commerce than sabotage is. It is also more cooperative.

Subversion is more cooperative because it appeals to sympathetic audiences or fellow travelers. These cooperative conspirators may have a shared interest in opposing the regime or increasing political polarization. A degree of cooperation, ironically, can erode cohesion. Subversion can also help adversaries with a shared interest in avoiding escalation to "face off" while "saving face."[125] Open secrets, fig leaves, and "implausible deniability" give unresolved actors an excuse to avoid reacting to provocation.[126] For example, when Russia invaded Crimea in 2014, nobody doubted that "little green men" without insignia were Russian soldiers, but Kyiv and Brussels had no interest in confronting Moscow directly at that time.[127]

A lot of subversion is bullshit, in the technical sense. According to Harry Frankfurt, "The fundamental aspect of the essential nature of bullshit" is that "it is produced without concern with the truth," and thus "it need not be false."[128] The goal of bullshit is to manipulate rather than inform. Whereas liars care enough about the truth to hide it, "bullshit is a greater enemy of the truth than lies are."[129] Bullshitters communicate in bad faith. As Jean-Paul Sartre writes, "Bad faith apprehends evidence but is resigned in advance to not being fulfilled by this evidence, to not being persuaded and transformed into good faith."[130] Signaling in bad faith is a form of epistemological subversion that undermines the value of signaling altogether.[131]

But subversion can also be stabilizing, surprisingly enough. Secret diplomacy between two political actors can be understood as a subversive conspiracy that hides collusion from outside audiences such as foreign governments or domestic constituencies. States may suppress evidence of treaty violations to maintain the public viability of the treaty.[132] Subterranean dealing enables adversaries to negotiate understandings, or helps allies avoid public disagreement.[133] This is the international equivalent of dissembling in the workplace to avoid workflow disruptions or to deflect unhelpful criticism.[134]

As this discussion suggests, subversion is the most liminal or ambiguous form of secret statecraft. This is why it occupies a central position in figure 1.2. Subversion can be secretive like espionage (though discretion is harder), or it can communicate information like coercion (though signals are more ambiguous). It can be destabilizing like warfare (though less overtly violent) or stabilizing like governance (though less legitimate). The line between covert influence and open propaganda or marketing is very blurry.

Subversion can weave together overt and covert uses of information technology, for conflict and cooperation, in international and domestic politics.

COUNTERINTELLIGENCE

Counterintelligence, finally, provides defense against the dark arts. Targets and intruders alike use it to detect and deflect their competitors. While the term "counterintelligence" is sometimes used narrowly to describe law enforcement investigations of foreign spies, I use it broadly here to describe any sort of security policies and operations that defend against hostile espionage or covert action.

Counterintelligence is a form of organized deception because it deceives deceivers. Security professionals hide valuable assets from prying eyes via encryption, classification, compartmentalization, camouflage, and other forms of operational security (OPSEC). Counterspies employ espionage via hidden cameras, silent alarms, undercover stings, and TECHINT to detect and track intruders. Counterintelligence units can also use subversion to feed disinformation to spies, turn double agents, infiltrate enemy intelligence organizations, and sabotage them. Counterintelligence, or fears of counterintelligence, can paralyze an organization with paranoia.

All forms of espionage discussed above can support friendly counterintelligence, and all espionage must evade hostile counterintelligence. This is why these complementary strategies are adjacent in figure 1.2. Michael Herman points out that intelligence "is part of a contest with opposing security systems," while counterintelligence "takes the form of a set of sub-contests, subordinate to the main intelligence-security contest, which fit inside it and inside each other like Russian dolls."[135] A cyber example of this matryoshka doll appeared during the opening ceremonies of the 2018 Winter Olympics in Pyeongchang, in which a cyber attack turned out to be a Russian operation disguised as a Chinese operation disguised as a North Korean operation, probably intended to confuse (or intimidate) commercial incident responders.[136] Intelligence must worry about counterintelligence, which in turn must worry about counter-counterintelligence, and so on. Offense must play defense because defense plays offense, piling on new measures to counter the countermeasures. As Erving Goffman observes in his meditation on expression games, "Each seeker is therefore doubly a concealer, and each concealer is doubly a seeker."[137] These security imperatives create overhead costs that eat into the efficiency gains of institutions (and the usurpation of them).

Counterintelligence is closer to governance in figure 1.2 than any other type of secret statecraft is. It improves the institutional functions of monitoring and enforcement by detecting, blocking, and redirecting hostile threats. It is also the most visible dimension of secret statecraft, because organizations require personnel to submit to background checks, complete security training, and accept workforce surveillance. Other forms of counterintelligence, such as double agent operations, are more secretive. The interaction between espionage and counterintelligence is also rather sensitive, as in the "Vulnerabilities Equities Process" through which the United States determines whether the NSA should conceal vulnerabilities for a private SIGINT advantage or disclose them to vendors for a public cybersecurity advantage.[138]

Most cybersecurity is basically counterintelligence. And most cybersecurity firms are basically private counterintelligence units. Counterintelligence in cyberspace is enabled by concepts like computer network defense, information assurance, emissions control, public key infrastructure, network security monitoring, operational technology security, physical controls, airgaps, software patching, reverse engineering, malware analysis, attribution analysis, content moderation, and deep packet inspection. Defense can also play offense with honeypots, sinkholes, reverse deception, threat hunting, active defense, counter–cyber operations, or the US doctrine of "defend forward."

Authoritarian governments and other paranoid regimes rely heavily on counterintelligence. Censorship, surveillance, and propaganda amplify the authority of the regime, discourage dissent, and enhance the effectiveness of internal security forces. I discuss this further in chapter 7 on China. Even in democratic societies, many digital security and content controls bear more than a passing resemblance to authoritarian censorship and control systems.

COMPLEX OPERATIONS

The bewildering jargon encountered above reflects the growing complexity of deception in cyberspace. Nonetheless, the four logical types of secret statecraft are mutually exclusive and collectively exhaustive in terms of institutional means and competitive ends. The main security threats of cyberspace in this basic scheme are the erosion of information advantage through systematic digital espionage, the sabotage of critical infrastructure through cyber warfare, the subversion of social cohesion through internet influence campaigns, and the weakening of civil society through authoritarian censorship and counterintelligence. But institutions and intentions are almost always mixed in practice. The variety of secret statecraft in practice emerges through complex combinations and implementations that mix differing degrees of cooperation and institutionalization in different areas and scales.

Secret statecraft—by any means and in any era—works by usurping collective action. Cooperative actors make good-faith decisions to create and maintain common institutions and shared infrastructures in order to improve the efficiency of transactions. But political competitors can make a strategic decision to cooperate in bad faith. They can employ organizational deception specialists to convert the cooperative efficiency of institutions into an unfair competitive advantage. The general promise of secret statecraft in this sense is efficiency—doing more with less. But the peril is ineffectiveness—failing to get the job done.

The efficiency advantages of deception may vanish because of operational missteps, unforeseen consequences, or aggressive counterintelligence. Actors who want to preserve the strategic benefits of cooperation thus have incentives to counter deception. But this means that deceivers in turn have incentives to hide from or dupe the counterdeceivers. The offense must play defense because defenders play offense. This strategic intelligence contest is what drives the cutting edge of innovation in cybersecurity. And this carries us from the strategic rationale for secret statecraft to the complexities of operational implementation. The next chapter thus turns from the *why* of secret statecraft to the *how* of intelligence performance.

CHAPTER 2

A Theory of Intelligence Performance

The ancient Chinese strategist Sunzi is bullish about intelligence, "for it is what the armies depend upon in their every move."[1] But *The Art of War* concedes that spying is hard in practice: "Only the most perceptive and wise generals—those who can get the most intelligent men to be their spies—can fulfill their destinies and accomplish great things."[2] Incompetent agents or unforeseen events may turn a covert gambit into a strategic disaster. A ninth-century commentator on Sunzi thus offers an important qualification: "Just as water, which carries a boat from bank to bank, may also be the means of sinking it, so reliance on spies, while productive of great results, is often the cause of utter destruction."[3]

Deception has upsides and downsides. This chapter explains what makes the difference. The previous chapter discussed secret statecraft at the strategic level. I explained how organized deception usurps collective institutions in order to carry out strategies of espionage, sabotage, subversion, or counterintelligence. This chapter focuses on intelligence performance at the operational level, where secret statecraft is implemented. Espionage can provide a decision advantage only if collectors can gain access to and make sense of valuable data. Covert action can influence the balance of power only if operators can access and manipulate targets. Counterintelligence can protect friendly institutions only if protectors can spy on spies and deceive deceivers. This means that intelligence contests can provide information advantages only if the contestants can collect, affect, and protect information.

The operational foundation of secret statecraft is the ability to gain, maintain, and contest secret information channels. The implications of information technology, accordingly, are most apparent at the operational level. Improvements in the ability to measure, store, process, or communicate data affect the ability to protect or discover secrets. Indeed, the state of the art in technology determines the art of the possible in deception. But in any given case, there is always a gap between technical possibility and operational performance. Advanced techniques may be misused or countered, while simpler or outdated tech can be effectively employed. Intelligence performance is always contingent on dynamic institutional conditions, not simply the sophistication of information technology.

This chapter describes these general conditions, and the next chapter returns to the problem of increasing technological complexity in cyberspace. Here I proceed in three parts. First, I define intelligence performance by comparison to military effectiveness. Second, I explain why it depends on *vulnerable institutions* and *clandestine organization*. I conclude with a discussion of the empirical research design of the book.

The Operational Level of Intelligence

Intelligence performance refers to the relative ability of deception specialists to secretly establish and contest information channels. By deception specialists I mean intelligence services, reconnaissance units, counterintelligence agencies, cybersecurity firms, private investigators, organized criminals, or any entity that implements secret statecraft. These organizations specialize in managing secrecy, just as militaries specialize in managing violence. Deception specialists use secret channels to gather useful data (exfiltrating information for intelligence collection) or shape relevant behavior (infiltrating information for covert action), while preventing rivals from doing the same.

But what counts as "useful data" or "relevant behavior"? That depends on the broader strategic context. Success at the strategic level is usually more complicated than success at the operational level. Intelligence contests provide indirect information advantages in political, economic, or military contests.[4] But what do policymakers or commanders need to know in the first place? How will they use this knowledge? What are the risks of ignorance or miscalculation? What behaviors of which allies or adversaries should be influenced? What is the theory of influence that translates covert influence into political results? How will domestic or international audiences respond to successful, unsuccessful, or compromised operations? The answers to these questions depend on historical circumstances.

No matter how we answer these guiding questions, however, deception specialists still must gain and maintain secret channels to implement secret statecraft. Access to targets is the operational basis for success in espionage, sabotage, subversion, or counterintelligence, no matter what motivates them at the strategic level. The core competency of an organizational deception specialist, therefore, is achieving and contesting secret access, and doing so persistently.

Persistence is not just a simple structural imperative of cyberspace but rather an ongoing achievement in an intelligence contest.[5] Technology is neither necessary nor sufficient for persistence. Human spies like Kim Philby may persist in place for years if they are skilled and lucky. Network intrusions will not persist if they are blocked, mismanaged, or abandoned. Motivated intruders may be repeatedly detected and ejected, using new accesses and exploits every time. Such an intruder can be described as "persistent" even as individual intrusions do not persist through the target's mitigation efforts. The only difference between cyberspace competition and traditional intelligence contests in this sense is the greater institutional complexity of the conditions that enable operational persistence.

To successfully implement strategies of secret statecraft, spies and hackers alike must be able to reliably and repeatedly exfiltrate data or infiltrate instructions, which entails negotiating barriers and avoiding counterintelligence traps. I will return to the problems of measuring this achievement in the last section of this chapter.

COMPARISON WITH MILITARY EFFECTIVENESS

Intelligence performance is analogous to military effectiveness on the battlefield. While there are important differences, the similarities are instructive. Military campaigns link weapons and battles to political objectives and outcomes. But operational success is distinct from political success. Militaries can win battles but lose wars for many reasons. The weaker side may be more resolved, or the stronger may decide winning is too costly. Politicians may fail to capitalize on military outcomes, or diplomats may give away battlefield gains for political concessions. Nevertheless, military effectiveness in battle improves the prospects of success in coercive diplomacy.

Likewise in secret statecraft, intelligence campaigns link secret sources and methods to political interests. But policymakers can ignore or misuse accurate intelligence. Political developments can offset or overshadow the results of covert action. Nevertheless, successful intelligence performance makes it more likely that leaders will gain an efficient information advantage through secret statecraft.

The literature on military effectiveness emphasizes that technology alone does not determine battlefield performance. Institutional factors explain more variance in battlefield outcomes than the quality or quantity of weapons.[6] Healthy institutions can compensate for weaknesses in the quality or quantity of weapons, while dysfunctional institutions can undermine the advantages of large forces and modern weaponry. Scholars thus stress the importance of civil-military relations,[7] combined-arms doctrine,[8] command relationships,[9] and learning processes.[10]

Scholars who study intelligence also highlight the importance of institutional factors. The relationships between policymakers and intelligence agencies can be healthy or politicized.[11] Organizational cultures and processes affect the ways in which agencies collect and communicate intelligence or conduct covert action.[12] Analytical methods can improve over time or become more biased.[13] Later I will introduce the umbrella concept of *clandestine organization* to describe these sorts of "internal" institutional factors. But intelligence performance further depends on "external" factors, which I will describe as *vulnerable institutions*. Reliance on external institutions is what distinguishes intelligence performance from military effectiveness, even as they both rely on internal institutions.

Another relevant insight from scholarship on military effectiveness is that technology rarely determines battlefield advantage in war. The classic literature on offense-defense theory assumes that military technologies provide systemic advantages—for instance, mobile tanks improve offense and thus make war more likely, but fortification improves defense and thus makes war less likely.[14] The widespread assumption that offense dominates defense in cyberspace is consistent with this classic perspective.[15] But technology is only one factor in the offense-defense balance in practice. Military advantage ultimately depends on a net assessment of the local, dyadic balance in any given case, which includes not only the quantity and quality of weapons but also the institutional factors mentioned above.[16] Contingent institutional context likewise affects the cyber balance in any given case.[17]

Indeed, we should expect the offense-defense balance in *any* intelligence contest to be complicated for at least two reasons. First, each side of a contest is playing both offense and defense. Intelligence attackers also hide, and counterintelligence defenders also seek. If technology gives advantages to the offense in intelligence, then defenders can enjoy the same advantage in counterintelligence. Second, institutions play a fundamental role in secret statecraft, which works by usurping the efficiency benefits of collective institutions. If institutions condition the offense-defense balance for war, then the effects of institutions should be even more pronounced for intelligence contests.

CONTRASTING INTELLIGENCE AND WAR

The key difference between intelligence performance and military effectiveness is the constitutive role of institutions in secret statecraft. Intelligence relies on cooperation in a fundamental way that combat does not. Spies usurp collective institutions to collect or affect information, while soldiers use force to destroy enemy institutions and impose their own. Intelligence and combat are very different logically, even though many deception specialists wear uniforms in practice.

To use the terms of IR theory, war is an extreme form of anarchic competition between hierarchic cooperators.[18] Institutions matter a lot in war, but they are generally not shared across enemy lines. Commanders have some control over their own doctrine, administration, command, communications, logistics, and so on, but they do not control the enemy's institutions. In a pure or ideal-type battlefield duel (illustrated in figure 2.1), the military opponents are self-contained competitors who struggle to batter down resistance and forcibly impose their will on one another. Contact between their organizational institutions tends to be superficial, with a violent zone of contact separating mutually inaccessible rear areas. As bombardment expands the contact zone or armed thrusts penetrate further, enemy institutions become less coherent. I will relax this assumption later in my discussion of intelligence-enabled combat (illustrated in figure 2.3), but first it is helpful to contrast the logically pure types of combat and intelligence.

An intelligence contest, in contrast to war between autonomous organizations, is a form of deceptive competition within mutually entangled institutions (illustrated in figure 2.2). This is why secret statecraft appears further along on the institutionalized axis of figure 1.2 in the previous chapter. Imagine that spies infiltrate an enemy camp. They get inside the rival organization without destroying the institutions that enable their deception. They speak the same language, wear the same uniform, comply with the same bureaucratic procedures, gain the trust of enemy comrades, and generally avoid arousing suspicion. But they also do a little extra on the side. They memorize conversations, copy documents, take pictures, or monkey-wrench the equipment. They also communicate with outside handlers through dead drops, cutouts, and secret signals that remain hidden within the enemy camp.

The entangled institutions of figure 2.2 (the overlapping area) both enable and constrain deception. Our spies are in mortal danger if caught. They can be overpowered by internal security services and perhaps tortured or executed. To survive in this extremely unfavorable balance of power, they must create a favorable balance of knowledge instead. They do this by using deception to usurp enemy strengths. Yet deceivers can be deceived. Enemy counterspies can monitor their movements, learn about their subterranean infrastructure, feed them disinformation, persuade them to become double agents, or quietly trade them for their own captured spies. These dangers encourage our spies to double down on deception, which gives rise to the "hall of mirrors" quality of spy-versus-spy contests. Unable to win an outright battle of strength or resolve, spies must win a battle of wits.[19]

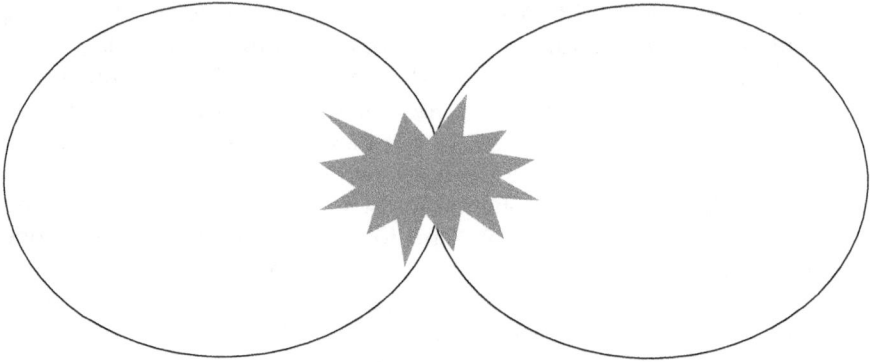

Figure 2.1. Combat between autonomous institutions

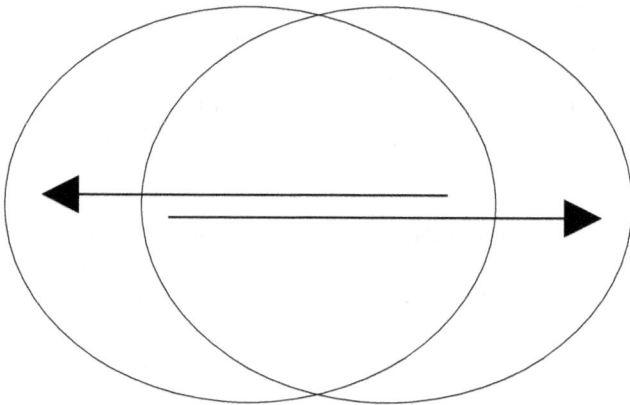

Figure 2.2. Intelligence contest within collective institutions

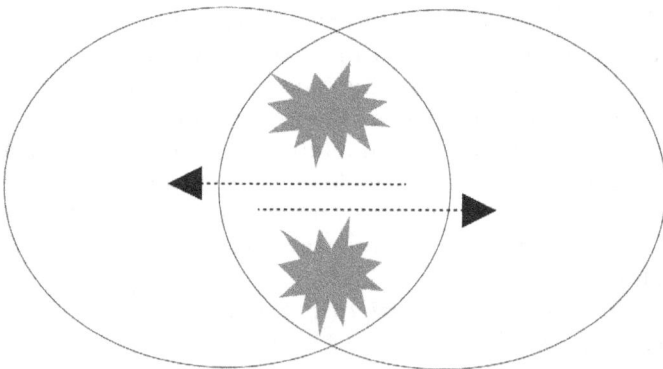

Figure 2.3. Hybrid intelligence-enabled combat

In a purely cooperative organization of trusting and transparent actors (i.e., a perfect Lockean commonwealth), the overlap in figure 2.2 would be complete. But the overlap is incomplete in an intelligence contest, which is a source of uncertainty and potential danger. The nonoverlapping regions on either side of figure 2.2 represent things that competing spies cannot access, understand, or directly influence. This inaccessible space—in remote headquarters, secure spaces, safe houses, or suspicious minds—provides maneuvering room that enables spies and counterspies to organize and adapt in secret. Thus, while intelligence competitors share some rules and tools in common (the overlapping region), they also control others autonomously (the nonoverlapping regions). I describe these logically distinct resources as "vulnerable institutions" and "clandestine organization," respectively.

THE HYBRID CASE OF INTELLIGENCE IN WAR

As an aside, the analytic distinction between war and intelligence helps to explain why combat is so uncertain, even in the era of high-tech command, control, communications, computers, intelligence, surveillance, and reconnaissance (C4ISR). Intelligence relies on collective institutions, but war occurs in anarchy. A fuller discussion of the institutional basis of knowledge is beyond my scope here (but can be found in my 2020 book *Information Technology and Military Power*).[20] I simply wish to emphasize that knowledge relies on cooperation. As Paul Edwards points out, the words "true" and "truce" have the same root in Middle English, linking agreement with facts to agreement with actors.[21] Information systems, likewise, depend on the harmonization of representational processes and protocols, which provides epistemological stability for actors across space and time. In the anarchic realm of war, however, the common institutions that underwrite reliable representation are weak or missing. This helps to explain why Clausewitz is so skeptical of intelligence.[22] As he famously observes, "All action takes place, so to speak, in a kind of twilight, which, like a fog or moonlight, often tends to make things seem grotesque or larger than they really are."[23]

The "fog of war" persists because modern war still occurs in anarchy. So how is it possible for commanders to know anything at all? Why are battlefield surveillance and reconnaissance even possible? The basic answer is that Clausewitzian "real war" is more complicated, constrained, or restrained than "absolute war."[24] Combatants at a minimum are constrained by geographical circumstances and material limitations, and they usually are further constrained by common cultures, shared infrastructure, open standards, emergent norms, or even explicit agreements.[25] These mutual constraints provide the scaffolding for battlefield entities to become legible and controllable. Warfare that is more "informatized" or "network-centric" or "cyber enabled" is far more institutionally constrained than an absolute Clausewitzian duel. This implies that the "fog of war" will vary with the degree of anarchy, or, conversely, that C4ISR will work better in more institutionalized circumstances.[26] This means that there are important but underappreciated political conditions that must be in place for states to realize the promise of the "revolution in military affairs."[27] It also means that surveillance is more feasible within societies than across them, a point to which I will return in chapter 7 and the conclusion.

The good news is that viable information infrastructure takes the edge off anarchy, but the bad news is that war in anarchy undermines the reliability of C4ISR. In the nether region between perfect institutionalization and absolute anarchy, battlefield entities become partially knowable yet incompletely controllable. Intelligence-enabled warfare (figure 2.3) is a hybrid of the pure intelligence model (figure 2.2) and the pure combat model (figure 2.1). Forces that rely on advanced C4ISR can project more precise fires and conduct leaner combat operations, but anarchic combat creates fog and friction that destabilize C4ISR systems. Figure 2.3 depicts, with smaller "explosions," improved efficiency relative to figure 2.1, but it also depicts, with broken information channels, degraded effectiveness relative to figure 2.2. Sources of information friction include incompatible interfaces, biased data, inadequate methodologies, glitchy systems, dropped connections, failing power, and bureaucratic miscommunication. Military organizations attempt to control these breakdowns by piling on additional layers of management, redundant control systems, more information specialists, and reserve forces. This additional complexity makes C4ISR systems challenging and costly to operate, offsetting the operational efficiency they are supposed to provide. The hybrid model tries to be both efficient and effective, but it usually ends up sacrificing some of each.[28]

Explaining Intelligence Performance

Sunzi describes espionage as a "net devised by gods of immense value to the ruler."[29] But divine networks still depend on human operators. At the operational level of intelligence in any era, it is necessary for deception specialists to gain and maintain secret channels. This is the basic operational achievement that makes it possible to collect secrets or inject instructions.

Gaining and maintaining persistent secret access to targets depends on two institutional conditions. First is the "external" institutional environment that an intruder shares with its target: Table 2.1 summarizes variation in vulnerable institutions. Second is the intruder's "internal" institutional ability to manage its intrusion: Table 2.2 summarizes variation in clandestine organization. Because an intelligence contest takes place in overlapping institutions, the "inside" of one organization is the "outside" of the other, and vice versa, which is why I use different terms to distinguish them.[30] Table 2.3 summarizes the interaction of these two factors, which gives rise to four different patterns of intelligence performance. The best performance is achieved by the most proficient actors in the most permissive environments.

Intelligence is obviously complex. It is easy to tease political scientists for trying to explain complex phenomena with a two-by-two table, as I do below. But one virtue of a two-by-two table—an interaction of two dichotomous variables—is that it is the simplest way to say that the world is indeed complex. Almost all generalizations about cause and effect in politics are conditional (e.g., democracies are less likely to go to war, as Immanuel Kant famously argued, but empirically this holds only for pairs of states that are both democracies).[31] A single important condition on a generalization helps to convey the intuition that context matters and to explain important exceptions to a historical trend (e.g., the United States is a democracy that goes to war a lot, which disconfirms the unconditional version of democratic peace theory, but it usually goes to war against nondemocracies, or only covertly against other democracies, which is more consistent with a conditional version of the theory).[32] Intelligence performance likewise depends on factors that condition the effects of technology.

A popular generalization about cybersecurity is that cyberspace makes offense easy. Sometimes it does. But offense may fail even in extremely vulnerable environments if attackers are incompetent. And very creative attackers may succeed even in secure environments. Any generalization about the ease of attack is at least conditional on the proficiency of the attacker. The distinction between an actor and its environment is about as simple and intuitive as it is possible to get. I thus explain intelligence performance as an interaction between an operational environment and an intelligence actor, or vulnerable institutions and clandestine organization, respectively. I also break each factor down into two components to describe a more complicated texture of variation. The first encompasses technical connectivity and social vulnerability, while the second encompasses administrative capacity and operational discretion. Many more nuances could be explored, and will be explored in the campaign studies that follow, but these two compound conditions are enough to make the basic point that institutions condition operational performance.[33]

VULNERABLE INSTITUTIONS

The most vulnerable institutions are densely interconnected, and they have social or technical imperfections. I describe these components as connectivity and vulnerability. *Connectivity* encompasses the informational and coordination advantages of information systems in the absence of exploitation (i.e., systems doing what they should). *Vulnerability* refers to institutional flaws in monitoring and enforcement functions that create the potential for exploitation (i.e., systems doing something they should not). The diminishment of either component makes intelligence performance harder by making the operational environment less permissive.

Table 2.1 summarizes variation in vulnerable institutions, with symbols indicating greater degrees of permissiveness for intelligence exploitation: (i) collective institutions with more connectivity and vulnerability are most *exposed* to exploitation, which is the most permissive operating environment; (ii) it is harder for intruders to reach *disconnected* vulnerabilities, but they can still exploit them if they find a way to create access in a somewhat permissive environment; (iii) connected institutions with robust monitoring and enforcement practices are more *secure*, but advanced threats may still find a way in through an only somewhat permissive environment; (iv) secure institutions with robust barriers to connection are virtually *inaccessible* to intruders, which is the least permissive environment.

Connectivity, broadly construed, is the reason to have information systems in the first place. It encompasses much of what vendors and users find attractive about digital applications, for managing work, coordinating operations, or communicating information. While the word "connectivity" has a technical connotation, I also use it more broadly here to refer to cultural practices that enable interaction and exchange. Connectivity is whatever provides reliable information channels for actors with compatible interests in communication and collective action—the institutional benefits of governance. Interconnected institutions provide efficient benefits for a cooperative community of technology designers, system users, and content consumers. These actors have shared interests in the design, adoption,

Table 2.1. Variation in vulnerable institutions

	More connectivity	*Less connectivity*
More vulnerable (Weak monitoring and enforcement)	i. Exposed[*]	ii. Disconnected[‡]
Less vulnerable (Robust monitoring and enforcement)	iii. Secure[‡]	iv. Inaccessible[†]

[*] Most permissive environment
[‡] Somewhat permissive environment
[†] Least permissive environment

maintenance, and repair of information systems (which should be understood to include both automated processes and social practices, as discussed further in chapter 3). Collective sociotechnical institutions provide connectivity that the deceiver requires to access the target. Systems that are open, trusting, accessible, and uncontrolled are most exposed to malicious intelligence threats. An example of a well-connected yet highly vulnerable target is a naive business without a security policy, or the public internet in the 1980s.

A lack of connectivity, conversely, creates barriers to access. Before the advent of satellites, for example, it was very hard to learn about what was happening within a closed society like the Soviet Union. Border guards, internal police, and paranoid targets made it hard to infiltrate human spies, unless clandestine services were very careful and lucky. Access barriers in cyberspace may be created by system partitions, security controls, or physical airgaps. Glitches and incompatibilities create additional unforeseen barriers that are hard to anticipate. It is harder to exploit systems that are disconnected, even if they are vulnerable, which perhaps explains why there are so few reported instances of malware attacking across airgaps.[34]

Most institutions have monitoring and enforcement functions. Monitoring provides information about what people and machines are doing; enforcement ensures that they are doing the right thing. Monitoring encompasses surveillance, investigation, and reporting systems that make it possible to discriminate loyal cooperators from defectors, traitors, or failures. Enforcement encompasses policing, physical controls, financial inducements, and other policy measures that create incentives for cooperation, impose sanctions on defection, and correct errors or malfunctions. These functions are essential for gathering data and improving control in social institutions and technical infrastructures.

Robust monitoring and enforcement functions reduce vulnerability. They ensure that people and machines behave as expected, and they make it easier to detect and correct exceptions. In the cyber realm, for example, organizations with a comprehensive information security policy, disciplined security practices, and active counterintelligence posture are harder to infiltrate and exploit. They are more likely to find and patch vulnerabilities and to detect and respond to intrusions, while enabling an organization to enjoy the benefits of connected systems. Secure systems—connectivity without vulnerability—are the dream of every CISO (chief information security officer), usually more honored in the breach. But it may be prudent to disconnect extremely sensitive systems altogether. Systems with limited connectivity and reduced vulnerability, such as nuclear command, control, and communication, are, or should be, more inaccessible to unauthorized actors.[35]

Weak monitoring and enforcement, however, increases vulnerability. Put simply, vulnerability is an agency problem. Principal-agent problems emerge when there is a divergence of interests between principals and agents (e.g., leaders and bureaucrats, or the public good and elected officials) and when monitoring and enforcement functions are unable to detect and correct the divergence. Unprincipled agents—human or otherwise—can behave deceptively when deception cannot be detected or policed. Agency problems also emerge when actors with the ability to improve security are not motivated to do so, or when path-dependent historical choices no longer serve the public interest. For instance, intelligence agencies may have institutional "birthmarks" that reflect the interests of founding bureaucrats but that later leaders may be unable to change, even as the strategic environment changes.[36] Software vendors often focus on functionality more than security to capture lucrative network effects, which locks in dependencies on insecure systems.[37]

Any unconstrained degree of freedom in monitoring and enforcement is a potential vulnerability. Recall that institutions, by definition, are human-devised constraints on social interaction. Constraints can be embodied in normative rules or material tools. Monitoring and enforcement functions ensure the integrity of institutional constraints. Unconstrained freedom in these functions, however, provides maneuver room for deception. For example, the spy Kim Philby (discussed in the introduction) looked and acted like a loyal member of British intelligence, but he was a traitor who did a little extra on the side, passing information to the Soviets. Philby exploited organizational blind spots that SIS monitoring and enforcement failed to control. In computer science, the excess functionality of software can be described as a "weird machine."[38] Software developers intend their systems to do only certain things, but, due to oversight or incompetence, they may encode the logical potential to do other things as well. Hackers who discover this surplus functionality can program systems to perform unintended behaviors.[39] In this sense, spies and hackers are somewhat like devious lawyers who exploit loopholes without technically breaking the law. This is fundamentally different from warfare, which batters down constraints rather than working within them.

Intelligence exploitation is possible whenever organizations or systems have the logical potential to do things that designers, members, managers, defenders, or users do not expect. Vulnerabilities provide the raw material for deception—the institutional risk of usurpation. They can be social or technical depending on whether rules or tools are exploited. A gullible secretary with the combination to the chairman's safe is a social vulnerability. A hardware component that leaks information about software encryption is a technical vulnerability.

Vulnerabilities can also be features or bugs. Incomplete contracts and modular tools are features that enable actors to adapt in good faith to unforeseen circumstances, but spies can adapt them in bad faith. Incompetent security officers and buffer overflows, by contrast, are bugs: Their defects are not intended by those who create or employ them. Features are in some ways more challenging than bugs. While most people can agree on fixing bugs, if they can find them, they have to make judgments about whether to sacrifice the convenience or functionality of features in the name of security.

To sum up, the most permissive environment for intelligence exploitation is when systems are densely interconnected and uncontrolled degrees of freedom in institutional constraints create potential vulnerabilities. Many accessible vulnerabilities are often hiding in plain sight until an attacker comes along to exploit them. In this sense, vulnerability is a relational property (affordance) that links loose institutional constraints to a creative adversary.[40] A key point here is that the intentional features that make information systems useful (connectivity) and unintentional weakness in monitoring enforcement functions (vulnerability) create only the potential for deception. Permissiveness is possibility, but acting on this possibility requires something more.

CLANDESTINE ORGANIZATION

A clandestine organization converts the deceptive potential offered by a vulnerable institution into a secret intelligence campaign. The most proficient organizations can use permissive environments to improve intelligence performance. The two key components that affect the operational proficiency of a clandestine organization are capacity and discretion. *Capacity* refers to the management of technical and organizational resources balanced with the ability to adapt to emerging threats and opportunities. *Discretion* refers to the ability to protect this sensitive capacity by using operational security (OPSEC) measures and exercising restraint. Diminishment of either degrades intelligence performance because deception specialists will be more likely to fumble opportunities or provoke counteractions.

Table 2.2 summarizes variation in clandestine organization, with symbols indicating greater degrees of proficiency in intelligence exploitation: (a) the most *sophisticated* organizations have considerable operational capacity to gain and maintain discreet access to targets, which describes highly proficient intelligence threats; (b) more *dependent* organizations rely on third parties for capacity and thus accept more operational risk of compromise or mission failure, which implies less proficiency; (c) *noisy* organizations betray their clandestine capacity, which may be considerable, through indiscreet or complacent behavior, which also undermines proficiency; and finally, (d) *incapable* organizations lack sufficient capability and discretion to gain and maintain persistent secret access to targets, which describes the least proficient threat actors.

Table 2.2. Variation in clandestine organization

	More capacity	*Less capacity*
More discreet (Good OPSEC and little signaling)	a. Sophisticated*	b. Dependent‡
Less discreet (Poor OPSEC or more signaling)	c. Noisy‡	d. Incapable†

* Most proficient actor
‡ Somewhat proficient actor
† Least proficient actor

The intelligence business is more than just spying and hacking. Deception specialists must do a lot of important but boring things too—the administrative scutwork of anarchy. A clandestine organization must recruit, train, and coordinate capable personnel to perform a variety of technical, analytical, and management tasks. Vulnerabilities must be discovered and mastered, and tradecraft or toolkits must be developed and tested against them. Surveillance and reconnaissance systems are needed to research and monitor targets. Analysts must interpret collected data and build up corporate memory. Control and logistics networks must be established to coordinate and resupply assets in the field. Operations must be planned, rehearsed, executed, and continuously evaluated. Security policy must be enforced, risks monitored, and incidents investigated. Administrators and lawyers keep the enterprise afloat by procuring resources, managing people, and ensuring compliance. Leadership must coordinate with other government agencies, coalition partners, and contractors.[41]

Capacity is not just about acquiring tools and talent, moreover, but also about coordinating two very different styles of organizational behavior. First, centralized management provides stability and predictability to offset the uncertainty of an intelligence contest. Second, decentralized adaptation enables clever operatives and analysts to respond to fleeting opportunities in the operational environment. In *Information Technology and Military Power* I describe this balancing act as "adaptive management."[42] Others describe it as "ambidextrous organization."[43] Clausewitz likewise extols the commander's "genius" and "coup d'oeil" while acknowledging the necessity of "routine" and "constant practice."[44] The doctrine of "combined-arms warfare" or the "modern system" relies on a similar hybrid of independent initiative and shared operational concepts.[45] But operational art entails the hybrid dilemma of effectiveness and efficiency mentioned above: Too much central control makes a fighting force too rigid, while too much decentralized freedom creates friction and fratricide. Likewise in intelligence, too much administration imperils responsiveness to evolving threats or opportunities, while too much initiative heightens the risk of security compromise or operational failure. A capable intelligence actor must be both carefully managed and competently adaptive. Chapter 3 examines the improbable success of Bletchley Park in this regard.

Not every would-be spy has the resources or administrative agility to conduct successful secret operations. Nation-state intelligence agencies tend to have more resources, experience, political protection, and legal authority for running sensitive operations. But even highly capable agencies confront challenges in analyzing, absorbing, and applying any intelligence acquired, especially as the volume and complexity of digital data increase.[46] Given these organizational hurdles, experienced spy agencies like the United States' NSA, Russia's SVR, or Israel's Mossad tend to be the most *sophisticated* clandestine organizations. They are able to combine sociotechnical capability and operational discretion to achieve a high degree of proficiency in intelligence operations. This reality is at odds with the popular assumption that cyberspace makes hacking cheap and easy for weaker actors; on the contrary, such actors face steep barriers to entry for conducting complex operations against sensitive targets.

Capable actors occasionally make mistakes, however, or behave negligently. If they did not, then we would know little about them. Most of the high-end threat activity reported by commercial threat-intelligence firms comes from *noisy* organizations that are capable but careless. Chinese threats in the early 2010s, for example, cast a wide net of exploitation but had weak OPSEC. Sophisticated SIGINT agencies like the NSA are less likely to be detected, but they may be exposed by indiscreet mistakes (e.g., the public compromise of Stuxnet) or internal treachery (e.g., the leaks of Edward Snowden). Noisy actors that neglect OPSEC sacrifice proficiency.

Proficiency can also be impaired when clandestine organizations become *dependent* on third parties or off-the-shelf tools they cannot control. Less capable deception specialists, including underfunded intelligence agencies and criminal gangs, tend to be especially dependent on tools and services provided by others. Advanced intelligence agencies may also run afoul of dependencies on civilian software infrastructure that leave behind compromising clues (such as the undeleted build records at SolarWinds that betrayed the Russian SVR, as mentioned in the introduction). As dependencies increase complexity and uncertainty, efforts to be discreet may be betrayed by indicators of compromise produced by remote applications and organizations.

Discretion is vital for protecting costly investments in operational capacity that is both valuable and fragile. Unique sensitive sources, developed and nurtured for years at great cost, may have to be liquidated to protect other assets in the field. Offensive toolkits, carefully built and maintained over an extended period, may be lost or "burned" if compromised. Future options may be foreclosed. Targets may retaliate. Careful attention to OPSEC reduces the likelihood of these unwanted outcomes.

By the same token, reliance on sensitive sources and methods complicates their use for signaling to an adversary. Unattributed mishaps, anonymous damage, and other ominous threats of unspecified harm are too easily confused with bluffing. An actor with something to hide may not seem resolved enough to follow through on a threat. Even worse, the very act of threatening to use a secret capability enables remediation of the threat: Signaling today precludes operations tomorrow. This can cut both ways, as when, for example, public attribution of a cyber threat to bolster deterrence forces an attacker to stop using its compromised tools but also results in a loss of attribution capability for the defender as the attacker adapts. This coercive problem may be alleviated somewhat if it is costly or time-consuming for the target to react to disclosure, or if the coercer has a stock of redundant capability to offset the loss of whatever is disclosed.[47] Intelligence consumers, in turn, must trade off the gains of future intelligence performance when capabilities remain concealed against the loss of capabilities when they are revealed by acting on intelligence. Practitioners know this trade-off as the "intelligence gain/loss" or "conceal-or-reveal" problem.

The operational imperative for secrecy turns the conventional wisdom about secrecy and deterrence on its head. Deterrence seems to be ineffective or irrelevant when threats are secret or anonymous, which is a big problem for cyberspace. But reliance on secrecy implies fear of consequences. Much as the shadow of violence hangs over political negotiation,[48] the shadow of compromise hangs over intelligence operations. Deterrence by disclosure, so to speak, encourages spies to exercise restraint in order to avoid compromise or counteraction.[49] Restraint in intelligence means exploiting fewer targets, exploiting less sensitive targets, limiting the severity of exploitation, hiding one's tracks, or biding one's time. The incentives for exercising restraint increase in a more dangerous counterintelligence environment (i.e., amid more robust monitoring and enforcement practices). The implicit threat of compromise—deterrence by disclosure—may not prevent deception, but it does shape its expression.

To sum up, sociotechnical capability and operational discretion improve the proficiency of clandestine organization. The absence of either degrades proficiency. Actors with neither of them are relatively *incapable* of intelligence exploitation. Incapable actors—amateur hackers, petty cybercriminals, and so-called script kiddies—may still get lucky against extremely exposed targets, and there is a lot of low-hanging fruit in cyberspace. Yet low-grade cybercrime is both easier to conduct and easier to defeat.

INTELLIGENCE PERFORMANCE OUTCOMES

The interaction of vulnerable institutions and clandestine organization shapes intelligence performance. This refers to the ability to gain and

Table 2.3. Variation in intelligence performance

	Vulnerable institutions are exposed[*] (i)	Institutions are disconnected[‡], secure[‡], or inaccessible[†] (ii–iv)
Clandestine organization is sophisticated[*] (a)	1. Persistent secret access to intelligence targets[*]	2. Greater requirement for operational complexity[‡]
Organization is dependent[‡], noisy[‡], or incapable[†] (b–d)	3. Greater risk of losing operational control[‡]	4. Successful penetration unlikely or infeasible[†]

[*] Best performance
[‡] Reduced performance
[†] Worst performance

maintain persistent access to target organizations while preventing hostile actors from doing the same. Espionage extracts information through secret channels, while sabotage and subversion inject information from the same channels. Counterintelligence protects an organization by blocking or co-opting hostile channels. Intelligence contests focus on enabling and contesting these channels. Channels can be used in current operations or reserved for future collection or surprise attacks. They can also be revealed or dropped in order to send strategic signals. But the first order of business is securing secret channels into and out of valuable targets in the face of counterintelligence defenses.

Table 2.3 summarizes this interaction. The columns and rows are labeled with values from table 2.1 and table 2.2, respectively. For simplicity I aggregate all the degraded dichotomous conditions together (those with symbols other than asterisks), to emphasize by contrast the factors most conducive to performance (those with asterisks).

The best outcome (for the attacker—and the worst for the target), is when vulnerable institutions are exposed and clandestine organization is sophisticated (quadrant 1). The combination of permissiveness and proficiency improves performance. This means that the target environment has both connectivity and vulnerability, and the deception specialist has both capacity and discretion. These restrictive conditions enable the attacker to gain and maintain persistent secret access to its targets with lower risk of compromise or counterexploitation. Espionage that collects secrets without disturbing the target is most likely to remain in this quadrant. Covert action is more likely to disturb the enabling conditions. Sabotage that culminates in catastrophic destruction, for instance, is a notable indiscretion. Subversion that relies on domestic audiences and proxy actors, likewise, must embrace dependency.

Intelligence is hard. Most of the variation that is possible in the two conditions is concentrated in the right column and bottom row of table 2.3 (which contain all non-asterisk conditions from tables 2.1 and 2.2). This means that there are more logical ways for the attacker to fail than succeed (as success requires both asterisk conditions). If the target's institutions are inaccessible, disconnected, or secure, then even a sophisticated organization will have to work much harder to gain and maintain access (quadrant 2). The less permissive institutional environment can be exploited only by more complex operations, which in turn carry more potential for fog and friction. The disciplined organization has even more incentives to exercise discretion to manage the additional complexity, while the administrative trade-offs between managed and adaptive practice become even more difficult. If, conversely, the attacker's organization is dependent, noisy, or incapable, it may still be possible to exploit the exposure of a vulnerable institution, but there is greater risk that the attacker will lose control of the operation (quadrant 3). The eventual strategic outcome may or may not accord with the strategic objectives of the attacker, but the attacker cannot control the process, since it is shaped by other actors. Third parties or wider conspiracies may co-opt or redirect operations, which are more likely to be compromised and provoke reactions by targets and external audiences. Hostile domestic factions may respond with counternarratives, fact-checking, and other counterintelligence measures. There is an inevitable trade-off across the ability to control a subversive operation, the scale of subversion, and the intensity of effects.[50]

The worst outcome (for the attacker—and the best for the target) is when vulnerable institutions are not exposed and clandestine organization is not sophisticated (quadrant 4). There is neither sufficient exploitable cooperation in the environment nor sufficient ability in the organization to implement exploitation. Successful intelligence penetrations become unlikely or practically infeasible. Many compromised operations—the intelligence and cyber campaigns that we know about—end up in this quadrant after starting off in one of the others. The Philby and SolarWinds cases from the introduction illustrate a movement from persistent success to operational failure (quadrant 1 to 4) with changes in the counterintelligence environment and OPSEC discipline.

Indeed, the goal of counterintelligence is typically to put intelligence threats into quadrant 4, by enhancing monitoring and enforcement to control connectivity and limit vulnerability. Counterintelligence actors first exploit attacker dependencies and indiscretions to detect the threat, and then they impose barriers and close vulnerabilities to block access. More active forms of counterintelligence may also employ double agents or hack the hackers. The same conditions for intelligence performance apply when defense plays offense.

INTELLIGENCE COMPETITION

Any intelligence contest is a complicated relationship. A spy agency wants to control a target that does not want to be controlled. Gaining and maintaining a secret information channel is like trying to shine a flashlight on a fugitive acrobat while running through a dark forest in the rain. A slower or immobile target will be easier to illuminate, but a fast and agile acrobat will keep jumping out of the light. A skilled pursuer will anticipate evasive maneuvers and lead the target, compensating for any trees in the way, but even the best will occasionally slip in puddles and run into branches. So much the worse if the fugitive pulls out a pistol and starts shooting.

Each side in an intelligence contest would like to stay in quadrant 1 and avoid quadrant 4. Each side seeks an advantage in exploitation while trying to avoid being exploited. Intruders infiltrate systems while hiding their intrusions. Security professionals protect systems by monitoring and misleading intruders. And each side must maintain the administrative and analytic infrastructure that makes all this possible. Each side in the contest plays offense and defense, at different times and in different ways, to shape and reshape the operational environment. This competitive dynamic generates friction for all, and it tends to increase system complexity over time.

The constitutive entanglement of institutions in an intelligence contest implies that one actor's efforts to improve performance will affect the performance of others. To the extent that an attacker gets "inside" the target, an alteration to the target organization alters the attacker's "outside" environment, and vice versa. Counterintelligence improvements may limit the connectivity and vulnerability the attacker can exploit, but attackers may respond by improving capacity and discretion (for instance, overcoming access barriers with undercover agents or retooling to exploit new vulnerabilities). Each side takes initiative to alter the structure of the intelligence environment for the other. The very nature of intelligence competition is destabilizing for intelligence performance.

This is precisely why discretion is so important. Secrecy slows down this destabilizing dynamic by obscuring incentives for change. To protect investments in sensitive capacity, it is necessary to hide activity, obscure agency, or discourage counteraction. Discretion conceals the presence of a competitor in the reassuring guise of cooperation. But at the extreme, perfect discretion becomes perfect inaction. As the intruder becomes more paranoid about hostile monitoring, it ceases to be much of an intelligence threat. Successful secrecy thus may discourage counteractions or restrain activity, but the end result is the same: The operational environment does not change as fast.

This competitive dynamic has several implications. First, intelligence contests tend to turn inward. Hiders and seekers can become more worried about each other than about whatever they are supposed to protect or discover. Deception specialists may become so obsessed with intelligence rivals that they lose sight of whether and how intelligence matters in the broader political contest. James Jesus Angleton, the hyperparanoid CIA counterintelligence officer who never got over Kim Philby's betrayal, is a cautionary tale in this regard.[51] Cyber and intelligence professionals work tirelessly to outwit their adversaries, but the political and economic effects of this contest may seem elusive. Practitioners struggle in the trenches while outside observers scratch their heads. If defenders did not contest hostile cyber and intelligence operations, however, then attackers might gain a real competitive advantage in politics. Active contests between capable adversaries tend toward dynamic stalemate.

Second, intelligence contests generate information friction.[52] Deception specialists routinely encounter unexpected resistances, uncertainties, incompatibilities, and breakdowns. The presence of an adversary makes these routine frictions more problematic and suspicious. Friction is problematic because accidents and uncertainties can undermine the constraints of secret information channels. Friction is suspicious because intelligence threats can hide within noisy institutional constraints. This has ambiguous implications for intelligence performance. While it is never possible to eliminate friction, it may be possible to make a rival suffer relatively more of it.[53] As Matthew Monte writes, "The effect of frictions can be reduced through expertise, training, process, and technologies, but the frictions themselves can never be eliminated. Both Attacker and Defender must craft a strategy that recognizes and accommodates frictions while seeking to increase those of their opponent."[54]

Third, intelligence contests become more complex over time. The dynamic interaction of measure and countermeasure, mitigating friction while inflicting it on rivals, encourages innovation in deception. Defenders introduce new rules and tools for monitoring and enforcement, while attackers discover new ways to subvert them. A general effect of competition is to ratchet up the complexity of information practice over time.[55] Competitive innovation is a bit like Lewis Carroll's Red Queen race, where you must run as fast as you can to stay in the same place.[56] The complexification of information practice is even more pronounced in intelligence, which is a form of information practice that exploits the information practice of others. Clandestine organizations become more complex over time in order to exploit more complex vulnerable institutions, which in turn pile on more complex institutional controls to defeat them. Everyone suffers more friction as a result.

Indeed, cybersecurity friction caused one of the most severe computer outages of all time. On July 19, 2024, CrowdStrike released a routine update to its Falcon platform, which was intended to improve threat monitoring. But there was a bug in Falcon's quality control process.[57] The update accidentally crashed millions of Windows machines around the world, leading to thousands of flight cancellations, delays, and reverberating economic shock waves.[58] Cybercriminals then piled on to exploit the chaos with fraudulent help sites.[59] In the intelligence performance framework, interconnections and interdependencies between a noisy CrowdStrike and a vulnerable Microsoft put commercial counterintelligence operations into quadrant 3, resulting in a dramatic loss of control over the information system. Friction in the pursuit of efficient counterintelligence at scale reduced the effectiveness of systems worldwide. The irony is thick: Security safeguards undermined societal safety.[60]

Fourth, the endogenous growth of information friction and sociotechnical complexity in intelligence contests creates new opportunities for political competition. Greater societal reliance on vulnerable information systems encourages more investment in clandestine organizations, creating more opportunity for secret statecraft. But this means that governments must worry more about intelligence and covert action in addition to their traditional preoccupations with commerce, diplomacy, and war. This is not necessarily a bad thing insofar as intelligence competition in cyberspace provides a pressure-release valve for geopolitical tensions.

Measuring Intelligence Performance

Measuring success in politics or war is notoriously complicated. Intelligence performance introduces additional complications. Operational success on the battlefield can be measured in terms of territorial control, movement of frontage, and exchange ratios. Even these measures are extensively debated.[61] But the geographical advance of autonomous organizations in combat (figure 2.1) is less relevant for intelligence contests between entangled institutions (figure 2.2). Battlefield interactions also tend to be more observable than secret intelligence contests, even as data about each are imperfect.

I conceive of intelligence performance in terms of persistent secret access to valuable targets. Persistent access enables the attacker to extract or inject information in secret over time without interference from other deception specialists. This makes it possible to assess the results of operations and adjust them, leverage results to build cumulative knowledge about the target, and make reliable plans for future operations. It is possible to study this narrowly scoped operational achievement in cases where empirical data are available. This obviously limits case selection. Specific empirical indicators of performance, moreover, will depend on historical nuances.

With those caveats, my basic measurement strategy in any given case is to evaluate evidence of reliable and repeatable access to valuable resources in the target organization—access that a clandestine organization can validate and control, free from counterintelligence interference. This means that clandestine organizations should be able to create secret information channels. These channels should connect to critical information processes in the target organization—that is, processes related to a target's operational or strategic decision-making. Clandestine organizations should be able to develop and maintain these channels over time, using them to develop a cumulative intelligence picture of the target and protect options for future collection, disruption, or influence. Clandestine organizations should endeavor to link intelligence activity to intelligence consumers, although what decision-makers do with intelligence is a different matter. Finally, targets should remain in the dark about secret channels, either overlooking suspicious activity or failing to respond to it. After taking this sort of evidence into consideration, I make a qualitative judgment as to the sustained viability of secret channels to relevant targets for collection or influence.

This notion of intelligence performance is narrowly operational. Additional effort is required to connect persistent access to political advantage, which means that assessing success in secret statecraft is more complicated as well. Assuming that intelligence agencies are able to acquire valuable data (or ensure access for influence), analyze its significance (or validate theories of influence), and deliver it to decision-makers (or create means for influence), decision-makers must be able, in turn, to act on intelligence (or initiate covert influence) in coordination with other political, military, or commercial activities. Intelligence may thereby improve the efficiency of action, either by making leaders smarter or by making rivals dumber, but this is often a long-term cumulative process that depends on sustained intelligence performance against politically or militarily relevant targets. Leaders can ignore or misuse intelligence, and covert activities can be overcome by events. Even in the best circumstances, successful collection or covert action usually plays only an indirect or supporting role in politics. The inherently ambiguous relationship between intelligence performance and strategic outcome must be assessed on a case-by-case basis.

QUALITATIVE CASE STUDIES

My basic empirical claim is that vulnerable institutions (a permissive operational environment) and clandestine organization (a proficient operational actor) improve intelligence performance (persistent secret channels). The presence of both conditions makes it more likely that deception specialists will succeed in an intelligence contest, which in turn makes it more likely that secret statecraft will provide an efficient competitive advantage in politics or war. The absence of either condition degrades intelligence performance, which makes successful strategic outcomes less likely.

An implicit competing theory is that technology is the main determinant of operational outcomes. If this is true, then systemic technical developments that expand "the attack surface" for defenders (i.e., create more avenues of attack against digital systems), or that provide more sophisticated technical tradecraft for attackers, should produce more sustained secret access to relevant targets.[62] Technology should thereby increase the chances of successful secret statecraft. I argue, however, that the increasing socio-technical complexity of institutions has ambiguous implications. Institutional conditions can change while the technological state of the art does not, and nonpermissive conditions can negate technical capabilities. Technology does not determine intelligence performance.

One might test these claims by looking for statistical correlations between variables. But data on secret intelligence operations are missing or messy. Cybersecurity datasets are fraught with problems of definition (incidents do not have clear boundaries), secrecy (victims may not detect or report incidents), and selective reporting (public sources have motivated biases).[63] There are also serious endogeneity problems in my theory, insofar as intelligence competition tends to alter the institutional conditions that enable it. Information systems span multiple actors and infrastructures, moreover, so it is hard to systematically code their attributes. Complexity is a major theme of this book, and it is also a major methodological challenge.

Qualitative research offers several advantages here. The complexities, contradictions, and contingencies that bedevil quantitative datasets can become useful virtues in qualitative case studies.[64] A rich historical case provides evidence across space and time and at multiple levels of analysis. Qualitative researchers use this evidence to trace processes of interaction and identify complicating influences. Process tracing explores, in detail and over time, the relationship between explanatory conditions (such as vulnerable institutions and clandestine organization) and the phenomenon of interest (such as intelligence performance). The analytical focus is on the mechanisms that link variables, not just their statistical correlation.[65]

Qualitative research can thereby improve confidence in general explanations, even with a small number of cases.[66] The reason is that a rich body of empirical evidence provides a rich mosaic of constraints. A good theoretical explanation must fit the complicated set of constraints embodied in the historical events and relationships of the case. Not every explanation will be consistent with the evidence. Alternative explanations that do not fit the facts become less credible. But when explanations remain consistent with more evidence about the case and its context, our confidence in them increases. Explanations should be ruthlessly interrogated, therefore, until they break against the contradictions of evidentiary constraints. Explanations that survive interrogation, even in just a few complex cases, are more likely to prove illuminating for a larger universe of cases.[67]

CASE SELECTION

This book focuses on a few "critical cases" that are intrinsically important in the history of cybersecurity.[68] These cases have featured prominently in the development of, or debates about, the role of intelligence and cyber

Table 2.4. Comparative case studies

Historical cases	Secret statecraft	Intelligence performance
Internet security (chap. 3)	Counterintelligence	Mixed
Bletchley Park (chap. 4)	Espionage	1. Persistent access
Stuxnet (chap. 5)	Sabotage	2. Operational complexity
2016 election (chap. 6)	Subversion	3. Loss of control
China (chap. 7)	Combined	Mixed

operations in world politics. Any theory of intelligence performance *must* be able to explain these cases. They all have a rich evidentiary record, moreover, so explaining them can improve confidence in the generality of the explanation. Table 2.4 summarizes cases and outcomes. While the cases are not perfectly comparable, they do illustrate the broad applicability of the theory. They illustrate all four types of secret statecraft discussed in chapter 1. They vary across the intelligence performance outcomes summarized in table 2.3. They also vary across technological eras in order to assess the alternative claim that technical sophistication boosts performance. The book's conclusion also provides a summary table of other "shadow cases" in the book. These cursory tests of correlation lack the same level of detailed process tracing as the main case studies but help to expand historical coverage up through 2024.

Chapter 3 takes a broad view to examine the historical growth of the cybersecurity ecosystem. It does not focus on a single operational campaign, and it does not illustrate a pure outcome. Instead it addresses the problem of increasing technological complexity in intelligence contests, which helps to provide context for the case studies of technology-enabled intelligence campaigns in chapters 4–6. Chapter 3 shows how counterintelligence success (i.e., intelligence failure in quadrant 4) has become both harder and easier along different dimensions over time. Digital devices have become more ubiquitous, but security practices have become more mature. I survey the development of institutional conditions over time and find no systemic technical advantage for offense or defense in cyberspace. To assess intelligence advantage, we must turn to the strategic and operational context of specific campaigns.

Most histories of cyber conflict start with the growth of the internet, reasonably enough.[69] There are also important insights to be gained from studying the tapping of telegraph wires in the nineteenth century.[70] Between these extremes is the SIGINT contest of World War II, a key confluence in the histories of both intelligence and computation. Indeed, the SIGINT revolution at Bletchley Park anticipated modern cyber exploitation at scale.

Rich archival data on this case also provide insight into organizations on both sides of an intelligence contest, which is harder to come by in modern cyber cases. Chapter 4 examines this classic case of successful intelligence performance. Breaking the Enigma code gave the Allies unprecedented access to Germany's internal communications (quadrant 1 in table 2.3). There is wide agreement among historians that Bletchley Park was a successful intelligence organization. The theory of intelligence performance explains why: The conditions of vulnerable institutions and clandestine organization were sustained throughout most of the war, with a few revealing exceptions. Since the oldest campaign in this book is also the most successful, there is clearly something other than technology at work.

Few modern cyber operations have been as extensively investigated as Stuxnet (chapter 5) and the 2016 US election (chapter 6). Why do we need another study of them? The answer is that they are intrinsically important and have had an outsized influence on our (mis)understanding of cybersecurity. It is important to get these cases right, and this book helps to correct several popular misconceptions about them. These seminal cases are also rich in data. The prominence of civilian victims and commercial threat intelligence has produced more evidence about these cases than we have about most secret intelligence contests (if we have any at all). This makes it possible to trace the interactive institutional complexity that is often obscured in quantitative datasets.

Stuxnet is a case of complex operations enabling chronic subtle sabotage (quadrant 2). A coalition of sophisticated clandestine organizations in the United States and Israel attempted to sabotage a hard target—the Natanz Fuel Enrichment Plant in Iran—that was mostly disconnected from the internet and protected by state security services. They were successful for a while, from a narrow operational perspective, but they did not affect Iranian enrichment in any meaningful way. But the same operation also enabled secret diplomacy to discourage Israel from starting a preventive war. Yet friction within the coalition ultimately compromised the operation. Mixed conditions required greater operational complexity and produced mixed outcomes.

The Russian influence campaign in 2016 exemplifies the opposite mixture. Russian actors completely lost control of an operation that exploited the highly exposed US media ecosystem (quadrant 3). Russia had a target-rich, and perhaps too permissive, environment. It was dependent on local actors like the Trump campaign, and it was undisciplined in its operational security. If Russian intervention altered the outcome of the election, which is highly debatable, then Russia did not achieve this by itself. Domestic actors willingly *and wittingly* amplified Russian disinformation after it was publicly attributed. Mixed conditions muddied the causal linkage between the Russian campaign and the election outcome.

Chapter 7 turns to the problem of long-term strategic competition with China. Much like chapter 3, this study is not limited to a specific campaign, though I will touch on several shadow cases, extending the empirical timeline of this book to 2025. Chapter 7 is more of an application of the theory than a test of it, showing how international and domestic institutional conditions both constrain and enable Chinese cyber power. I find that institutional conditions tend to produce mixed outcomes for various manifestations of Chinese cyber power. The book's conclusion touches on several additional cases, including the war between Russia and Ukraine (ongoing as of this writing), to connect the theory of intelligence performance to the reality of wartime cyber operations. An important theme is that the fit between institutions and organizations is particularly hard to finesse in war.

THEORY BUILDING

The case studies in this book provide confirming tests of its theory. But this book is perhaps better understood as a theory-building project. The theoretical account you have just read is the result of a long empirical odyssey, not its starting point. To save my readers from years of wandering, however, the logic of presentation differs from the logic of discovery.

Many positivists would argue that the cases that inspire theories should not be used to test them. Science as such is idealized as a rational method that moves deliberately from hypothesis generation to empirical testing. But behind the scenes, the scientific process is much messier.[71] Researchers often start with an example of a phenomenon, then draw on their background knowledge to derive general theories, and later revisit the same motivating examples.[72] This method is known as "abduction," as distinguished from pure logical deduction or naive induction. Abduction is a pragmatic method that iterates between empirical research and theory construction.[73] Even hard-core positivists rely on abduction in practice, even if they hide it in public presentations. Interpretivists may be more forthcoming about the reflexive interventions of the researcher, but their work is often harder to understand for the same reasons. In other words, positivism may offer a useful rhetorical strategy for presenting the discoveries of a messier interpretive process.

My theory of intelligence performance emerged through abduction.[74] My prior interest in military information practice broadened into an interest in intelligence practice in cyberspace. Immersion in international relations scholarship and cybersecurity policy debates acclimatized me to important ideas and cases. The process of researching, analyzing, writing, and rewriting a few critical cases enabled me to develop the theory that explains the same cases. This process translated a more heuristic focus on the importance of institutions and deception in cybersecurity into the more refined conditions of intelligence performance. The process culminates in a series of analytic narratives that illustrate general mechanisms by explaining important cases.[75] The result is a constitutive theory of secret statecraft in the twenty-first century that embraces complexity, rather than eliding it. The next chapter tackles the complexity of cyberspace directly.

CHAPTER 3

Security in Cyberspace

A popular myth about the internet is that its founders ignored security.[1] As Walter Isaacson writes in his hagiography of the computer revolution, "The protocols of the Internet were devised by peer collaboration, and the resulting system seemed to have embedded in its genetic code a propensity to facilitate such collaboration."[2] Isaacson's index does not contain a single entry for "security" or any cognates, suggesting that it was either a sideshow or an afterthought. To some extent, internet pioneers themselves encouraged this view. Several of them wrote a "Brief History of the Internet" in 1997 that did not mention security at all.[3]

In this view, the tech economy exploded in the roaring 1990s, and the world discovered a common web. Liberal values spread through cyberspace, or at least through the pages of *Wired* magazine. Techno-libertarian narratives lost their luster only in the new millennium. Airport ads about global networks gave way to security marketing, and surveillance capitalism transformed the business of Silicon Valley. The internet of things became stranger, and darker.

But it is incorrect to suppose that security did not matter before. Indeed, the US Department of Defense Advanced Research Projects Agency (ARPA) funded internetworking research to improve military communications and strategic deterrence. In the development of the ARPANET, the forerunner of today's internet, ARPA program managers partitioned communication from security to enable *both* research in networking by civilian scientists *and* end-to-end encryption for government agencies. The problem was not that the ARPANET ignored security but that the ARPANET security solution did not scale. During the dramatic commercial growth of the internet in the 1990s, threat actors exploited open networks with abandon. Market and government actors, in turn, piled on patches and created new security communities. As cyberspace became more complex, it created new options for everyone. The United States and its tech companies became even more powerful in the process, despite being frequent targets of attacks.

This chapter describes the historical evolution of security institutions in cyberspace. It thus focuses on the counterintelligence variant of secret statecraft. The following chapters will focus on the espionage, sabotage, and subversion variants, respectively. This chapter deals with broad historical trends associated with the emergence of the internet and its implications for the conditions for intelligence performance (vulnerable institutions and clandestine organization). The next three chapters will use these conditions to explain the outcomes of particular intelligence campaigns. As such, this chapter provides an empirical segue from the theory in the previous chapters to the case studies in the following chapters. It supplements my institutional theory of secret statecraft with an institutional interpretation of cyberspace. Readers who are eager to get into the details of historical intelligence contests should feel free to skip ahead. But readers who are looking for a better understanding of cyberspace or are curious about why it is so insecure should read on. In the following pages I will develop the idea of cyberspace as an institution, describe the increasing complexity of cybersecurity, and consider the role of cyberspace in the global liberal order built (and perhaps dismantled) by the United States, with all the contradictions that implies.

Cyberspace as an Institution

What is cyberspace? Science fiction author William Gibson coined the word in the early 1980s, writing of a "consensual hallucination experienced daily by billions of legitimate operators. . . . Lines of light ranged in the nonspace of the mind, clusters and constellations of data. Like city lights, receding."[4] The cyberpunk aesthetic went mainstream with the *Matrix* movies, and it lives on today in the cyber-marketing tropes of steaming ones and zeros, glowing keyboards, ethereal circuits, and deviant hackers.[5]

The US Department of Defense defines "cyberspace" less romantically as "a global domain within the information environment consisting of the interdependent networks of information technology infrastructures and resident data, including the Internet, telecommunications networks, computer systems, and embedded processors and controllers."[6] The Pentagon's definition says nothing about the countless people and organizations that make cyberspace work. The emphasis is squarely on technology.

The geographical metaphors of "virtual terrain," "digital commons," and "the cyber domain" are as misleading as they are widespread.[7] Cyberspace is a network not just of data and devices but of people and organizations, all working in real places with real concerns. I thus use the word "cyberspace" reluctantly, and ironically, to gesture toward the social and technical infrastructure of the information age. But if cyberspace is not a space, what is it?

CYBERSPACE IS NOT ANARCHY

Eric Schmidt, the former CEO of Google, once described the internet as "the largest experiment in anarchy that we have ever had."[8] John Perry Barlow, a lyricist for the Grateful Dead, rhapsodized likewise about digital anarchy: "Governments of the Industrial World, you weary giants of flesh and steel, I come from Cyberspace, the new home of Mind. . . . You have no sovereignty where we gather. . . . I declare the global social space we are building to be naturally independent of the tyrannies you seek to impose on us."[9] General Michael Hayden, a former director of the NSA, took a darker view of anarchic cyberspace: "The cyber domain had never been a digital Eden. It was always Mogadishu."[10]

Anarchy, in IR theory, describes the absence of an overarching, legitimate, effective government. In an anarchic political system, there is no one to call on when a neighbor tries to steal resources or inflict harm. With no higher authority to adjudicate disputes, actors have to help themselves. According to Kenneth Waltz, each actor "decides for itself how it will cope with its internal and external problems, including whether or not to seek assistance from others and in doing so to limit its freedom by making commitments to them."[11] But cyberspace is decidedly not a self-help system in this sense.

Computer users rely on other actors for everything they do. We all rely on the help of software vendors, service providers, public utilities, banks, insurance firms, law enforcement agencies, and government regulators. None of these actors rely on themselves, either. All benefit from the relative predictability of interactions within a highly interdependent system that nobody can understand in detail. All benefit from technical protocols and complicated bodies of law in various jurisdictions. The illusion of a seamless web depends on the ongoing interventions of countless human beings. From the perspective of IR theory, therefore, it is profoundly mistaken to describe cyberspace as anarchy.

On the contrary, cyberspace is the largest experiment in institutions that we have ever had. Even mundane activities like viewing the news on a website are triumphs of institutional coordination. Billions of web pages are served up daily. Each must pass through numerous "control points" that affect whether a web page is available from a server, an internet-connected system is available to the user, the system is configured to access the web page, reliable connections are negotiated with the server, security credentials are authenticated, datagrams are routed and reassembled, the page is retrieved and rendered, and so on.[12] All these everyday miracles depend on the institutionalized coordination of countless actors, including telecommunications utilities, internet service providers, technology vendors, content creators, government regulators, and other stakeholders.

THE RULE OF PROTOCOL

The internet is a packet-switching network. This communication concept contrasts with traditional telecommunication networks that rely on centralized switchboards. Packet switching uses a more decentralized process to route data from senders to receivers. Information packets (also known as datagrams) can carry data for any application (finance, entertainment, intelligence, etc.) across networks that are owned and operated by many different entities (universities, service providers, governments, etc.).

A datagram is sort of like a standardized shipping container that can carry anything (food, clothing, narcotics) via many types of vehicles (trucks, ships, trains) across many jurisdictions (cities, states, countries).[13] The multimodal freight system relies on packers, stevedores, sailors, truck drivers, engineers, maintainers, administrators, regulators, and even diplomats to move containers around the world. Internetworking, likewise, depends on an unsung host of network operators, service providers, security professionals, technicians, clerks, administrators, bureaucrats, academics, and hobbyists, to say nothing of big tech platforms, regulatory agencies, and multistakeholder organizations.[14] In each case, global coordination is enabled by common technical standards and protocols (i.e., institutions).

The protocol stack of the internet is often represented as an hourglass, with many software applications at the top and many hardware implementations at the bottom (figure 3.1). At the narrow neck is Transmission Control Protocol and Internet Protocol (TCP/IP), a lingua franca that enables many actors to connect many things in many ways. A TCP/IP network that is administered by a single entity is known as an autonomous system (AS). Multiple AS networks connect to each other through internet exchange points (IXPs) via Border Gateway Protocol (BGP). The Domain Name System (DNS) provides an intuitive human interface into the internet by translating a uniform resource locator (URL) like www.google.com into an IP address like 64.233.160.0. Thousands of other standards and protocols enable all kinds of devices (from mobile phones to factory robots) to run all kinds of applications (from streaming video to industrial control software) across all kinds of physical links (from fiber-optic cables to satellite relays) used by all kinds of organizations (from public utilities to private firms) in all kinds of social endeavors (from entertainment to warfare). The internet is a network of networks that makes it possible to have a general-purpose, universal, global information infrastructure.

Internet protocols like TCP/IP and BGP are institutions. Organizations that adopt them can improve information and coordination. Much as the rule of law constrains those who consent to be governed by it, the rule of protocol constrains those who consent to adopt it. But these constraints

Applications

*Email, browsing, voice, video,
gaming, command & control . . .*

Middleware

*DNS, BGP, directory, storage,
file formats, security . . .*

Network

TCP/IP

Communication

*Broadband, ethernet, Wi-Fi,
LANs, WANs, cellular . . .*

Physical infrastructure

*Fiber-optic, twisted pair, radio,
satellites, submarine cables . . .*

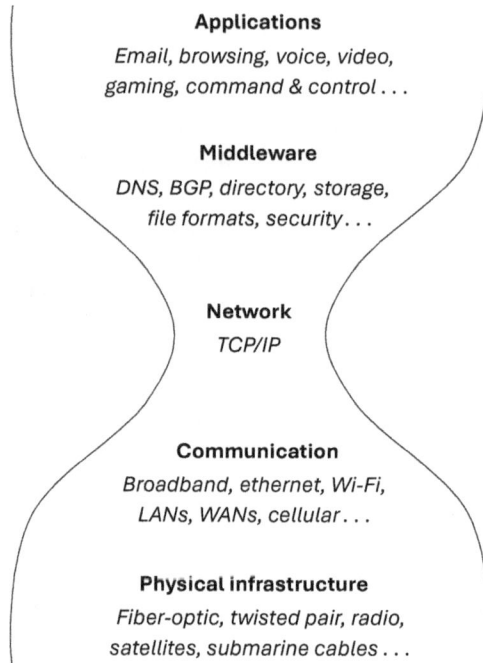

Figure 3.1. The internet protocol hourglass mapping many applications to many implementations

are not absolute. Indeed, the implementation of networks and applications is unconstrained by design. The administrators of AS networks can implement their own features and security protocols. In economic terms, the internet is an incomplete contract that gives AS administrators discretion to adapt to local needs. Incomplete contracts provide flexibility for the contracting parties to negotiate unforeseen circumstances. This compromise, like all compromises, is not perfect. Unconstrained networking enables innovation, growth, and resilience, but this same "interpretive flexibility" is also a source of friction, incompatibility, and vulnerability.[15] As discussed in the previous chapter, both institutional features and implementational bugs create uncontrolled degrees of freedom that threat actors can exploit. In both law and code, incomplete contracts open the door to usurpers.

RULES AND TOOLS

An obvious objection to this framing is that technologies are artifacts, not institutions. In Douglass North's famous sports analogy, institutions are the *rules of the game*, while individuals and organizations are the players.[16]

Technologies must then be the *tools of the game*. North distinguishes institutions from technology to explain "why there is such an enormous gap between the rich countries and the poor countries when the technology is, for the most part, available to everyone."[17] He shows that Spanish Latin America and British North America had access to the same machinery, but their economic performance diverged because Spanish and British colonists inherited different property rights schemes.[18] In cyberspace, likewise, firms that develop different business models and administrative processes may realize very different results with the same digital technologies.[19]

But rules and tools are not as easily separable as North's analogy suggests.[20] If institutions are "the humanly devised constraints that shape human interaction,"[21] then constraints can be normative or material. Normative constraints are social constructions: Traffic laws regulate driving speeds. Material constraints are architectural constructions: Speed bumps make it hard to drive fast. Rarely do we find a system that is purely normative or material. The purest possible idea (a mathematical theorem) emerges via notepaper, blackboards, and seminar rooms.[22] The simplest possible instrument (a stone hand axe) provides archaeologists with evidence of hominid culture. Courts rely on courthouses, and militaries on weapons. Even the machine tools in a lone tinker's workshop have a cultural history that constrains and enables her tinkering.

In short, all institutions are sociotechnical systems. Alternately, all technologies are sociotechnical institutions.[23] As Langdon Winner points out, "Technology is itself a political phenomenon."[24]

The distinction between rules and tools vanishes completely when *tools are rules*. Ronald Jepperson notes that a "microcomputer's basic operating system [OS] appears as an institution relative to its word-processing program (especially to a software engineer)."[25] Software systems, after all, are a set of rules governing the behavior of computing tools. They perform the classic institutional functions of measurement (gathering data), coordination (managing processes), and enforcement (controlling behavior). Indeed, the basic terminology of computer science is strikingly bureaucratic, with its files, folders, processes, procedures, protocols, registries, and programs.[26] It is telling that Alan Turing's seminal paper on computing theory (i.e., Turing Machines) asks readers to imagine automating the work of a punctilious clerk.[27] The automation of bureaucracy contrasts sharply with popular images of deviant hackers in cyberspace.

CONTROL SPACE

Gibson was just riffing off "cybernetics" when he dreamed up his "consensual hallucination." The cybernetics movement was inspired by the military problems of fire control, ship navigation, and cryptography during World War II.[28] Cybernetics went on to influence the development of computer science and cognitive psychology,[29] as well as organizational analysis and decision theory.[30] The word "cybernetics" is a neologism from the Greek word for pilot (κυβερνήτης).[31] The same root (κυβερ/cyber) appears in the English verb "to govern." Just as pilots steer ships, governors steer the ship of state, and governor valves regulate steam engines. From this perspective, "cyber" just means "control."

Centuries of improvement in the methods and instruments used to transmit and process information, from the filing cabinet to the server farm, have enabled human beings to exert greater control over corporate and government affairs.[32] Thomas Hughes points out that "the information revolution . . . arose in part because of the search for the means to control large technological systems."[33] James Cortada observes that "more than any other recent class of technology, [information technology] facilitated control and increased productivity."[34] James Beniger thus describes the emergence of the digital economy as "the control revolution."[35]

The institutional functions of monitoring and enforcement predate digital technology, but digital technology makes them more efficient. Indeed, North's conception of institutions owes a clear debt to cybernetics: "The computational limitations of the individual are determined by the capacity of the mind to process, organize, and utilize information," and thus "rules and procedures evolve to simplify the process."[36] It is thus not surprising that institutional concepts apply so well to cyberspace. It would be shocking if they did not. Cyberspace is a complex control system that reduces the transaction costs of information processing at scale. We can even think of computers as a way of *controlling control*, or using digital monitoring and enforcement to expand the scope and scale of political and economic influence.

The means of control are never politically neutral. Technical measures to improve control raise a number of questions, such as, most obviously, who controls what? Who decides what and how to control? Whose interests do control systems advance, and whose are ignored or suppressed? Who gets to design, repair, change, or remove the controls? Cybernetic control is inherently political.[37] As Paul DiMaggio and Walter Powell point out, "Institutions are not only constraints on human agency; they are first and foremost products of human actions. Indeed, rules are typically constructed by a process of conflict and contestation."[38] Or as Geoffrey Bowker and Susan Leigh Star put it, channeling Karl Marx, "Software is frozen organizational and policy discourse."[39]

For the same reasons, control systems usually become contested. Some forms of contestation are overt, as in the politics of internet governance.[40] Some forms of contestation are covert, as in secret statecraft through cyberspace. Cybersecurity, accordingly, is preoccupied with covert control contests via digital rules and tools. Cyberspace is an institutionalized control space, and cybersecurity contests it.

The Complexity of Cybersecurity

Since cyberspace is an institution, an institutional theory of secret statecraft is useful for making sense of cybersecurity. This means that basic concepts from political economy (such as the historical path dependence of institutional development and the trade-offs between markets and governments) should apply to cyberspace.[41] Because cyberspace is a terrifically complex institution, moreover, intelligence contests among a variety of deception specialists are complex as well.

Digital deception specialists include spy services, military units, mercenaries, organized criminals, private investigators, law enforcement agencies, commercial threat-intelligence companies, corporate security departments, academic researchers, and digital rights activists. Some are state agencies, and others are market actors. Some contribute to the public good, and others undermine it. All these various attackers and defenders contest control over digital devices, data, and networks, in different ways and to differing degrees. This contestation causes intelligence contests to become more complex over time, along a historically contingent path. The increasing complexity of both intelligence performance conditions—vulnerable institutions and clandestine organization—means that offense dominance cannot be taken for granted. Contrary to popular belief, neither offense nor defense maintains a systemic advantage in the sociotechnical institution of cyberspace.

THE FOUNDING COMPROMISE

Most institutions have birthmarks, or traces of founding moments that endure long into the future. Internet architecture, likewise, was shaped by its military beginnings. Paul Baran (with the RAND Corporation) developed a packet-switching concept for the Air Force as early as 1961.[42] An ARPA deputy director stated flatly that the ARPANET project's "goal was to exploit new computer technologies to meet the needs of military command and control against nuclear threats, achieve survivable control of US nuclear forces, and improve military tactical and management decision making."[43] Janet Abbate points out that "military concerns and goals were built into the Internet" and that its design "favored military values, such as survivability, flexibility, and high performance, over commercial goals, such as low cost, simplicity, or consumer appeal."[44]

Given the military origins of the internet in the 1960s, it beggars belief to suppose that ARPA somehow forgot about security while in the midst of the Cold War and at the height of the Vietnam War! On the contrary, the same Information Processing Techniques Office (IPTO) that managed the ARPANET also organized a "Task Force to study and recommend hardware and software safeguards that would satisfactorily protect classified information in multiaccess, resource-sharing computer systems."[45] In 1970, the task force led by Willis Ware produced a landmark Defense Science Board report on multilevel security. The Ware report's insights on threat vectors and best practices still resonate today, especially its emphasis on social vulnerabilities in networked systems (figure 3.2).[46] The first nodes of the ARPANET, moreover, came online in 1970 at UCLA and the Stanford Research Institute, both hotbeds of computer security research.[47] Far from ignoring network security, IPTO helped to advance the state of the art in both networking and security at the same time.

What actually happened is that ARPA partitioned communication and security research. A fully classified networking project was prohibitive. Most of the academic experts in networking did not hold clearances. Asymmetric encryption did not yet exist. IPTO thus empowered civilian scientists at academic centers and commercial firms such as Bolt, Beranek and Newman (BBN) to work on the hard problems of packet switching in a fully unclassified environment. Meanwhile, ARPA pursued a complementary program for securing government applications on the ARPANET. The Private Line Interface (PLI) program connected KG-34 encryption peripherals, developed by the NSA, to internet routers (IMPs). Figure 3.3 depicts the shielded PLI and KG devices between a classified (red) system and an unclassified (black) IMP. A successor program named BLACKER provided

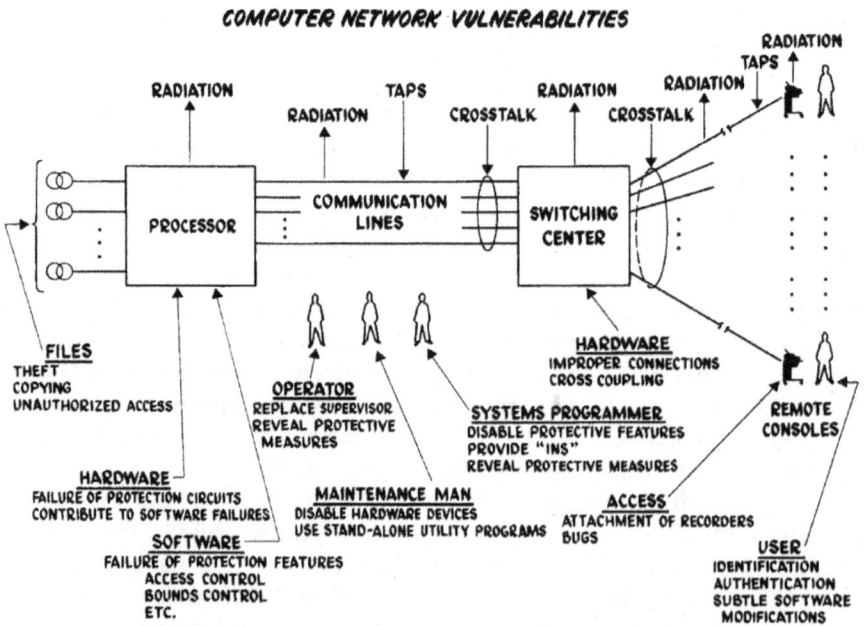

Figure 3.2. A diagram of "threat points" in Ware 1970, 6.

end-to-end encryption for the Community Online Intelligence Service (COIS) and Automated Defense Network (AUTODIN).[48]

This arrangement worked because the incentives of key stakeholders aligned. Civilian scientists received government support but had considerable freedom in designing the ARPANET.[49] Military and intelligence organizations, meanwhile, absorbed the costs of encrypting a packet-switched network. The partition of insecure communication from secure computing seemed reasonable given the set of interests and expectations when the ARPANET was created.

Report No. 2816   Bolt Beranek and Newman Inc.

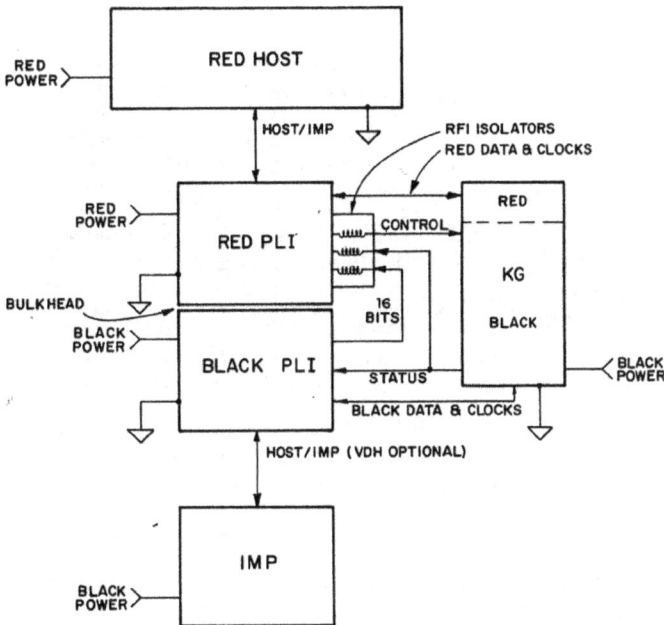

All cables and cabinets fully shielded

Figure 1   PLI Configuration.

7

Figure 3.3. Schematic of Private Line Interface (PLI) for end-to-end ARPANET encryption (source: BBN Report 2816, April 1974)

This arrangement also combined two very different management models. The management of secure government infrastructure (PLI, BLACKER, COIS, AUTODIN, etc.) was thoroughly bureaucratic. Program offices negotiated with contractors and executive agencies in a classified environment, and everything took longer than planned. By contrast, academic scientists and commercial partners adopted a famously open, informal, consensus-based form of governance. They discussed internet standards and behavior through Request for Comment (RFC) emails, edited and distributed informally by Jon Postel at UCLA, and hashed out in the "multistakeholder" working groups of the Internet Engineering task Force (IETF).[50] David Clark captured the informal ethos of the community in a landmark talk at the 1992 meeting of the IETF: "We reject: kings, presidents and voting. We believe in: rough consensus and running code."[51]

VULNERABLE INSTITUTIONS AT SCALE

The vulnerability of the unprotected civilian portion of the ARPANET was apparent as early as 1973, the same year that ARPA initiated the PLI program. Bob Metcalfe noted in an RFC that "at least two major serving hosts were crashed under suspicious circumstances by people who knew what they were risking; on yet a third system, the system wheel password was compromised—by two high school students in Los Angeles no less. We suspect that the number of dangerous security violations is larger than any of us know is growing."[52] The ARPANET was so exposed that even barely capable teenagers could hack it. By the same token, amateur miscreants' indiscretions were easily detected and mitigated (i.e., quadrant 3 of table 2.3). More capable threats might remain hidden (quadrant 4).

As the ARPANET matured, the US National Science Foundation (NSF) built a new TCP/IP backbone in the 1980s called NSFNET.[53] Internet service providers like Verizon then built and leased commercial backbones in the 1990s. The emergence of hypertext protocol (HTTP) in 1991 catalyzed an era of extraordinary growth—the World Wide Web. Internet penetration expanded dramatically in the late 1990s, especially in leading OECD countries such as the United States, Japan, and Germany. A second wave followed in the late 2000s in emerging economies such as China, Russia, India, and Brazil.[54]

Global growth of the internet roughly followed national income groups as coded by the World Bank and plotted in figure 3.4. Wealthy democracies were early adopters. Authoritarian states such as Russia and China lagged until the 2000s. As I will discuss in chapter 7, autocrats figured out how to capture the economic benefits and control the political risks of the internet. The upshot is that the internet became increasingly essential for the global economy, even as its liberalizing effects proved to be exaggerated. The dip in US data corresponds with the global financial crisis of

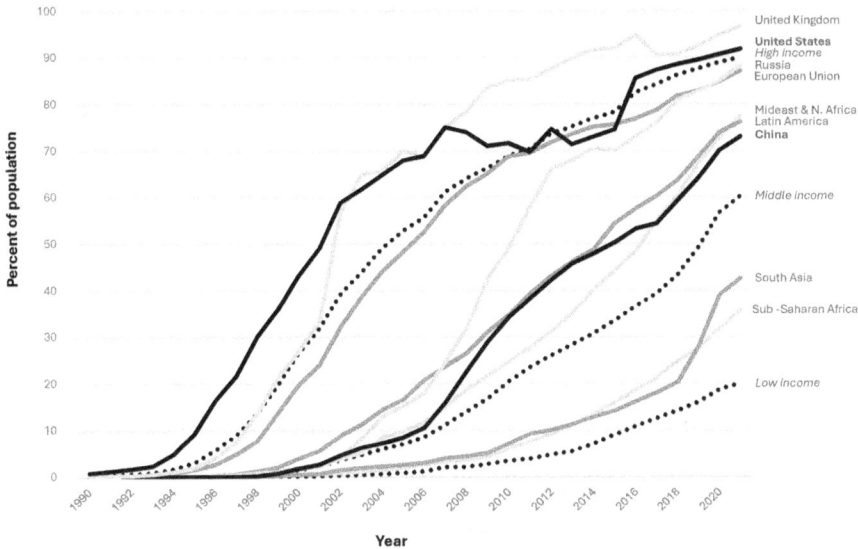

Figure 3.4. Individuals using the internet by percent of population in representative countries or regions clustered by income (data: World Bank)

2008 and its aftermath, which is suggestive of risks inherent in US internet dominance. The greatest beneficiary of connectivity was also exposed to uncontrolled shocks.

Serious cybersecurity problems began to emerge as the economic context changed but technical architecture did not. Early architectural choices became locked in as more networks and applications became dependent on them. A classic example is the transition from IPv4 to IPv6, which was intended to preempt a depletion of IP addresses; the transition proceeded decades slower than anticipated due to backward compatibility and switching costs.[55] The founding partition between security and communications that was embodied in the PLI solution also became locked in. By the 1990s, the PLI concept had been replaced by public key infrastructure (PKI), enabled by the advent of asymmetric encryption. PKI provided end-to-end encryption for civilian and military networks alike, but an important PLI legacy persisted. Both PLI and PKI encrypt data packets, but TCP/IP requires unencrypted metadata to route them. This architectural legacy became a matter of international controversy in 2013, when NSA contractor Edward Snowden leaked documents that revealed a large-scale program for the bulk collection of metadata.[56] Revelations that the United States was exploiting its advantageous position in the global internet—in effect usurping a collective institution—encouraged other countries to implement limits and controls on open connectivity. Tussles over internet privacy roiled US-European relations, and US criticisms of Chinese surveillance began to ring hollow.[57]

One must be careful not to overstate the original sin of the ARPANET partition of security and communication. Open protocols are just one source of insecurity; the functionality built on top of them is a much bigger problem. In a counterfactual world in which core internet protocols were more secure, buggy applications and gullible users would still undermine the promise of security. In our actual world, moreover, it is still possible to build secure applications on legacy protocols. The entire discipline of security engineering is predicated on this possibility. But technocratic ideals are elusive because cyberspace is a human institution, and institutions are inevitably imperfect.

An overarching theme in the economics of information security is that the root causes of software insecurity are perverse incentives and market failures.[58] The tech economy rewards vendors who are first to market, which enables them to build larger user communities.[59] Users, meanwhile, value the direct benefits of functionality, while they discount the indirect risks of insecurity.[60] Vendors who spend time and money on security engineering, therefore, risk being outcompeted by vendors who do not. The positive externalities of networks thus generate negative externalities for security.[61] Even if consumers do value security, moreover, insecurity is notoriously hard to measure.[62] The inability to tell the difference between secure and insecure products leads to a "market for lemons" in security.[63] The basic problem is that the costs of security engineering are concentrated on vendors, but its societal benefits are diffuse. This is a recipe for collective action failure.[64]

The internet boom, accordingly, was a happy time for hackers. Cyberspace was exposed—highly connected and extremely vulnerable. Hackers leveraged the same features that enabled legitimate innovation, and they exploited the bugs that were rife in popular software. Cybercrime, spam, website defacement, and identity theft soared in the 1990s, raising concerns about systemic vulnerability. An infamous example is the Morris worm, a coding experiment by a Cornell University graduate student in 1988 that temporarily crashed the internet. In the same IETF talk where Clark praised "rough consensus and running code," he also worried that the Morris worm heralded "the decade of the cyber-terrorist."[65] Clark sounded a dire warning for internet governance: "Lack of security means the END OF LIFE AS WE KNOW IT!!"[66] He was worried less about what harm hackers might inflict than about what the backlash against market failure might mean for meritocratic internet governance.

COUNTERINTELLIGENCE AT SCALE

The internet did not end, of course. Hackers exploited exposed systems, but the internet grew anyway. Why? The mixed architecture of the internet is part of the answer. The same layered architecture of the internet that enabled hackers to develop malware (and the NSA to conduct bulk surveillance) also encouraged innovation in computer security. To some extent, hacking was too easy on the early internet. As indiscreet deceivers attracted more attention, counterdeceivers emerged to raise security barriers and mitigate vulnerabilities. In response to the Morris worm, for example, the Department of Defense created the first Computer Emergency Response Team Coordinating Center (CERT/CC) to facilitate common responses to systemic internet threats. Similar organizations appeared in many countries to coordinate transnational incident responses, and to develop new security protocols, on an informal and voluntary basis. The 1990s thus saw the rise of a decentralized, collaborative, global community of practice for cybersecurity.[67]

A series of incidents in the late 1990s galvanized the attention of US policymakers. These included Eligible Receiver in 1997 (in which an NSA red team hacked the US military), Solar Sunrise in 1998 (in which California teenagers breached military systems), and Moonlight Maze in 1999 (in which Russian hackers breached US systems). The military services began creating information warfare units to defend against cyber threats, and some of them became new threats themselves. The Department of Defense eventually created US Cyber Command in 2010 to consolidate cyber activities, and it became a fully fledged unified combatant command in 2018.[68]

The classic solution for market failure is public policy. But governments can fail too, or at least create inefficiency and coordination problems. There are many stakeholders in US cyber policy, including the Departments of Commerce, Defense, Homeland Security, Justice, and State, and their authorities, missions, and priorities are not always compatible. While diplomats promote international norms to discourage hacking, the NSA is the most capable offensive cyber threat in the world. While offensive operators discover and exploit secret vulnerabilities, network defenders report and patch them. While national security agencies focus on foreign threats, commercial industry bears the brunt of foreign attacks. Contradictions in the goals of different institutional actors encourage the development of new administrative processes to coordinate them. In the early decades of the twenty-first century, a series of bureaucratic reforms in the United States and elsewhere piled on new operational capacity, additional layers of management, and new advisory and oversight bodies.[69] Domestic politics can inject additional friction. For example, President Donald Trump created the Cybersecurity and Infrastructure Security Agency (CISA) in 2018 to coordinate federal efforts and interface with the private sector, but CISA later became a pariah among Trump supporters because of its efforts to combat disinformation under President Joseph Biden, which led to calls to hobble CISA during the second Trump administration.[70]

Cyber policy is especially complicated because some market actors act like governments too. In 2020, boosted by widespread dependence on digital services during the COVID-19 pandemic, five US tech platforms (Apple, Microsoft, Alphabet-Google, Meta-Facebook, and Amazon, which might be collectively called AMAMA) accounted for 22 percent of the S&P 500, with a combined annual revenue of $1.2 trillion, increasing to 25 percent by 2025.[71] These massive global platforms are a perennial target of antitrust suits. Yet the AMAMA firms also play a quasi-regulatory role.[72] Microsoft products, for example, are a systemic source of vulnerability in the global cyber ecosystem, yet Microsoft has also emerged as a major counterintelligence actor to police it, which in turn encourages US government oversight.[73] Maha Rafi Atal points out that platform firms are simultaneously "private platforms and public spheres" that exploit "the institutional cracks of the regulatory system" to shape their own environment.[74] As Laura DeNardis observes, "Internet governance is a potent and complicated form of governance because it involves the technical mediation of the public sphere and the privatization of conditions of civil liberties."[75]

A key development in the history of counterintelligence has been the rapid rise of the global cybersecurity industry. As in the tech industry generally, US firms have dominated. By 2016, there were thirteen thousand cybersecurity firms worldwide; three-quarters of them emerged only after 2000, and most were American.[76] Some developed and sold antivirus software and firewalls. Others offered incident response and threat intelligence services. By 2024, the global cybersecurity market was valued at $210 billion and was growing at 12 percent annually; it was forecasted to reach $314 billion by 2028.[77] The commercialization and professionalization of cybersecurity, on balance, has improved the ability of firms and governments to reduce digital risk and respond to digital threats.[78] Innovation in cyber insurance has also enabled firms to transfer risk to insurance markets, while also reintroducing classic problems of moral hazard (disincentivizing investment in security) and imperfect information (difficulty assessing security and pricing premiums).[79]

Indeed, new market security solutions often create new security problems. As private platforms scale up, they tend to recapitulate government coordination problems. Public and private organizations alike now rely on a bewildering array of middleware for encryption, authentication, threat detection, vulnerability mitigation, and so on. This means that organizations and individual users must spend more time debugging interoperability and access frictions. Even worse, the commercial interests of security firms sometimes diverge from public interests. Commercial threat reporting, for example, focuses on high-end threats to corporate and government customers, but hackers also ravage journalists, activists, and nongovernmental organizations.[80] The rise of the cybersecurity industry has also raised familiar concerns about a military-industrial complex, uncontrolled arms markets, private security contractors, and mercenaries.[81]

CLANDESTINE ORGANIZATION AT SCALE

Some private deception specialists have capabilities that rival those of state spy agencies. An infamous example is NSOGroup, an Israeli company that employed veterans of Unit 8200, Israel's analogue to the NSA.[82] NSOGroup developed numerous "zero click" exploits that provided remote access to Apple iPhones without any user interaction.[83] This was an impressive feat because Apple iOS had a well-deserved reputation for taking security seriously. NSOGroup ostensibly marketed its Pegasus spyware and back-end support services for counterterrorism and national security missions, but several authoritarian regimes purchased its services to spy on political dissidents and journalists. The Benjamin Netanyahu government had authorized the sale of Pegasus spyware to help curry favor with Gulf states and other countries. Pegasus spyware was later linked to the killing and dismemberment of *Washington Post* journalist Jamal Khashoggi by Saudi agents in Istanbul.[84] Pegasus was also implicated in the disappearance and murder of journalists and activists in Mexico.[85]

Academic researchers at Citizen Lab at the University of Toronto were the first to discover NSOGroup's exploits.[86] The intelligence contest between Citizen Lab and NSOGroup even featured in-person counterintelligence stings.[87] Investigative journalists built on the work of Citizen Lab to reveal the extent of NSOGroup's skullduggery.[88] These efforts prompted the Biden administration to blacklist NSOGroup, along with another Israeli firm named Candiru, which prevented US firms from selling to them or their subsidiaries.[89] These firms then relocated, changed their names, and reconstituted capabilities. Nongovernmental deception specialists play an increasingly important role in counterintelligence.

The conditions for intelligence performance are complicated in this case. The iPhone provided ubiquitous connectivity, but iOS had excellent security protocols (e.g., BlastDoor); nevertheless, there were subtle vulnerabilities. I would code vulnerable institutions as mostly secure or slightly exposed. NSOGroup had world-class capacity and operational security, but its business model created dependency on unsavory and overzealous customers, and blended operations combining digital surveillance and physical security services created further complexity. I would code clandestine organization as mostly sophisticated or slightly dependent. These mixed conditions enabled NSOGroup to operate in quadrant 2 of figure 2.3 much of the time: A sophisticated organization used complex operations to overcome nominally secure institutions. But over time, the environment became less permissive as operational complexity produced friction and noise that counterintelligence entities like Citizen Lab could exploit. Intelligence performance then shifted toward quadrant 4 as sustained secret access became less feasible.

The strategic implications are nuanced. In contrast to the claim that cyberspace empowers the weak against the strong, Pegasus helped to make strong regimes even stronger and weak victims more vulnerable. While the cyberwar narrative tends to emphasize threats *to* the state (national security), NSOGroup's clients highlight threats *from* the state (human security). Critics of the cyberwar narrative sometimes argue that hacking has never killed anybody, but Pegasus shows how intelligence operations can complement lethal action, somewhat like a high-powered sniper scope. This is an important qualification to the claim that secrecy makes cyber operations unsuitable for coercion. The "cross domain" combination of Pegasus and authoritarian security services created a chilling effect on dissidents and journalists.

This is not your father's secret statecraft. NSOGroup was a commercial intelligence company, employing state-level technical capabilities, exploiting a ubiquitous commercial platform, supporting economic statecraft for a democratic state, contracting services to authoritarian regimes to target nonstate actors, violating human rights worldwide, revealed by nongovernmental organizations, and provoking international sanctions. The institutional entanglements between a wide variety of public and private actors are complex, transnational, and sociotechnical. This case exemplifies the transformations of secret statecraft in the twenty-first century: Tradecraft relies on more digital tools and techniques; the scale of operations is unprecedented; commercial and other civilian actors play an outsized role; and digital tools can be used to enable physical violence. Cybersecurity is an intelligence contest that is more digitized, supersized, civilianized, and weaponized.

The Infrastructure of Liberal Order

This chapter has advanced an institutional interpretation of cyberspace. The "cyber domain" is not like the physical environments of land, sea, air, and space. Cyberspace—control space—is better understood as an assemblage of rules and tools that enhance measurement, coordination, and enforcement at scale.

Because cyberspace is an institution, insights from political economy are essential for understanding it. First, institutions are path dependent. This means that their design reflects their founding moments. The security imperatives of the Cold War inspired the search for more resilient communications, so the Pentagon invested in the ARPANET. Administrators and scientists did not forget about security, but rather agreed to partition the development of packet-switched routing and end-to-end encryption. An enduring legacy of this compromise is encrypted data and unencrypted metadata.

Second, markets and governments shape the path-dependent evolution of institutions. Economic imperatives have encouraged the growth of the internet, interconnecting a more diverse global community. Malicious hackers have exploited connectivity and vulnerability in the same network, which has encouraged market actors and government agencies to invest more in security. More effective local defenses, in turn, have encouraged attackers to exercise more discretion, while a heterogenous collection of defenders have discovered compatible interests in collective information security.

Political philosophers emphasize different views of institutions. The tradition of Locke argues that commonwealths emerge to improve the common good. The tradition of Rousseau argues that institutions reflect and reinforce unequal power relations. The internet embodies elements of both. Actors voluntarily do adopt open protocols and participate in internet governance to improve mutual connectivity and prosperity. But cyberspace has also amplified the advantages of larger corporations and more capable states, and it has contributed to growing economic inequality and various social ills. Indeed, tussles within and between US government agencies and US tech giants had an outsized influence on the development of the internet. Cyberspace may be a technological construct, but it is also a political institution, at once a digital commonwealth and an engine of inequality.

CYBER HEGEMONY

To paraphrase Charles Tilly, America made the internet, and the internet made America. Cyberspace may even be described, with little exaggeration, as the infrastructure of liberal hegemony. The internet emerged from and continues to bolster the dominant geopolitical position of the United States. Contrary to the techno-libertarian hype of the 1990s, commercial innovation in information technology has not flattened or undermined US power. On the contrary, digital systems have amplified the military power and economic prosperity of the United States, and of many other countries besides.[90]

The development of cyberspace recapitulates a familiar pattern of market-driven and technologically enabled US preeminence. And yet the same technology becomes embroiled in global controversies about privacy, monopoly, and toxic content. In the world of cybersecurity, US entities can play the role of victim, facilitator, protector, and threat, sometimes all at the same time. But this, too, is not unusual. Cyberspace tends to amplify all the complexity and contradictions of its national origins.

The US Constitution concentrates responsibility for national security and interstate commerce in the federal government, but American federalism distributes policy sovereignty and internal security across fifty different states. The US economy is supercharged by innovative firms that compete relentlessly in global markets, but economic competition depends on government regulation and centralized monetary policy. Each aspect of this mixed market has strengths and weaknesses: Decentralized markets promote innovation and efficiency, but they also enable pollution and monopoly; centralized governments can regulate market failures, but they are also lumbering and corruptible. This is the American way.

Cyberspace, likewise, is a complex mixture of self-organization and formal management. On the supposedly anarchic internet, any user can type any website address into a browser. But all websites rely on a hierarchical DNS to resolve addresses. Any network operator can reconfigure an AS, but all connect through IXPs via standardized BGP. Any country can connect its government and industry to the internet, but they inevitably come to depend on dominant US software platforms (AMAMA). The internet may be a universal blessing, but it benefits some countries and companies a lot more than others. For better and for worse, cyberspace—vibrant, flexible, and contested—reflects the global liberal order that the United States built in its image.

Neither cyberspace nor global capitalism is completely ungoverned. They are just not governed very efficiently. Much like the so-called liberal order, cyberspace is managed through a complex mixture of state regulation, nonstate governance institutions, international norms, corporate policy, and market forces.[91] The United States' role in this management may or may not be necessary (IR scholars debate this), but it is always contested.

Coordination for cybersecurity, likewise, has long had a recognizably American flavor. Many major and historical players in cyberspace are US corporations. Many countries have counterparts to the US cybersecurity agencies, but US agencies have comparatively greater global impact. In regulating the US tech industry, US agencies indirectly regulate global cyberspace as well. The dominance of US tech giants as key platform governors is recapitulating the hegemonic role of the United States as the first among equals in international institutions.

A paradoxical feature of the digital liberal order is that it interconnects its own challengers. Liberal hegemony invites challenges from rising states, resentful states, angry orphans, and, improbably enough, the hegemon's own government.[92] Chapter 7 will return to this theme by examining how China managed to repurpose liberal means for illiberal ends. As of early 2025 when this book went to press, the destabilization of global liberal order by the United States itself puts the viability of cyberspace in question as well. The key point for now is simply that cyberspace amplifies institutional dynamics, including the contestation of institutions.

AMBIGUOUS CONDITIONS FOR INTELLIGENCE PERFORMANCE

Cybersecurity is not just about technology. Threat actors—as well as their victims, service providers, and counterintelligence adversaries—are human organizations in a human-built world. Cyber intrusions, therefore, are not simply network links between remote attackers and victim systems. Intrusions are social relationships between complex organizations mediated by the global economy. This perspective has at least two important implications for understanding cyber threats.

One is that technical capabilities and vulnerabilities are created by social actors who pursue power, profit, or status. Software developers are human employees of capitalist firms competing in global markets regulated by national governments in an international system on an interconnected planet. Malware developers are similarly situated. It is imperative for threat analysts to consider the political and economic interests that motivate, and the incentives that shape, the behavior of all relevant actors in this system. This also goes for the cybersecurity industry, which is hardly a neutral defender against all cyber threats. Politics shapes both threats and threat hunting.

Another implication is that no actor or analyst can fully understand this bewilderingly complex dynamic system. For threat actors, the imperfection of knowledge about operational conditions can be a source of opportunity (because ignorant victims can be deceived). But ignorance is also a source of friction (because ignorant attackers can deceive themselves). For threat analysts, much knowledge about the threat landscape comes from commercial intelligence reporting of uneven quality, some of it essentially just marketing material. Even where misaligned incentives for data sharing can be resolved, technical facts alone cannot tell the whole story. Many facts remain hidden, and some of the most important facts are not technical at all. This is why theory is important.

Because cyberspace is a sociotechnical institution, an institutional theory of secret statecraft is useful for understanding cybersecurity. The historical evolution of cyberspace exemplifies the path-dependent logic of institutional development generally. As in all institutions, the rules and tools of cyberspace are shaped by political and economic interests and the incentives created by markets and governments. The greater salience of automated "tools" in cyberspace (devices and infrastructures) just increases the relevance of its social "rules" (norms and practices). The coordination of computational functionality relies everywhere on human beings to design, use, maintain, adapt, debug, and repair it. The root causes of exploitable vulnerability in cyberspace are perverse incentives and inefficient transactions in its coordination.

Cyberspace is more complex than most institutions, in part because it connects everything else. The most complex system of control ever devised by humanity, in turn, gives rise to the most complex contests of deception in history. A wide variety of deception specialists—spy agencies, security firms, criminal networks, digital activists—operate on different sides of multiple overlapping contests. The systemic implications for intelligence performance are profoundly ambiguous. Technical and social features are both improving and degrading the two enabling conditions of intelligence performance in different ways.

First consider the principal components of vulnerable institutions: connectivity and vulnerability. Cyberspace provides connectivity at scale, and software monocultures are full of features and bugs that can be exploited. But connectivity is not absolute, because internetworks are fragmented by numerous physical and logical barriers. Vulnerability is also not absolute, because there is a thriving global cybersecurity ecosystem, and firms and governments are gradually, albeit unevenly, improving their cyber defenses.

Next consider the principal components of clandestine organization: capacity and discretion. Cyberspace enables distributed teams to use modular platforms to manage complex intrusions, and there are many ways for threat actors to obfuscate their activity amid the complexity of cyberspace. But this improvement in capacity is neither absolute nor universal. Many deception specialists also find themselves dependent on third parties, outside vendors, and public infrastructure. Discretion is also not absolute, because there are many ways for attackers to make mistakes, leave clues, and compromise operations.

Given all this complexity and contingency, information technology does not create any simple (systemic) advantage for offense or defense. Put simply, cyberspace is not offense dominant. Analysts must look instead to the details of specific cyber campaigns to assess the (dyadic) offense-defense balance between particular competitors in specific circumstances. This will always be a more limited and contingent judgment. Technological implementation does constrain the art of the possible for cyber threats, so it is always essential to understand what is or is not technically possible, but technology does not constrain outcomes uniquely. In secret statecraft in any era, institutional circumstances usually explain more than the technological state of the art does. To drive home this point, the next chapter circles back to a less digital milieu at the dawn of the computer age.

PART II. SECRET STATECRAFT IN PRACTICE

CHAPTER 4

Espionage

Bletchley Park and the Mechanization of Intelligence

During World War II, the British Government Code and Cypher School (GC&CS) at Bletchley Park broke the Enigma cipher, which Germany had considered to be unbreakable. The "Ultra" intelligence derived thereby provided Allied commanders with unique insight into Axis plans and operations.[1] This accomplishment was enabled by a new mathematical approach to cryptography and new computing machines that could process data at scale. Bletchley Park thus set important precedents for modern cyber security.

GC&CS is rightly celebrated as one of the most successful intelligence organizations of all time. This makes Bletchley Park a critical case for any theory of intelligence success. There is also an abundance of archival evidence available about signals intelligence (SIGINT) in World War II. This is useful for illuminating organizational processes that are harder to study in modern cases. This chapter does not add new historical facts about the well-studied case of Bletchley Park, but it does offer a new interpretation of why GC&CS was so successful: Bletchley Park was a sophisticated organization that exploited Germany's exposed institutions, which together enabled persistent secret access. Bletchley Park is a clear case of successful intelligence performance, and both of the necessary conditions for success are indeed present. As such, the theory in this book passes an important "hoop test."[2] Process tracing further shows how and why these conditions mattered.

Many cyber actors today struggle to consistently meet these same conditions, but Bletchley Park met them for years. This provides an invaluable basis of comparison for evaluating modern cases, and it also helps to show how even the best operational conditions do not guarantee strategic outcomes. Intelligence success at Bletchley Park was only an indirect factor in Allied military success. Victory in World War II cannot be attributed to any one element, let alone intelligence. Still, when commanders knew how to use Ultra, they could plan better operations and receive better feedback on their progress. As historian Paul Kennedy writes, "Far, far better to have it than not, but by the very nature of the intelligence war with Germany it could only produce mixed results, not miracles."[3] Cyber operations today, conducted in far more complex sociotechnical conditions, can still produce only indirect political effects.

This chapter unfolds in five parts. First, I discuss the relevance of Bletchley Park for cybersecurity. Second, I show how German institutions were vulnerable to exploitation. Third, I show how a British clandestine organization was able to exploit them. Fourth, I discuss the combined effect of these conditions for British intelligence performance. Fifth, I conclude with a discussion of contingency and complexity.

The First Cyber Campaign

It may seem anachronistic to describe Bletchley Park as a cyber organization. Yet the very idea of "cybernetics" emerged from the wartime problems of fire control, navigation, and cryptography.[4] Bletchley Park's star cryptographer, Alan Turing, published a seminal article on computing theory right before the war, and he made additional contributions during it.[5] An American cryptographer at Bell Labs, Claude Shannon, developed the basic ideas of information theory during the war.[6] These two founding fathers met each other during Turing's 1942 trip to the United States to improve Allied cryptographic collaboration. Shannon recalled, "Turing and I used to talk about the possibility of simulating the entirety of the human brain. . . . We both thought that this should be possible in not very long, in ten or 15 years."[7] Two SIGINT pioneers were excited about AI. Cyber was in the air.

Cyber competition is essentially a digitized, supersized, and civilianized intelligence contest, and Bletchley Park is a key historical inflection point in these developments. GC&CS invented electromechanical marvels such as the Bombe machines that emulated Enigma, and novel electronic devices such as Colossus that attacked the Lorentz teleprinter cipher. GC&CS standardized the term "SIGINT" in October 1943 to refer to the integration of radio interception, cryptography or codebreaking, and intelligence analysis.[8] GC&CS performed all these activities at unprecedented scale. University professors, telecommunications engineers, and corporate managers at Bletchley Park pioneered new analytic and administrative methods, often borrowing best practices from civilian industry and academia. By digitizing, supersizing, and civilianizing SIGINT, Bletchley Park waged a cyber campaign before cyberspace.

FROM SIGINT TO CYBER

Before Bletchley Park, quirky puzzlers in the black chambers of foreign ministries decrypted individual incepts by hand. After Bletchley Park, professional intelligence bureaucracies used automated tools to decrypt entire cryptosystems. The SIGINT competition between the Allies and the Axis thus became a duel of computing machines—Enigma versus Bombe, Lorentz versus Colossus. Colossus may or may not have been the first programmable computer, but it certainly set important precedents in the history of digital computing.[9] This makes Bletchley Park the earliest possible candidate for an electronically mediated intelligence contest, or secret statecraft in proto-cyberspace.

GC&CS set the template for modern SIGINT agencies such as the British Government Communications Headquarters (GCHQ), its direct descendant, and the US National Security Agency (NSA), its wartime collaborator. GCHQ and NSA went on to become some of the most capable cyber organizations on the planet. A 1942 report from the director of GC&CS stated, "We believe that we should try to read every enemy signal, neglecting none however apparently unimportant."[10] Seventy years later, documents leaked from the NSA expressed similar sentiments: "Collect it all, tag it, store it."[11] Since cyberspace has supercharged SIGINT, it is helpful to know how SIGINT began.

There are obvious differences between midcentury SIGINT and twenty-first-century cyber espionage. Only government agencies had access to highly controlled electromechanical encryption devices back then, but today everyone has access to robust public encryption (PKI). While 1940s SIGINT was mainly a governmental affair, commercial actors play an outsized role in cybersecurity today. In classic SIGINT, radio signals are passively collected without affecting target communications, but cyber intrusions actively consume bandwidth and memory on target networks. For the same reasons, cyber intrusions can also influence or disrupt network operations, while classic SIGINT techniques focus exclusively on collection. Bletchley Park was a wartime SIGINT agency, but many (or most) cyber campaigns occur in peacetime.

But all this makes Bletchley Park even more interesting as a basis for comparison. This book is about secret statecraft *and* cybersecurity, after all. I am interested in both the continuities of organized deception and its transformations in the digital era. Bletchley Park is also an attractive case because it is so well documented.[12] The availability of data is an attractive feature given that so many modern cyber campaigns are shrouded in secrecy. Declassified archival documents provide rich detail about the inner workings of intelligence organizations in World War II. Comparable detail is hard, if not impossible, to recover from technical forensics alone when most state cyber activity remains highly classified. Organizational behavior changes more slowly than information technology, so insights gleaned from the twentieth-century case of Bletchley Park are likely to remain relevant for cybersecurity in the twenty-first. Indeed, there is enough information available about Bletchley Park to provide a tentative basis for generalization to a larger universe of intelligence campaigns.

INTELLIGENCE PERFORMANCE

In the typology of chapter 1, Bletchley Park is a case of espionage, which uses organized deception to collect secrets to gain an information advantage. Counterintelligence is an important secondary theme here. German counterintelligence was less effective than British counterintelligence, which advantaged British espionage. Covert action is less prominent in this case study, although Ultra was used to support Allied deception, including the successful strategic feint before D-Day. Below, I will briefly touch on Operation Fortitude as a shadow case, which provides a helpful basis of historical comparison for the discussion of modern information operations in chapter 6.

The essence of deception, for any purpose and in any era, is cooperation-enabled competition. Unlike brute force or open negotiation, deception relies on the voluntary assistance of the deceived. As Sir Michael Howard writes in the fifth volume of the official history *British Intelligence in the Second World War*, "Deception can never be effective either in love or in war, unless there is a certain willingness to be deceived, and the London Controlling Section could never have succeeded as well as it did had it not possessed, at the highest level of the German Command, its unconscious sympathizers."[13]

All intelligence contests are duels of deception. Success relies on the unconscious collusion of the deceived. But cooperation is especially hard to achieve in war, where competitors are trying to destroy each other. GC&CS was doubly successful in this regard. Britain systematically decrypted German communications while keeping Germany completely in the dark. Howard thus argues that Great Britain "enjoyed two extraordinary, possibly unique, advantages; advantages so extraordinary that one would be rash to assume that we or indeed anyone else could ever possess them in comparable measure again."[14]

If luck is when preparedness meets opportunity, then Bletchley Park was very lucky. Its enemy offered a golden opportunity by broadcasting a large volume of traffic that was protected by vulnerable cryptosystems. GC&CS was prepared to exploit this opportunity through able management, adept adaptation, and disciplined security. Not every deception specialist is so fortunate. Many are not. Without vulnerable institutions and a clandestine organization that can exploit them, successful intelligence operations are impossible.

Bletchley Park met both conditions of intelligence performance for years on end. Target institutions were exposed. German reliance on radio provided pervasive connectivity, while German design flaws and security lapses created exploitable vulnerability. GC&CS was also sophisticated. It had the operational capacity to balance formal management and creative adaptation, while a cult of security improved discretion to protect its valuable yet fragile achievements. These conditions enabled Bletchley Park to gain and maintain persistent access into German organizations for most of the war. Cumulative success in SIGINT provided the Allies with an indirect efficiency advantage. Military commanders who were willing and able to use Ultra improved their operational performance, even as they still had to fight the war in order to win.

Exposed Institutions

The most exposed institutions are those with a lot of connectivity and vulnerability. Connectivity refers to the information channels and interface protocols that enable a social group to communicate and coordinate more efficiently. Connectivity provides access for threat actors who usurp institutional efficiency. Vulnerability refers to flaws in the monitoring and enforcement mechanisms that afford intelligence exploitation. An important characteristic of vulnerability is that the intelligence target creates it willingly but unwittingly. Technical design flaws and lax security postures provide unwitting cooperation with hostile threat actors.

RADIO CONNECTIVITY

Radio produced a connectivity revolution in the early twentieth century. Radio connectivity, together with supporting protocols for sending and receiving messages, dramatically improved Germany's ability to project power.[15] While the German military was large, the Continent was vast. Germany's grand strategy of conquest required movement beyond fixed landlines. Germany solved this problem through the wide adoption of mobile radio sets, which enabled its geographically dispersed forces to combine air, armor, and infantry units into coordinated mobile offensives, or blitzkriegs. Radio also enabled the Kriegsmarine to direct U-boats to intercept Allied convoys, which would otherwise have been lost in the vast Atlantic.

The institutions of radio communication and tactical intelligence improved the efficiency of German combined arms warfare and naval operations. But intelligence gleaned from German radio also improved the efficiency of British defenses. At the beginning of the war, Britain was isolated, overmatched, and utterly dependent on vulnerable sea lines of communication. Germany fielded a formidable army and air force, and its power grew with every conquest. Britain, by sharp contrast, did not have enough force to defend everywhere. Intelligence improved the efficiency of British defenses by helping decision-makers figure where to concentrate or avoid. British innovation SIGINT (and radar) was a functional response to its acute demand for information. In effect, the British efficiency advantage in SIGINT offset the efficiency advantages of radio for German war fighting. David Kahn goes further to suggest that "while intelligence is necessary to the defense, it is only contingent to the offense."[16]

Radio has the economic characteristics of a public good. Anyone within range of a transmitter can passively listen to a radio broadcast (it is non-excludable), and the activity of listening does not diminish the signal for other listeners (it is nonrival). These features are useful for military forces that need to solve the collective action problems of large-scale campaigns. But the nonexcludability and nonrivalry of radio is also a boon for intelligence. Radio makes it possible for hostile intelligence to directly access the internal communications of remote adversaries. High-power, long-distance radio waves propagate in all directions at the speed of light, which makes it hard to deny access to enemy eavesdroppers. These intelligence risks became obvious to all combatants well before World War II.[17] All took steps to protect communications using encryption, using both manual methods and mechanical devices, although not always with the same proficiency.

CRYPTOGRAPHIC INSTITUTIONS

Cryptography and communication are closely related, historically and mathematically. In 1945, in a classified paper for Bell Labs, Claude Shannon published the first mathematical theory of cryptography.[18] Cryptography encodes messages from a source that can be decoded by a receiver but not by an eavesdropper in between (figure 4.1). Cryptographers try to

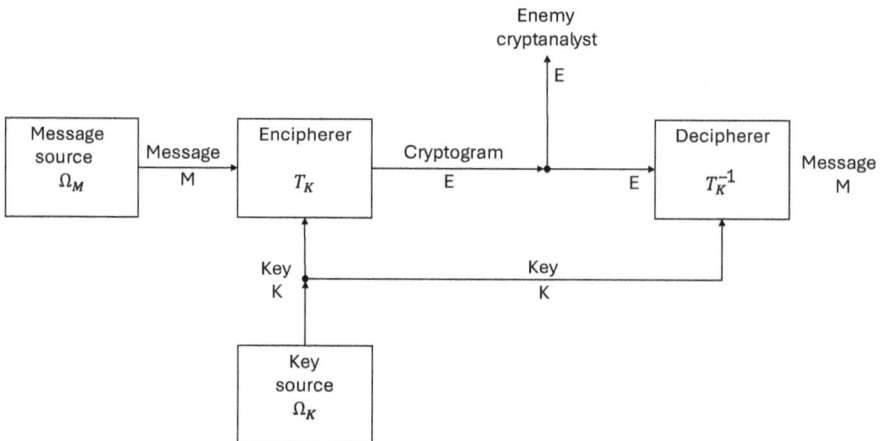

Figure 4.1. Shannon's model of symmetric cryptography, based on *A Mathematical Theory of Cryptography* (1945)

eliminate uncertainty for the legitimate receiver while maximizing it for the eavesdropper. Shannon later published a paper on the mathematics of communication in 1948.[19] Information theory is preoccupied with reducing uncertainty in a noisy channel (figure 4.2).

As the similarity of the two figures suggests, the mathematics of deception and the mathematics of coordination are one and the same. Logically, communication comes first, enabling deceptive exploitation of it. Historically, cryptography came first, preoccupied with protecting communications from exploitation. Encipherment, from the perspective of information theory, is a manufactured source of noise for the eavesdropper. A receiver with the right key, however, can decipher the message noiselessly. A clever enemy may even be able to discover the key if the noise source is not completely random.

Communication and cryptography depend on institutions. The only difference between informational coordination and cryptographic deception, from this perspective, is the guiding intentionality. Pure communication is cooperative, but cryptography is competitive. Encryption protocols are institutions for communication that enable selective exclusion, not universal access. Cryptography works by partitioning a communication system into *public connectivity* and *private content*. This is somewhat like the distinction between open internet metadata and encrypted datagrams discussed in chapter 3.

From the perspective of *all* actors in a competitive system, encrypted content has the properties of a private good. The cryptosystem excludes unauthorized actors who could negate the value of the information. Enemy knowledge of a secret attack plan, for instance, would enable the enemy to defeat the plan. Secret content is rival in this sense because enemy counteractions can lessen its operational value, even as radio connectivity is nonrival in the sense that many people can receive the same bits of information.

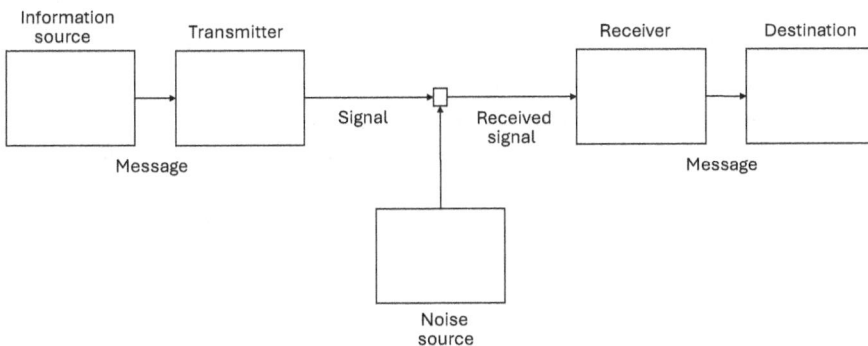

Figure 4.2. Shannon's general model of communication, based on "A Mathematical Theory of Communication" (1948)

From the perspective of just the legitimate communicators, moreover, a good cryptosystem can also be interpreted as a club good: It excludes adversaries while providing friendly access to nonrival content. Friendly communicators use a shared key to decrypt traffic and coordinate collective action, while enemy eavesdroppers without the key are excluded.

CRYPTANALYTIC EXPLOITATION

The technical partition of public connectivity and private content presents two distinct intelligence opportunities. The first is *traffic analysis*, which examines patterns of connectivity rather than communication content. Encryption offers little defense here. Traffic patterns are a (nonexcludable) public good. The strength, volume, timing, and call signs of enemy traffic, in turn, can reveal information about the structure and concentration of enemy forces.[20] Radio-direction-finding techniques can triangulate enemy units, especially ships that would be otherwise unobservable.

The second opportunity is *cryptanalysis,* or codebreaking, which attempts to recover the content of messages. Cryptography and cryptanalysis are the offensive and defensive twins of *cryptology.*[21] The former disguises a signal to look like noise, while the latter recovers the signal from the noise. The successful cryptanalyst steals the club good of encrypted content.

GC&CS wove both methods together. Traffic analysis could improve cryptanalysis by suggesting probable unit identities and communication topics. Cryptanalysis could improve traffic analysis by identifying relevant units and frequencies.

Another institutional feature that aided cryptanalysis was common knowledge of encryption protocols. Enigma was invented by a civilian engineer, who applied for a patent in 1918. The German military adopted modified Enigma machines in the late 1920s.[22] But the general principles of Enigma were well understood. Allied machines such as Typex and Sigaba worked similarly. The US Patent Office even approved a patent for Enigma in 1928 (figure 4.3).[23] When Allied cryptanalysts encountered new codes they couldn't break, therefore, they could make educated guesses about the machines that had produced them. Common scientific knowledge helped cryptanalysts and electrical engineers to establish bounds on their reverse-engineering problem. Because the general principles of mechanical encipherment were well understood, only the daily settings of the machine and some architectural details stood out as intelligence gaps. Filling these gaps was the major goal of Allied cryptanalysis.[24]

ENIGMA SECURITY

For centuries before World War II, codebreaking was a craft. Cryptanalysts focused on only the most promising messages because manual decryption was a long and tedious process. Even GC&CS did not pay much attention to machine decryption prior to 1939.[25] Mechanical encryption machines like Enigma changed the game. They improved the efficiency of field communications by enabling radio operators to quickly send and receive highly secure messages. The flood of encrypted traffic overwhelmed manual methods.

Enigma implements a system of electromechanical rotors, wires, plugs, and other settings (e.g., figure 4.3). Each rotor wires one logical alphabet to another. The press of a typewriter key (the plaintext input) completes an electrical circuit, which passes through several rotors and back again, to light up a different letter (the ciphertext output). Each keypress also advances the rotors to a new setting, which means that a subsequent press

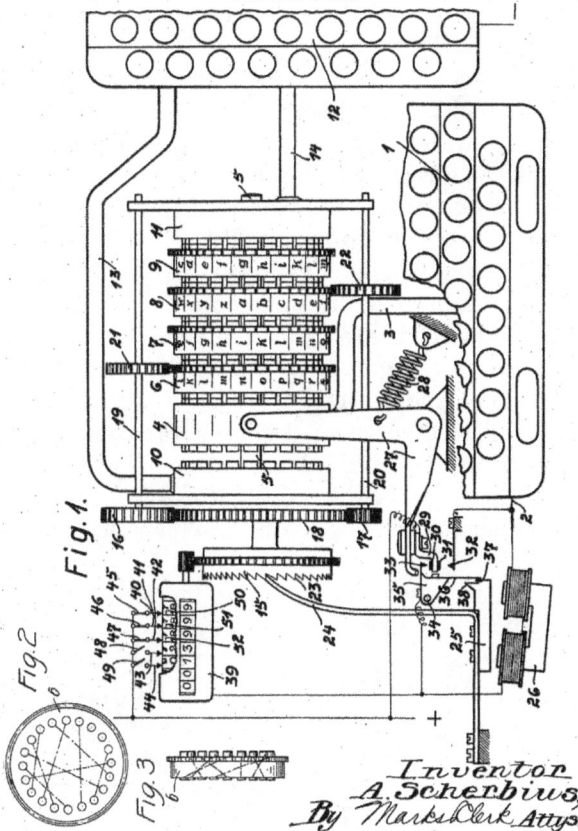

Figure 4.3. Schematic of the commercial variant of Enigma, 1928 (source: US Patent Office)

of the same key completes a different circuit through the rotors, which lights up a different letter. The resulting ciphertext appears nearly random. More randomness (entropy) is better.[26]

But Enigma output is not truly random. The mapping of plaintext to ciphertext can be reversed by a deterministic process. This is what enables decryption. Keying in the same sequence of ciphertext letters, starting with the same initial settings, outputs the original sequence of plaintext letters. The design of the machine thus embodies a symmetric encryption algorithm, and the initial settings embody the key. This means that even if an Enigma machine falls into enemy hands, security is still assured so long as the key remains secret. The separation of public algorithm from private key is known as Kerckhoffs's principle.[27]

The Germans were justifiably confident in the theoretical security of Enigma. In principle, the three-rotor military Enigma could produce 3×10^{114} machine states, or keys. The four-rotor naval Enigma expanded this to 2×10^{145} states. In practice, some settings were fixed or rarely changed, so British cryptanalysts faced only 10^{23} possibilities, but this was still a vast search space.[28]

Symmetric protocols such as Enigma require senders and receivers to use the same key, which is embodied in the initial settings of the machine. Key material must be delivered through a private channel that is not exposed to hostile interception. This is known as the key distribution problem, and it is a perennial headache for symmetric encryption, especially in large distributed organizations.[29] Germany outfitted units with standardized Enigma machines and rotors. Security clerks then visited field units on a regular basis to drop off copies of a codebook listing daily key settings. German doctrine required Enigma operators to choose three out of five rotors (or more) in a different order every day, and to reset the plugboard (Stecker) on the device. They also changed rotor ring settings every month. Operators then selected unique rotor settings for every message, enciphered using the initial daily settings from the codebook. The receiving operator used the same daily settings from a copy of the same codebook to decipher the message setting, which was then used to decipher the message.[30]

It is possible for an adversary to attack the key distribution channel directly, which, if successful, obviates the need for cryptanalysis. The British did this by "pinching" key material from disabled German ships and U-boats whenever possible. They crafted cover stories to let the Germans believe that all key material went down with the sinking ship. Stealing key material bypassed the tedium of cryptanalysis, but the benefits would be temporary if the British could not ensure persistent access to fresh keys. Ensuring persistence required cryptanalysis.

ENIGMA VULNERABILITY

Germany, despite all its war-fighting prowess, and in part because of it, was a cooperative intelligence target. Germany tended to prioritize tactical intelligence to support its offensive operations while neglecting intelligence for defense.[31] In terms of OPSEC, Germany was centralized where it should have been decentralized and fragmented where it should have been integrated. Germany unwittingly created predictable patterns that Allied SIGINT could exploit through a combination of its standardized doctrine and OPSEC complacency in the field. German counterintelligence organs, meanwhile, were too disunified and fractious to recognize and correct the danger.

The architecture of Enigma provided a lot of entropy, or uncertainty about the key. But any source of nonrandomness in ciphertext reduces entropy. Statistical information—the opposite of entropy—aids the search for keys. Mistakes by Enigma operators and other constraints effectively reduced entropy. The French acquired an Enigma manual from a German traitor in 1931, which enabled Polish cryptanalysts to begin reconstructing the internal wiring of three Enigma rotors. They were able to decrypt messages, with the help of an electromechanical Enigma emulator, because of subtle cycles in the ciphertext. But Polish methods were overwhelmed by the introduction of two additional rotors in 1938, and invasion destabilized the intelligence process.[32]

Yet even with more secure cipher machines, German operators still failed to paraphrase, pad, or reorder messages that they retransmitted across different networks. They used easy-to-guess keys for multipart messages (e.g., HIT+LER or ROM+MEL) that the British called "cillies."[33] Occasionally operators simply gave away settings in plaintext sessions with other operators.[34] Key material for most Luftwaffe networks was apparently prepared by one single individual, who lazily reused portions of previous lists that GC&CS was quick to recognize.[35] According to historian Ralph Erskine, "Germans had continually to make a lot of mistakes every day for [GC&CS] to succeed against them."[36]

British cryptanalysis also became adept at guessing "cribs," or plaintext phrases suspected to be in the ciphertext. For instance, it might be possible to guess the plaintext elements of a weather report of known weather patterns, or a reconnaissance report of a known British patrol, or a standardized greeting or doctrinal phrase.[37] Cribs were especially useful against Enigma, because the machine never enciphered a letter as itself, and it always enciphered reciprocally (e.g., A as F and F as A). Cryptanalysts exploited these constraints to construct "menus," or graphs linking letters in an intercepted ciphertext and a plaintext crib. These logical graphs could be used to plug up real electrical circuits on the electromechanical Bombe machines, which performed a brute-force search for Stecker (plug) settings.[38] The British effort to exploit these subtle flaws was a major organizational undertaking, as I will discuss below.

The same volume of Enigma traffic that overwhelmed manual cryptanalysis thus provided a wealth of data for Bletchley Park's new approach to SIGINT. British cryptographers realized that even trivial messages were useful if they provided clues about keys and algorithms. Instead of just attacking messages that seemed to have important content, GC&CS attacked the entire cryptosystem. German chatter within and across different military services and civilian agencies throughout the Third Reich generated a massive volume of traffic. Enigma encrypted most of it, and all of it was potentially useful for British cryptanalysis. Uniformly formatted units, call signs, and reporting procedures created predictable traffic. Operators passed similar messages at the same time each day to the same recipients with the same message headers and preambles. British personnel were able to match cribs to cryptograms by identifying individual U-boats based on traffic analysis, analyzing the behavior of specific skippers and boats, and fingerprinting individual radio transmitters and vessels.[39] According to an internal history of Bletchley Park, "It was often upon the trivial or boring small items, when accumulated, that some of the most important long-term pieces of intelligence were built up. . . . [M]uch of the red-hot tactical Intelligence could have been jettisoned without irreparable harm, but the long-term things, nearly always less spectacular, often individually very trivial, were yet indispensable, and unique in the history of intelligence."[40]

Germany's sociotechnical implementation of Enigma thus provided security against manual cryptanalysis, but it embodied inadvertent cooperation for mechanized cryptanalysis. Bletchley Park tracked nearly two hundred different networks throughout the war, but most were just different settings for the same basic cryptosystem. When cryptographers broke any one of the sixty ciphers it monitored on a given day, the others soon followed.[41] Even when units upgraded Enigma security (e.g., adding a fourth rotor to naval Enigma), they had to forego the extra security when communicating with other organizations using standard machines. The British described identical German messages transmitted in two different keys as "kisses."[42]

GEOGRAPHICAL CONNECTIVITY

Geographical constraints can amplify or reinforce institutional constraints. Geography enhanced British connectivity to German communications. Conversely, it limited German connectivity to British communications.

As Germany went on the offensive, the Wehrmacht left landline terminals behind and produced a larger volume of radio traffic. German radio communications on the Continent and across the oceans overlapped with listening stations in the Home Islands and colonial outposts. The British, by contrast, could rely on protected landline connections from listening posts (known as Y-branch stations) to Bletchley Park (also known as station-X), which were both shielded from German intelligence access. As war loomed in 1939, GC&CS relocated to Bletchley Park, a bucolic manor located halfway between the intellectual centers of Oxford and Cambridge and on the main trunk line to London. From this relatively safe and central location, GC&CS was able to gather, compare, correlate, and combine a mass of historical and current intelligence to learn about German operations.

Another geographical advantage for connectivity was the west-to-east pattern of European weather, which provided Bletchley Park with advance notice of weather patterns that German operators on the Continent would soon be reporting. The net effect was that it was easier for Britain to get inside German communication networks while simultaneously maintaining some of its own organizational capabilities out of German reach. This is consistent with the heuristic of figure 2.2, which highlights the role of nonoverlapping institutional resources in sustaining information channels through the institutions that overlap with the enemy.

TELEPRINTER CIPHERS

In addition to Enigma, Germany used higher-grade encryption for headquarters communications. The Lorentz-Schlüsselzusatz 40/42 teleprinter relied on a system of twelve rotors rather than Enigma's three (or four). Whereas Enigma produced ciphertext by substituting alphabetic letters, Lorentz performed binary arithmetic on characters that were digitally encoded using the International Teleprinter Code, or Baudot code, implementing a stream cipher.[43]

Baudot protocol and teleprinter principles were common knowledge. Yet Lorentz traffic was harder to access than Enigma. Broadcasts from Enigma operators were easier to transcribe than the faint non-Morse teleprinter traffic of Lorentz. Collection and faithful transcription of Tunny required a dedicated array of massive aerials, and hundreds of personnel, at a GC&CS intercept facility in Kent.[44] This anticipates a theme in the next chapter: When connectivity is challenging (when barriers are higher), organizations must compensate with more operational complexity.

Traffic encrypted with Lorentz was harder to break. GC&CS never encountered a physical Lorentz machine until after the war; its traffic was known simply as "Tunny." Breaking Tunny depended on a single mistake: A German operator carelessly retransmitted a single long message twice with the same key, which provided just enough redundancy for John Tiltman to deduce the key stream that had been added to the plaintext. Lorentz produced a new key for every message, of course, so Tiltman's feat was not operationally useful by itself. But in one of the greatest mathematical feats of the war, the Canadian Bill Tutte leveraged the Tiltman break to deduce the design of all twelve Lorentz rotors, sight unseen, from a single message.[45]

Max Newman used Tutte's insight to identify a critical design flaw in the Lorentz machine: a systematic staggering of the rotors used to generate ciphertext from plaintext through bitwise addition. Newman's team devised an attack to subtract out the effect of half the Lorentz rotors, which, combined with the frequency distribution of letters in the German language, revealed a faint statistical signal in the distribution of Baudot-encoded data.[46] GC&CS then automated this attack with a novel electronic machine named Colossus, discussed further below.

GERMAN COUNTERINTELLIGENCE FAILURES

In many ways, wartime intelligence is harder than peacetime collection, since there are big incentives to avoid cooperating in any way. The danger of enemy exploitation should encourage attention to monitoring and enforcement. Counterintelligence units should monitor for indications of cryptosystem breaches. Security enforcement should limit connectivity and vulnerability. Some institutions fail to respond to strategic imperatives, however.

German cryptography, like German intelligence generally, was underresourced. Germany had no centralized analogue to Bletchley Park, and civilian academics were not well integrated into the intelligence effort. German intelligence neglected high-grade Allied cryptosystems such as Typex and Sigaba on the assumption that Enigma was invulnerable. They assumed that similar machines were a waste of time as well.[47]

German counterintelligence was limited by bureaucratic specialization and fierce interservice rivalry. Germany prioritized intelligence support for offense over support for defense. Service and government intelligence agencies rarely shared information, and investigations of suspicious incidents often missed anomalies noted across previous inquiries. German analysis always found a way to exonerate the security of Enigma after surprising Allied successes. No one in Berlin wanted to hear that the Reich's communication security was categorically compromised. Intelligence officers succumbed to groupthink and told their customers what they wanted to hear.[48] Nazi coup-proofing measures, such as the replacement of Abwehr professionals with SS loyalists, further degraded performance. German officers on the Western Front also tended to exaggerate British strengths in order to limit the hemorrhage of German units to the Eastern Front.[49]

In the SIGINT contest of Word War II, the rival organizations were nearly mirror images of each other. German intelligence was insular, while British intelligence was managed. British organizations were adaptable, while German complacency was problematic. The GCHQ history points out that "the Western Allies multiplied each other's strengths" in intelligence collaboration, while "German and Axis agencies divided them."[50] As a result, Britain was better able to take advantage of the opportunities created by radio communications and mechanized cryptography in ways that the enemy failed to detect or systematically disrupt. The Allies did experience several notable intelligence failures, of course, such as missing preparations for the Battle of the Bulge and the V-weapon programs.[51] Overall, however, Allied intelligence organizations were relatively more successful.

To sum up so far, Bletchley Park operated in a permissive environment for espionage. Exposed institutions—radio connectivity and cryptosystem vulnerability—created the potential for intelligence exploitation. To turn potential into reality, however, required a clandestine organization.

Sophisticated Organization

Sophisticated deception specialists have administrative and technical capacity, and they exercise discretion to protect it. They are well managed enough to plan complex operations and ensure operational security, but they are flexible enough to repair breakdowns and adapt to enemy countermeasures. In *Information Technology and Military Power*, I described this general combination of opposites as "adaptive management."[52] This balance is hard to strike, especially in an entangled intelligence contest. But Bletchley Park was able to do so.

Two radically different images are often used to describe Bletchley Park: "a university and a factory."[53] On one hand it was like an Oxbridge common room where eccentric fellows noodled over puzzles. On the other it was like a regimented sweatshop where an army of clerks sorted paperwork and maintained machinery. Christopher Grey shows that the traditional dichotomy of formal centralization versus informal decentralization fails to capture the reality of GC&CS. Bletchley Park was not simply a hybrid of bureaucracy and adhocracy but rather a "twisting together" of mutually supporting modes of work.[54]

THE SIGINT FACTORY

Bletchley Park was a human organization that processed information like a machine. It might also be described as an organizational computing system that inputted radio intercepts and outputted high-grade SIGINT. Its data storage and processing equipment ranged from the humble index card and tabulating machine to computational marvels such as the Bombes and Colossi. Like a mechanical computer but with human circuits, Bletchley Park relied on standardized and modularized processing, indexing and memory, error handling, and resource-allocation processes.[55]

GC&CS first broke into Luftwaffe Enigma in January 1940 by manual cryptanalysis. That March it installed the first electromechanical Bombe machine, which could emulate three sets of three-rotor Enigmas.[56] Many more followed, which dramatically increased the volume of Enigma decrypts. By fall 1943, Bletchley Park was processing three thousand signals per day, encrypted in ninety different ciphers.[57] By D-Day in 1944, GC&CS operated over 160 Bombes at outstations throughout the United Kingdom; the US Navy operated additional Bombes customized to emulate the four-rotor naval Enigma machine. Ninety of these were linked by wire directly to Bletchley Park.[58]

This level of effort required an industrial-style production line for decryption and analysis. Y-branch intercepts from over six hundred receiving sets were sent via teleprinter to Hut 8 (naval traffic) or Hut 6 (air and land traffic).[59] They sorted traffic into different cipher systems and prioritized traffic for the cryptography watch. The "Fusion Room" analyzed Y-intercept logs to search for traffic patterns, reencipherments, and cribs. Cryptanalysts in the huts used cribs to create menus, which they then hand-carried to the Bombe rooms. Promising results from the Bombes were tested on an Enigma clone and indexed. Readable decrypts were then passed to Hut 4 (naval) or Hut 3 (air and land) for translation and intelligence analysis. Unreadable "duds" went to Hut 11A for further processing and identification of Enigma modifications.

Intelligence analysts built and used a large database. It was embodied in a room full of handwritten index cards stored in shoeboxes that catalogued archived decrypts, network settings, German units, radio call signs, and individual operators.[60] These data could be searched with Hollerith punchcard sorting machines that had been originally developed for business applications. Decrypted messages and GC&CS analyses were reencrypted on British Typex machines for distribution. Special Liaison Units from GC&CS deployed to the field with an exclusive communications network to pass Ultra.[61]

This organization did not emerge overnight; there were tussles and growing pains along the way. The early part of the war for GC&CS was a period of learning characterized by "friction everywhere," according to the official history by John Ferris.[62] When Bletchley Park cryptographers complained in October 1941 that they were underresourced, Prime Minister Winston Churchill responded with his famous "Action this day" memo: "Make sure they have all they want on extreme priority and report this has been done."[63]

The intervention of the prime minister and the chief of the Secret Intelligence Service (MI6) led to a major reorganization in 1942. The old-school chief of GC&CS, Alastair Denniston, was replaced by the ruthlessly efficient Edward Travis. GC&CS received more authority and consolidated control of intercept stations that were previously managed by the military services. This sort of centralizing reform is a typical bureaucratic response to the friction of coordination problems. By mid-1942, GC&CS combined radio interception, traffic analysis, cryptanalysis, intelligence analysis, and OPSEC in a single vertically integrated organization—the very model of a modern SIGINT agency.

CREATIVE HACKERS

Bletchley Park's Y-stations, Bombe rooms, Hollerith room, and Typex rooms were Taylorist factory operations. A host of nearly ten thousand clerks and technicians (mostly women) toiled at Bletchley Park by the end of the war. They performed repetitive, mundane, exhausting, endless work without ever understanding its true purpose.[64]

By stark contrast, the cryptographers, analysts, and engineers of Bletchley Park (mostly men) led a more free and informal existence. They conversed with each other casually and experimented with new approaches to cryptanalysis. They drew on personalized relationships and prewar friendships to coordinate Bombe time, intelligence analysis, and cryptologic resources.[65] Never before had so much of the world's computational expertise been concentrated in the service of intelligence; nor has it been since.

Bletchley Park's most famous cryptographer was Alan Turing, an eccentric mathematician from Cambridge. Before the war, Turing had published a landmark paper laying the foundation for theoretical computer science.[66] Turing also had a penchant for tinkering with machines, which informed his mathematical achievements. During the war, Turing personally designed the Bombe machines that Bletchley Park used to speed up the search for Enigma keys.[67] He also invented new statistical methods for cryptanalysis, playfully known as "Banburismus" and "Turingery," that anticipated the empirical Bayes methods used in modern AI.[68] After the war, Turing and his mentor Max Newman, who designed Colossus to attack Lorentz, built one of the first working stored-program computers at Manchester University.[69] Turing's ruminations on the nature of AI continue to resonate today.[70] Curious, unconventional, and awkward, Turing would not be out of place at a modern hacker convention like DEF CON or Black Hat.[71] This is all the more reason to describe Bletchley Park as the first cyber campaign.

Turing was hardly Bletchley Park's only unconventional hacker. Dilly Knox, an old-school cryptanalyst trained in classics, led the initial attack on Enigma. Colleagues Margaret Rock and Mavis Lever broke into the Abwehr Enigma.[72] John Tiltman and Bill Tutte cracked Tunny, and Max Newman designed algorithms to exploit it. One cryptographer in the "Newmanry" recalled that "tea parties were started; anyone could call one, ideas were bandied about, you came if you could and you brought your own tea. Tea parties didn't decide things but they led to action on all fronts. Newman ran a comfortably democratic and friendly section."[73] Every member could make suggestions in a "Yellow Book" to be discussed by peers, much as in an informal Slack group today.[74]

To implement Newman's attack on Tunny, a talented engineer named Thomas Flowers at the Post Office Research Department at Dollis Hill designed an optical scanning machine (Heath Robinson) and an electronic machine (Colossus).[75] Flowers was one of only a handful of experts in the world on the practical applications of "electronic valves," as vacuum tubes were known. He spent personal funds to acquire components for these contraptions. Many engineers assumed at the time that vacuum tubes were too fragile for large-scale use, but Flowers took the contrarian view that they would work reliably if machines were rarely switched off. This condition was not a problem for cryptanalysis, which required long searches through vast data. Colossus first ran at Dollis Hill in December 1943 with over 1,500 valves; it became operational at Bletchley Park the next month.[76]

An improved Colossus II with nearly 2,500 valves entered service on June 1, 1944, just in time for D-Day. Flowers built more flexibility into Colossus than was required by Newman's design. Thus, while Colossus was initially designed to find a key setting given known wheel settings, it was later modified to find wheel settings too.[77] This change enabled the Newmanry to defeat a German change introduced after D-Day, whereby Germany started changing wheel patterns daily.[78] Throughout the war, GC&CS decrypted 13,500 out of 168,000 intercepted Lorentz messages.[79]

Remarkably, Bletchley Park's informal hacker culture coexisted within an austere OPSEC environment. One of Newman's colleagues described "a group identity . . . in which extraordinary freedom and extraordinary discipline [were] combined."[80] Personnel cleared for ULTRA were empowered to collaborate informally and received back-channel feedback on their successes.[81] This worked in part because personnel faced a common enemy and were motivated by a common national purpose. The broader intelligence alliance was also characterized by a high degree of openness and collaboration among British, Canadian, and US intelligence units.

DISCIPLINED DISCRETION

This highly capable organization was fragile. An effective German counterintelligence response could have destroyed Britain's investment. German intelligence organizations had their own problems, as we have seen, but the dangers of compromise were real. The intelligence performance of Bletchley Park, after all, was founded on Germany's inadvertent cooperation.

GC&CS had a culture of extreme secrecy. OPSEC was rigorously enforced through background investigations, personnel indoctrination, the signing of the Official Secrets Act, classification, and compartmentalization.[82] Many personnel did not even realize that Bletchley Park was a codebreaking organization, and the press acquiesced to official requests to keep mum. Ultra was often sanitized so that it might appear to come from some other source, such as a human spy or aerial reconnaissance. The Allies seriously debated the risks and benefits of acting on Ultra, sometimes foregoing opportunities to attack Germans without a plausible alibi. Thus, for instance, according to John Ferris's official history, "fear of tipping the Allied hand hampered photo-reconnaissance."[83] This is known today as the intelligence gain/loss problem.

Beyond GC&CS, however, Allied OPSEC was not as disciplined. Germany deployed listening stations across Europe to monitor Allied communications.[84] By April 1940, German naval intelligence (B-Dienst) was reading over half of intercepted Allied traffic, and this increased to 80 percent by December 1942.[85] Germany initially enjoyed considerable SIGINT success against Allied forces, particularly in identifying targets for offensive operations.[86] In unrestricted submarine warfare, SIGINT was vital for directing U-boats to Allied convoys and away from escorts. The Kriegsmarine was especially effective against Allied convoy communications, at least until the Allies implemented new codes and procedures in June 1943. This improvement came partly as a result of Bletchley Park's insights into German SIGINT successes and Allied OPSEC failures.[87]

PROACTIVE BRITISH COUNTERINTELLIGENCE

Bletchley Park actively targeted German intelligence communications, continually searching for evidence of Ultra's compromise. It never found any.[88] Other than John Cairncross, one of the Cambridge Five, there is no other evidence of a serious security breach, and no evidence of Axis penetration.[89] Ultra derived from German intelligence, moreover, provided GC&CS with feedback about British security measures and British deception operations.

Bletchley Park was not just a passive SIGINT collector. Sometimes it coordinated active operations to protect or enable Ultra. When Ultra discovered the locations of German U-boats, for example, the British vectored reconnaissance flights over them to encourage U-boat commanders to assume that a lucky patrol had discovered their location.[90] Then the U-boat could be attacked without risking compromise of Ultra. Bletchley Park sometimes conducted military operations in view of German observers for the purpose of generative intelligence opportunities. A larger volume of chatter on networks monitored by GC&CS about a known topic would simplify the search for "cribs" and "depths." The British might mine channels recently swept by German vessels, for example, in the hope that this would provoke a flurry of emergency messages from German communicators in both dockyard and naval ciphers; this lateral move from an easier to a more difficult cipher was called "gardening" for "kisses."[91] German operators thus became inadvertent assistants to British cryptanalysts.

Even more sportingly, the British sometimes sent false communications to German radio operators encrypted in legitimate Enigma keys, so that benighted soldiers might pass misleading messages to enemy commanders. According to Ferris, "When deception worked, it was the most precise and devastating form through which Ultra damaged its enemy."[92]

Nevertheless, GC&CS was first and foremost a collection agency: It was in the business of espionage rather than covert action. Protecting the conditions that enabled espionage was of paramount importance. This focus on quietly collecting without altering target institutions contributed to successful intelligence performance. More provocative British operations to influence German behavior had to be carefully evaluated to avoid disabling SIGINT successes. SIGINT success, in turn, enabled more active counterintelligence operations.

By the end of 1940, Britain had identified every human agent that the German Abwehr had sent to the Home Islands. British counterintelligence (MI5) turned many of them into double agents who fed disinformation back to the Abwehr.[93] The so-called Double Cross network was used to send false indications of an impending invasion at Pas-de-Calais in support of Operation Fortitude, the plan to mislead Germany about the D-Day landings at Normandy.[94] MI5 relied on Ultra to vet the reliability of double agents and verify that the enemy had swallowed the bait.[95]

SUPPORTING SUBVERSION

The overall Allied deception plan was known as Operation Bodyguard. It included Operation Fortitude, the scheme to mislead German commanders about Allied intentions in summer 1944.[96] If SIGINT at Bletchley Park anticipated cyber espionage, Bodyguard anticipated influence operations through cyberspace. Bodyguard was surprisingly successful. Fortitude in particular, which encouraged Germany to thin its defenses in Normandy, is often held up as a superb example of what military deception can accomplish. But it is important to understand the historical conditions that made this possible. Subversion carries more operational risk than espionage, as it actively shapes enemy perception instead of just passively collecting information. British deception planners were able to control these risks by building on the intelligence performance of Bletchley Park. And most importantly, Germany was a cooperative target. Once again, similar conditions explain performance: connectivity to a vulnerable audience via a disciplined and capable organization.

While the Allies could not disguise the fact that an invasion was imminent, they could disguise its location. Fortitude reinforced German assumptions that the Allies would land at Pas-de-Calais and Norway rather than Normandy. To achieve this remarkable outcome, the London Controlling Section had to consistently produce credible content for German audiences for months (and in some cases years) on end. The Allies used double agents to trick German HUMINT, bogus radio traffic to trick German SIGINT, and decoy equipment to trick German aerial reconnaissance (IMINT). Ultra from Bletchley Park, in turn, provided Fortitude with confidence that German intelligence officers and commanders had swallowed the bait. Fortitude was a long con of the entire German information system. It was not purely clandestine, because its target had to observe its products, but it had to be completely covert, because its target would adapt to compromise.

Fortitude was a successful covert disinformation campaign because it met the conditions for intelligence performance. Britain had connectivity to gullible eyes and ears through controlled channels, most notably complete control over Germany's entire HUMINT network in Britain through the Double Cross program. Britain exploited the preconceptions and confirmation biases of an obligingly vulnerable target with dysfunctional intelligence organs. The London Controlling Section was a capable clandestine organization that centralized British counterintelligence and military deception operations while granting officers considerable freedom to explore unconventional methods. Britain was ruthlessly disciplined about operational security, using reliable feedback from Ultra to watch for signs of German suspicions.

In bargaining theory, costly signals are credible because they enable a perceiver to discriminate true types from fakes.[97] Costly signaling works because it is hard for mimics to produce the same signals, because they lack either the resources or the resolve. The goal of covert disinformation, however, is to produce precisely these signals, which appear outwardly costly and thus credible. In reality, the forged signals pool with the noncredible deceiver, but that reality must be hidden from the deceived. It may be easier to fool marks when the stakes are low and the penalties associated with being fooled are not great, but when the stakes are high, fraudulent signals must be of extremely high quality to persuade a mark to act (or fail to act) against their own interest. Germany had strong interests in repelling the Allied invasion, so it had to be persuaded to voluntarily do something that was very costly. Fortitude, remarkably enough, was able to simulate (apparently) costly signals for the Germans that enabled them to (wrongly) discriminate the (false) landing site from (true) alternatives.

Simulating costly signals is itself a costly problem! The Allied deception campaign was neither cheap nor easy. For example, the imaginary First US Army Group (FUSAG) was "commanded" by the real General George Patton. This ruse, in the context of other confirming clues supplied by Fortitude, helped to encourage the Germans to discriminate an apparently true situation (which was false) from a bluff (which was true). Why else would the Allies assign their top man to the job? Why else would Germany's most productive HUMINT agents and SIGINT collectors provide so much corroborating evidence? The price tag of deception further included the significant investment in Bletchley Park, without which the British would not have been able to discriminate genuine German credulity from the motivated speculation of British deception officers.

The gamble paid off. The Germans reinforced Pas-de-Calais, against their best interests, and thinned defenses at the actual landing beaches. Fortitude was so successful that Germany held back units of the Fifteenth Army and the First SS Panzer Division for weeks after D-Day, believing that Normandy was a feint covering the real landing at Pas-de-Calais.[98] As late as October 1944, German intelligence still clung to the fiction that fourteen nonexistent British Army divisions threatened to land.[99]

Successful subversion in high-stakes competition requires not only a vulnerable audience but also extensive organizational infrastructure and security discipline. It is a mistake to assume that cheap disinformation can produce dramatic results. There is no free lunch in deception, especially when the price of being deceived is very high for the target. Chapter 6 will return to these problems in the Russian influence campaign of 2016, which had very different technical and political circumstances compared to Bodyguard. Russia did not have to be as discreet in 2016 as Bodyguard did in 1944, and the imperatives for operational control were far less. Portions of the US electorate were far more sympathetic with Russia than the Axis was with the Allies.

Successful Performance

Bletchley Park was able to meet both performance conditions for years on end. Radio provided reliable connectivity with enemy communication institutions, which were systematically vulnerable. GC&CS had the organizational capacity to exploit German vulnerabilities, and Britain protected its fragile investment with disciplined discretion. As a result, GC&CS was able to create, maintain, and repair secret information channels into German communications for years on end.

British intelligence advantage in the SIGINT contest with Germany generally emerged from sustained collection and cumulative analysis, moreover, and not from individual decrypts. GC&CS worked methodically to be successful, to be sure, but it was also very fortunate. Germany unwittingly provided an incredible intelligence opportunity.

The detailed circumstances of intelligence opportunity varied throughout the war, at different times and for different targets. Bletchley Park's intelligence performance also varied, accordingly, as did Allied commanders' willingness and ability to use Ultra. Intelligence success did not automatically lead to military advantage. Material logistics, operational doctrine, and hard fighting mattered more.[100] But in the right circumstances, the efficiency advantages of Ultra intelligence improved Allied military effectiveness too.

VARIATION IN INTELLIGENCE PERFORMANCE

Table 4.1 summarizes the impressive performance of GC&CS against Enigma ciphers.[101] Of the 183 network ciphers identified, all but 10 were broken, an incredible success rate of 95 percent. There is notable variation across services (where the "other" category includes railroad, Abwehr, and Gestapo ciphers). Luftwaffe ciphers, the largest proportion, were broken early and often. Luftwaffe operators made the most mistakes, and air operations generated the most traffic. Naval Enigma, by contrast, was the most challenging, with the most unbroken ciphers (7 of 10). The sea services practiced much better OPSEC. As the theory expects, cryptologic performance dipped with less cooperative targets.

Admiral Dönitz understood well that reliance on centralized radio communications made his submarines vulnerable to Allied SIGINT. After all, Dönitz relied on his own SIGINT to target Allied convoys to deadly effect, at least until the Allies overhauled their OPSEC in 1943. But German wolf pack tactics were simply not possible without radio coordination, even as breaking radio silence was anathema for the silent service. Dönitz thus invested in customized Enigma machines with extra security (additional rotors and a fourth slot), water-soluble ink for printing key material, a method of specially encoding geographical coordinates, and numerous other organizational procedures. As David Kahn points out, "By the start of the war, the Kriegsmarine had in place an extremely well thought out cipher system."[102]

One of the darkest periods of the naval SIGINT contest for Bletchley Park was Germany's introduction of four-rotor naval Enigma (codenamed Shark), which locked out GC&CS for most of 1942. The British

Table 4.1. GC&CS success rate against German Enigma networks

	Air Force	Army	Navy	Other	Total
Enigma ciphers identified	77	62	26	18	183
Ciphers never broken	1	1	7	1	10
Average months in use	21	14	27	30	20
Average time readable	83%	71%	46%	77%	73%

managed to adapt new methods and new machines to get back in, fortunately, before the climactic convoy battles of 1943. Toward the end of the war, Germany even began using unique keys for individual U-boats, which seriously stressed GC&CS.[103]

The crisis of naval Enigma throughout 1942 and its resolution in December illustrates the value of Ultra. When GC&CS was reading naval traffic in the last half of 1941, U-boats sighted only one out of ten convoys on average, sinking 600,000 tons. In the last half of 1942, by stark contrast, U-boats sighted one out of three convoys and sank 2,600,000 tons.[104] The United States' entry into the war at the same time provided Germany with many Allied targets with poor OPSEC; German submariners described this as "the happy time." Bletchley Park was finally able to break in again, thanks to a Short Weather Cipher code book recovered from a disabled German U-boat. Allied tonnage lost in January and February 1943 dropped to half the total for November and December.[105] Further Allied improvements in SIGINT and OPSEC by mid-1943 caused Germany to slip behind in the intelligence contest for good.

CUMULATIVE INTELLIGENCE SUCCESS

Figure 4.4 lists individual German networks by the date each cipher was first broken. Once broken, German nets tended to remain readable for the life of the key, on average twenty months, and some much longer. The highly productive Luftwaffe "Red" network, for example, was readable for the duration of the entire war. Army keys were generally used for a shorter duration compared to other services because keys were used for specific land campaigns.

Even after networks became readable, however, GC&CS still had to break into daily keys afresh. Sometimes ciphers were broken within hours, but others required many days. Lower-priority networks, therefore, were not read continuously, and some only sporadically. Breaking Enigma, and all the other Axis cryptosystems, was necessarily an ongoing process.[106]

Cyber theorists highlight cumulative effects as an important feature of persistent engagement in cyberspace.[107] But cumulation is a much more general feature of intelligence performance. GC&CS maintained a synoptic view of German operations by patiently combining SIGINT from multiple networks and nurturing deep analytical familiarity with German behavior. Intelligence performance in this case exemplifies what J. C. Wylie describes as a cumulative rather than sequential strategy.[108] Indeed, the inspiration for Wylie's distinction is Allied success in the antisubmarine warfare campaign, in which Ultra played an important supporting role. Cumulative intelligence success is vital for building up analytical infrastructure, managing complex operations in strict secrecy, and maintaining persistent access to enemy secrets.

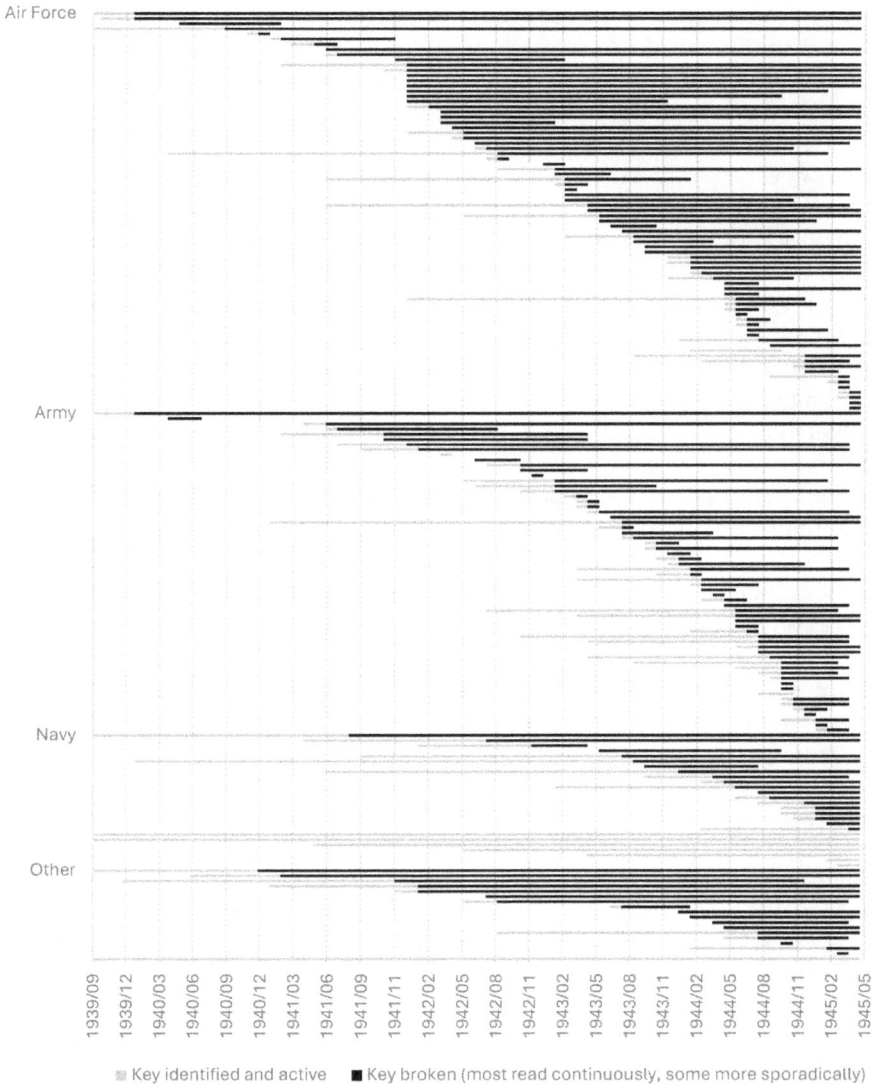

Figure 4.4. Enigma networks of German military service detected and broken by GC&CS throughout the war (data: Hinsley et al., *British Intelligence in the Second World War*, vols. 2 & 3.1–3.2)

INDIRECT CONTRIBUTIONS TO VICTORY

Even in the best conditions, intelligence performance does not automatically translate into political advantage. Meeting the performance conditions means only that a secret information channel for collection or influence can be established and maintained indefinitely. This achievement provides a relative information advantage, but decision-makers still must act to exploit it, and they must do so in circumstances full of friction and contingency. Some Allied commanders leveraged Ultra well, but they still had to fight the war. They also fought it with an evolving portfolio of weapons and tactics. In such dynamic political and military contexts, intelligence operations can provide at best an indirect competitive advantage.

This means that simple correlations of intelligence success and military behavior can be misleading. GC&CS was reading naval Enigma in mid-1941. In July and August 1941, merchant sinkings fell to a third of the total for May and June. Yet this was not necessarily because of any radical improvements in SIGINT: Allied destroyer crews got better, air patrols were increased, convoys sailed faster, and some U-boats were reallocated to the fight against Stalin.[109]

Bletchley Park was not the only game in town. The Allies made improvements in radio direction finding and vessel fingerprinting (ELINT). The United States added more destroyer escorts and long-range patrol aircraft, eventually closing the Atlantic gap in coverage. In spring 1943, Allied aircraft and ships began carrying centimetric radar sets that German U-boats could not detect. Aircraft also began using Leigh Lights to spot U-boats that were recharging their batteries on the surface at night.[110]

Some senior Allied leaders praised Ultra. Churchill stated, "I attach more importance to [intelligence reports] as a means of forming a true judgment of public policy in these spheres than to any other source of knowledge at the disposal of the State."[111] Eisenhower said that Ultra had "priceless value to me. It has saved thousands of British and American lives and, in no small way, contributed to the speed with which the enemy was routed and eventually forced to surrender."[112] But others ignored or misused Ultra. Bletchley Park decrypted German invasion plans for Crete in May 1941; however, British commanders were unable to respond effectively.[113] Allied commanders committed to Operation Market Garden in September 1944 (as depicted in the film *A Bridge Too Far*), even as Ultra revealed German preparations for an airborne landing in Holland.[114] The Ultra advantage, according to John Ferris, was irrelevant whenever "the British were good at intelligence and bad at operations."[115] Strategic bias could also offset intelligence success. Douglas MacArthur often ignored intelligence that did not support his preconceived beliefs.[116] Josef Stalin had a similar problem.

Ultra could even encourage complacency. General Bernard Montgomery's intelligence chief reflected that Ultra "was dangerously valuable . . . not only because we might lose it, but because it seemed the answer to an intelligence officer's prayer. . . . The information purveyed was so remarkable that it tended, particularly if one were tired or overbusy, to engulf not only all other sources, but that very common sense which forms the basis of intelligence."[117] And sometimes it was simply impossible to act on Ultra. Even though Poland broke the Enigma first, it lacked the military power to repel a German blitzkrieg.

Historians offer mixed assessments of Ultra. John Keegan weights operational improvements over intelligence performance.[118] Paul Kennedy finds that Ultra "seems a less decisive factor in the Battle of the Atlantic once a detailed analysis of the key convoy battles of 1943 has been undertaken."[119] Max Hastings counters that "the evidence shows that knowledge of the enemy's motions made a more important contribution to the Western Allied war effort than Kennedy allows, especially at sea, both in the Pacific and Atlantic theaters."[120]

A full accounting of Allied intelligence success must consider the offsetting effects of enemy successes. Ferris finds that Ultra "was a tiebreaker in individual engagements, but across the board it aided both sides equally, which most helped the stronger navy."[121] Moreover, "U-boats ambushed twice as many convoys when B-Dienst was effective and Ultra was not, than vice versa."[122] Ferris concludes that Ultra overall "budged the balance of attrition towards the Allies. The quality of Allied intelligence, and its superiority over the Axis, provided much certainty to Anglo-American assessment and planning and let them use their forces with remarkable precision against an enemy which increasingly was ignorant, uncertain and outgunned."[123]

Beyond the vital Battle of the Atlantic, Ultra made important contributions to campaigns in North Africa and Europe, provided targeting and combat assessment information for the strategic air campaigns, and offered insight into the strategic intentions of the Axis powers.[124] In the air, according to Robert Ehlers, the "intelligence effort paid huge dividends in discerning, targeting, and assessing damage to oil and transportation assets, the Reich's most vital target sets."[125] Allied bombing also drove Germans to communicate more by radio, so "a relative trickle of Ultra intercepts regarding heavy-bomber effects turned into a torrent," but Ehlers hastens to add that the impact of Ultra was conditional on the availability of other sources of intelligence and analytical fusion: "Only when combined with photointelligence-based products and technical-expert intelligence did it yield the kind of fidelity that came to be the norm by spring 1944."[126]

On the ground, Allied commanders incorporated Ultra into operational planning to a historically unprecedented degree.[127] David Kenyon finds that "access to more recently declassified material—including GC&CS's own internal orders of battle, as well as other non-ULTRA material—has shown that in fact Bletchley's understanding of the enemy's dispositions was much more detailed and complete than was hitherto appreciated."[128] He concludes that Ultra "was of vital importance to the planning process prior to the start of the battle [of Normandy]; however, once the fighting was under way in some respects its usefulness diminished."[129] Ultra was invaluable but not miraculous.

The combination of Germany's exposed institutions and Britain's sophisticated organization improved Allied intelligence performance throughout the war. Axis targets made systematic mistakes in communication and counterintelligence, while Allied SIGINT worked systematically in secrecy. GC&CS still experienced a lot of information friction, but the balance of friction favored Bletchley Park. Bletchley Park thus succeeded in one of the most lopsided contests in the history of intelligence. Its unprecedented success, however, provided only an indirect military advantage.

Bletchley Park was lucky. The British found themselves on the right side of a revolution in cryptology enabled by mathematics and mechanization. Their German adversary did not understand the full potential of SIGINT at scale. The British wisely made the most of their opportunity, and the Germans helped them do it. The German Enigma was supposed to cloak communications in secrecy, but Ultra turned Enigma into an oracle for the British. These "extraordinary" circumstances are hard to reproduce reliably or at will. There is no free lunch in secret statecraft, but states that are lucky and capable enough may dine at a discount.

Bletchley Park met the conditions for success with flying colors. Performance conditions today are usually more mixed. One irony is that the first cyber campaign may have been more successful than anything that has followed. This is hard to say with any confidence, of course; successful campaigns are necessarily discreet, so we have little public knowledge of them. But it is reasonable to suspect that cyber operations are not getting easier as a straightforward consequence of technological progress. On the contrary, contingent institutional context determines intelligence performance, and sociotechnical context has become fantastically more complex for all sides in an intelligence contest. To explore the greater complexity of intelligence performance in the digital era, the next chapter turns to the infamous case of Stuxnet.

CHAPTER 5

Sabotage

Stuxnet Reinterpreted as Secret Diplomacy

The most famous case of cyber-enabled sabotage to date, as of this writing in early 2025, is still the Stuxnet attack on Iranian nuclear centrifuges, which was first reported in 2010. This is also a precious case. Cyber attacks that create significant physical damage are as rare in the empirical record as they are prominent in the cyberwar narrative. This is puzzling: Stuxnet remains an outlier in the empirical record of cyber conflict, even as states have invested in cyber warfare capacity and competed fiercely in cyberspace for many decades now. Why? Is serious sabotage too hard? Is it not politically useful? Is it just well hidden? The answers are both complicated and instructive.

Stuxnet has been extensively studied, but there are still many misconceptions about it. This important case deserves a second look for several reasons. More information has become available since 2010, and subsequent experience with cyber conflict helps to put Stuxnet in context. From this perspective, Stuxnet is better understood as a saga of secret statecraft than as an episode of cyber warfare. Stuxnet may seem unusual in the annals of cyber conflict, furthermore, but it is consistent with patterns of covert action in the Middle East. The United States, Israel, and Iran have long cooperated and competed in the shadows in various ways, pursuing national interests while avoiding escalation. The Stuxnet attack, ironically enough, helped to stabilize this triangle rather than undermine strategic stability.

Stuxnet also illustrates a pattern of intelligence performance that contrasts with the case of Bletchley Park in chapter 4. Stuxnet was a joint product of US and Israeli SIGINT agencies, two of the most proficient cyber actors in the world. This coalition can be described as a sophisticated organization, much like Bletchley Park (adjusting for contemporary technology, of course). But the difference is that Bletchley Park could exploit the relatively exposed institutions of German radio traffic, while the Stuxnet coalition had to exploit the more disconnected institutions of a remote industrial control system (ICS). The combination of sophisticated organization and disconnected institutions heightened operational complexity. Complexity, in turn, created friction for the coalition, and friction eventually compromised the operation. Whereas Bletchley Park maintained persistent access to German communications for years, Stuxnet first gained and then lost access to its target. This had ambiguous strategic implications.

As a technical sabotage operation, Stuxnet did not meaningfully alter Iranian enrichment trends; however, Stuxnet was also an instrument of secret diplomacy. The United States used covert action to dissuade Israel from starting a preventive war, and it also encouraged Iran to enter diplomatic negotiations, which ultimately did more to limit Iranian enrichment than covert sabotage ever did. While Stuxnet may have failed in its operational goal of limiting Iranian enrichment, it succeeded in contributing to success at the strategic level. Mixed conditions produced mixed results.

This chapter begins with the context and historiography of Stuxnet. Then I discuss the complex institutional environment and the complicated coalition that exploited it. I next assess operational and strategic outcomes. I conclude by updating my own earlier interpretation of this case from 2013.[1]

Revisiting Stuxnet

Most studies of Stuxnet draw on reporting that emerged shortly after its discovery. The basic story is well known: In mid-2010, a computer in Iran began rebooting itself. This led to the discovery of a suspicious file by a technician with an antivirus company in Belarus.[2] He uploaded it as "Rootkit.TmpHider" to an antivirus database, and malware analysts at Symantec later named it "Stuxnet" based on code artifacts. Kaspersky, Symantec, ESET, Langner, and other cybersecurity companies assessed that Stuxnet was designed to infiltrate the ICS at an Iranian fuel enrichment plant (FEP) located in Natanz, an underground facility located about three hundred kilometers south of Tehran.[3] Arms control analysts drew on data from International Atomic Energy Agency (IAEA) inspections to suggest that Stuxnet had destroyed a thousand centrifuges, or 11 percent of the total installed at Natanz.[4] Investigative journalists later reported that Stuxnet was part of a joint covert action program by the United States and Israel, code-named "Olympic Games."[5]

Thanks to all this reporting, we know more about Stuxnet than we do about most other cyber campaigns (with the important exception of Russian intervention in the 2016 US election, discussed in Chapter 6). But the significance of this seminal case remains contested. Stuxnet has been used both to demonstrate the plausibility of cyberwar and to illustrate its limits. But the most famous case of cyberwar is not really a case of war at all. The forensic timeline of relevant artifacts and events spans almost two decades, which is more reflective of a chronic twilight struggle than a single militarized crisis.

A Cyber Revolution?

Stuxnet redefined the state of the art for cyber operations. Commercial analysts recall "a dizzying period of discovery that made the industry realize that malware-based digital espionage was not only going on, but had been going strong, unnoticed for years. The tranquil days of reverse engineering banking trojans were pierced by Stuxnet, Duqu, Flame, Gauss, and MiniFlame."[6] Some hailed Stuxnet as a revolution in cyber warfare as well.[7] As General Michael Hayden observed, "This is the first attack of a major nature in which a cyberattack was used to effect physical destruction. . . . Somebody crossed the Rubicon."[8]

Skeptics (including myself) objected that Stuxnet did not support popular narratives about cyberwar.[9] Stuxnet was developed by a coalition of powerful states, hardly an asymmetric advantage for the weak. It was neither cheap nor easy to deploy, complicating claims about offense dominance.[10] And it did not affect Iran's output of enriched uranium, raising questions about the effectiveness and destructiveness of cyber operations.[11] Indeed, Stuxnet was never intended to produce catastrophic destruction, but just to create a little friction for Iranian engineers. Its world-class architects also made several mistakes that compromised their operation, which is why we can talk about it today.

The focus on cyberwar risks overlooking the bigger nuclear context of Stuxnet. The uncertain prospects of cyber warfare pale beside the obvious dangers of nuclear war. The United States and Israel have long pursued a policy of limiting nuclear proliferation, often using covert action to support this objective. Seen from this perspective, Stuxnet appears as less of a disruptive revolution in warfare and more of a continuous evolution of secret statecraft.

Stuxnet does not fit cleanly into just one of the categories of secret statecraft. American and Israeli engineers clearly designed the malware to sabotage Iranian centrifuges. Tactically, it had little other purpose. But this also required a lot of supporting espionage for target reconnaissance and operational assessment. All these various intrusions had to evade Iranian and commercial defenses. The primary US motivation for Olympic Games, finally, was secret diplomacy with Israel, which I described in chapter 1 as the conspiracy variant of subversion. Stuxnet was a complicated solution for a complicated problem.

THE THREE-BODY PROBLEM

Political interests drive secret statecraft. The previous chapter showcased a relatively straightforward opposition of wartime enemies. Theoretical treatments of cyber operations, likewise, typically discuss a stylized contest between attacker and target. But the case of Stuxnet features an interdependent system of state and nonstate actors with overlapping interests. Stuxnet was a coalition effort of allies whose interests did not completely align, and the interests of their targets did not completely diverge. All sides of this multisided contest relied on the technology of outside vendors and service providers. The reliance on third-party technology contrasts with Bletchley Park's reliance on its own Bombes and intercept stations to exploit Germany's Enigma machines.

Stuxnet was a cyber operation motivated by nuclear strategy. Iran had signed the Treaty on the Non-Proliferation of Nuclear Weapons in 1970, but by the mid-2000s it was not in compliance. Multiple United Nations Security Council resolutions authorized sanctions and IAEA inspections. Iran publicly maintained that its nuclear program was peaceful, but the breakout time to a bomb steadily decreased. Iran's growing stocks of low-enriched uranium (LEU) for nuclear energy could be further enriched into weapons-grade material for a bomb.[12] Tehran could not fail to notice the untimely demise of Iraq's Saddam Hussein and Libya's Muammar Qaddafi, who each gave up their weapons of mass destruction (WMD) programs, or the survival of North Korea's Kim regime, which did not. Iran thus pursued an ambiguous strategy of nuclear latency, which enabled Iran to enjoy some of the benefits of deterrence (since it could sprint for a bomb), while Israel and the United States enjoyed some of the benefits of prevention (since it did not have one).[13]

Given the rhetorical hostility of Iran, Israel viewed the prospect of an Iranian bomb as an existential threat.[14] Israel had long been resolved to prevent regional adversaries from acquiring the bomb, as demonstrated by unilateral airstrikes on Iraq in 1981 (Operation Opera) and Syria in 2007 (Operation Orchard).[15] The Israeli Air Force (IAF) reportedly used a cyber-enabled electronic warfare tool to blind Syrian radars in its 2007 raid on a Syrian research reactor.[16] This is an example of cyber operations improving the efficiency of air operations. The IAF planned Orchard in strict secrecy to avoid alerting Syrian defenses, which precluded ex ante signaling, but the subsequent fact of the raid *could* be used ex post. The operation thus provided a direct benefit of limiting Syrian proliferation, and an indirect benefit of demonstrating resolve to multiple audiences. The raid was cleverly designed to enable Syrian president Bashar al-Assad to save face: Assad did not acknowledge the program and Israel did not acknowledge the raid.[17] The raid also put the United States on notice that Israel would act unilaterally if something was not done about Iran.

Israel sought US assistance for preventive strikes on Iran, which was a difficult operational problem with serious potential for escalation.[18] But there was daylight between the two allies. Israeli Prime Minister Ehud Olmert asked President George W. Bush to consider military action in May 2008. Bush reportedly responded, "I am unequivocally against an attack."[19] The US military was already fighting two unpopular wars in Afghanistan and Iraq, both of which neighbor Iran. The Bush administration had justified the invasion of Iraq on faulty intelligence about WMD.[20] The declassified judgments of a 2007 US National Intelligence Estimate (NIE) later assessed "with moderate confidence Tehran had not restarted its nuclear weapons program."[21] Another preventive war for WMD was politically untenable for Bush.

Secret statecraft offered a third option between war and doing nothing. Bush and Olmert thus agreed to deepen intelligence collaboration and sabotage Iran's program.[22] Sharing secrets enabled the United States to reassure Israel that it was committed to countering Iran while sidestepping audience costs associated with the NIE. For the same reasons that secrecy complicates signaling to an adversary (the cyber commitment problem discussed in chapter 1), it can improve credibility with an ally. Shared secrets bind conspiracies together through the unspoken threat of mutual betrayal. The United States did not offer an empty promise to hack Iran, moreover, but rather a mature SIGINT program and an advanced suite of exploit tools that it was already using for technical reconnaissance in Iran. Covert coordination with Israel also enabled the United States to monitor, and potentially influence, Israeli preparations for unilateral military action against Iran.

Olmert's successor, Benjamin Netanyahu, worried that Bush's successor, Barack Obama, was less committed to preventive action. Israel quietly prepared unilateral military options to hedge against the failure of covert action and to put pressure on the United States. For example, the IAF conducted a hundred-aircraft exercise in June 2008 that US intelligence was sure to monitor, followed months later by a two-thousand-mile practice run to Gibraltar.[23] According to Israeli journalist Ronen Bergman, Netanyahu "ordered the IDF [Israel Defense Forces] and the intelligence arms to prepare for Operation Deep Waters: an all-out air attack, supported by commando forces, in the heart of Iran. Some $2 billion was spent on preparations for the attack and for the anticipated ensuing war."[24]

Obama doubled down on secret diplomacy through Olympic Games. From the Bush administration, he retained Secretary of Defense Robert Gates, who was opposed to military action against Iran. Gates traveled to Israel in July 2009 and was followed by a parade of other officials throughout the year. According to an under secretary of state, "Our message was that we understand your concerns, and please don't go off on a hair trigger and start a war, because you're going to want us to come in behind you."[25]

Netanyahu's intransigence encouraged the Obama administration to initiate secret talks with Iran in late 2010, not long after the public compromise of Stuxnet. Iran warmed to the opportunity to quietly negotiate with the United States (the greater military threat) while maintaining open hostility toward Israel (the greater ideological threat).[26] The Obama administration offered sanctions relief in return for international safeguards. Secret talks intensified throughout 2012, eventually blossoming into the open P5+1 process in 2013; that process led to the Joint Comprehensive Plan of Action (JCPOA) in 2015.[27] The JCPOA effectively limited Iranian enrichment (until US President Donald Trump scuttled it in 2018).

The United States thus pursued a dual strategy of secret diplomacy. On one hand it acted to influence Israel through its secret collaboration in Olympic Games. On the other it acted to influence Iran through secret talks in Oman as Olympic Games unraveled. The United States and Israel shared an interest in prevention but differed in their willingness to risk war. Iran and the United States shared a tacit interest in keeping Israel from launching a preventive air strike. Israel and Iran shared an interest in getting the United States to moderate the behavior of the other, although in opposite directions. All parties tacitly tolerated Iranian nuclear latency and US and Israeli covert action without escalating into open warfare.

AN EXTENDED TIMELINE

If the strategic context of Stuxnet is complicated, so is the forensic record. More information has come to light since 2010, but much remains unknown. We now know that Stuxnet was part of a larger ecosystem of clandestine tools, built with multiple software development kits, employed by multiple intelligence agencies, sometimes together and sometimes independently, for numerous intelligence operations, some prior to Olympic Games and others after it. This is more consistent with an extended saga of secret statecraft than with a brief episode of cyber warfare.

Symantec's "Stuxnet Dossier" describes a self-replicating worm that can cross physical barriers (airgaps) via removable media, spread through a Microsoft Windows network while evading security protocols, send and receive messages through a peer-to-peer network of infections, verify the configuration of Siemens Step7 equipment at Natanz, implement a rootkit to hack a programmable logic controller (PLC), and thereby manipulate centrifuge valves and rotors.[28] Symantec initially reported three waves of infections in 2009–10, which remains the canonical dating of the Stuxnet attack. Symantec later reported registrations of command-and-control (C2) servers in 2005, supporting an earlier version of Stuxnet compiled in 2007.[29]

The United States reportedly appropriated $300 million in 2007 for "joint covert projects" targeting Iran.[30] The presence of artifacts predating 2007 suggests that Olympic Games was not the beginning of Stuxnet but rather an acceleration of a long-existing program to exploit Natanz. There are timestamps in Stuxnet's PLC code blocks and Step7 libraries dating to 2000–2003.[31] Kaspersky reports activity from Equation Group—a euphemism for US cyber exploitation, mainly by the NSA with some CIA collaboration—going back to the late 1990s.[32] A reconnaissance tool dubbed Fanny, which shared exploits with Stuxnet for navigating airgaps, was active in the wild in 2008.[33] It is reasonable to speculate that Fanny or something like it informed the 2007 NIE by providing the NSA with technical intelligence about the capabilities of Natanz. The secret means that deception specialists use for collection can be repurposed for covert action.

At the other end of the timeline, cybersecurity companies reported on several later operations that were related to Stuxnet. Spyware tools known as Flame and Duqu reused functionality that appeared in samples of Stuxnet; new versions of both appeared in 2014–15.[34] Journalists reported, furthermore, that the United States prepared a serious cyber-warfare plan, reportedly code-named Nitro Zeus, in case Israel started a war with Iran.[35] Unlike Olympic Games, which was a peacetime intelligence operation, Nitro Zeus was a military contingency plan. Yet its enabling technologies continued to be used to collect intelligence well after 2010, when Stuxnet was compromised.[36] I will return to this later.

The expanded timeline of Stuxnet-related functionality spans nearly two decades. This is a key period in cybersecurity history. As early debates about cyberwar in the 2000s emphasized the vulnerability of the United States, US agencies secretly developed a potent offensive capability. US Cyber Command debuted in 2010, but the groundwork for cyber disruption was laid long before.[37] As US cyber-strategy discourse shifted from its early preoccupation with deterring cyberwar to its later emphasis on "persistent engagement" beneath the threshold of armed conflict, the open rhetoric was just catching up with covert activity.[38] As Russian and Chinese espionage campaigns grabbed headlines in the 2010s and Stuxnet became old news, several reconnaissance tools in the Stuxnet family remained active. In short, the new history of Stuxnet is much bigger than Stuxnet.

The history of covert action in the region is also bigger than Stuxnet. The United States and Israel have repeatedly attempted to sabotage the Iranian nuclear program by different means. The CIA ran a Russian scientist, code-named Merlin, who was directed to provide Iran with deliberately flawed nuclear trigger designs.[39] The CIA also recruited a family of Swiss engineers (the Tinners) to provide intelligence on the Iranian program (beginning in 2000) and introduce faulty components (in 2003 and 2006)—overlapping with Olympic Games.[40] Covert action also continued after the revelation of Stuxnet. Israel assassinated a half dozen or more Iranian scientists between 2007 and 2020.[41] The killings not only degraded Iranian nuclear science but also reinforced Israeli diplomatic warnings to US officials that the IDF was ready to strike. And Mossad operatives brazenly heisted nuclear documents from a vault in Tehran in 2018.[42] Stuxnet was part of a much broader, chronic, covert struggle with Iran.[43]

Iran was hardly a passive victim in all this. Iranian penetration of CIA communications led to several arrests and executions in 2009.[44] This made the CIA even more dependent on Israeli HUMINT on Iran.[45] Also in 2009, the Iranian Green Movement erupted over allegations of fraud in the reelection of Mahmoud Ahmadinejad. Heightened Iranian paranoia regarding

Western conspiracy raised the counterintelligence threat to Western operations. Then in the years after Stuxnet, Iranian offensive cyber campaigns ramped up. Waves of DDoS attacks hit US banks.[46] Disruptive wiper attacks targeted Gulf rivals.[47] Iranian hackers disrupted city services in Atlanta with ransomware attacks in 2018.[48] Iranian cyber espionage became more persistent.[49] While Stuxnet may have helped to control military escalation by providing a covert option for alleviating tension, it also may have encouraged more threat activity in the cyber domain.

All actors in this strange triangle were playing multiple games for high stakes. This complicated context shaped the conduct of covert cyber operations. Ambiguous goals at the strategic level, moreover, contributed to ambiguous performance at the operational level.

Disconnected Institutions

Using the intelligence performance framework, I code the institutional environment of Stuxnet as partially *disconnected*, with nuances and qualifications aplenty. While I make a logical distinction between an actor and its environment, it is impossible not to discuss some of the operational choices made by the attackers here. The technical details of Stuxnet provide important insight into its institutional operating environment. We can assess, for instance, that the malware had to overcome barriers in order to exploit vulnerabilities in commercial software while hiding its tracks. At least, it had the capabilities to do so.

In this section I first describe the tactical challenges of infiltrating Natanz. Then I describe the broader international infrastructure that enabled and constrained infiltration. The following section describes the attackers in more detail.

ACCESS BARRIERS

Stuxnet is rightly celebrated for its technical wizardry. Its tactics are also the most knowable aspect of Olympic Games. Traditional weapons destroy themselves on the battlefield, but malware samples contain their operating instructions. Figure 5.1 illustrates the basic concept of operations, which I liken to a commando raid in three phases: insertion of operators into the target area, stealthy infiltration through defenses to the target, and actions on the objective. The special operations metaphor should also call to mind the back-end planning and support required for such a caper.[50]

The insertion phase was complicated by the so-called airgap. Stuxnet's target—the Natanz ICS—was not directly connected to the internet. Remote operators had to infiltrate malware through C2 servers on the public internet to the ICS network and then exfiltrate status and intelligence reports

```
┌─────────────────────────┐  ┌─────────────────────────┐  ┌─────────────────────────┐
│ 1. Insertion into target│  │ 2. Infiltration to the  │  │ 3. Actions on the       │
│ area                    │  │    target               │  │    objective            │
│                         │  │                         │  │                         │
│   Remote cyber operations│ │  Peer-to-peer network for│ │     Mask feedback       │
│           ▲             │  │  updates and status     │  │     to human            │
│           │             │  │       reports           │  │     operators           │
│           ▼             │  │                         │  │                         │
│  ┌───────────────────┐  │  │  ┌───────────────────┐  │  │  ┌───────────────────┐  │
│  │ Command and control│ │  │  │ Microsoft Windows │  │  │  │ Programmable logic│  │
│  │ infrastructure    │  │  │  │ enterprise network│  │  │  │ controllers       │  │
│  └───────────────────┘  │  │  └───────────────────┘  │  │  └───────────────────┘  │
│                         │  │                         │  │                         │
│   Internet connection   │  │  Controlled replication │  │  Tailored rootkit payload│
│   and/or human agents   │  │  and network mapping    │  │  ┌───────────────────┐  │
│                         │  │                         │  │  │ Centrifuge operations│ │
│  ┌───────────────────┐  │  │  ┌───────────────────┐  │  │  └───────────────────┘  │
│  │ Iranian industrial│  │  │  │ Siemens Step7     │  │  │ Overpressure  Rotor speed│
│  │ firms             │  │  │  │ industrial control│  │  │ attack (2007): attack (2009):│
│  └───────────────────┘  │  │  │ system            │  │  │ Alter sensors  1. Speed up│
│                         │  │  └───────────────────┘  │  │ Close valves   2. Normal │
│   Removable media to    │  │     Verify target       │  │                3. Slow down│
│   span the airgap to    │  │     configuration       │  │                4. Normal │
│   Natanz                │  │     (or abort)          │  │                5. Repeat │
└─────────────────────────┘  └─────────────────────────┘  └─────────────────────────┘
```

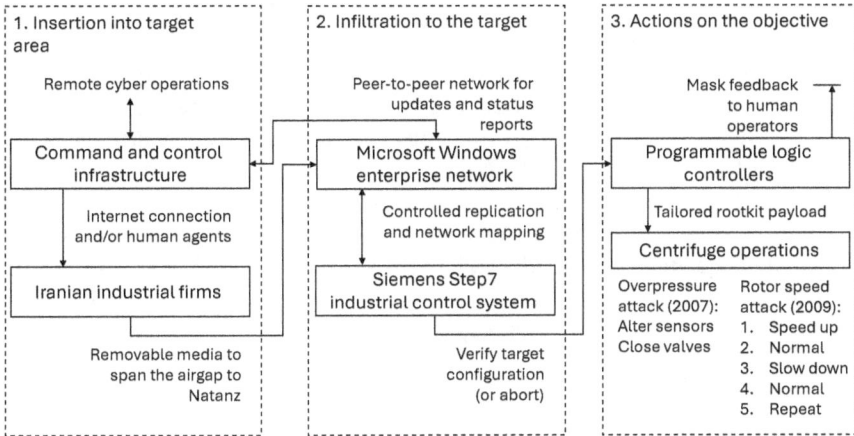

Figure 5.1. The Stuxnet intrusion as a special operation

back. Maintaining control of an intrusion across an airgap is so challenging that fewer than twenty cases of airgap-crossing malware were identified between 2000 and 2015, and a quarter of them were related to Stuxnet.[51] Few organizations appear to have the ability or willingness to sustain cyber campaigns across an airgap. Stuxnet in this sense is not representative of most cyber campaigns, but this says something about the capacity required for high-end exploitation. More complex problems often require more complex solutions.

Complicated access barriers—physical or logical—require organizational scaffolding to restore connectivity for intelligence access. Olympic Games relied on the witting or unwitting assistance of human beings to connect removable media such as a USB memory stick or maintenance laptop. The CIA and Mossad reportedly requested assistance from Dutch intelligence (AIVD) in 2004 to gain access to Natanz. By 2007 AVID had recruited an Iranian engineer who provided detailed intelligence used to develop Stuxnet and who later connected an infected USB flash drive to the Iranian network. According to an anonymous source, "The Dutch mole was the most important way of getting the virus into Natanz."[52] Meir Dagan, former director of the Israeli Mossad, hints that Mossad assets also played a role.[53] Later infections relied on other pathways through five industrial locations associated with the Iranian nuclear industry.[54] In effect, clandestine infrastructure restored institutional connectivity.

Next, the infiltration phase exploited internal connectivity within the enterprise network of Natanz. Stuxnet propagated through Microsoft Windows and Siemens Step7 software by exploiting multiple unpatched vulnerabilities (zero-days) to copy itself. Each copy kept a log of its lineage.

The network of infections also implemented a clandestine peer-to-peer communication network. This enabled Stuxnet to transmit progress reports back to remote operators and receive updates back through the airgap.

In the final phase, the payload triggered only when precise conditions were met (the malware verified the right version of Simatic Step7 software and the right model of PLC). Stuxnet manipulated PLC controls, but it did not inflict catastrophic breakage on centrifuges. Instead, it subtly increased the malfunction rate of centrifuges by manipulating rotors or valves. The IR-1 centrifuge design was already inefficient, so Stuxnet just marginally reduced efficiency a bit more.

SECURITY CONTROLS

The whole operation was engineered with considerable attention to discretion. Olympic Games planners patiently conducted reconnaissance for years in advance. They carefully tailored the intrusion and payloads to the specific configuration of Natanz. Each new infection checked its host for popular antivirus products and varied its behavior accordingly. The extensive proliferation controls in Stuxnet's code (such as verifying target configuration, limiting the number of reinfections, and ending the operation by a certain date) bely the involvement of national security lawyers.[55]

The payload also suggests that discretion was a high priority. Symantec initially described a subtle attack on centrifuge rotors in a version of the worm that had been compiled on June 2009—Stuxnet version 1.0.[56] The primary attack sequence worked by speeding up centrifuges for fifteen minutes, returning to normal for a month, slowing down for an hour, returning to normal for another month, and then repeating indefinitely. This had the effect of reducing the efficiency of enrichment and creating mechanical stress on centrifuges. Stuxnet also provided bogus feedback to ICS operators to mask any alert signals from the PLCs (the equivalent of using looping surveillance camera footage to distract the security guards from the bank robbers in the movie *Ocean's Eleven*). A reasonable inference is that Stuxnet's designers wanted the operation to remain hidden, so that it would be viable for an extended amount of time and minimize the risks of compromise.

Symantec later discovered an earlier version—Stuxnet 0.5—that had been uploaded to a virus database in November 2007.[57] It implemented a different attack sequence, which worked by closing centrifuge valves to prevent gas from escaping and create dangerous overpressure. The valve attack was disabled in version 1.0 and replaced with the rotor attack. Perhaps security-conscious architects thought that the more aggressive valve attack was more likely to be detected than the subtle rotor attack. They also may have decided that the simpler manipulation of rotors was a more reliable form of sabotage than the virtuoso sequence of valve manipulations.[58]

Nevertheless, the disconnected institutions of the environment posed a serious problem for intelligence performance. While the random walk of infections increased the likelihood of finding the intended target, it also increased the number of malware samples in circulation. Sure enough, despite all the security controls, the self-replicating infection accidentally spread beyond Natanz. This enabled civilian security companies to obtain samples, redirect C2 traffic to local sinkholes, and gather forensic data. For example, each instance of the worm kept an internal map of its lineage and then communicated its progress to its remote handlers, but the same graphs enabled incident responders to trace the spread of the infection. Stuxnet was caught in a classic trade-off between efficiency and effectiveness. The same design features that enabled Stuxnet to efficiently penetrate closed industrial facilities became an open book to commercial counterintelligence agents.

To borrow a slogan from US Special Forces, Stuxnet worked "by, with, and through" civil society. Local proxies can expand the reach of small teams of special operators, but proxy forces sometimes act negligently or treacherously. For Stuxnet, likewise, reliance on third-party commercial technology both improved operational efficiency and created operational risk. Figure 5.2 depicts the entire institutional ecosystem that both enabled and constrained Stuxnet. Note that the technical operation depicted in

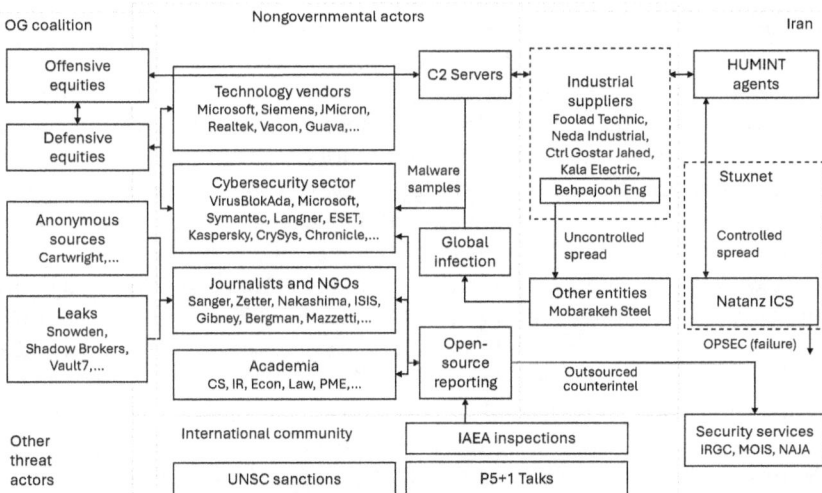

Figure 5.2. The institutional ecosystem of Stuxnet

135

figure 5.1 fits almost entirely within the box labeled "Stuxnet" on the right side of figure 5.2. Yet operations traversed and exploited civilian technologies around the world. This infrastructure was not simply "virtual terrain" to be navigated by a threat actor but an institutional system shaped by national governments, international organizations, commercial businesses, and other nongovernmental actors. Many of these agents embodied counterintelligence threats to Olympic Games.

Obama's 2011 *International Strategy for Cyberspace* decried "aggressive acts in cyberspace" and called for international norms for "preserving global network functionality and improving cybersecurity."[59] Obama reportedly worried that "American acknowledgment that it was using cyberweapons—even under the most careful and limited circumstances—could enable other countries, terrorists or hackers to justify their own attacks."[60] Legal experts debate whether Stuxnet qualifies as a use of force in violation of international law or, on the contrary, was a legitimate effort to enforce international sanctions.[61] But better not to have this debate in the open, since it would expose the United States to charges of hypocrisy.[62] Sure enough, Chinese diplomats seized on the revelation of Stuxnet, and later the Snowden leaks, to counter American moralizing about Chinese network intrusions. Worse, Stuxnet's code provided a public template for ICS attack that could come back to bite the United States.

Stuxnet thus found itself constrained by disparate policy goals. There was tension between the US government's role in protecting public infrastructure and privately exploiting it. The Olympic Games coalition (described further in the next section) fits roughly within the box labeled "Offensive equities" at the top-left corner of figure 5.2. Yet the same governments had defensive equities in cybersecurity too. US agencies also protected government networks, regulated the technology industry, managed public safety, and so on. While the NSA openly coordinated "information assurance" to secure US government networks, it secretly ran offensive cyber operations through its Tailored Access Operations (TAO) unit.[63] While the US government coordinated public-private partnerships with industry to improve defensive cybersecurity, it also subverted their products for offensive cyber operations. Exploits kept secret for private advantage could not be revealed to vendors for the public good.[64]

For example, Ukrainian criminals independently discovered one of the technical vulnerabilities used by Stuxnet (MS08–067); it was incorporated into the notorious Conficker internet worm, discovered in November 2008.[65] In principle, the NSA could have reported it to Microsoft when it was first discovered, which might have preempted Conficker and improved cyberspace for all. Other vulnerabilities associated with Stuxnet (exploited by Fanny and Flame) were independently patched by Microsoft in 2009. This did not interrupt operations, as Stuxnet's architects simply switched to other secret exploits to achieve the same functions.[66] This suggests that the

NSA had a large stockpile of Microsoft exploits available. In principle, all these undisclosed vulnerabilities could have improved public cybersecurity against criminal threats like Conficker. Instead they provided the NSA with an operational reserve.

The initial revelation of Stuxnet in 2010 obliged Microsoft to patch four hitherto unknown vulnerabilities, or zero-days. Others were documented later. Table 5.1 summarizes software vulnerabilities in Microsoft and Siemens software that were exploited by some version of Stuxnet.[67] There are almost certainly other versions of Stuxnet that have not appeared in public virus repositories, and they may contain additional exploits. These exploits

Table 5.1. Stuxnet zero-days in the common vulnerabilities and exposures (cve) catalog and corresponding microsoft patches

Software vulnerability (and patch)	Exploit functionality and Stuxnet versions
CVE-2008–4250 (MS08–067)	Windows arbitrary code execution in v1.0/1.1 and Conficker[1]
CVE-2009–1123/4/5/6 (MS09–025)	Windows privilege escalation only in v1.0 and Fanny & Flame[2]
CVE-2010–2568 (MS10–046)	Windows remote attack execution via .LNK shortcut file in v1.1[3]
CVE-2010–2729 (MS10–061)	Windows print spooler remote execution in v1.0/1.1[4]
CVE-2010–2743 (MS10–073)	Windows keyboard layout vulnerability in 1.1[5]
CVE-2010–2744 (MS10–074)	Windows privilege escalation in Kernel Mode Drivers[6]
CVE-2010–2772	Siemens Simatic hard-coded password in v1.0/1.1[7]
CVE-2010–3338 (MS10–092)	Windows privilege escalation in task scheduler[8]
CVE-2010–3888 (MS10-092)	Windows privilege escalation via "unknown vectors" in 1.1[9]
CVE-2010–3889 (MS10-092)	Windows unspecified vulnerability[10]
CVE-2012–3015	Siemens Step7 insecure library loading in V0.5/1.0/1.1[11]

1 Falliere et al., "W32.Stuxnet Dossier," 24.
2 Gostev, "Back to Stuxnet"; GReAT, "Fanny Equation."
3 Falliere et al., "W32.Stuxnet Dossier," 25.
4 Falliere et al., "W32.Stuxnet Dossier," 23; Muñoz, "Emerald Connection."
5 Falliere et al., "W32.Stuxnet Dossier," 15.
6 Industrial Control System Cyber Security Institute, "Stuxnet—Understanding, Demos, References," SCADAhacker, January 21, 2014, https://scadahacker.com/resources/stuxnet.html.
7 "CVE-2010–2772 Detail," National Vulnerability Database, National Institute of Standards and Technology, September 8, 2010, https://nvd.nist.gov/vuln/detail/CVE-2010-2772.
8 Industrial Control System Cyber Security Institute, "Stuxnet."
9 "CVE-2010–3888 Detail," National Vulnerability Database, National Institute of Standards and Technology, September 8, 2010, https://nvd.nist.gov/vuln/detail/CVE-2010-3888.
10 "CVE-2010–3889 Detail," National Vulnerability Database, National Institute of Standards and Technology, September 8, 2010, https://nvd.nist.gov/vuln/detail/CVE-2010-3889.
11 McDonald et al., "Stuxnet 0.5," 2.

are almost certainly just a small sample of the offensive stockpile available to the Olympic Games coalition. Stuxnet's architects identified and operationalized at least a dozen vulnerabilities and were willing to use them in the same operation. This is no mean feat, suggestive of both organizational capacity and the high priority of the target.

Table 5.1 reflects an implicit intelligence contest between a US spy agency (the NSA) and a US company (Microsoft). Such are the conundrums of secret statecraft in cyberspace. Microsoft found itself in the crosshairs of its own government because its products were used by Iran, a political adversary of the United States. But this also meant that Microsoft's efforts to patch its vulnerabilities implicitly benefited Iran as well. Microsoft (and Siemens) publicly provided software patches and advice to mitigate a global infection. They acted to protect corporate products and reputations, of course, but they improved public safety in the process. This same effort inadvertently helped Iranian counterintelligence and harmed US intelligence.

CIVIL COUNTERINTELLIGENCE

Stuxnet was much more than a three-body problem, which is unpredictable enough. Its operating environment also included security firms and other nongovernmental actors, such as the IAEA inspectors who provided data on Iranian centrifuge operations. Their presence made the operating environment less permissive for persistent access.

Commercial cybersecurity firms were the first responders. When Stuxnet was first detected, it was not immediately obvious what its purpose was—only that it was infecting computers worldwide, with a heavy concentration in Iran. Stuxnet samples provided a blueprint of its operational design and a rich source of epidemiological data for cybersecurity researchers. Symantec documented the spread of Stuxnet in three waves, targeting five Iranian suppliers of centrifuge and ICS technologies.[68] It appears that uncontrolled propagation began with the March 23, 2010, infection of Behpajooh Engineering Company, an Iranian ICS vendor implicated in illicit technology transfer. This inadvertently infected computers at Mobarakeh Steel Company, a large industrial concern with international business. This single accident led to a global epidemic of Stuxnet infections.[69]

Speculation about attribution began as soon commercial analysts revealed the wizardry of Stuxnet and the nature of its target. The pool of likely suspects quickly narrowed to the United States and Israel based on an assessment of means, motive, and opportunity. Journalists soon found anonymous sources in the US government who were willing to provide information. Former STRATCOM commander General James Cartwright later pled guilty to lying to the FBI during its Stuxnet investigation.[70]

Government spies hacked commercial tech, and industry adapted. The private sector created, maintained, and repaired the institutional environment that Stuxnet exploited. Commercial firms were sources of connectivity and vulnerability, yes, but they also enhanced defensive monitoring (information about Stuxnet) and enforcement (patching and mitigation). Table 5.1 can thus be read as evidence of the enduring presence of software vulnerabilities in mature commercial products, but it can also be read as evidence of community processes in place to identify threats and close vulnerabilities.

History and historiography mingle in this case. Public reporting on Stuxnet confirmed the suspicions held by Iranian counterintelligence agencies that Western spies were targeting nuclear sites. Commercial patches aided Iranian incident response. Public compromise prompted threat actors to take evasive measures, tear down supporting infrastructure, and adapt technical methods. More information trickled out later, much of it too late to matter operationally but useful nonetheless for understanding the overall campaign. All of this same information then filters into historical case studies like this one.

The public revelation of Stuxnet was followed a few years later by a series of damaging leaks. NSA contractor Edward Snowden leaked a tranche of classified documents to journalists that revealed the NSA's discreet partnerships with, and clandestine exploitation of, major US tech firms, creating a firestorm of controversy.[71] Then during the 2016 election influence campaign, a Russia-linked hacker group known as the Shadow Brokers released a large amount of internal code, purportedly divulged by another contractor, Harold T. Martin III, who had worked in the NSA's TAO.[72] The Shadow Brokers material provided additional data on and cross-validation of NSA tooling.[73] Another tranche of data on US cyber operations was passed to WikiLeaks by former CIA officer (and child pornographer) Joshua Schulte, who had worked for the CIA's Information Operations Center (IOC).[74] All these leaks were at least illicit, and some of them could have been Russian influence operations (recruiting traitors and doxing the United States). This makes them problematic as sources, but they do provide circumstantial evidence to supplement other sources to fill in the overall picture.

Sophisticated Organization

The initial Symantec report concluded that "Stuxnet is of such great complexity—requiring significant resources to develop—that few attackers will be capable of producing a similar threat, to such an extent that we would not expect masses of threats of similar in [sic] sophistication to suddenly appear."[75] If anything this assessment was too cautious. Stuxnet was the product of multiple platforms run by multiple agencies in multiple nations.[76]

I code the clandestine organization of Stuxnet as mostly *sophisticated*, with the major caveat that there were significant dependencies embodied in the coalition relationships and technical tooling that ultimately undermined operational discretion. Sovereign state agencies were free to operate unilaterally in their national interests. Olympic Games did not, and probably could not, completely control the risks of dependency and disclosure.

EXPLOIT PLATFORMS

Software platforms are a double-edged sword for malware developers. Hackers are programmers too. Like any software engineer, they rely on dynamic link libraries, application programming interfaces, and software development kits. Developers recombine and reconfigure this functionality in custom applications without having to write and debug code from scratch. This improves the efficiency of malware development. But code reuse and dependencies also increase counterintelligence exposure for offensive hackers. Incident responders and reverse engineers can use these dependencies to learn about the capabilities of the attacker.

This, of course, is the classic logic of deception in both directions. First, malware developers usurp the efficiency of legitimate commercial software systems. Flexible development platforms are incomplete contracts—features that become vulnerabilities for malicious actors. But second, counterintelligence analysts usurp the usurped efficiency of the attacker. An attacker's poor OPSEC is a bug that defenders can exploit.

Figure 5.3 is my synthesis of the technical reporting on Stuxnet's malware ecosystem. Boxes with double borders at the top describe development platforms used by US or Israeli intelligence agencies. Links between technical components indicate code dependencies and reuse. Boxes with bold borders in the bottom half depict zero-day exploits, per table 5.1. This functionality was incorporated into four known versions of Stuxnet at the bottom of figure 5.3. Other boxes throughout depict other malware components created with the same platforms. There are almost certainly more versions of Stuxnet and other tools that have not been reported to public antivirus repositories or described in public reporting. Stuxnet is not one thing, and we do not know everything.

Kaspersky first reported on the "Equation Group" platform in 2015, revealing "operations dating back to 2001, and perhaps as early as 1996."[77] Leaked internal CIA commentary clarifies that "the Equation Group as labeled in the report does not relate to a specific group but rather a collection of tools (mostly TAO some IOC)."[78] The same source highlights the internal security failures that Kaspersky and other firms were able to leverage: "The bigger issue is in breaking ties between tools (or at a minimum

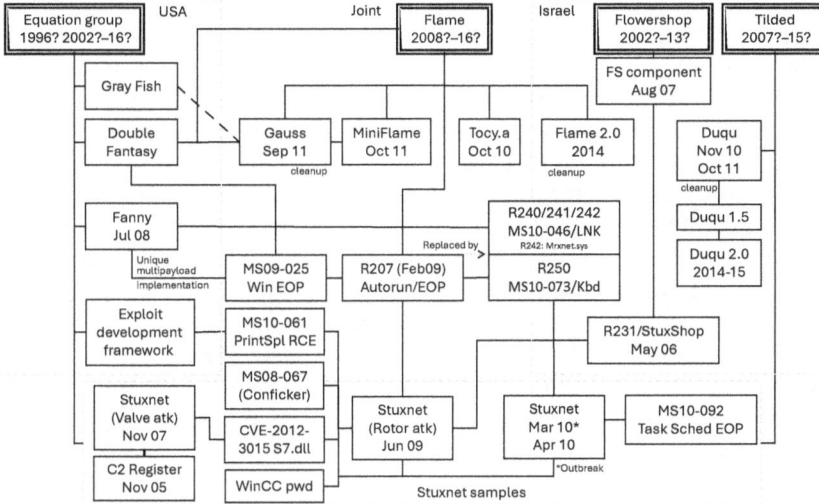

Figure 5.3. Forensic dependencies across development platforms (double border), zero-day exploits (bold border), and various malware in the Stuxnet family

tracking them), and not reusing tools with compromised techniques/ exploits."[79] This is a version of the classic efficiency-effectiveness trade-off discussed in chapter 2. The same tools that improved the efficiency of malware development at the TAO and IOC provided evidence for counterintelligence analysts and thus degraded malware effectiveness. Kaspersky describes several Equation Group tools associated with Stuxnet, including a scripting tool and a print spooler vulnerability.[80] Fanny, the reconnaissance tool for crossing airgaps, is exclusively associated with Equation Group and contains a unique implementation of an exploit that later appeared in a version of Stuxnet.[81] Equation Group capability likely predates collaboration with Israel on Stuxnet.

The "Flame" platform, by contrast, appears to be a joint US-Israeli project, according to reporting in *The Washington Post*.[82] A joint exploit platform would have enabled the NSA or CIA to offer a collaboration platform to allies while holding back the best of Equation Group for US-only operations.[83] Kaspersky first discovered Flame after the UN invited it to investigate reports of a mysterious data wiper attack targeting Iran. This led to the discovery of Flame and "Gauss" spyware. Flame is a distinct suite of espionage tools that shares little with Stuxnet, but one version of Flame (tocy.a) shares a module with the June 2009 version of Stuxnet (reimplementing a Fanny exploit).[84] Another version of Flame (miniFlame) shares functionality with the Gauss trojan, which uses sophisticated encryption techniques characteristic of Equation Group.[85]

The other two platforms are likely Israeli. "Tilded" is Kaspersky's name for a platform (named for files starting with "~d") that was used to create the trojan known as "Duqu." Later versions of Stuxnet share naming conventions, modular structure, injection mechanisms, and driver reuse with Duqu.[86] Tilded most likely belongs to Israel's Unit 8200, the elite SIGINT agency in the IDF intelligence directorate (Aman).[87] "Flowershop" is an older exploit platform that has been linked to a single module in the June 2009 version of Stuxnet.[88] This version marks an important juncture in Stuxnet's developmental history. Symantec assesses that the November 2007 version of Stuxnet was implemented differently from the 2009–10 version: The "platform code bases are different enough to suggest different developers were involved."[89] This rearchitecting is consistent with the time frame in which US-Israeli intelligence collaboration increased following a May 2008 meeting between Bush and Olmert in Jerusalem.[90] This is probably a forensic shadow of the divergence of US and Israeli efforts, as discussed further below.

Olympic Games actors reacted to their compromise by burning capabilities and altering behavior. Kaspersky's discovery of Duqu, Gauss, and Flame prompted their operators to shut down intrusions and C2 infrastructure. Kaspersky witnessed an attempt to clean up Flame before Kaspersky even released its report, raising the possibility that Kaspersky was under surveillance.[91] Flame seemed to have been abandoned after May 2012, but in 2019, Chronicle analysts discovered that a new version dating to February 2014 had been circulating. "While the malware is clearly built on the Flame source code," they noted, "it includes new counter-measures against researcher meddling."[92]

Duqu 2.0, similarly, reappeared several years after the cleanup effort with a new memory-only implementation. Kaspersky reported that Duqu 2.0 infections from 2014–15 were "linked to the P5+1 events and venues related to the negotiations with Iran about a nuclear deal. The threat actor behind Duqu appears to have launched attacks at the venues for some of these high-level talks."[93] Duqu 2.0 infections seemed to be unilateral Israeli efforts: "One of the victims appear [sic] to have been infected both by the Equation Group and by the Duqu group at the same time; this suggests the two entities are different and competing with each other to obtain information from this victim."[94] This demonstrates how intelligence collaborators can also compete.[95]

I draw four main inferences from commercial threat intelligence reporting on Stuxnet. First, the sabotage tool was just one part of a larger malware ecosystem. Second, multiple national development efforts contributed to this system. Third, the agencies behind these efforts were highly sophisticated, both technically and operationally. Fourth, however, the dependencies across tooling and operations were a major counterintelligence liability. The ability to reassemble something like figure 5.3 from open-source reporting is reflective of imperfect discretion in the clandestine organization that developed all that capability.

BUREAUCRATIC CAPACITY

As the operation's code name suggests, Olympic Games was a multinational effort.[96] The Netherlands, the United Kingdom, Germany, and perhaps France also aided efforts led by the United States and Israel.[97] It is unclear from the available evidence how the multinational coalition was managed. Spy agencies from different countries would have had to coordinate not only technical experts but also a cadre of administrators, systems integrators, skilled intelligence analysts, experienced operational planners, and competent commanders, not to mention a raft of lawyers.[98]

There is more information available about the US role in Olympic Games than about the Israeli role, in part because the US national security bureaucracy is leakier and in part because the leading partner had more to leak. Olympic Games combined the efforts of the US intelligence community, Department of Defense, and National Laboratories in the Department of Energy (DOE). The CIA, which has the legal authority for most covert action in the United States, allegedly initiated Olympic Games via a secret presidential finding in late 2007 or early 2008, although there were informal discussions as early as 2006.[99] The NSA performed most of the technical work, primarily through TAO, drawing on Equation Group capabilities already in place.[100] The CIA also provided technical support through the IOC, which, according to a report in *The Washington Post*, specializes "in computer penetrations that require closer contact with the target, such as using spies or unwitting contractors to spread a contagion via a thumb drive."[101]

A complex operation like Stuxnet had to be carefully engineered, debugged, tested, and rehearsed. The Oak Ridge National Laboratory (ORNL) had acquired Libyan centrifuges as the IR-1 by March 2004; the ORNL reportedly set up a test FEP ("The Hill") the following year.[102] Another DOE facility, the Idaho National Laboratory (INL), ran an ICS security program known as Aurora, which was supported by Siemens.[103] It is unknown whether this collaboration influenced the design of the Stuxnet attack on Siemens ICS, but a leaked State Department cable suggests that the German Ministry of Foreign Affairs was not opposed to sabotaging the Iranian program.[104] At the same time that the INL was publicly demonstrating the dangers of cyber-physical attacks for defensive purposes, the ORNL was privately testing Stuxnet and breaking centrifuges for offensive purposes.

Israel had its own sophisticated organizational and technical capabilities. It also had deep expertise in SIGINT and covert operations, and it had built a test FEP at the Shimon Peres Negev Nuclear Research Center in Dimona.[105]

This could be used to develop and test tailored Israeli variants of Stuxnet (or something else). As discussed above, the IAF was planning preemptive military action against Iran (Operation Deep Waters), both to goad US covert action and to hedge against its failure. This divergence of interests in the secret conspiracy created operational risk for Olympic Games.

COALITION DEPENDENCY

In Symantec's assessment, "Stuxnet clearly escaped the original organizations due to collaboration with partner organizations."[106] David Sanger reported in *The New York Times* that an uncoordinated Israeli modification in the code apparently caused Stuxnet to replicate beyond Iran.[107] The details, timing, and responsibility for this specific breakdown, as well as the overall architecture of the joint operation, are profoundly unclear. It is premature to conclude that any nation or organization was solely or even mainly in the driver's seat of this operation. Nonetheless, the available evidence supports an assessment that the malware development effort forked. The United States and Israel ended up managing different versions of Stuxnet.

Stuxnet activity intensified in 2009, and there was an uptick in Flame infections in 2010. It is possible that Israel began taking liberties with tools it acquired from the United States. According to an unnamed NSA source, "We operated at a low profile. . . . The Israelis, on the other hand, constantly pushed to be more aggressive."[108] This is consistent with a description of Israeli cyber culture as "chutzpah gone viral," whereby "accepted norms, practices and sources of authority are constantly questioned and improvisation, creativity and innovation are highly prized values."[109] There is also some forensic evidence that the development effort forked. Stuxnet appears to have been rearchitected starting with the June 2009 version. The samples described in figure 5.3 migrated from the Equation platform to Duqu (i.e., from the United States to Israel), borrowing a few functions from Flowershop and Flame along the way. This means that most of the versions of Stuxnet found in the wild may in fact be Israeli variants of a once common project.

Israel also had a motive to fork the project. Suggestively, Obama and Netanyahu clashed in May 2009 over how aggressively to attack Iran.[110] In September 2010, Netanyahu reportedly told Dagan, the director of the Mossad, "I have decided to place the IDF and you at 0 plus 30," meaning Israel should be ready to execute a military operation against Iran in a month.[111] By November 2010, Israel's military chief of staff informed Netanyahu that the IDF still did not have an "operational capability" for a unilateral strike on Iran.[112] Dagan thus stepped up the Mossad's own covert alternative, including the assassination of Iranian scientists in January and November 2010, July 2011, and January 2012. Seen in this context, the intensification of Stuxnet activity in 2009 and its compromise in mid-2010 is a leading indicator of the growing Israeli willingness to unilaterally to preventive action.

While this interpretation is admittedly speculative given the thin evidentiary record, I assess that the compromising outbreak of Stuxnet was an unintended consequence of an Israeli push to intensify the disruption of Natanz in late 2009. Another possibility is that the Israelis deliberately compromised Stuxnet to send a signal to Iran (that its nuclear program was reachable) or to the United States (that it was time to try something else). But if signaling were really the goal, then the nuanced breakage of a few centrifuges was a very anemic signal. After all, Stuxnet could have been reprogrammed to cause much more visible and catastrophic damage, even as this would neutralize years of expensive effort and preclude ongoing operations. A more parsimonious interpretation, on the principle that we should not attribute to malice things that can adequately be explained by stupidity, is that the Stuxnet team made a mistake. Divergent goals and independent development centers within the covert coalition undermined the coordination of clandestine operations.

CYBER WARFARE PLANS

According to a report in *The New York Times*, Israeli threats of unilateral action compelled the Obama administration "to develop its own military contingency plans in the event of such an attack, including destroying a full-size mock-up of an Iranian nuclear facility [Fordo] in the western desert of the United States with a 30,000-pound bomb."[113] Preparations reportedly included a US Cyber Command contingency plan called "Nitro Zeus" that aimed, according to another *Times* report, to "turn off critical elements of the Iranian infrastructure without firing a shot."[114] Cyber saboteurs also targeted another nuclear suite in Fordo, but they curtailed operations in 2013 as public talks with Iran got underway.

In the event of war with Iran, Nitro Zeus could have boosted the efficiency of US military operations by disrupting Iranian systems or confusing defensive responses to a US attack. This may be likened to a scaled-up version of Operation Orchard, the cyber-enabled electronic warfare operation that supported the IAF air strike in Syria discussed above. This is a very different concept of operations compared to Stuxnet. Whereas Olympic Games was a peacetime covert action in lieu of war, Nitro Zeus was a military contingency plan for precisely that war. Nitro Zeus hedged against the possibility that unilateral Israeli prevention might drag the United States into the very war that Olympic Games was designed to avoid.

While it does not make sense to describe Stuxnet as cyber warfare, Nitro Zeus was most definitely a cyber warfare plan. It is unknown whether US policymakers had any confidence in the plan, or whether it would have worked as planned. According to one anonymous participant, "This was an enormous, and enormously complex, program. . . . Before it was developed, the U.S. had never assembled a combined cyber and kinetic attack plan on this scale." The effort "involved thousands of American military and intelligence personnel, spending tens of millions of dollars and placing electronic implants in Iranian computer networks to 'prepare the battlefield.'"[115] This additional complexity is suggestive of the challenges of using cyber operations, which always rely on institutions shared across competitors, in wartime conditions, which involve lethal combat between autonomous institutions.

The fog and friction of war probably would have undermined the planning assumptions of Nitro Zeus. Indeed, the peacetime context of Stuxnet helps to explain its viability: Commercial institutions stabilized the institutional connectivity that was the condition for its possibility. Even in these slightly more permissive conditions, however, Stuxnet did not degrade Iranian enrichment, and the operation was compromised. If Stuxnet was a hard operation, then Nitro Zeus would be even harder, perhaps prohibitively so.

Mixed Performance

Stuxnet was a complex operation conducted by a mostly sophisticated organization within partially disconnected institutions. These mixed conditions produced mixed performance. As the United States shared more capability with Israel, Israel became more willing to engage in unrestrained cyber operations. The public compromise of Stuxnet then increased Israel's willingness to take unilateral military action. But it also increased the United States' desire to find nonmilitary options—namely, secret diplomacy with Iran. Diplomacy ultimately succeeded where cyber operations had failed, but cyber operations encouraged key parties to give diplomacy a chance.

ENRICHMENT CONTINUES

The data on Stuxnet's effects on Iranian enrichment are poor. Most studies cite IAEA inspection data analyzed by the Institute for Science and International Security (ISIS), a nonprofit arms control organization based in Washington, DC. ISIS assessed that Stuxnet caused the Iranians to disconnect and replace one thousand IR-1 centrifuges at Natanz by early 2010.[116] Figure 5.4 reproduces two ISIS figures from 2015 that informed contemporary public debate.[117] The correlation of IAEA data and Symantec reports is suggestive but hardly definitive.

Figure 5.4a reveals a dip in the ratio of centrifuges installed and fed with uranium hexafluoride (i.e., actively enriching) from mid-2008 to 2011. This is plausibly due to the reduced efficiency caused by Stuxnet. A larger ratio (bigger dip) indicates less efficient enrichment or perhaps more effective sabotage. Figure 5.4a also shows a leveling off in total centrifuges starting in mid-2009. This is plausibly due to more aggressive Israeli infections that ultimately compromised the operation. The dip in December 2009 is the famous thousand centrifuges that ISIS attributed to Stuxnet. The global outbreak was detected in summer 2010; it then took several months for Iran to clean up the infection, after which efficiency improved.

Whatever the temporary effects of Stuxnet in centrifuge input, figure 5.4b shows that the cumulative output of LEU continued to increase throughout

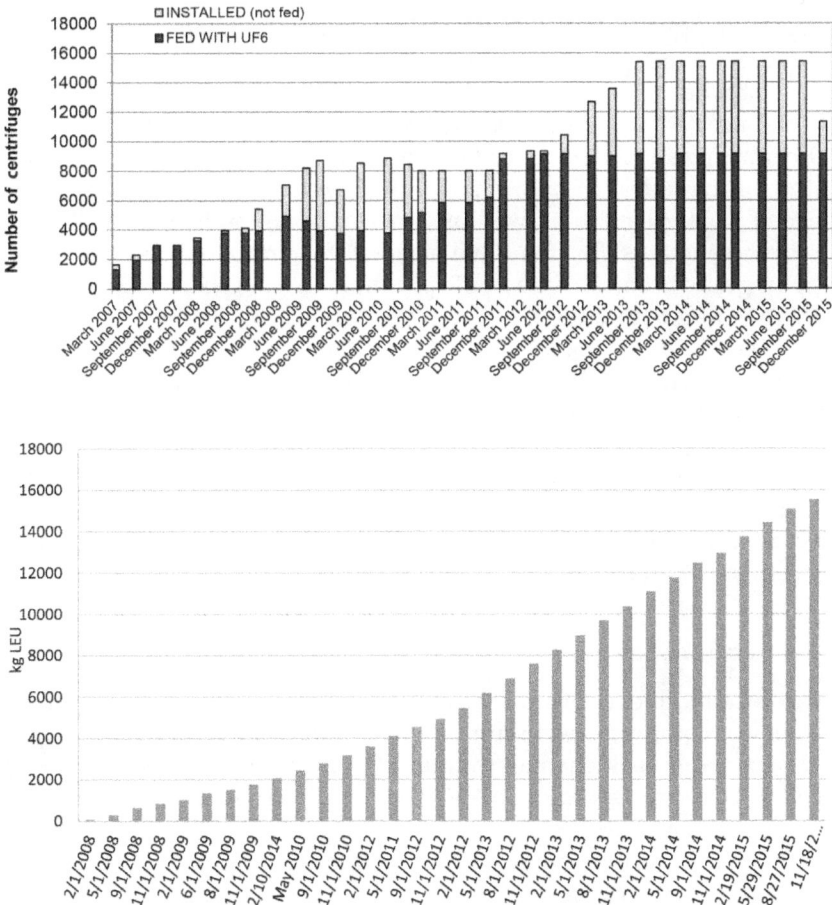

Figure 5.4. IAEA data on Natanz centrifuge trends over time, showing (a) centrifuges installed and enriching at the Natanz fuel enrichment plant, and (b) Iran's steadily increasing cumulative production of lightly enriched uranium (source: Institute of Science and International Security [mislabeled years in the legend of figure 5.4b are typos in the original document])

the Olympic Games campaign. According to IAEA inspection data, further-more, the damaged centrifuges were removed from the least productive cascades (no cascades in Module A28 and only some cascades in Module A26 were fed with uranium hexafluoride gas), while the most productive cascades do not seem to have been affected (all cascades in Module A24 were fed).[118] It is unknown whether this discrepancy was the result of delib-erate targeting (to keep a low profile and improve discretion by targeting only spares) or an artifact of Stuxnet's random spreading (which missed the most lucrative target in A24 altogether). The former would be consistent with incentives for restraint, while the latter would be consistent with the frictions of remote operations. Either way, the result was that Natanz con-tinued to accumulate LEU at a steady rate.

By 2012 in figure 5.4a, the number of centrifuge installations has returned to the pre-Stuxnet growth rate, plausibly due to Iran's successful mitiga-tion of Stuxnet. The number of actively fed centrifuges then reaches its all-time high. By late 2013, Natanz has nearly quadrupled the number of IR-1 centrifuges installed since Olympic Games began. Iran also installed prototype cascades of more advanced centrifuges (IR-2/4/5/6) that enriched at 20 percent, as well as a new underground FEP at Fordo.[119] Breakout estimates for the time needed for Iran to produce enough weapon-grade uranium for a bomb plummeted from six months in 2009 to nearly one month in 2013.[120]

Iran was closer to a bomb after Stuxnet than before it. Sabotage did not slow or meaningfully disrupt Iranian enrichment. It is plausible that Stux-net degraded long-term efficiency at Natanz by cutting into spare centri-fuge supplies, raising error rates, and undermining the confidence of Iranian engineers, but the discovery of Stuxnet may also have increased Iranian resolve to further improve its latent nuclear capability. Stuxnet's direct effects as a sabotage operation cannot be considered successful except in a very narrow, tactical, and temporary sense.

IRAN NEGOTIATES

Stuxnet's indirect strategic effects, by contrast, may be more significant. Stuxnet was compromised in summer 2010. Later that same year, the United States opened a back channel to Iran. This eventually blossomed into the open P5+1 process leading to the JCPOA in 2013. The relationship between these events is murky.

US overtures to Iran predate the compromise of Stuxnet, and Iran had other reasons to consider them. Diplomats in the US State Department had been advocating for talking to Iran since 2008 and met with senior Iranian officials in fall 2009.[121] Obama had even sent a secret letter to Iranian supreme leader Ayatollah Ali Khamenei in summer 2009, but this feeler was eclipsed by Tehran's crackdown on the Green Movement.[122] As the IAEA reported increasing enrichment levels at Fordo and Natanz, the United States ramped up economic sanctions throughout 2010. At the same time, the sultan of Oman was helping to mediate negotiations to release three American backpackers who had been detained by Iran under suspicions of espionage. In late 2010, Obama envoys gave a message to the Omani leader, to be conveyed to Khamenei, according to *The New York Times*, that the "United States thought there was a chance for a peaceful denouement to the nuclear standoff with Iran but was prepared to take military action if Iran rejected diplomacy."[123]

Did the compromise of Stuxnet affect Obama's decision to send this message? Did it improve the credibility of the message? Did it affect the Iranian decision to respond positively to it? Without more detailed evidence, we cannot answer these questions definitively. Yet the timing is intriguing. The revelation of Stuxnet, which was widely suspected to be the work of US intelligence, would have enabled Iran to draw several conclusions. First, the United States was willing and able to penetrate one of Iran's most secure facilities. Second, the United States wanted to keep this penetration secret. Together these implied that the United States was both serious about counterproliferation and motivated to avoid escalation. Third, however, Iran could now mitigate Stuxnet, thanks to the public cybersecurity response. This took away this particular US covert option but not the demonstration of US resolve. The United States could thus credibly offer, and Iran could accept, secret talks to take the place of sabotage. While secret diplomacy had several other causes in this case, it is plausible that Stuxnet helped it along.

The talks were kept secret from Israel, presumably to help Iran save face and to avoid Israel acting as a spoiler. But Israeli SIGINT detected the talks in mid-2012. Netanyahu responded with a defiant speech in September at the UN General Assembly declaring a redline for Iranian enrichment past the threshold required for a bomb. Israel used the threat of unilateral prevention to encourage US counterproliferation efforts: "In the summer of 2012," according to *The New York Times*, "American spy satellites detected clusters of Israeli aircraft making what seemed to be early preparations for an attack."[124] But Netanyahu was bluffing. As the diplomatic JCPOA process took shape, the United States increasingly opposed military action. In October, Netanyahu quietly canceled IDF planning for a preventive strike. The United States also dialed back on cyber operations associated with Nitro Zeus.[125]

In June 2013, Iranians elected as president Hassan Rouhani, who was more moderate than his predecessor, Mahmoud Ahmadinejad. In a historic phone call in September, Obama and Rouhani agreed to reinvigorate P5+1 negotiations (i.e., the permanent members of the UNSC plus Germany) to hold Natanz at 15,420 centrifuges. The plateau in figure 5.4a corresponds to the first open phone call between Obama and Rouhani in September 2013. The diplomatic process culminated in the JCPOA in July 2015, followed in October 2015 by the removal of 4,112 centrifuges, or four times as many as are attributed to Stuxnet. The final drop in figure 5.4a corresponds to the official adoption of the JCPOA in July 2015. Notably the JCPOA included a clause committing the signatories to "cooperation through training and workshops to strengthen Iran's ability to protect against, and respond to nuclear security threats, including sabotage," which is suggestive of the role played by Stuxnet in encouraging talks in the first place.[126]

I will hazard four tentative conclusions about the political impact of Olympic Games. First, as long as cyber sabotage was a viable option, Israel was unable to secure US support for a strike, and Israel was also more willing to put off preventive war. Second, Stuxnet might have accomplished more had it remained both clandestine (hiding activity) and covert (hiding agency), as its architects intended, but it came to a premature end. Third, diplomacy ultimately had a more significant direct effect than covert action in limiting the Iranian program. Fourth, covert action probably had an indirect effect by buying time for diplomacy and making it more attractive to all parties. Richard Maher similarly assesses, "While sabotage and covert action may not have been the most important factors in Iran's decision to accept limits and restrictions on its nuclear program, they contributed to the overall coercive approach the United States and other countries used against Iran."[127]

CHRONIC COVERT CONFLICT

The reverberations of Stuxnet provide additional insight into the stabilizing role of secret statecraft. All three states continued to target each other with cyber operations more or less continuously. Within the cyber domain, this may be described as escalatory.[128] But for politics writ large, cyber operations appear to have been calibrated to avoid escalation.

Iranian cyber attacks on the United States and regional rivals intensified noticeably throughout the 2010s, encouraged in part by the revelation of Stuxnet.[129] A hacktivist group calling itself "the cutting sword of justice" claimed responsibility for a wiper attack (Shamoon) that disabled thirty thousand computers at Saudi Aramco and displayed images of burning American flags. Tehran denied responsibility, but there was much speculation that Shamoon was retaliation for Stuxnet.[130] If so, then it was a very ambiguous and indirect signal, targeting Iran's regional rival rather than the United States. In his infamous "cyber Pearl Harbor" speech, US Secretary of Defense Leon Panetta claimed that "the Shamoon virus was probably the most destructive attack that the private sector has seen to date." Panetta unsurprisingly did not mention Stuxnet, which was definitely more destructive and more interesting to industry, but the subtext was unmistakable: "These attacks mark a significant escalation of the cyber threat and they have renewed concerns about still more destructive scenarios that could unfold."[131] In both Stuxnet and Shamoon, however, we see important elements of restraint.

Also in 2012, a series of DDoS attacks, known collectively as Operation Ababil, were attributed to Iran. Ababil hit dozens of commercial- and financial-sector targets in the United States and Middle Eastern countries, causing millions of dollars in lost revenue. I interpret Ababil, much like Shamoon, as a face-saving protest. Both were public but unavowed Iranian responses to a compromised but unavowed US attack. Escalation in the cyber domain was calibrated to avoid cross-domain escalation.

US reactions to Iranian campaigns appear likewise calibrated to control escalation. The Obama administration eventually blamed the Islamic Revolutionary Guard Corps (IRGC) for Ababil, but it did not indict Iranian hackers until after the JCPOA deal was completed. The 2016 indictment also accused Iran of infiltrating the Bowman Avenue Dam ICS in Rye Brook, New York. Iranian hackers were not able to cause any damage because the dam was under repair and critical components were disconnected at the time—foiled by friction.[132] Iran conducted several violent attacks in 2019, including attacks on oil freighters and cruise missile strikes on a Saudi refinery. The United States opted against kinetic options and instead relied on nonlethal cyber options to interfere with IRGC C2 and intelligence capability for several months.[133] According to *The Washington Post*, "President Trump approved an offensive cyberstrike that disabled Iranian computer systems used to plan attacks on oil tankers in the Persian Gulf, even as he backed away from a conventional military attack in response to its downing Thursday of an unmanned U.S. surveillance drone. . . . The operation did not involve a loss of life or civilian casualties."[134] This operation may be interpreted as an accommodative signal to defuse a crisis.[135] The choice *not* to do something is also informative: A capable actor who leaves options on the shelf communicates that it does not care enough to send the very best. Thus, the United States withheld high-end military options and engaged in low-end hassling to respond to Iranian aggression without provoking further reprisals.

This recessed pattern of chronic covert conflict preceded Stuxnet, and it is likely to continue indefinitely. Traditional bombs and assassins still have their place in this intelligence contest as well. Mossad agents thus cut their way into safes in Tehran in 2018 to steal nuclear-related documents, which Netanyahu hoped would persuade Trump to scuttle the nuclear deal.[136] Israel assassinated several nuclear scientists in Iran.[137] Israel even employed a semiautonomous sniper system to kill Iran's head nuclear scientist in 2020.[138] Mysterious explosions and blackouts continued to rock Natanz a decade after Stuxnet.[139] An Israel-linked hacktivist group, or a front for Israeli intelligence, caused a serious fire at an Iranian steel factory in 2022;

interestingly, the hackers waited until workers were absent to attack and later posted online to advertise their discretion in sparing the innocent.[140]

Secret statecraft—both cooperative and conflictive—has long been attractive in this triangle. Secrecy, obfuscation, and ambiguity have enabled the United States, Israel, Iran, and other actors to address contradictory imperatives without risking too much in the process. This unholy trinity has tolerated chronic covert conflict as a way of pursuing power while avoiding escalation. Tacit imperatives for mutual restraint dominate the pure logic of security competition.

This is an uncomfortable situation. There is no guarantee that the pattern of mutually acceptable chronic covert conflict will persist indefinitely. Indeed, hostilities between Israel and Iran broke out into the open as Iran launched massive (conventional) ballistic missile salvos in April and October 2024 in reprisal for an Israeli air strike on an Iranian embassy in Syria and on Hezbollah leadership in Lebanon.[141] But at least during the historical period in which Stuxnet was developed, deployed, and curtailed, the interactions among the United States, Israel, and Iran hovered in the gray zone between peace and war. Secret statecraft helped to keep things there.

The Limits of Cyber Warfare

I published an article in 2013 entitled "Stuxnet and the Limits of Cyber Warfare." It hit a chord with readers for challenging the conventional wisdom about cyberwar at the time. I argued that Stuxnet was the first and only opportunity to empirically test the revolutionist thesis that cyberspace "gives militarily weaker actors asymmetric advantages, that offense is becoming easier while defense is growing harder, and that the attacker's anonymity undermines deterrence." I found that "the empirical facts of Stuxnet support an opposite interpretation; cyber capabilities can marginally enhance the power of stronger over weaker actors, the complexity of weaponization makes cyber offense less easy and defense more feasible than generally appreciated, and cyber options are most attractive when deterrence is intact."[142]

The theory and practice of cyber conflict have moved on since 2013. In retrospect, Stuxnet appears to be a precious operation tailored for a very specific purpose in unique historical circumstances. Subsequent cyber campaigns have revealed a boundless variety of other possibilities in cyberspace. Military cyber units and intelligence agencies have also conducted numerous computer network operations in combat zones. Their experience of using cyber during actual wars has reshaped doctrinal ideas about cyberwar, leading to new doctrines like "defend forward" that stress "persistent engagement" and "agreed competition" beneath the threshold of armed conflict.[143] And cyber scholarship has moved on from its early debates about cyberwar to analyses of the more moderate patterns of cyber conflict that we observe in the wild.[144] These developments may suggest that Stuxnet is of limited use for generalizing about cybersecurity.

The same trends, however, provide some support for the arguments that I made in 2013. If Stuxnet was a rare event then, it appears even rarer today. Stuxnet stands out as an outlier in patterns of cyber conflict. We have seen only a handful of episodes of cyber-physical sabotage since, almost all of them the work of capable nation-state spy services—overwhelmingly in the United States, Israel, and Russia, with serious developments in China (discussed in chapter 7). The rarity of serious cyber-physical sabotage suggests that there are still significant barriers to weaponizing high-end offensive cyber operations. Indeed, the new evidence available since 2012 suggests that Olympic Games was even more complicated than it appeared when I wrote my article. The commercial threat-intelligence industry today is also much more advanced, while the potential for friction in cyberspace is greater than ever. A modern Stuxnet would have to be even more sophisticated—and even luckier—to inflict useful targeted sabotage.

The big problem with my 2013 article, however, is its framing of Stuxnet as a case of cyber warfare. I described Stuxnet as an "offensive fizzle" because it did not slow down Iranian enrichment, but this was unfair. In retrospect, counterproliferation was not Stuxnet's sole or even its primary strategic objective. As I have argued in this chapter, Olympic Games was an instrument of alliance management. Its lackluster operational achievements and eventual failure even helped to set the conditions for a diplomatic deal that did limit Iranian enrichment. Stuxnet did not impose this strategic outcome, but it did create a political opportunity that key actors were willing and able to recognize. Explaining these complex events requires close attention to a shifting mosaic of intentions and institutions over an extended period.

The article also did not explain in any generalizable way how and why Stuxnet had the political effects that it did. I audited the contemporary conventional wisdom with a single historical case, testing and rejecting some popular assumptions, but I did not replace them with a new story to explain this and other cases. The theory of secret statecraft now provides a better and more general explanation. The strategic system in this case was a complicated three-body problem, and secret diplomacy provided a pressure-release valve. Stuxnet thus provided influence without escalation. The operational problem was complicated by institutional access barriers and commercial counterintelligence risks, while the organizational solution was complicated by coalition politics and security failures. The result of these mixed conditions was a complex operation that achieved mixed results. The performance of Stuxnet as sabotage was disappointing at the operational level, but it provided helpful support to secret diplomacy (conspiracy/subversion) at the strategic level. This provides a more satisfying interpretation of why Operation Olympic Games succeeded as long as it did, and why the risks embodied in complexity finally caught up with it.

In 2013 I offered only a negative argument about what Stuxnet was *not*—cyberwar. I did not provide a clear account of what it was—secret statecraft. I did suggest that strong states have real advantages in engineering cyber intrusions to work around their opponents' deterrence policies, and I still think this is true. Yet the new interpretation helps to clarify why such states may be motivated to work around deterrence in the first place, why assurances to allies may complement coercive diplomacy, and why cyberspace is generally more attractive for activities other than physical destruction.

We now know that Stuxnet was not a *discrete* incident of cyber warfare lasting only a year or two but rather a *discreet* episode in a twilight struggle spanning decades. Stuxnet was not a prelude to war but an alternative to it. Stuxnet was also not a policy failure but a minor contribution to a political outcome that turned out better than many of the alternatives. Stuxnet was neither a revolution in cyber warfare nor a failed revolution, but rather an ongoing evolution in secret statecraft.

This chapter has thus expanded the temporal scope of the case by including a number of other cyber operations besides Stuxnet. Some cases, such as the electronic warfare component of Israel's Operation Orchard or the US Nitro Zeus plan, can accurately be described as cyber warfare. Many others, such as Flame and Duqu, were clearly espionage. The same two conditions of intelligence performance help to make sense of these other operations as well, which improves confidence in the utility of the theory—and the highly qualified utility of cyber sabotage.

The definitive history of Olympic Games has yet to be written. There is so much unknown about the timing, extent, motivations, and effects of Stuxnet that anyone should be cautious in drawing any conclusions. Nevertheless, even though new revelations cannot be ruled out, the accumulating evidence paints a remarkably consistent picture of mixed motives and mixed implementations in a multipolar dance of secret statecraft.

We can never rule out the possibility of catastrophic cyberwar from a purely technical perspective. But the theory of secret statecraft suggests that cyberspace is more useful for other things. Stuxnet is a rare event that teaches us much about its rarity. Institutional factors help to explain why cyber-physical sabotage is rare in cyberspace, and they also help to explain why subversive disinformation is more pervasive. A better exemplar of modern secret statecraft in this respect is Russia's disinformation campaign to influence the 2016 US presidential election, the subject of the next chapter.

CHAPTER 6

Subversion

The 2016 US Election and the Demand for Disinformation

Expert opinion remains divided on whether Russia tipped the scales in the 2016 US presidential election, even though the basic facts of the case are clear. Russia conducted a wide-ranging influence campaign throughout 2016 that combined hacking, disinformation, and propaganda. Most Russian messaging was aligned with the Republican campaign of Donald J. Trump and against the Democratic campaign of Hillary R. Clinton. Clinton, a former secretary of state and first lady, was widely favored to win the election, and she did carry the popular vote on November 8, 2016. But Trump, an eccentric business tycoon and television celebrity, won more delegates in the peculiar institution of the Electoral College and thus won the election. The US intelligence community later assessed that Russia deliberately intervened in support of Trump and against Clinton.

The interpretation of these facts, however, is far less clear. Almost everyone was surprised by the outcome of the election, probably even the Russians. Many jumped to the conclusion that Russia had tipped the scales of the election. If it is true that Russian hackers and trolls really did help to elect Trump, then they performed the most efficient regime change of all time. In the words of Sunzi, "To take the enemy state whole is ideal."[1] But as every student of statistics knows, correlation is not causation. There were so many confounding factors in this unusual campaign season that we may never know for sure whether Russia swung the election. What is more certain is that Russian meddling reverberated in US politics through several years of controversial investigation and litigation. The legitimacy of the Trump presidency became a lightning rod in an increasingly polarized electorate.

Russian influence operations also transformed the public debate about cybersecurity, which had been previously preoccupied with Stuxnet-style cyberwar. This chapter pivots, accordingly, from sabotage to subversion, or from hacking machines to hacking minds. Whereas Stuxnet attempted to prevent the separation of uranium isotopes, Russia attempted to encourage the separation of American voters. As before, it is important to examine not just the technologies of exploitation but also their institutional context.

While it is easy to focus on the technical supply of disinformation, the political demand for bullshit is often more important.[2] In 2016, US media consumers were already buying what Russian trolls started selling. Throughout the election season, the campaigns and partisan media were already peddling similar content, and in far greater quantity. Some political entrepreneurs continued to endorse Russian content even after the public identification of its foreign source. Russian content was less a source of persuasion than a resource for partisan mobilization. In the counterfactual world in which Russia did not intervene in 2016, there would still have been a lot of bullshit in US cyberspace. Indeed, platform controls and counterintelligence operations limited Russian influence after 2016, but homegrown subversion became an even bigger problem after the 2020 election. The wellspring of disinformation was always the US electorate itself.

This chapter uses the 2016 election to explore the role of cooperation in subversion, or the demand for disinformation. It also showcases a different configuration of intelligence performance conditions. The previous chapter, on Stuxnet, examined a mixture of sophisticated clandestine organization and disconnected vulnerable institutions, which increased operational complexity and produced mixed results. This chapter examines the converse combination of a noisy and dependent organization and highly exposed institutions, which in this case increased the risk of Russia losing control of its operation and becoming irrelevant to political outcomes. Indeed, Russian subversion is neither necessary nor sufficient for explaining the outcome of the election.

I proceed in five parts. I begin with an overview of the case and review the concept of subversion. I next discuss Russian operations and assess intelligence performance conditions. I then show how American political polarization and local entrepreneurs boosted the Russian signal, willingly and wittingly. Fourth, I review the inconclusive debate about the effects of the Russian campaign. I conclude with some dilemmas of demand-driven disinformation.

Significance of the Case

Russian election meddling in 2016 is the most investigated cyber campaign of all time. Postmortem reports include two volumes from special counsel Robert S. Mueller III and multiple volumes from the House and Senate Intelligence Committees.[3] Additional information has emerged through public indictments from the Department of Justice, extensive investigative journalism, commercial threat-intelligence reporting, and academic studies.[4] This chapter provides a new interpretive synthesis of the evidence.

In the final weeks of Barack Obama's presidency, on January 6, 2017, the US intelligence community publicly accused Moscow of aiding the Trump campaign. The director of national intelligence released a "declassified version of a highly classified assessment" that had been "drafted and coordinated among The Central Intelligence Agency (CIA), The Federal Bureau of Investigation (FBI), and The National Security Agency (NSA)."[5] Democrats saw it as a damning account of unfair influence, while Republicans saw it as a political smear job. Among its key judgments:

> We assess Russian President Vladimir Putin ordered an influence campaign in 2016 aimed at the US presidential election. Russia's goals were to undermine public faith in the US democratic process, denigrate Secretary Clinton, and harm her electability and potential presidency. We further assess Putin and the Russian Government developed a clear preference for President-elect Trump. We have high confidence in these judgments. . . . Moscow's influence campaign followed a Russian messaging strategy that blends covert intelligence operations—such as cyber activity—with overt efforts by Russian Government agencies, state-funded media, third-party intermediaries, and paid social media users or "trolls." Russia, like its Soviet predecessor, has a history of conducting covert influence campaigns focused on US presidential elections that have used intelligence officers and agents and press placements to disparage candidates perceived as hostile to the Kremlin.[6]

Four years later to the day, on January 6, 2021, the first Trump presidency culminated in a violent riot at the US Capitol. Trump supporters attempted to interrupt congressional certification of the election, and they clashed with law enforcement officers, resulting in injuries and fatalities. A Russian Federation Council member relished the moment: "The celebration of democracy is over. America no longer forges that path, and consequently has lost its right to define it. Much less force it on others."[7] The day before the riot, coincidentally, the US government had blamed Russia for the SolarWinds breach. Russia bookended Trump's stormy first term in office.

Trump was an unusual candidate and an even more unusual president. In his first term, he sparked a nuclear crisis with North Korea, started a trade war with China, suspended a nuclear deal with Iran, upended diplomatic relations with Europe, fomented an immigration crisis on the Mexican border, mishandled the COVID-19 pandemic, and polarized the American public. His administration was racked with scandal and criminal indictments. Trump himself was impeached twice by the US House of Representatives and was later indicted or convicted on multiple counts in various state and federal courts. Trump lost the election in 2020 to Joseph Biden, an elder statesman who campaigned on a promise to restore normalcy to the United States. Widespread dissatisfaction with Biden then contributed to Trump's election in 2024 to a second term, which began even more dramatically than the first. Had Clinton been elected president instead, it is reasonable to believe that US policy during a critical period, and the trajectory of US leadership worldwide, would have been very different. If Russia deserves any credit for electing Trump, then a foreign cyber campaign changed the course of history.

At the very least, Russia transformed the debate about cybersecurity. Before 2016, technical cybersecurity and information operations (IO) were usually treated separately, at least in Western countries.[8] Headlines about cybersecurity focused on espionage campaigns and sabotage threats. Security professionals focused on technical threats to the confidentiality, integrity, and availability of computer systems. The civility, veracity, and contagion of content were secondary concerns. This changed dramatically in mid-2016. Disinformation in cyberspace suddenly seemed like a greater threat to democracy than technical threats such as Stuxnet.[9] Stuxnet may have been a big deal in the cybersecurity community, furthermore, but it was a rather minor episode in world politics. Meddling in the 2016 US presidential election, by contrast, was far more significant, and its implications longer lasting. The cyber-policy conversation thus pivoted from technical intrusion to political disinformation, or from bad bugs to bad ideas.

SUBVERSION AND LOCAL AGENCY

It may be helpful at this point to round up a few relevant insights developed throughout this book. In chapter 1, I described subversion as a form of covert action that uses deception to alter beliefs and opinions. Sabotage and subversion both work indirectly to weaken institutional strengths from the inside, but sabotage targets capabilities while subversion targets ideas. Subversion is more common than sabotage. Classic means of subversion include propaganda, disinformation, forgeries, smear campaigns, vandalism, agitation, intimidation, and sponsorship. Many studies emphasize the importance of local proxies—and the problems of monitoring and enforcement they entail.[10] Local conspirators, fellow travelers, and receptive audiences may accept support from and amplify the messages of a foreign intelligence agency, but they actively pursue their own interests as well.

Chapter 2 argued that dependency is a liability for intelligence performance. An organization that depends on third parties for its capability gives up some control. While outsourcing improves flexibility, it complicates management and discretion. Agency problems within a clandestine organization are a boon for counterintelligence adversaries. The very feature that makes subversion more feasible—connectivity to a sympathetic local audience—threatens to undermine the capacity and discretion of clandestine organization. Using this framework, I assess Russian intelligence agencies as dependent and indiscreet, while the US media ecosystem was connected and vulnerable. As we shall see, this combination produced performance dynamics that Russia did not, and could not, control.

Chapter 3 explored the digital infrastructure of liberal hegemony. Open networks dramatically improve connectivity for foreign threats. Freedom of expression is both a democratic feature and a subversive vulnerability. During the Cold War it was much easier for Soviet intelligence agencies to access American audiences than vice versa. Western efforts such as Voice of America and Radio Free Europe had to broadcast from the periphery, but Soviet provocateurs could stir up local dissent and plant news stories. At the same time, there was arguably more demand for Western information behind the Iron Curtain than there was for Soviet propaganda in the West. The Soviet Union thus relied on harsh internal counterintelligence to patch its ideological vulnerabilities. Liberal cyberspace makes it even easier for foreign actors to reach into open democracies (connectivity), but domestic actors still shape the demand for content (vulnerability).

Chapter 4 described a remarkably successful case of subversion: the Allied plan to mislead German commanders in World War II. Operation Fortitude, the deception plan for the D-Day landings in June 1944, was part of the larger Allied deception plan, Operation Bodyguard. These efforts spared no expense to create believable disinformation for German commanders and to control feedback from German intelligence. The Allies cultivated an elaborate system of double agents (Double Cross), performed SIGINT miracles at Bletchley Park, and orchestrated theatrical maneuvers for German reconnaissance. Germany was highly motivated to oppose the Allied landing, so it would have rejected Allied messaging if it had understood its true provenance. But careful coordination and disciplined discretion on the part of Allied deception planners preserved their fragile connectivity to vulnerable audiences. The contrast with 2016 is stark. Russia generated a large volume of disinformation at relatively low cost, but the campaign was compromised and attributed by the summer of 2016. By the standards of Bodyguard, indiscreet Russian subversion should have failed. Instead, as we shall see, US factions alternately embraced and decried Russian content, which boosted the signal of Russian influence operations. The big difference between these two cases is the degree of cooperation with the target audience. There was an alignment of interests between Russian subversives and American audiences that was entirely missing between the Allies and the Axis. Axis audiences did unwittingly cooperate with Allied deceivers, insofar as Bodyguard deliberately reinforced German biases, but it was imperative for the enemy to believe, mistakenly, that it was competing effectively with the Allies. The American audiences who cooperated unwittingly with Russian trolls, however, kept on cooperating even after the Russian campaign was publicly revealed and attributed.

Chapter 5 focused more on sabotage than subversion, but I argued that an important US motivation for Stuxnet was secret diplomacy to dissuade Israel from starting a preventive war. Israel also contributed important intelligence capabilities to the secret coalition. Secret diplomacy is the conspiracy variant of subversion, whereby actors with common interests hide their collusion from third parties. Olympic Games worked, to the extent that it did, only because Israel was willing to go along with it. Subversive collusion, which was hidden from Iran, enabled disruptive sabotage, which targeted Iran.

The overarching theme of this review is that the interests of local agents are a key factor in the performance of subversive campaigns. I will describe the *demand for disinformation* as high when the political interests of the subversive campaign and the target audience are openly aligned; demand is low, by contrast, when interests are not aligned. Demand in this sense was low in the case of Bodyguard but high in the cases of Olympic Games and the 2016 election.

THE DEMAND FOR DISINFORMATION

When demand is low, disciplined deception is more important. When interests are not aligned, suspicious or witting targets are more likely to reject the fraud. Effective subversion thus depends on hiding the truth about content, sourcing, or intent. When institutions are less vulnerable, therefore, an organization must be more capable in order to subvert them. Because enemy interests in 1944 were highly opposed, the London Controlling Section had to work very hard to dupe its targets. Bodyguard had to carefully manage the supply of disinformation to control every contingency and avoid compromising mistakes.

But when interests *are* aligned, then IO is more like commercial marketing—openly promoting messages from an easily identifiable source to shape consumer behavior. Subversive activities do not need to be carefully hidden when target audiences are openly willing to do more of the work. Recall from the typology of strategies in chapter 1 that subversion falls between sabotage and commerce on the spectrum of competitive interests (figure 1.2). Highly competitive subversion (such as Bodyguard) is closer to sabotage, while more cooperative campaigns (such as the 2016 campaign) are closer to marketing.

In the business world, marketing professionals cultivate demand. But if customers do not want what marketers are selling, then even the slickest promotions will not lead to repeat purchases. Coca- Cola advertisements may encourage consumers to "have a Coke and a smile," but those consumers will not keep smiling if the soda is not sweet. This is why military IO in counterinsurgencies so often falls flat: Messaging to support the government against the guerrillas is not persuasive if local populations are disillusioned with their government and afraid of the guerrillas.[11] Whenever customer demand is strong, by contrast, even relatively modest marketing can help customers learn where and how to make repeat purchases.[12]

Popular accounts of digital disinformation tend to overlook demand. The focus instead is on clever technical tricks, manipulated news feeds, and the massive volume of fraudulent posts and reposts. The assumption is that the technological supply of disinformation creates influence.[13] Without a doubt, cyberspace makes it easy to supply disinformation at scale. Accordingly, we observe a lot of fake news, deepfakes, trolling, doxing, and astroturfing. Not only is there a lot of supply-side activity in cyberspace, but it is also much easier to measure. Supply-side remedies, in turn, include fact-checking, content moderation, and exhortations to think critically. But it is a logical leap to assume that the technological supply of content translates directly into political influence at scale. Mass marketing will simply fall flat with audiences who reject an unsavory product or its exorbitant price.

This implies an empirical test. If the supply-side story is true, then limiting technological supply should limit foreign influence and improve civil discourse. If the demand-side story is true, however, then audiences will react differently upon learning about subversion. When demand is low, then the public compromise of a subversive campaign should limit its spread. Alerted audiences will be inoculated against the technological supply of disinformation. But when demand is high, the revelation of subversion should amplify its impact. The foreign supply of disinformation is less relevant because opportunistic audiences will just find another source when foreign supplies dry up.

Demand-driven disinformation encourages a pernicious pattern. The truth of content becomes less relevant than who embraces or rejects it. Disinformation becomes a loyalty test for polarized political factions. One side accuses the other of being duped by foreign trolls, while the other side reacts with indignation. The fervent repetition *and rejection* of bullshit, or speech indifferent to truth, boosts its signal. Charismatic exaggeration and doublespeak swamp civil discourse.[14] One should not assume that all disinformation is strictly untrue, insofar as selective truths can also be mobilized for political effect. The essence of bullshit is not truth but performance. The goal of demand-driven disinformation is competitive mobilization, not rational deliberation. Political bullshit becomes more consequential, ironically enough, once the bullshitter is exposed. This is exactly what happened in 2016.

Russian Supply

The Russian doctrine of "information confrontation" is a supply-side theory. State agencies employ "active measures" to achieve "reflexive control" over a target, encouraging voluntary behavior aligned with Russian goals.[15] While Russian agencies may believe this doctrine, one should not accept it uncritically. Activity is not productivity. Detection of a Russian influence campaign does not necessarily mean that Russia controls the campaign's targets, much less its operations.

The Russian IO campaign in 2016 mixed clandestine hacking, covert disinformation, and overt propaganda. The RT news network, for example, was deliberately overt, providing a platform for Western commentators on both the left and the right to criticize the US government. One might even argue that RT enhanced the ability of civil society to speak out against the state, a right enshrined in the First Amendment to the US Constitution. The overt media campaign illustrates an alignment of interests between Russian propagandists and some US audiences. The clandestine and covert elements, moreover, did not remain hidden for long.

CLANDESTINE ESPIONAGE

Russia had a mature platform for subversion, drawing on decades of experience in active measures from the Soviet era. The Russian Federal Security Service (FSB) and the Main Intelligence Directorate of the General Staff (GRU) adapted classic espionage and subversion techniques to cyberspace. They used technical exploits and social engineering to hack into the networks of the Democratic National Committee (DNC), the Democratic Congressional Campaign Committee (DCCC), and some Republican organizations as well.[16]

To take one notorious example, Clinton's campaign manager, John Podesta, received a phishing email that appeared to be from Google.[17] Podesta was suspicious and checked with an IT manager, who mistakenly replied, "This is a legitimate email. John needs to change his password immediately."[18] Podesta then clicked the link in the email and inputted his password. The GRU could then use his credentials to exfiltrate data and install malware. Russian hacking teams similarly targeted hundreds of email accounts and thereby gained access to hundreds of thousands of internal documents.

Dmitri Alperovitch with the cybersecurity firm CrowdStrike assessed, "Their tradecraft is superb, operational security second to none."[19] Russian hackers used native Windows tools wherever possible to avoid detection, performed lots of security checks, regularly swapped out tools to reduce their signature, and anonymously registered their command-and-control (C2) domains in advance using Bitcoin payments. But the FSB and GRU did not integrate their efforts. Russian spy services are notoriously rivalrous.[20] While each agency exercised some discretion, the lack of coordination between Russian agencies upset the delicate balance between administration and adaptation on which clandestine proficiency depends. Flaws in organizational capacity made errors in discretion more likely.

The hacking operation was almost compromised in September 2015, when an FBI agent notified the DNC that it had been hacked by "the Dukes" (a.k.a. the FSB).[21] The FBI received a tip from Dutch intelligence agencies that were able to observe Russian hackers in real time.[22] The DNC did not act on this tip because a part-time tech at the DNC mistakenly believed that the FBI calls were a prank. But on April 29, 2016, the DNC IT team finally received clear evidence of a breach and initiated an incident response. The DNC called in CrowdStrike, which collected intelligence on the breach throughout May. Malware tools and other forensic signatures almost immediately provided convincing evidence for CrowdStrike that it was looking not only at a Russian operation but at multiple FSB and GRU intrusions. CrowdStrike worked with the DNC to roll back the intrusions and deny access to Russian hackers, completing its remediation on June 13. CrowdStrike and the DNC publicized the intrusion the next day.[23]

The US government had received early intelligence that Russia was intervening to help Trump and harm Clinton. But Obama was reticent to act publicly, lest he be accused of trying to aid his own party in the election. His desire to maintain an air of executive impartiality translated into tacit toleration of Russian interference—a form of vulnerability that Russia exploited. As summarized by the Senate Intelligence Committee,

> the administration was constrained in its response to Russian meddling by (1) the heavily politicized environment; (2) the concern that public warnings would themselves undermine public confidence in the election, thereby inadvertently helping the Russian effort; (3) the unknown extent to which the Russians could target and manipulate election systems; (4) the delay in definitive attribution of some efforts to Russia; (5) the time and resources required to compose policy options prior to execution; and (6) challenges in how to address WikiLeaks. These constraints affected the response options available, as well as the timing and sequencing of their implementation.[24]

COVERT INFLUENCE

Public attribution of the operation to Russia ended its hacking phase. The next phase of the operation—doxing stolen data—was not as sensitive. In the covert leaking phase, which continued throughout the rest of the campaign, the Russians released documents through web fronts such as DCLeaks and WikiLeaks and the online persona Guccifer 2.0.[25] The revelation of infighting within the Democratic Party, including disparaging comments about progressive candidate Senator Bernie Sanders, prompted the resignation of DNC chair Debbie Wasserman Schultz.

The United States had some advance warning, but there was not much the DNC could have done. In May 2016, according to press reporting, US intelligence intercepted a Russian officer bragging that the GRU "was getting ready to pay Clinton back for what President Vladimir Putin believed was an influence operation she had run against him five years earlier as Secretary of State. The GRU, he said, was going to cause chaos in the upcoming U.S. election."[26] But the Russians had already copied hundreds of thousands of sensitive documents during the clandestine hacking phase. There was no way for the victims to get these data back after the compromise. While knowledge of sensitive sources and methods may undermine the use of the same tradecraft in the future, it does not preclude the use of anything taken or affected prior to compromise.

The DNC and CrowdStrike publicized the Russian intrusion on June 14, 2016, and the GRU countered the next day with the Guccifer 2.0 persona, who posted DNC documents on a WordPress blog and claimed to be a lone Romanian hacker. Cybersecurity antibodies massed, and Guccifer 2.0 was quickly and convincingly identified as a Russian cover.[27] From that point forward, public evidence began to accumulate of Russian involvement, and Russian fronts continued to dump documents. The ShadowBrokers hacking group—widely believed to be a Russian front—dropped its first batch of NSA tools on August 15.[28] Plausible deniability became increasingly implausible.

The Internet Research Agency (IRA) "troll farm" in St. Petersburg had been featured in *The New York Times* in June 2015.[29] Its social media content was barely covert; its messaging covered the waterfront. To encourage audiences on the right, Russian trolls posted social media content with evangelical, xenophobic, and security themes. To discourage audiences on the left, Russian trolls highlighted government racism, police brutality, and the marginalization of progressive voices such as Jill Stein and Bernie Sanders.[30] IRA ad buys on Facebook were crafted to exacerbate existing fears and exploit local events such as the Black Lives Matter protests.[31] Russian astroturfing—the simulation of grassroots organization—created online interest groups and in some cases encouraged people to turn out for small demonstrations. Figure 6.1 shows a few examples.

Kathleen Hall Jamieson points out that Russian themes aligned well with the Trump campaign's strategic needs.[32] Agenda setting and framing prime what voters think about. Messaging can be reinforced contagiously through interpersonal networks. It works best when it targets susceptible audiences, so long as opposing messaging campaigns do not cancel each other out. According to Jamieson, Russian trolls were thus able to "(1) engage in sufficiently widespread messaging; (2) focus on issues compatible with Trump's strategic needs; (3) address constituencies he had to mobilize and

Figure 6.1. Examples of Russian content on Facebook (source: US House of Representatives)

demobilize; (4) employ persuasive content that was amplified in swing states, was visually evocative, and whose power was magnified by sharing, liking, and commenting; and (5) target their appeals well."[33] Jamieson argues in effect that Russia influenced the election by doing the sorts of things that have been shown to be persuasive in other elections. A key enabler of this strategy was the openness of the US information environment.

OUT OF CONTROL

The first condition of intelligence performance was easily met. The United States' vulnerable institutions were highly exposed in 2016. The

Russians had abundant connectivity to American audiences. Open networks and liberal norms made it very easy for Russian hackers, bots, and trolls to access millions of US media consumers in 2016. Digital platforms like Facebook were open by design, with liberal posting policies and limited content moderation.[34] News media outlets could publish almost anything. The permissive connectivity and exposed vulnerability of the US media ecosystem in 2016 created a golden opportunity for Russian deception specialists.

The second condition was not met, however. Russian clandestine organization was both dependent on US audiences and proxies, and it was quite indiscreet. Open networks provided Russian access to the American electorate, but they also created exposure to commercial and government counterintelligence actors. The broad scope of Russian activity produced abundant clues about attribution and activity that could be accessed and assessed by US agencies, journalists, cybersecurity firms, and individual citizens.

The theory of intelligence performance predicts a loss of operational control under these circumstances, which is what happened. Thomas Rid quips that Russian active measures were "more active than ever but less measured."[35] Russia depended on open platforms and countless actors who could not be controlled directly. Its indiscreet operations created a large signature that undermined plausible deniability. Investigations and recriminations reverberated for years.

The theory is ambiguous about what operational loss of control means for political outcomes. In low-demand situations, where deception is essential for influencing targets that do not want to be influenced, loss of control makes it more likely that a subversive campaign will fail. But in high-demand situations, where target interests are aligned, loss of control may not undermine, and may even promote, political outcomes that are desirable for both parties.

By the same token, a subversive campaign may be irrelevant to the political result. Russian content simply reflected beliefs that many Americans already held, and would continue to hold, because it was socially useful to hold those beliefs. Indeed, it may be more accurate to say that Russian content reflected rather than caused the predispositions of target audiences. This would imply that Russian marketing promotions were neither necessary nor sufficient for "repeat purchase" decisions by US audiences to endorse, forward, or act on problematic content.

US Demand

The litmus test for supply-driven subversion is that audiences should reject deceptive content after learning about its true nature. Deception disclosed is deception defeated. To interpret Russian intervention in 2016 as a clever form of deception, therefore, we would need to observe *unwitting* receptivity to Russian influence. Targets exposed to Russian content should end up believing something they would not otherwise believe, and they should be chagrined about learning they have been duped.

No doubt, many Americans did not realize they were viewing and forwarding Russian content when they were first exposed to it. The audiences most receptive to Russian content, however, were not really fooled into believing anything. The most sympathetic segments of the US electorate—concentrated on the right end of the political spectrum—were already generating and forwarding similar content themselves. The revelation of Russian provenance, by and large, did not reduce its attractiveness; on the contrary, political entrepreneurs made the most of it.

POLITICAL POLARIZATION

The US electorate was highly polarized in 2016. The US marketplace of ideas, as Trevor Thrall points out, has long tended to divide itself into "countervailing factions based on competing sets of values and competing frames of the issues at hand."[36] US cyberspace, Thrall and Andrew Armstrong note elsewhere, is "expansive, noisy, full of propaganda and misinformation of domestic origins, and slow to correct itself at the best of times."[37] 2016 was not the best of times.

Yochai Benkler, Robert Faris, and Hal Roberts document a pronounced bimodal distribution of ideological bias in the US media ecosystem.[38] They find a normal distribution of left-leaning and centrist sources (indicative of diverse viewpoints that balance each other) and a highly skewed distribution at the rightmost extreme (indicative of more homogenous views that amplify the signal). They argue that this is the product of a perfect storm of media deregulation, broadband connectivity, and the rise of partisan media outlets like Fox News prior to 2016. The upshot is that conservative media "outlets offered an ideological coordination point, a cathartic experience of shared anger, and a platform for disciplining political elites who did not hew to the pure message produced by these new right-wing media."[39] In this environment, Russian-sourced material became politically useful for fully informed right-wing media consumers: "There is a part of the American media ecosystem for which knowing that the origin of a story is Russia is no reason to ignore it, as long as it aligns with the tribal narrative they are pushing. Willing embrace of divisive Russian propaganda, not innocent error because of Twitter and Facebook manipulation, is the core challenge."[40]

I argue that political polarization was the root cause of the strong demand for disinformation. The Russians did not create this demand; American demand for bullshit predated Russian meddling. The same US audiences that Russia targeted were already wittingly repeating falsehoods to demonstrate factional loyalty. When disinformation is obvious or unsubtle, it provides a solution to an important political problem: separating friend from foe.

If everyone you meet is potentially a member of the opposing political faction, how can you recruit like-minded people to form a political movement? One possibility is to look for people who are willing to repeat obvious disinformation and conspiracy theories. Those who repeat and repost obvious lies will identify themselves as fellow travelers, while those who reject and ridicule the lies identify themselves as political opponents. The performative repetition and rejection of dubious information thus enhances solidarity and aids mobilization, for both sides. Fact-checking and ostracization by liberal outgroups, in turn, encourage conservative ingroups to keep repeating falsehoods.[41]

This dynamic is similar to Thomas Schelling's famous "tipping point" in a racially polarized neighborhood.[42] When there is nothing as obvious as race to discriminate ingroups from outgroups, factions need another way to distinguish like-minded allies from rivals they view as dangerous or defective. Disinformation provides this signal. The repetition of disinformation becomes a loyalty test to identify fellow travelers. Attempts to debunk disinformation then raise the credibility of the signal for screening friend from foe. The actual source or content matters less than the willingness of partisans to repeat and reject it. Indeed, more outrageous bullshit makes for a better loyalty test, since only the truly committed will repeat it.

This sorting mechanism should not be conflated with the "echo chamber" or "filter bubble" theory of social media. Filter bubbles are a story of gullible tragedy rather than willful conspiracy. There is weak empirical support for the idea that people self-isolate in filter bubbles. What often happens instead is that intensive exposure to communities in conflict heightens the polarization of identities by encouraging people to take sides and reproduce affiliative performances. Factional sorting is driven by interaction across groups rather than isolation within them.[43]

Factional sorting in a polarized society explains the high demand for disinformation in 2016. It also explains why disinformation persisted after the disinformation campaign was attributed to Russia. Instead of assuming that Russian interference caused American beliefs, it may be more reasonable to see US polarization co-opting the Russian campaign. Americans exercised agency in the events of 2016, and Americans deserve the credit—or blame—for their outcome.

"I LOVE WIKILEAKS"

Sure enough, the revelation of Russian meddling became yet another lightning rod in an increasingly polarized electorate. Reactions to the public attribution of the disinformation campaign to Russia split cleanly along partisan lines. Democrats were more likely to condemn revelations of Russian intervention, while Republicans were more likely to deflect attention or make use of Russian-sourced content.[44] Attitudes toward Russian content became a useful marker of partisan loyalty.

To use a poker metaphor, public revelation of the disinformation campaign called the Russians' bluff, but American players remained in the game. Even after all the cards were on the table, they continued to raise the stakes. This suggests that they were playing a different game.

Indeed, Trump's promotion of Russian material went into overdrive. In a July 2016 news conference, he encouraged Russia to keep looking for more of Clinton's emails: "Russia, if you're listening, I hope you're able to find the 30,000 emails that are missing. . . . I think you will probably be rewarded mightily by our press."[45]

On October 7, 2016, after extensive media reporting on Russia's role, the US director of national intelligence and the Department of Homeland Security issued a joint statement: "The U.S. Intelligence Community (USIC) is confident that the Russian Government directed the recent compromises of e-mails from US persons and institutions, including from US political organizations. The recent disclosures of alleged hacked e-mails on sites like DCLeaks.com and WikiLeaks and by the Guccifer 2.0 online persona are consistent with the methods and motivations of Russian-directed efforts."[46] Yet Trump praised WikiLeaks material throughout the final month of the campaign in numerous rallies and tweets: "I love WikiLeaks," "This WikiLeaks is like a treasure trove," and so on.[47]

According to a lengthy investigation by the US Senate Select Committee on Intelligence, "The Trump Campaign publicly undermined the attribution of the hack-and-leak campaign to Russia and was indifferent to whether it and WikiLeaks were furthering a Russian election interference effort."[48] The Trump campaign alternately deflected charges of Russian interference and embraced the publicity that the interference generated. A question about "the cyber" came up in the first debate with Clinton, and Trump provided a classic answer:

I don't think anybody knows it was Russia that broke into the DNC. She's saying Russia, Russia, Russia, but I don't—maybe it was. I mean, it could be Russia, but it could also be China. It could also be lots of other people. It also could be somebody sitting on their bed that weighs 400 pounds, okay? You don't know who broke in to DNC. But what did we learn with DNC? We learned that Bernie Sanders was taken advantage of by your people, by Debbie Wasserman Schultz. Look what happened to her. But Bernie Sanders was taken advantage of. That's what we learned. Now, whether that was Russia, whether that was China, whether it was another country, we don't know, because the truth is, under President Obama we've lost control of things that we used to have control over. We came in with the Internet, we came up with the Internet, and I think Secretary Clinton and myself would agree very much, when you look at what ISIS is doing with the Internet, they're beating us at our own game. ISIS. So we have to get very, very tough on cyber and cyber warfare. It is—it is a huge problem. I have a son. He's 10 years old. He has computers. He is so good with these computers, it's unbelievable. The security aspect of cyber is very, very tough. And maybe it's hardly doable.[49]

Russia could not have asked for a better spokesman. Trump supporters and media boosters took his cues and boosted the signal. Russian meddling just provided them with another opportunity among many to highlight the deficiencies of the Democrats.

Putin, meanwhile, deflected attention away from Russian sourcing and toward incendiary content. As he said in an interview with Bloomberg News, "It doesn't really matter who hacked this data from Mrs. Clinton's campaign headquarters. . . . The important thing is the content was given to the public."[50] Putin cynically pretended to be improving political discourse in the United States by offering alternative perspectives to competing political factions. He thus highlighted a harmony of interests between Russian active measures and the US electorate, or parts of it.

The Mueller report and congressional investigations documented extensive collusion between Russian operatives, Russian operations, and the Trump campaign. To borrow a phrase from the ancient Sunzi, Trump became "the operative to be treated with particular generosity."[51] This is not to imply that Trump was some sort of Manchurian candidate controlled by Russian spymasters, as if any case officer could control so mercurial a personality.[52] Rather, Trump was an opportunistic narcissist whose political instincts aligned conveniently with Russian goals. The "Additional Views of Democratic Senators" section of the Senate committee's report (in the volume titled "Counterintelligence Threats and Vulnerabilities") alleged extensive collusion:

> The Committee's bipartisan Report unambiguously shows that members of the Trump Campaign cooperated with Russian efforts to get Trump elected. It recounts efforts by Trump and his team to obtain dirt on their opponent from operatives acting on behalf of the Russian government. It reveals the extraordinary lengths by which Trump and his associates actively sought to enable the Russian interference operation by amplifying its electoral impact and rewarding its perpetrators—even after being warned of its Russian origins. And it presents, for the first time, concerning evidence that the head of the Trump Campaign was directly connected to the Russian meddling through his communications with an individual found to be a Russian intelligence officer.[53]

Any claim that Russian active measures elected Trump, therefore, must come to grips with the active measures conducted by the Trump campaign itself, and by its activist base. Russia was an opportunistic source of disinformation in 2016 that political entrepreneurs knowingly amplified to mobilize partisan support. Had Russia refrained from intervening, American bullshit artists would not have run out of material. But because Russia did intervene, political entrepreneurs like Trump could take advantage of it.

"STOP THE STEAL"

Events after 2016 cast some additional light on the existence of a local demand for disinformation and its contribution to factional sorting. During the US-Russia summit in Helsinki in 2018, for example, Trump endorsed Putin's denial of Russian meddling over the clear assessment of Trump's own intelligence agencies: "My people came to me—[Director of National Intelligence] Dan Coats came to me and some others—they said they think it's Russia. I have President Putin; he just said it's not Russia. I will say this: I don't see any reason why it would be, but I really do want to see the server."[54]

In one breath, Trump cast doubt on Russian culpability and deflected attention to an old scandal involving his defeated rival, Hillary Clinton. He was communicating as much as dissembling. The messages to the media and to his supporters were: Don't talk about this, talk about that; Russia is not the adversary, but the Democrats are. This messaging was all the starker because there was not really any doubt among any of the parties in the room—Trump, Putin, and press—that Russia meddled in 2016.

After the experience of 2016, US government agencies and social media platforms implemented countermeasures to protect elections from foreign meddling.[55] This included content moderation and active counterintelligence operations. The United States' vulnerable institutions became slightly less vulnerable in this regard. Accordingly, Russian influence was a nonstory during the 2018 midterms and 2020 presidential election.[56] This looked like a success story for the new US doctrine of defending forward in cyberspace. As the commander of US Cyber Command, General Paul Nakasone, testified, "Our efforts in defense of the 2018 elections taught us the value of persistent engagement to contest adversary campaigns, the power of enabling partners, and the ability to impose costs."[57] Coordination to counter "foreign malign influence threats" across the whole US government was even more robust by 2024.[58]

These countermeasures provide a test of the demand-driven disinformation hypothesis. If disinformation in 2016 was driven by foreign supply rather than domestic demand, then US cyberspace should have become a bit more "truthy" after curtailing the Russian supply. If digital deception from Russia was the primary source of disinformation, then limiting Russian access to American audiences should have limited harmful disinformation in subsequent elections. But this is obviously not what happened.

Fake news and alternative facts continued to flourish in US cyberspace. Laudable efforts to curtail Russian interference did little to stem the flood of homegrown disinformation. The endogenous sorting mechanism gathered steam throughout Trump's term, with little input from Russia. The Republican and Democratic Parties continued to align around identity politics more than other issues. I interpret this as evidence that Russian intervention was always more of a symptom than a cause of the underlying factional sorting that boosted US demand for disinformation.

Factional sorting went into overdrive during the first Trump term, and it contributed to his winning a second term as well. A study by John Sides, Chris Tausanovitch, and Lynn Vavreck, drawing on a comprehensive battery of opinion polls, found that US politics in 2020 became "calcified." This means that "policies where Democrats and Republicans might find some common ground were not as important as those where they strongly disagreed. . . . [T]he farther apart Democrats and Republicans were, the more important the issue was to Americans overall."[59] Calcification was resistant to shocks that might have been expected to produce common ground, such as the COVID-19 pandemic, the economic crisis in its wake, and a significant racial justice movement. Disinformation did not cause the underlying preferences that drive polarization, but the selective repetition of disinformation by party leaders and their constituents (together with efforts from the other side to publicly counter it), according to Sides, Tausanovitch, and Vavreck, simplified the "ability to perceive those differences." Calcification was reinforced by "clear differences between what the Democratic and Republican parties stand for" and by "voters' increasing ability to perceive those differences and to know which side they prefer."[60]

Trump lost the November 2020 election to Biden, but he did not clearly and unequivocally concede defeat. His supporters then embraced his suggestion that the election had been stolen. These allegations were convincingly refuted by many investigations and official hearings, but the "big lie" continued to be repeated by conservative media personalities and Republican politicians.[61] The "stop the steal" movement breached the Capitol in a violent riot on January 6, 2021, and roiled US politics for years afterward.

Any controversy over politicized truths can amplify a separative signal. Thus, well after the 2020 election, "stop the steal" became a rallying cry for the American right. As more evidence accumulated that nothing was stolen at all, "stop the steal" became an even better litmus test for political loyalty. By 2024, as Trump faced multiple criminal indictments in state and federal courts, large swaths of the Republican electorate had rewritten the narrative of the 2020 election. Questioning the election and exonerating the rioters became a staple of Republican rallies, while Democrats used the same events to mobilize opposition to Trump. One of Trump's first acts upon returning to the White House in 2025 was to pardon 1,500 rioters whom he described as "patriots" attending a "day of love."[62] Russia was irrelevant in this denouement. The Trump phenomenon had emerged from underlying conditions in the US body politic, not from some foreign contagion.

Marginal Effects

Scholars do not lack information about disinformation, but teasing out its effects is challenging.[63] Multiple studies find evidence that exposure to Russian-sourced content had a short-term effect on online behavior such as forwarding or retweeting, mainly by users with a prior ideological predisposition toward the content.[64] But this suggests that influence can run in the other direction too: Russian active measures may be an epiphenomenal reflection of the preexisting beliefs and behaviors of the target audience. Indeed, Russian Facebook ads that appealed to racialized fear lagged the appearance of Black Lives Matter protests in 2016, which suggests that Russia acted opportunistically to take advantage of preexisting divisions in US society that Russia did not create.[65]

Disinformation apparently spreads faster through cyberspace than the truth does.[66] But multiple mechanisms can explain this. One possibility is that gullible people are readily duped into unwittingly spreading emotionally salient content. The alternative developed here is that some audiences wittingly believe that emotionally salient bullshit will get more attention. Supply-side mechanisms emphasize the agency of deception specialists and their high-tech tools, while demand-side mechanisms emphasize the agency of the information audiences.

Most elections are overdetermined: Economics, identity, campaigning, and policy may point in the same direction. The determinants of public attitudes and mobilization patterns are many and varied, and it is possible that disinformation could have affected a few of them. The 2016 election had more than its share of confounding factors, or alternative explanations that may be more compelling than Russian intervention.[67] Social scientists will probably keep debating the impact of Russian meddling for years to come.

Many experts view the Russian campaign as totally unnecessary for explaining the election. Other factors seem both significant and sufficient for explaining Trump's victory. John Sides, Michael Tesler, and Lynn Vavreck point to the rising salience of identity politics in Democratic and Republican coalitions between 2012 and 2016. Preference changes were activated by candidates' choices to focus on diversity (racial, ethnic, gender, religious, ideological) as either a national asset (Clinton) or a mortal threat (Trump).[68] Economic anxiety among Republican voters was high, even though the economy was performing well during Obama's presidency. Republican perceptions were refracted through racialized perceptions of immigration and globalization.[69]

Nate Silver stresses that Trump enjoyed a demographic advantage among white voters without college degrees in swing states, amid a socioeconomic climate that was generally favorable to a Republican challenger, while liberal media bias contributed to exaggerated expectations of a Clinton victory.[70] Silver is agnostic about the effect of a relatively small amount of Russian content in the face of so many confounding factors.[71] Changing socioeconomic context is sufficient for explaining US politics, while Russian meddling was a small rock thrown into a churning sea.

It is easy to overstate the salience of Russian disinformation by ignoring similar content from other sources. The Russian IRA allegedly had a monthly budget of $1.25 million.[72] Russia may have purchased only $100,000 worth of ads on Facebook.[73] Some might say this represents influence at a bargain. But the national campaigns spent orders of magnitude more than Russia did. The Trump campaign spent $546 million and generated a lot of similar content.[74] Campaign finance figures do not begin to account for similar content generated by partisan media outlets, political action committees (PACs), nongovernmental organizations, commercial firms, and affiliative movements.

Russian content was thus a small drop in an overflowing bucket. At best its effects were extremely indirect and more likely irrelevant.[75] A study of Russian disinformation on Twitter in 2016 found "no evidence of a meaningful relationship between exposure to the Russian foreign influence campaign and changes in attitudes, polarization, or voting behavior," in part because exposures were concentrated on a tiny fraction of Twitter users who were exposed to a large volume of similar content from other sources.[76]

A key assumption of supply-side accounts is that messaging matters. But if political advertising by itself were decisive, Clinton should have blown Trump out of the water. She spent twice as much ($955 million) and maintained an advantage in ad airings throughout the campaign.[77] A study of campaign advertising by Joshua Kalla and David Broockman finds, however, that "the best estimate of the effects of campaign contact and advertising on Americans' candidates choices in general elections is zero."[78] If political advertising is so ineffective in general, why should we expect a tiny amount of Russian content to tip the scales? Once again, intelligence operations do not necessarily produce strategic effects.

Campaign antics ultimately spoke louder than all the political advertising of 2016. Both candidates created their own controversies, from

Clinton's description of Trump supporters as "a basket of deplorables" to Trump's misogynistic comments on an *Access Hollywood* tape. These self-inflicted wounds generated more furor than any Russian data dump. Trump in particular generated colorful news coverage throughout the election season, which provided lots of free publicity.[79] It would have been a chaotic media circus even without any Russian meddling at all.

Strategic disinformation may have moved the needle in a few instances. WikiLeaks released its second major tranche of documents on the same day as the *Access Hollywood* scandal broke, and this was quickly followed by a US government statement on Russian interference. This gave Republicans more evidence of Clinton malfeasance and Democrats more evidence of Russian influence, which blunted the negative effect of *Access Hollywood* on Trump. Conversely, the effects of the first WikiLeaks tranche in July were dwarfed by the DNC convention bump for Clinton.[80] No one media event was decisive, and their effects often canceled each other out.

The most likely candidate for a point event affecting the election is FBI Director James Comey's announcement on October 28 that the FBI was reopening the investigation into Clinton's misuse of a personal email server while serving as Obama's secretary of state. This announcement resulted in a drop in Clinton's lead in the polls from 4.5 to 1.7 percentage points between October 28 and November 4.[81] Kathleen Jamieson argues that Comey's decision was indirectly influenced by the Russian leak of emails about the FBI investigation, which influenced Comey to speak publicly about the case in July, which in turn influenced his decision to go public again in October.[82] This would be a very indirect effect indeed, not to mention utterly unforeseeable by any disinformation planner.

Jamieson presents perhaps the strongest possible case for Russian effectiveness.[83] Her major premise is that a large body of empirical scholarship on political communication has demonstrated that emotions and psychology shape voting behavior. Her minor premise is that there was a strong fit between Russian messaging and these general conditions. Ergo, Russian influence is likely. This argument is plausible based on what we know about political messaging. Jamieson concludes that "Kremlin-tied interventions functioned in each of these areas in ways that in past elections have produced discernible effects, many of them larger than the one required to alter the 2016 outcome."[84]

Dov Levin offers a different perspective on plausibility.[85] Based on a dataset of 117 electoral interventions between 1946 and 2000 by the United States and the Soviet Union/Russia, Levin finds "that electoral interventions, with some exceptions, seem to be an effective foreign policy tool benefitting those they are designed to help [. . . but] overt interventions are significantly more effective than covert interventions."[86] His statistical model estimates that Russian intervention accounted for 2 percent of the national vote count and that, but for that intervention, Clinton would

have won key battleground states in the Electoral College.[87] Levin emphasizes that "electoral interventions are 'inside jobs,' occurring only if a significant domestic actor within the target wants, or is willing, to be aided in
this manner by a great power."[88] The Trump campaign provided "inside"
assistance, consistent with the demand-side model.

It is extremely difficult, and perhaps impossible, to rule out the significance of Russian intervention for the outcome of the election as a point of
historical fact. The effects are too indirect, there are too many confounding factors, the data are too noisy, and there is no representative control
sample that was not exposed to Russian-sourced content. Interpretations
thus depend on assumptions. Every interpretation reviewed above
depends on theoretical assumptions that go beyond the facts of the case—
assumptions about, for instance, the mechanisms of media influence,
democratic voter behavior, or great-power intervention. At best, Russia
found a perfect patch of soil for its active measures to flourish. At worst,
Russian disinformation was a minor symptom of a major problem in US
politics, and thus largely irrelevant to the chaos that Americans inflicted
upon themselves.

We may never empirically settle the question of Russian effectiveness
once and for all. This is why it is so important to pay close attention to the
theoretical mechanisms of subversion. In this chapter I have laid out a
demand-driven theory of disinformation implied by the intelligence performance framework. I find that the case of 2016 passes a key test for
demand-driven subversion. Public disclosure of Russian interference in
mid-2016 did not undermine the campaign; instead it generated emotionally salient drama and had reverberating effects. If Russian content mattered at all, it was because Americans made opportunistic use of it to
mobilize fellow travelers and stigmatize rivals.

Demanding Disinformation

Russian intelligence performance in 2016 was mixed. Russia was able to
exploit a densely interconnected and highly vulnerable information ecosystem, but its clandestine organization was dependent on American political
entrepreneurs, and Russian discretion was undisciplined. The result is that
Russia could easily conduct a subversive campaign at scale, but it quickly
lost control of it. The campaign had at best minor marginal independent
effects in an unusually turbulent election season. The domestic demand for
bullshit trumped the foreign supply.

Demand-driven subversion is not about changing hearts and minds.
Consumers of bullshit already know what they want, and foreign messaging campaigns just show them how to get it. Political behavior
changes, if at all, because of the endogenous dynamics of domestic

politics, not the exogenous shock of foreign intervention. Kate Starbird and colleagues thus stress that most disinformation is collaborative, organic work. Online conspiracy theorists, they write, do "not wait for an external disinformation agent to give them the signal to start theorizing. Instead, each new event becomes interpreted through the same lens, and becomes a catalyst for another round of conspiracy theorizing. . . . The online nature of their activity allows for an epistemic community to take shape around these conversations. . . . Thus, this activity can act to recruit others into the community and teach them the social rules of participating there."[89]

Public efforts to limit Russian activity from mid-2016 onward turned Russia into a political litmus test. The creation of access barriers to exclude Russian influence after 2016 merely encouraged Trump supporters to rely more on homegrown disinformation. Indeed, locally sourced bullshit was available in large quantities in 2020 and 2024.

This has a troubling policy implication: The measures that work to limit supply-driven disinformation may help to promote demand-driven disinformation. Efforts to block, debunk, or limit access to problematic content can provide a protective barrier against covert disinformation. Yet the same measures have the perverse effect of amplifying the attractiveness of overt disinformation to polarized political communities. Because there is demand for disinformation, publicity boots the signal. More effective fact-checking and content controls just make the repetition of obvious falsehoods more effective as a separative signal. Only loyal members of the ingroup will repeat the lie, precisely because it becomes more costly for members of the outgroup to repeat it. Breathless media coverage of controversial narratives then makes it easier for political actors to sort friend from foe. The more blatant the lie, the more effective it is for signaling the loyalty of the liar.

The remedies in each case contrast starkly. For supply-driven subversion (where interests are not aligned, audience demand is low, and threat actors must carefully manipulate their targets), sunlight is the best disinfectant. But for demand-driven disinformation (where interests are aligned, demand is high, and audiences care little for provenance), it may be better to ignore it until it goes away. Calling attention to and limiting access to problematic foreign content just encourages domestic audiences to generate their own disinformation, politicize the fact-checking process, and decry content moderation as an assault on free speech. Getting the diagnosis right is critical because different etiologies require different remedies.

This is a genuine dilemma for disinformation defenders. The things one might do to limit covert disinformation, such as blocking dubious content and public fact-checking, can help to publicize overt disinformation. Ignoring and downplaying overt disinformation, on the other hand, leaves the door open for foreign influence and abets the spread of covert disinformation. To further complicate the situation, many subversive IO campaigns mix covert and overt disinformation, as did the Russian campaign.

From Prohibition to the War on Drugs, supply-side solutions have been applied to demand-driven problems. Supply control may be attractive for organizational and political reasons. It is usually easier to measure seized material and incarcerated felons. Supply-side interventions may also help to alleviate violence caused by drug gangs, at least in the short term. But sanctions also raise the value of banned substances and encourage the growth of illicit infrastructure at home. Policy alternatives such as drug legalization and social programs to alleviate poverty or addiction are rarely politically popular. It is usually easier to create a consensus for law enforcement than for social engineering. An analogy between content control and drug control is suggestive: As bullshit junkies were cut off from their Russian dealers in 2018 and 2020, American addicts just sourced their own sauce.

No one has figured out a humane remedy for toxic political polarization. It is not obvious that most Americans want it to be remedied. It is much easier for disinformation warriors to focus on filtering content and taking down botnets in cyberspace. Because disinformation is more easily countered than deterred, such remedies are necessary in the short term for countering foreign influence and domestic terrorism. As with any intelligence contest, it is best to keep efforts to counter disinformation as discreet as possible to avoid amplifying the polarizing dynamics of collective bad faith. But the underlying problem of disinformation is a wicked one that cannot be solved by technocratic intervention alone.

As this book went into production, the US government announced plans to counter Russian influence campaigns during the 2024 election.[90] Once again, the Kremlin favored Donald Trump over a female Democratic candidate (Kamala Harris rather than Hillary Clinton) in an unusual election. But this time, the incumbent Democratic administration (of Joseph Biden rather than Barack Obama) proactively countered foreign influence by indicting RT employees and Russian hackers, taking down suspicious websites, removing Russian malware, imposing financial sanctions, issuing public service announcements, coordinating with big tech firms, and conducting counterintelligence operations. These efforts largely succeeded in limiting foreign influence. The US electorate, however, was even more polarized than in 2016, with vocal elements on the right denouncing government efforts to counter foreign influence as a tyrannical suppression of free speech. With Trump and Harris polling in a dead heat, the right stoked fears of a stolen election while the left stoked fears of election violence, which led the Biden administration to beef up physical security around polling stations.[91] The domestic demand for disinformation was greater than ever, and efforts to counter it just amplified its spread. This time, however, Trump won both the popular vote and the Electoral College. Both sides accepted the legitimacy of the result, but that probably would not have happened had the election gone the other way. With the benefit of hindsight in 2024, the sorting dynamics of 2016 seem even more obvious.

The scope and scale of Russian influence in 2016 was dramatic, but that is true of almost everything in cyberspace. Cyberspace has supersized not only subversive campaigns but also political advertising, media coverage, and the spectacle of ochlocracy (mob rule). The Russian intervention was shameless and brazen, to be sure, but it was upstaged by the constant drama created by Trump, Clinton, and the US electorate. There were so many confounding factors in 2016 that we still cannot say decisively whether Russian intervention really did change the course of history. But the intensification of polarization in 2020 and 2024 suggests that 2016 was indeed an inside job.

It is tempting to blame foreign trolls for ugly ideas in society. Yet disinformation is ultimately a symptom of the domestic political preferences that drive voter behavior. I'll let comedian Dave Chappelle have the last word on this topic: "Is Russia making us racist? Oh my God, thank goodness. I thought it was us."[92]

CHAPTER 7

Cyber Power

China and the Contradictions of Cybersecurity

In December 2024, Chinese hackers gained access to computers used by the US secretary of the treasury and the Office of Foreign Assets Control (OFAC). OFAC would have been an attractive target given its role in administering sanctions against China. A hacking group known as Silk Typhoon, associated with the Ministry of State Security (MSS), the Chinese version of the KGB, got in through a cloud-based service run by a cybersecurity company named BeyondTrust, ironically enough. As I have argued throughout this book, trust in cyberspace is a constitutive condition for cyber insecurity, and threat actors usurp it by going beyond the institutional constraints of system architects and users. To compound the irony, the company had previously issued a press release titled, "BeyondTrust Reinforces Commitment to a Safer More Transparent Digital World by Signing CISA's Secure by Design Pledge."[1]

This case has a rhyming similarity with the SolarWinds breach, which was discussed in the introduction to this book. In 2020 the Russian SVR, a descendant of the KGB, exploited a trusted administrative service to access SolarWinds clients, including the US treasury department. In both cases, a vulnerable software intermediary that was supposed to improve security instead opened the door to spies. The BeyondTrust hack, furthermore, came on the heels of a massive telecommunications breach that surpassed SolarWinds in scope and scale, and which also subverted security controls. The Biden administration acknowledged that Salt Typhoon, another MSS-linked group, had "compromised private companies, exploiting vulnerabilities in their systems as part of a global Chinese campaign that's affected dozens of countries around the world," providing access to the unencrypted cell phone data and metadata of a "large number of Americans."[2] Victims included Verizon, AT&T, T-Mobile, and Lumen Technologies, and through them the trusted devices of many government officials as well as presidential candidate Donald Trump and running mate J. D. Vance. Salt Typhoon exploited the wiretapping mechanisms that telecommunications firms were required to implement for lawful intercept under the Communications Assistance for Law Enforcement Act (CALEA) of 1994. The Chinese continued to exploit US telecommunications even months after all the increased counterintelligence attention.[3] To use the terms of this book, a sophisticated organization exploited an exposed institution to maintain persistent access.

The exploits of the Typhoons bore out a US intelligence assessment from earlier in 2024, which stated that "China remains the most active and persistent cyber threat to U.S. Government, private-sector, and critical infrastructure networks. Beijing's cyber espionage pursuits and its industry's export of surveillance, information, and communications technologies increase the threats of aggressive cyber operations against the United States and the suppression of the free flow of information in cyberspace."[4] As with SolarWinds, the US response to large-scale hacking was not military but economic. OFAC announced (more) sanctions against Chinese individuals and companies associated with the Typhoons.[5] Once again, secret statecraft in cyberspace implicated commercial entities in an international intelligence contest at breathtaking scale.

Yet there is always a military edge to the economic relationship between the United States and China. While trust and interdependence enable cyber competition between great powers, the shadow of cyber warfare encourages mistrust and barriers. FBI Director Christopher Wray warned in January 2024, "PRC [People's Republic of China] hackers are targeting our critical infrastructure—our water treatment plants, our electrical grid, our oil and natural gas pipelines, our transportation systems." Wray stated that Volt Typhoon, a hacking group linked to the Chinese People's Liberation Army (PLA), was preparing "to wreak havoc and cause real-world harm to American citizens and communities." Cyberwar was coming: "Low blows against civilians are part of China's plan."[6]

Claims that information technology provides China with an unfair advantage over the United States have been a staple of national security rhetoric for decades.[7] This threat narrative gains new urgency with China's doctrine of informatized warfare and its active probing of US infrastructure, which demonstrate both intent and capability. But as we have seen, weaponizing digital systems for geopolitical advantage is a nontrivial challenge. Sabotage at scale must overcome myriad institutional problems, and it is not obvious that Chinese deception specialists will be able to solve them in the turbulent conditions of crisis or war. The US military and intelligence community, by contrast, has much more experience with the operational challenges of cyber warfare and multidomain operations. Even if we focus just on peacetime espionage, the astounding scope and scale of Chinese intrusions may not translate into systematic competitive advantage. China must not only acquire data but also absorb, analyze, and apply it, and these tasks tend to increase the bureaucratic overhead for Chinese intelligence and industry. By optimizing for espionage rather than innovation, China may be specializing in second place.

Intelligence warnings can even be flipped on their head. The fact that we know so much about the extent of Chinese threat activity can also be interpreted as evidence of increasing Western ability to contest it. Chinese threat actors are indeed very active in the exploitation of commercial and government targets around the world. Yet a global cybersecurity community is also increasingly active in the detection, attribution, and mitigation of Chinese threats. Persistent Chinese threats have inspired, and warnings from US officials reflect, renewed interest and investment in counterintelligence in public and private sectors alike. One does not simply walk into an intelligence contest and win it. Cybersecurity is an interminable process of contesting the rules and tools of control.

The previous campaign studies in this book focused on intelligence performance at the operational level. This chapter does something different: It provides a holistic assessment of Chinese cyber power at the strategic level. I will briefly discuss the performance of a few Chinese campaigns herein, but the goal of this chapter is to revisit the themes of previous chapters in a different national context. This helps to extend the explanatory scope of the theory and show how different national institutions shape the goals and conduct of secret statecraft.

Cyber power is the digital dimension of all other forms of power, with an emphasis on interactions across them. David Betz and Tim Stevens define it "as the variety of powers that circulate in cyberspace and which shape the experiences of those who act in and through cyberspace. . . . [C]yber power is therefore the manifestation of power in cyberspace rather than a new or different form of power."[8] The dramatic growth of the information economy in recent decades has affected *all* instruments of national power—diplomatic, informational, military, economic, and so on. National cyber power in this sense sets the conditions for secret statecraft in cyberspace. It creates both the resources used in national cyber campaigns and the targets exploited by foreign cyber campaigns.

Throughout this book I have stressed that operational performance depends on the conditions of vulnerable institutions and clandestine organization. These conditions tend to vary over time and from case to case. This has uneven implications for different facets of cyber power. To understand the nature and limits of Chinese cyber power, therefore, it is important to understand how institutions both constrain and enable China's use and abuse of information technology. Indeed, an institutional perspective on secret statecraft helps to temper the conventional wisdom about Chinese cyber power.

The organization of this chapter retraces the conceptual arc of the book to this point, as mapped in table 7.1. First, I discuss China's appropriation of the digital infrastructure of US hegemony. Second, I discuss patterns of

Table 7.1 Secret statecraft in the Chinese context

Theme	Previous case study	Chinese cyber power
Security	Chap. 3—Cyberspace	Repurposing the internet
Espionage	Chap. 4—Bletchley Park	Industrial espionage at scale
Sabotage	Chap. 5—Stuxnet	Military informatization
Subversion	Chap. 6—2016 election	Information control

Chinese cyber espionage in comparison with the World War II SIGINT contest. Third, I discuss China's struggles to implement its doctrine of informatized warfare, which is predicated on very different institutional conditions compared to Stuxnet. Fourth, I discuss the most comprehensive system of counterintelligence ever built, as well as the reasons why Chinese domestic-influence operations are so much more effective than Russian foreign-influence operations. I conclude by highlighting the institutional contradictions of Chinese cyber power.

Co-opting Liberal Infrastructure

The digital infrastructure of the US liberal order is designed to encourage innovation. All kinds of actors can recombine open protocols and modular abstractions into countless applications. But this same flexibility enables nonliberal actors to innovate. Espionage and censorship are just apps on a flexible digital platform. Indeed, China shows how it is possible to unbundle economic and political liberalization. China repurposed cyberspace to both get rich and impose control.

For better and worse, information technology helped China to become a great power. Economic liberalization and global engagement have dramatically improved Chinese standards of living, even as China's distribution of wealth is highly uneven. China's thriving technology economy flourishes within a managed economy, which is distorted by state-owned enterprises and an inscrutable bureaucracy. The Chinese political system, which has been described as "fragmented authoritarianism," is run by striving officials who compete to curry favor with powerful elites while struggling to govern an unwieldy economy across a sprawling geography.[9] China's vibrant online community of "netizens" is not afraid to express their opinions in creative and outspoken ways, even as Beijing runs the world's most sophisticated system of internet censorship.

There are two important institutional trends in modern Chinese politics: a weakening of "liberal peace" abroad and a strengthening of "authoritarian peace" at home. While the global economy remains highly integrated, there are early signs of economic decoupling.[10] Barriers to travel and trade are gradually rising. Alternative regional coordination mechanisms are emerging. Governments are onshoring key economic resources. Balancing coalitions are forming. Meanwhile, China under the leadership of Xi Jinping has undergone a consolidation of autocratic control not seen since the days of Mao Zedong. These macrotrends reinforce each other. A more authoritarian China provokes counteractions to it, while a more hostile environment encourages Xi to increase control.

These entwined developments give rise to a distinctly Chinese approach to cyber power. In this section I discuss these institutional trends, their technological implications, and Xi's notion of "cyber superpower" (*wangluo qiangguo*). China thereby attempts to shape the environment for its own secret statecraft, notable for its distinct brand of national counterintelligence.

UNBUNDLING THE LIBERAL ORDER

The PRC under Mao Zedong was poor and isolated. In the 1980s, Deng Xiaoping oversaw the "reform and opening" of China to create a mixed-market economy, or "socialism with Chinese characteristics." Jiang Zemin and Hu Jintao largely embraced Deng's admonition to "hide strength and bide time" with their principles of "peace and development" and "peaceful rise," respectively. US-China relations soured temporarily after the 1989 Tiananmen Square massacre, the 1995–96 Taiwan Strait crisis, and the accidental US bombing of the Chinese embassy in Belgrade in 1999. But liberal optimists interpreted these as mere growing pains, expecting China to follow Eastern Europe out of benighted Communism to enlightened democracy.[11]

Indeed, the new millennium began on a promising note. China agreed to a series of liberalizing reforms and joined the World Trade Organization in 2001. This gave China access to global markets and foreign direct investment. China entered a remarkable period of sustained economic growth that lifted hundreds of millions of people out of poverty. Some became quite rich. Extensive legal reforms also enabled people to enjoy new civil liberties. The US and Chinese economies became increasingly integrated, realizing mutual interests in digitally enabled prosperity.[12]

But the Chinese Communist Party (CCP) remained firmly in control throughout the reform period. Construction of the "Great Firewall of China"—a euphemism for sweeping internet censorship and information control measures—helped China to capture the economic benefits of cyberspace while mitigating CCP paranoia about political liberalism. As the CCP quietly exchanged Communist ideology for capitalist prosperity, it also quietly encouraged the theft of data from Western governments, corporations, and civil society organizations. Prosperity by any means necessary became the foundation for CCP legitimacy. Meanwhile the PLA, which is formally the army of the CCP rather than the Chinese state, embraced networked "informatization" (*xinxihua*), and later automated "intelligentization" (*zhinenghua*), as the key to victory in future war.[13]

As economic globalization made China rich, the CCP became both more powerful and more insecure. Susan Shirk describes a process of logrolling among entrenched interests under the weak leadership of Hu Jintao, resulting in a more nationalist and assertive China beneath the veneer of its "peaceful rise."[14] China bolstered its security posture for the 2008 Beijing Olympic Games and weathered the global financial crisis better than most Western countries. US-China relations during the tenure of President Barack Obama were clouded by incessant allegations of Chinese cyber espionage and backlash against the Edward Snowden leaks, which revealed systematic NSA exploitation of not only US companies like Microsoft but also Chinese companies like Huawei.

Xi Jinping inherited China's growing sense of confidence in 2012, and its growing security apparatus. Xi's new philosophy of striving hard to realize the "Chinese dream" of national "rejuvenation" aimed to make China the leading world power by 2049, the one-hundredth anniversary of the founding of the People's Republic of China. Rather than hiding and biding, a newly powerful China required a "new type of great power relations."[15] But Xi also reverted to an old kind of autocratic politics. He consolidated CCP control over the state, and personal control over the CCP. He liquidated political rivals through anticorruption campaigns, imposed draconian controls on ethnic minorities, expanded internal security forces, reorganized the PLA, bolstered information control, crushed democratic protests in Hong Kong, and locked down Chinese society during the COVID-19 pandemic. The CCP confirmed Xi to a third term in 2022 after altering the Chinese constitution. PRC propaganda rehabilitated Mao Zedong and suppressed Deng Xiaoping, signaling a return to authoritarian rule away from liberal opening.[16]

STRATEGIC COMPETITION

Xi's consolidation of control at home was accompanied by more coercion abroad.[17] China began building islands in the South China Sea, expanding economically into Central Asia through the "Belt and Road Initiative," engaging in border skirmishing with India, and embracing "wolf warrior diplomacy" (a reference to Chinese action movies with American villains). China's assertive foreign policy inspired fear among its regional neighbors and encouraged balancing (e.g., the Quadrilateral Security Dialogue of Australia, India, Japan, and the United States and the AUKUS partnership between Australia, the United Kingdom, and the United States).[18] As Xi accelerated the conventional and nuclear modernization of the PLA, global observers worried more about the risks of war.

Simmering tensions mounted between China and the United States.[19] The first Donald Trump administration explicitly named China as a geopolitical rival, adopted a national security strategy of "great power competition," and initiated a trade war with China. The US banned government use of Huawei and ZTE telecommunications equipment, citing national security concerns, and encouraged other countries to decouple from Chinese tech firms as well. The Joseph Biden administration dialed back on the rhetoric but largely maintained a combative economic policy. The US imposed further rounds of economic sanctions to block Chinese access to sensitive US technologies, and to block Chinese platforms such as TikTok from the US market.[20] The 2022 US CHIPS Act, which limited Chinese access to US semiconductors used for advanced AI models, highlighted China's dependency on the United States, while also encouraging the US to limit its own reliance on China.[21]

China, meanwhile, adopted a "dual circulation" strategy to expand domestic consumption and insulate the Chinese economy from international interference. The "Made in China 2025" plan aimed to achieve dominance in high-tech manufacturing, while "China Standards 2035" expressed an ambition for the global adoption of Chinese technical standards and protocols. Both were built on China's long-standing desire to reduce foreign technological dependence through "indigenous innovation."[22] China emerged as a serious competitor in many areas, including quantum informatics, green energy, and mobile infrastructure (5G/6G).[23] In other areas, notably semiconductors, China remained reliant on US-dominated international supply chains and exposed to external shocks.[24]

As discussed in chapter 3, path-dependent network effects shape the information economy. The US information technology sector enjoyed a first-mover advantage that catapulted US tech firms to global dominance. Network effects exacerbated political battles over technical standards and protocols as China alleged an unfair US advantage. China advocated for an alternative principle of "cyber sovereignty" to govern the internet through the International Telecommunications Union.[25] This multilateral approach contrasted with a multistakeholder system of institutions (ICANN, IETF, etc.) that manage the internet through a network of private companies, industry groups, academics, nongovernmental organizations, and government delegates. Controversy over internet governance encouraged worry about a possible bifurcation of internet standards in the future, or a "splinternet."[26]

But the liberal system of internet governance remained deeply entrenched, even as the reelection of US President Trump posed new challenges for it. Chinese proposals for alternative norms and governance institutions found limited traction outside the authoritarian states of the Shanghai Cooperation Organization.[27] Xi's challenge as an institutional revisionist was that Chinese prosperity—and thus CCP legitimacy—was still dependent on integration into the US-led global liberal order. China, as Edward Steinfeld put it, was still "playing our game."[28] Liberal order is not a monolithic concept, furthermore, which means that China was able to accept or tolerate some kinds of order while challenging others.[29] This also suggests that the Trump administration will likely preserve some aspects of liberal order while dismantling others; time will tell. While such heterogeneity creates strain on interdependence, it is also a brake on decoupling. The common connectivity of cyberspace has thus remained invaluable for Chinese economic performance, even as the CCP was still able to appropriate its flexibility for political control.

CYBER SUPERPOWER

In a 2016 speech, Xi called on China "to increase investment, strengthen the construction of information infrastructure, promote the deep integration of the internet and the real economy, accelerate the digitization and intelligentization of traditional industries, make the digital economy bigger and stronger, and expand new space for economic development."[30] This would be implemented through an "Internet Plus" plan to network every sector of Chinese society. Internet Plus espoused such recognizably liberal ideas as "connecting everything" through an "open ecology" that is "innovation driven" and "integrated across borders" with an abiding "respect for humanity."[31] Yet the safety and stability of a decentralized open network also required centralized planning. As Xi was fond of saying, "There is no national security without cybersecurity, and no modernization without informatization."[32]

The phrase "cyber superpower" appeared regularly in Xi's domestic speeches on the internet and cybersecurity beginning in 2014. It was less frequent in foreign messaging. While Chinese diplomatic statements stressed win-win collaboration in cyberspace, domestic messaging portrayed cyberspace as a key arena for great-power competition that China should win.[33] This meant innovating world-leading information technologies and standards, ending dependency on foreign technologies, harnessing "civil-military fusion" to boost military power, and strengthening cybersecurity and defense against ideological subversion.

In July 2023, the Cyberspace Administration of China (CAC), which oversees censorship and propaganda, published *Introduction to General Secretary Xi Jinping's Important Thoughts on Cyber Superpower*.[34] It explains that informatization is a "golden opportunity" for China, which is advancing from a "major cyber power" (*wangluo daguo*) to a "cyber superpower" (*wangluo qiangguo*). Cyberspace thus becomes "the central front" for "ideological conflict," and "core technology" China's "most important weapon."

This requires China to "vigorously develop the digital economy," "lay a solid foundation for cybersecurity," and work "online and offline together like concentric circles." Ten principles stress the ideological dimension of cyber superpower:[35]

1. The CCP controls the internet.
2. CCP control of the internet benefits the Chinese people.
3. The people must uphold Xi's "new era of socialism with Chinese characteristics."
4. The CCP maintains control in internet planning, development, and security.
5. Maintaining "positive energy" in cyberspace is the "last word" and the "real skill."
6. The PRC must build a robust national information-security barrier.
7. The CCP drives informatization.
8. Internet users obey cybersecurity laws.
9. The PRC promotes a vision of a shared future in cyberspace for the international community.
10. The PRC must have a loyal, clean, and responsible cybersecurity and informatization workforce.

These principles are starkly at odds with the libertarian rhapsody of John Perry Barlow's "Declaration of the Independence of Cyberspace."[36] The mid-1990s may have been the era of peak liberalism in cyberspace, but China realized a very different model three decades later. "Cyberspace is not a lawless place," as the CAC put it,[37] and the CCP is firmly in control. But then again, "cyber" has always been about control. The seeds of networked authoritarianism were planted at the dawn of cybernetics.

At least one important feature of Chinese cyber superpower does not explicitly appear on this list. The PRC relies on cyber espionage to bolster the prosperity and security of the CCP, enabled by the same sociotechnical institutions that underwrite the liberal economic order.

Scaling Up Espionage

Michael Herman describes intelligence as "a significant part of the modern state and a factor in government's success and failure," arguing that it "constitutes its own particular kind of state power: *intelligence power*."[38] Intelligence power, to the extent that it exploits information technology, is a key component of cyber power. The main political benefit of intelligence, as discussed in chapter 1, is improving efficiency by usurping institutional efficiency. Better intelligence enables actors to identify threats and opportunities, act with more discretion, and make the most of limited resources while also limiting risk.

Chinese intelligence power has long been an important pillar of CCP control.[39] While Western intelligence services tend to focus on national security, authoritarian services often have a broader remit.[40] Chinese services not only spy on foreign targets but also target dissident groups, civil society organizations, and a wide range of industrial sectors. The preoccupation with internal security and economic policy supports the twin CCP imperatives to maintain control over perceived political dangers and promote legitimacy through economic growth. Secret statecraft via cyberspace supports these goals.

Intelligence contests with China have been an important factor in the improvement of Western cybersecurity capacity. Indeed, the modern term of art for cyber-threat actors—advanced persistent threat (APT)—was originally coined in the early 2000s as a euphemism for Chinese state hackers.[41] Widespread offensive Chinese operations, in turn, catalyzed innovation in network defense. We have China to thank, in no small part, for the professional state of the art in cybersecurity.

INDUSTRIAL ESPIONAGE

Commercial espionage has long been a point of contention in US-China relations. Most cases prosecuted under the US Economic Espionage Act of 1996 have been associated with China (even though the act was originally motivated by the illicit activities of US allies such as France and Japan). Hacking, moreover, was just a small part of China's extensive collection effort, which also leveraged good old-fashioned human intelligence and open-source collection.[42] According to the US National Counterintelligence and Security Center, China "continues to use cyber espionage to support its strategic development goals—science and technology advancement, military modernization, and economic policy objectives."[43]

Many early Chinese campaigns did not prioritize operational security, but neither did their targets. Other operations were quite sophisticated, such as the theft of RSA SecureID seed tokens enabling the breach of Lockheed Martin's Joint Strike Fighter program.[44] The Mandiant company released a report on "APT1" in 2013, marshaling an impressive body of evidence identifying a major PLA SIGINT organization in Shanghai targeting English-speaking entities.[45] This landmark report made public what US intelligence agencies had long known in private.[46] It also marked the zenith of widespread yet undisciplined economic espionage by the PLA.

PLA intruders had been notoriously indiscreet, leaving lots of clues for incident responders. But then in 2014, targeted intrusions attributed to China dropped dramatically.[47] As Mandiant testified to the US-China Economic and Security Review Commission, Chinese intrusions held steady at a much lower level thereafter (figure 7.1).[48] Three factors may explain this drop. First, the Department of Justice (DOJ) publicly indicted five PLA officers in May 2014 on counts of industrial espionage, drawing on some of the same intelligence that was in the APT1 report. This marked the beginning of US efforts to "name and shame" foreign threat operators. According to one participant in diplomatic talks, "The Chinese hated them [the US indictments]. They complained about them every time there was a meeting. They said there couldn't be any progress . . . until the indictments were withdrawn and we promised not to do them again."[49] Second, Xi and Obama publicly agreed not to conduct economic espionage in 2015, and a similar nonbinding agreement by the G20 followed later that year. The decrease in intrusions began in 2014, however, so the 2015 agreement at best only reinforced it. Third, the PLA created a new Strategic Support Force (SSF) in 2015 to consolidate space, cyber, and electronic warfare.[50] This reform refocused PLA SIGINT units on national security objectives rather than commercial espionage.

Yet the MSS continued to conduct economic espionage. In early 2016, for example, an MSS-affiliated group (APT3) acquired and repurposed US NSA hacking tools. This was prior to their public release by the Russian Shadow Brokers group in late 2016 and early 2017.[51] A 2018 indictment of

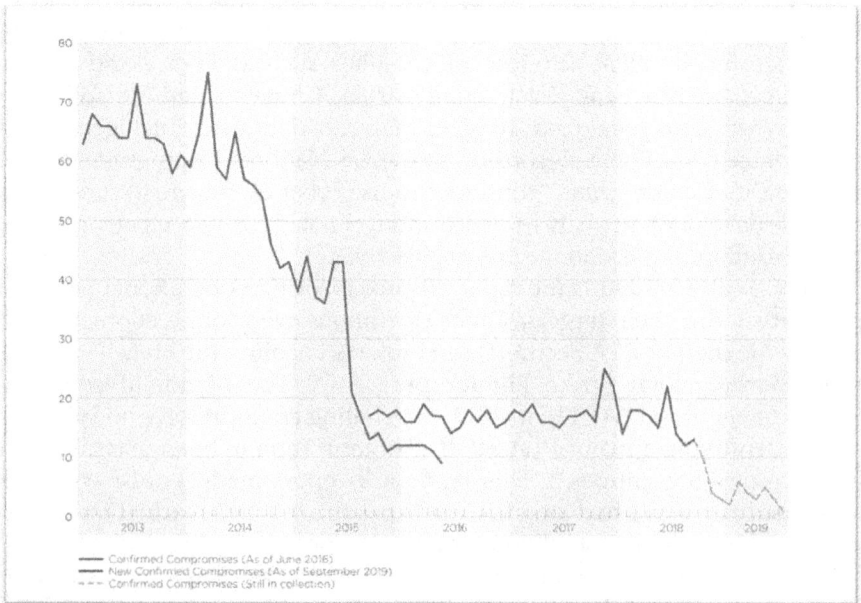

Figure 7.1. Active network compromises conducted by China-based groups by month, February 2013–June 2019 (source: Mandiant)

an MSS-associated threat group (APT10) described a cyber campaign targeting industries in the ten crucial sectors of the "Made in China 2025" initiative, prompting public criticism by the United States and twelve allies for China's violation of the 2015 agreement.[52] In early 2020, another prolific group (APT41) exploited enterprise networking and endpoint management devices to target over seventy-five companies in multiple sectors.[53] The French cybersecurity company Sekoia assessed that "APT40, APT41, APT31, Mustang Panda, Lucky Mouse, and APT10 are active China-nexus intrusion sets directly associated with the MSS."[54]

In early 2021, right on the heels of the SolarWinds breach, multiple Chinese actors exploited vulnerabilities in the Microsoft Exchange email server. Microsoft attributed the breach to the MSS-linked Hafnium group (later rebranded as Silk Typhoon, the same group that hacked OFAC in 2024).[55] Hafnium met both intelligence performance conditions for at least two months, and probably longer. The architecture of Microsoft's Exchange server was partitioned into an internet-facing "client access services" layer and a "backend services" layer to maintain backward compatibility and convenient maintenance. It accepted client connections unless the network was behind a VPN, so specially crafted email queries to the front end could deliver back-end server names and access tokens. The target institution—Exchange—was both connected and vulnerable. Hafnium performed reconnaissance to gain valid email accounts and tested and customized at least three zero-day exploits. This clandestine organization had the capacity to carefully synchronize this attack, and it exercised discretion by limiting the number of intrusions it could have feasibly undertaken, camouflaging the scope of its exploitation within Microsoft's patch cycle. Things changed abruptly on February 26, 2021. The number of intrusions scaled up to thousands per day (less discreet) as multiple other Chinese threat actors acquired the exploit for unclear reasons (more dependency and less controllable capacity). Microsoft responded by releasing patches (barriers to connectivity), and a US interagency Unified Coordination Group initiated a coordinated response (vulnerability reduction) in March. In May a federal grand jury in San Diego indicted four Chinese nationals with the MSS, and the US government publicly attributed the attack to the Chinese government in July.[56]

The MSS maintains partnerships with Chinese companies including Alibaba, Tencent, Huawei, ByteDance, Baidu, and ZTE.[57] Chinese corporations can provide data and analytic support to the MSS. Note that US intelligence agencies also have partnerships with US tech firms, ranging from overt contracting relationships to discreet data-sharing agreements, as dramatized in the Snowden leaks. Regional MSS offices sometimes form or co-opt shell companies that recruit civilian hackers from local universities.[58] This provides a cutout for the MSS, but outsourcing also creates agency and security risks. MSS clients may blend state espionage and criminal fraud.[59]

This kind of moonlighting is what encouraged Xi to rein in PLA hackers prior to 2015, refocusing them on their primary mission of informatizing war. Sloppy tradecraft or security by clients could also draw unwanted attention to the MSS, as happened in February 2024 when a large tranche of internal documents from the Sichuan branch of the I-Soon company was leaked through a GitHub repository. The leaks revealed a massive hack-for-hire operation with contracts let out to the MSS, the Ministry of Public Security (MPS), and the PLA.[60]

END OF THE HAPPY TIMES

The widespread and flagrant nature of Chinese espionage in the early twenty-first century encouraged Western governments and industries to invest more in cybersecurity. China's targets begin erecting defensive barriers, and the cybersecurity community began countering threats more actively. China, in turn, shifted responsibility for espionage away from the PLA and toward the MSS. Chinese intrusions became more sophisticated in the process. China had to develop better clandestine organizations in order to exploit a less permissive institutional environment, and Chinese operations accordingly became more complex.

Chapter 4 suggests a historical parallel. In the early days of the Battle of the Atlantic, Bletchley Park was locked out of naval Enigma, and Allied antisubmarine warfare capabilities had not yet matured. German submariners described a "happy time" during which convoys were easy to hunt. But German success encouraged Allied countermeasures. Antisubmarine warfare capability improved with convoy escorts, long-range aviation patrols, centimetric radars, and success against four-rotor Enigma. These improvements enabled Allied navies to go on the offensive against German wolf packs. The hunters became the hunted. The maritime domain gradually became less permissive for German U-boats and was downright prohibitive by the end of 1943.

In this analogy, the internet boom was a happy time for Chinese hackers. US policymakers in the early 2000s were preoccupied with the short-term challenges of counterterrorism and counterinsurgency in the Middle East, downplaying the long-term challenge in the Pacific and subsidizing the growth of a military rival.[61] Government and corporate networks were poorly defended, so Chinese hackers had a target-rich environment. But Chinese operations were noisy and brazen, which encouraged improvements in Western cybersecurity. A 2009 report from Citizen Lab on the "GhostNet" campaign targeting Tibetans in exile demonstrated the potential for civilian counterintelligence reporting on Chinese threats.[62] That same year, Chinese hackers breached Google and gained access to the Gmail accounts of Chinese human rights activists, prompting the dramatic exit of Google from China in 2010.[63] The trickle of commercial intelligence reporting on Chinese threats turned into a flood.[64] After the 2013 Mandiant report on APT1, Western targets began taking Chinese threats much more seriously. Potential victims started throwing up barriers to connectivity and shoring up sociotechnical vulnerability. Public and private counterintelligence actors also began to more proactively hunt for Chinese threats.

As the happy times came to an end, Chinese threat actors had to invest more in clandestine organization to compensate for the less vulnerable institutions they would exploit. Accordingly, Chinese threats began to exercise more discretion—quietly using local resources (or "living off the land"), cleaning up forensic evidence, and systematically using anonymization networks—which was necessary because defenders improved their capability to discreetly detect them.[65] One indication of China's increasing clandestine capability is that its use of zero-day vulnerabilities increased from ten between 2015 and 2020 to twenty-three between 2021 and 2023.[66] A new industrial policy also required firms to disclose software vulnerabilities to the China Information Technology Security Evaluation Center (CNITSEC) run by MSS.[67] This increase in the supply of capability must also be understood in terms of an increase in the demand for security. A steady stream of zero-days was needed to remain competitive in a more contested operating environment.

Chinese espionage obviously did not end as the institutional environment became less permissive, but the intelligence contest itself consumed more effort and resources. China kept up a relentless pace of intrusion, targeting numerous US interests, including hacking the email of the US secretary of commerce and the US ambassador to China in 2023, once again through a subtle vulnerability in Microsoft systems.[68] Microsoft Exchange had once again fallen victim to Chinese hackers. The US Cyber Safety Review Board concluded that "this intrusion was preventable and should never have occurred."[69] This episode encouraged further improvement of US counterintelligence efforts (such as a law enforcement operation in January 2025 to remove Twill Typhoon malware from over 4,200 infected US computers),[70] as well as the imposition of technical trade barriers (such as bans on equipment from Huawei and ZTE). China also kept up the pressure in other countries, which likewise redoubled cybersecurity efforts. For example, Chinese hackers burrowed deep into Japan's most sensitive networks, and Japan, according to *The Washington Post*, responded by "boosting the cybersecurity budget tenfold over the next five years and increasing their military cybersecurity force fourfold to 4,000 people."[71] The happy times were over, but the intelligence contest was not.

ORGANIZED HYPOCRISY

The ongoing exploitation of Western targets by the MSS underscores a general problem with public norms in secret statecraft. Any public promise not to engage in deception provides private motivation to engage in *more effective* deception. In a 2015 speech in Seattle, at the end of the happy times, Xi stated flatly, "China is a staunch defender of cybersecurity. China is also a victim of hacking attacks. The Chinese government will not participate in, encourage or support anyone in any form of theft of trade secrets. Whether it is cyber commercial theft or hacking of government networks, they are all illegal and criminal acts and should be cracked down in accordance with laws and relevant international conventions. The international community should work together to build a peaceful, secure, open and cooperative cyberspace based on the principles of mutual respect and mutual trust."[72]

Hypocrisy is hardly unusual in international politics. Michael Poznansky shows that the United States often uses covert action to avoid hypocrisy costs while maintaining a facade of compliance with international commitments.[73] Stephen Krasner goes so far as to describe sovereignty as "organized hypocrisy."[74] Secret statecraft is part of this dubious tradition. Denying deception is a basic tactic of deception. A liar is most likely to say, "I'm not lying."

There is an unspoken norm between sovereign governments that political and military espionage will be tolerated. Professional spies try to steal secrets without getting caught, and professional counterspies try to catch them. For example, the Chinese breach of the US Office of Personnel Management (OPM) was a counterintelligence disaster for the United States and an intelligence bonanza for China (because the MSS could use security clearance investigations from the OPM to identify Western agents and target espionage).[75] Yet the director of national intelligence, James Clapper, said, "You have to kind of salute the Chinese for what they did."[76] The implication is that the NSA would do the same, given the opportunity. This suggests that the United States has little interest in a comprehensive ban on espionage.

In the economic realm, however, US firms did not need to steal from Chinese competitors, because they were already market leaders, even if US intelligence agencies were to help them, which they legally could not. The United States thus had nothing to lose by agreeing not to engage in industrial espionage. The 2015 agreement between Xi and Obama and the G20 remained noticeably silent, however, on national security matters. While Mandiant's APT1 report revealed extensive Chinese hacking of both economic and national security targets, moreover, the DOJ indictments based on the same intelligence focused only on industrial espionage. The tacit message was that national security espionage remained fair game.

The distinction between commercial and political espionage is fuzzy in practice. US agencies might hack into a corporation like Huawei because its political targets use Huawei equipment. American spies have been known to hack American tech for that purpose.[77] US agencies might also hack into economic targets to assess national capabilities, or into defense firms to understand military capabilities. National counterintelligence efforts may improve the competitive position of US firms as well. The US delegitimization of economic espionage is narrowly scoped to intellectual property theft to give commercial firms a market advantage. China agreed to this publicly but honors it in the private breach.

ANALYTICAL INFRASTRUCTURE

Years of Western reporting on Chinese espionage feeds a narrative that China benefits commensurably with the scope of its hacking. China has indeed gained an unfair advantage in many sectors, including high-speed rail, wind turbines, and the defense industry. The 2017 US Commission on the Theft of American Intellectual Property estimated losses to the US economy in the range of $225 to $600 billion annually, much of it through hacking, and most of it to China.[78] The commission assessed that Chinese theft of trade secrets posed a serious threat to the long-term competitiveness of the US economy.

In 2020, FBI Director Christopher Wray described a "theft on a scale so massive that it represents one of the largest transfers of wealth in human history."[79] Wray's comments echo similar comments by NSA Director Keith Alexander a decade earlier.[80] But the same decade saw the longest expansion of the US economy on record, as well as a slowdown of Chinese economic growth. Chinese espionage did not paralyze the US economy, and it did not enable China to overtake it. As in secret statecraft everywhere else, the relationship between tactical espionage and economic advantage is not straightforward.

Intellectual property theft is only a first step on a long and winding road to commercial performance. Recall that Bletchley Park's intercept operations required extensive analytical and dissemination infrastructure; even then, SIGINT success affected military performance indirectly, only when commanders were willing and able to use Ultra. Similarly, industrial secrets must be not only acquired but also absorbed into industrial processes and applied in commercial interactions in order to have any economic effect.[81] A large quantity of stolen data does not create a large qualitative advantage without a lot of intermediary work.

It is much easier to measure intrusion activity than it is to link it to economic productivity. It is also much easier to steal text than context. Chinese intelligence actors steal a lot of data, and Western counterintelligence actors detect a lot of this theft (eventually). But innovation is much more than intellectual property. Innovation emerges from an ecosystem of technical labor, venture capital, higher education, property rights, civil liberties, supply chains, and even recreational opportunities.[82] Simply moving data from one society to another is like injecting DNA from one species into another. There is no reason to believe that genetic information will alter morphology or behavior if adequate epigenetic machinery is missing.

To the extent that China has indeed benefited from cyber espionage, this is testament to China's considerable investment in analytical infrastructure. Wray estimated that China employs more than fifty thousand hackers.[83] This technical talent, of potentially uneven quality, must be supported by severalfold more analysts and administrators. China also collects foreign scientific information through many legitimate pathways, such as open-source collection, participation in scientific networks, joint ventures with Western firms, and academic communities.[84] All these data do not interpret themselves. Illicit information is just a small part of the take, and there are additional transaction costs associated with acquiring, analyzing, and applying it. The analytical infrastructure of absorption necessarily eats into the efficiency of espionage. The costs of absorbing foreign data tend to increase, moreover, as collectors move up the value chain. China's struggles to reverse engineer a competitive equivalent of a fifth-generation fighter like the F/A-22 are illustrative.[85]

Cyber espionage may nevertheless augment Chinese military power in at least four ways. First, espionage may enable an actor to build better military forces in peacetime, subject to all the caveats above. Second, operational intelligence and reconnaissance can be used to guide the employment of military forces in wartime. Third, information channels can be reversed to produce disruptive effects, either as a complement to kinetic operations or as a substitute for them. Fourth, security failures that alert adversaries to the dangers of the prior three mechanisms may encourage arms racing to protect and offset military power. But all of these require complementary analytical infrastructure. There is no free lunch for Chinese espionage, or anywhere else in cyberspace.

Informatizing Military Power

Military power is perhaps the most intuitive form of power in international relations. It is nevertheless complicated to implement and measure.[86] Translating material capabilities into battlefield effectiveness depends on organizational institutions such as command-and-control arrangements, service cultures, operational doctrine, civil-military relations, the defense industry, and information practice.[87] As military operations become more complex (more speed, scale, specialization, precision, coordination, etc.), command and control institutions (C4ISR) become even more essential for efficient combat operations. The economic function of institutions in general, after all, is to reduce transaction costs and improve information and efficiency. The military component of cyber power attempts to gain efficient military advantages through both the use and the abuse of information technology.

China and the United States both view information technology—networks, drones, AI, cyber, satellites, and so on—as a key to victory in any future war. China sees space and cyberspace capabilities as vital for impeding US global power projection, while the United States looks to networked, automated, autonomous capabilities to offset a growing Chinese threat. As ever, institutional efficiency is a double-edged sword. If intelligence fails or friction is intense, then forces built for efficiency become vulnerable to defeat in detail.[88] Military efficiency and effectiveness are not equivalent, and institutions are needed to translate one into the other. But when it comes to the institutional implementation of military informatization, the PLA's reach exceeds its grasp.

RMA WITH CHINESE CHARACTERISTICS

China keenly observed the information technology revolution in military affairs (RMA) in the United States, taking special interest in the first Gulf War (1991) and the Kosovo air war (1999).[89] The evergreen dream of Chinese informatization (as with US network-centric warfare and its recent reincarnation as "Joint All Domain Command and Control," or JADC2), is to combine pervasive reconnaissance, responsive networks, precision fires, and cyber and information operations to improve both efficiency and effectiveness. Smarter forces should be able to act more quickly and precisely to accomplish their mission, with better feedback on operations and outcomes.

The PLA identified space and cyberspace as key enablers, and thus serious coercive vulnerabilities, of the American way of war.[90] The US leviathan would be dead in the water without the ability to connect sensors to shooters. Enemy units that rely on radars and radio communications become vulnerable to electronic attacks on physical circuits, or cyber attacks on software logic. Information-based attacks may be used as a substitute for kinetic weapons (for instance, by deactivating a radar site rather than bombing it), or more likely as a complement (for instance, by creating a window of opportunity for an air strike to evade enemy air defenses). The common theme throughout Chinese primary sources is that mastery of big data analytics and network warfare will position China to win future wars between great powers.[91]

The US outspends China on defense by almost threefold. It also spends a larger proportion of its GDP on defense. An important difference, however, is that PLA missions are largely concentrated in China's local region, while the US military has global commitments. The US military, in this sense, is an economy force that relies on technology and information to project power around the world, using fewer people and platforms to service more conflicts and commitments. Intelligence and communication networks become vital for US military hegemony on the cheap. The same networks, from a Chinese perspective, are an Achilles heel. Any US intervention in an East Asian conflict scenario will be at the end of an eight-thousand-mile logistics chain, while China will be fighting in its front yard. The United States may have enduring advantages over China at a global level,[92] but the regional balance of power increasingly favors the PLA.[93]

IMPLEMENTING INFORMATION WARFARE

Chinese strategists point out that informatized warfare "will not only be a confrontation of military strength, but also a competition of comprehensive national strength. . . . Different from any form of warfare in history, information warfare is . . . a system-to-system overall confrontation."[94] Therefore, "realizing the effective integration of various systems is the fundamental way to win information warfare." This perspective stresses the importance of integrating domains or spaces (*kongjian*), forces (*liliang*), levels (*cengji*), styles (*yangshi*), and means (*shouduan*).[95]

To improve integration in informatized war, the PLA reorganized in 2015 to centralize control of electronic and cyber warfare, network operations, and military space operations in the SSF. The SSF embodied the Chinese view of information as the key strategic resource in modern war, and it also consolidated political control over a key military resource.[96] Fionna Cunningham argues further that growing Chinese reliance on the internet in previous years (see figure 3.4) created greater vulnerability to US cyber operations, which encouraged China to adopt a calibrated escalation policy to mitigate the risks of uncontrolled PLA operations.[97] Then in April 2024, the SSF was dissolved into a new Aerospace Force, Cyberspace Force, and Information Support Force, all subsumed directly under the Central Military Commission (CMC) run by Xi Jinping.[98]

Two major reorganizations in under a decade are suggestive of a political imperative for control. The first reform (creating the SSF) might be explained as a response to an increasingly dangerous threat environment, but the second reform (disbanding the SSF) is not obviously an improvement in this regard and might even be counterproductive for efficient military coordination. Consider by contrast that US Cyber Command was given more authority to take operational initiative in its first decade.[99] The strengthened oversight of the CMC thus suggests a different motivation. Authoritarian governments often "coup proof" their militaries to ensure political loyalty at the expense of military effectiveness.[100] A similar dynamic could handicap the efficient coordination of Chinese cyber operations to ensure political information control. Recall that the capacity of a clandestine organization requires the ability to balance administrative management with agile adaptation. It is likely that administration will dominate adaptation given a higher degree of centralization under Xi, more administrative purges, and increasing emphasis on ideological discipline. The motivations of the 2024 reorganization remain unclear, but China may be creating a coup-proofed Cyberspace Force that will be run by hacks rather than hackers.

Not too long before the SSF was disestablished, cyber intrusions linked to the PLA were reported under the code name Volt Typhoon. The Five Eyes governments (the United States, the United Kingdom, Canada, Australia, New Zealand) released a coordinated advisory in May 2023 warning that Volt Typhoon was "living off the land, which uses built-in network administration tools . . . to evade detection by blending in with normal Windows system and network activities, avoid endpoint detection and response (EDR) products that would alert on the introduction of third-party applications to the host, and limit the amount of activity that is captured in default logging configurations."[101] Microsoft reported on Volt Typhoon the same day—an example of close public-private coordination in the United States. It found that technical reconnaissance of "critical infrastructure organizations in Guam and elsewhere in the United States" had shifted to the "development of capabilities that could disrupt critical communications infrastructure between the United States and Asia region during future crises."[102] CISA further reported that "Volt Typhoon's choice of targets and pattern of behavior is not consistent with traditional cyber espionage or intelligence gathering operations, and the U.S. authoring agencies assess with high confidence that Volt Typhoon actors are pre-positioning themselves on IT networks to enable lateral movement to OT [operational technology, or industrial control systems] assets to disrupt functions."[103] This is suggestive of the SSF preparing the cyber environment for future military contingencies—that is, intelligence power enabling military power.[104]

But while Volt Typhoon may demonstrate PLA preparation for cyber warfare, activity must not be confused with advantage. As Joshua Rovner points out, "What is possible at the operational level may fizzle as a strategic tool."[105] Reporting on Volt Typhoon reflects not only improved organizational capacity on the Chinese side but also improved counterintelligence capacity on the Five Eyes side. The intelligence contest is indeed a contest. Another challenge for Volt Typhoon and other PLA cyber warfare units, as discussed, is the recent subordination of cyber forces directly under the CMC. The turbulence of another reorganization is likely to create additional friction for Chinese cyber operations, improving political micro-management while degrading operational initiative. Increased political control should be expected to affect the quality of Chinese cyber commanders and operators at the same time as Western counterintelligence is on high alert.

THE BALANCE OF FRICTION

Strategists in both China and the United States expect that cyber warfare will be a feature of any future conflict. For China, cyber warfare is an attractive means of interfering with US C4ISR networks, which are vital for projecting power to the opposite side of the planet. For the United States, cyber warfare is an attractive means of preempting an increasingly unfavorable military balance in the Pacific. Both states see automation and robotics as essential enablers of military power.

But information systems are more than just technology, and information dominance is more than just doctrine. China's space, cyber, and electronic warfare capabilities have improved over the years, but they still recapitulate the general organizational pathologies of the PLA. A recurring theme in PLA studies is that serious institutional weaknesses hinder its ability to successfully conduct joint "system of systems" operations in "informatized conditions."[106] The PLA's institutional weaknesses include organizational structure (cumbersome staffing and political controls), organizational culture (ideology and corruption), and command structure (rigid training and fraught civil-military relations). Integrating increasingly complex weapons and platforms, along with inadequate personnel training, remains a key challenge for the PLA in all operational domains. Moreover, as the PLA itself becomes more networked or informatized, the Cyberspace Force loses any asymmetric advantage it may have had, especially against an increasingly capable US Cyber Command.

The balance of friction affects any intelligence contest, both in peacetime and in war. Combined-arms warfare, joint operations, and multidomain campaigning are extremely challenging operational activities. They require extensive training, flexible command systems, talented personnel, and a willingness and ability to adapt and repair information systems in the face of tremendous uncertainty. Translated into military cyber operations, cyber warriors need to be lucky. Luck is when preparedness meets opportunity: A sophisticated clandestine operation requires a lot of preparation, and exposed vulnerable institutions provide fragile opportunities. It is not clear that the PLA is lucky in this sense. Indeed, the US military may be luckier.

The PLA may not be able to conduct effective cyber operations in a complex and dynamic conflict with high political stakes. The US military may also not be as fragile and vulnerable as the PLA's information dominance narrative assumes. CCP coup proofing in peacetime—filling the PLA with Xi loyalists and political commissars—is likely to hamper the performance of PLA cyber operators in wartime. The US military, by contrast, has a long tradition of encouraging its junior personnel to take the initiative in combat. The US military and intelligence community have decades of experience working through information friction in wartime conditions, but the PLA has only begun to reckon with the coordination challenges of informatized military operations. Large, scripted exercises are perhaps better for propaganda than for operational readiness. Effective multidomain operations require flexible organization combining bottom-up initiative and enterprise management. A fragmented authoritarian regime with paranoid information controls may find this difficult.

I assess that the balance of friction in cyberspace favors the United States. But friction, by its very nature, is impossible to measure precisely. Doing so would require detailed assessments based on classified information, which would still inevitably be incomplete. It is reasonable to expect, however, that increasing military reliance on coordinating institutions in an extremely complex operational domain will increase uncertainty about the relative balance of power. The extreme secrecy associated with cyber warfare makes it even harder for enemy forces to measure the balance of power. This has troubling implications for strategic stability. Seduced by its own doctrine, the PLA may *overestimate* its abilities and overlook the difficulties of cyber warfare in practice. Intimidated by the same doctrine, the US military may *underestimate* its ability to mitigate combat friction. Anything that creates uncertainty is a potential source of miscalculation and war.

Reinventing Counterintelligence

While there are many open questions about the economic impacts of Chinese espionage and the viability of Chinese cyber warfare (i.e., sabotage), the most successful type of Chinese secret statecraft is, without a doubt, counterintelligence. Western analysts often focus on the cyber threat from China to other countries, but much of China's intelligence effort is internally focused. For example, over half the 120 contracts in the I-Soon leak were with provincial and city MPS units, compared to just 22 with MSS.[107] Moreover, according to Sekoia, most "cyber operations attributed to the MSS are linked to MSS-provincial bureaus rather than the central organ," with ten times as many personnel working in local agencies.[108]

China has pioneered the practice of "networked authoritarianism," which uses information systems to bolster state control over civil society.[109] Beijing uses censorship, surveillance, and curated content to selectively promote narratives that support the CCP, communicating to the population what is tolerable and what is not. This can also be considered a form of reverse subversion, whereby the state conducts internal influence operations to discourage and disrupt political dissidence. The autonomous coercive capacity of the MPS and the People's Armed Police (PAP), in turn, makes this form of messaging far more credible than anything we saw in chapter 6 on Russian influence operations against the United States. Chinese counterintelligence subversion reinforces CCP governance by discouraging political competition and compelling cooperation.

INFORMATION CONTROL

"Psychological warfare" is a key plank of the "Three Warfares" strategy that the CCP uses to control ideological narratives (along with "legal warfare" and "public opinion warfare").[110] The greatest fear of the CCP is the emergence of domestic political movements with the potential to overthrow the modern Mandarin emperor, as has happened so many times in Chinese history. A close second is fear of foreign invasion or subversion leading to the same result. Addressing these concerns is a vital precondition for any form of informatization for the CCP.

Information control is a form of influence that sends signals to citizens that (1) dissent and factionalism will not be tolerated, and (2) there is no exit from state control. It is a way of keeping Chinese society together and protecting it from foreign "hostile forces" and the domestic "three evils" of terrorism, separatism, and extremism.[111] The emphasis on sovereign control prioritizes institutional independence from the common international order. The emphasis on cracking down on dissent prioritizes cooperation with the CCP.

China repurposed the flexible modular architecture of the internet and other Western information technologies to build the Great Firewall, the most sophisticated national system of censorship, surveillance, and propaganda in the world. Protected from the ideological dangers of the liberal order, the internet is reconstructed as an engine of social harmony and CCP control. Xi's 2019 speech during "Cybersecurity Week" thus focused on safety, innovation, and international cooperation: "It is necessary to adhere to both safety and controllability and open innovation, maintain cybersecurity based on an open environment, strengthen international cooperation, and enhance the general public's sense of gain, happiness, and security in cyberspace."[112]

Both the supply-side and demand-side factors of Chinese domestic information campaigns are very different than in Russian foreign campaigns (e.g., those discussed in chapter 6). To return to the marketing analogy,[113] the "product" of information control is netizen conformity with official norms of online behavior. State interventions backed up by police action raise the "price" of accessing banned content. State-sponsored "promotion" of approved messaging floods online forums with comments aligned with official preferences, and shouts down and shames offending viewpoints. The pervasive "placement"' of active and passive controls thus gives netizens more opportunity to create a more harmonious society (*hexie shehui*). The net result is the sorting of society into a more ideologically homogenous and controllable mass by excluding ideas that the CCP finds threatening.

A study of 468 incidents on WeChat between 2014 and 2019 found that posts that spread unverified information, criticized the government, and called into question its credibility were more likely to lead to arrest, detention, or prosecution.[114] Another study found that Chinese netizens can express criticism of the government, but only if doing so does not mobilize demonstrations against the government.[115] The messaging of China's censorship and control regime is credible because it is backed up by coercive force, which is usually missing from many foreign IO campaigns. Censorship can discourage demonstrations, which netizens can reliably expect to be met with a police response. Compliance with CCP intentionality is the "product," and the coercive capacity of the MPS and PAP persuasively raises the "price" of noncompliance with IO messages, which the CAC "places" and "promotes" throughout Chinese cyberspace.

This is an important reason why information operations tend to be more effective when deployed against a state's own population rather than against foreign audiences. The conventional wisdom about disinformation expects foreign subversion to produce dramatic effects, but information control at home has a much better chance of succeeding. In foreign influence campaigns, disinformation and propaganda are basically cheap talk. Messaging usually has little effect unless the foreign audience is already motivated to co-opt it for its own purposes (as we saw in the case of the 2016 election). But in a domestic society, information control works by complementing internal security services to bolster government control. This turns the conventional wisdom about information operations on its head. Cyberspace may be less useful for foreign subversion than for reinforcing authoritarian stability.

FRICTION AND FLOODING

Chinese internet censorship relies on technical barriers and active interventions to filter out harmful digital content and block unwanted external interventions.[116] China also employs service denial attacks for ideological objectives, in one case using the Great Firewall infrastructure to attack servers in the United States hosting censorship-evasion tools.[117] Surveillance projects co-developed with Huawei and partner vendors include voice recording analysis, detention center monitoring, location tracking of political individuals of interest, police surveillance in the Xinjiang region, and corporate tracking of employees and customers.[118] To gain access to China's 750 million netizens, Western firms have also been known to facilitate Chinese information control, as demonstrated by censorship features on Google's Project Dragonfly, an Android search app in China.[119]

Chinese censorship incorporates elements of deception, or (im)plausible deniability, to complement open propaganda and security laws. Margaret Roberts shows that Chinese censorship relies more on *friction* and *flooding* than on fear.[120] Overt censorship threatens violators with punishments, but reliance on fear tends to provoke anger and can be difficult to enforce. Instead, Chinese censorship is deliberately ambiguous, meaning that it can be hard to distinguish between system outages and intentional filtering (friction), or between genuine support for the regime and intentional manipulation (flooding). Users learn quickly what is allowable and what is not, while the state's "implausible deniability" about censorship enables everyone to save face.[121] Deviants who want to circumvent the Great Firewall can find ways to do so, but then in the process, they self-identify as someone deserving more attention from the police. Officials who need information to do their jobs can also circumvent controls, even as they uphold the policies of the state. Ironically, the porousness of Chinese censorship makes it more robust!

Chinese information control implements a mixed influence strategy combining overt disinformation (sorting loyal citizens) and access denial (blocking harmful content). Chinese information controls create barriers by censoring forbidden content, blocking access to offensive websites, removing problematic discourse, and throttling offending connections. Chinese trolls employed or inspired by counterintelligence agencies masquerade as grassroots netizens (colloquially known as *wumao*, or "the fifty-cent army").[122] Chinese information controls embody a form of disclosure to the population about what the government will and will not tolerate.

Chinese internet-control measures have generally become more pervasive and robust under Xi Jinping. As Xi observed in 2016, "Cybersecurity and informatization are mutually complementary. Security is the precondition of development, development is the guarantee of security, security and development must progress in step. We must absolutely understand that throughout all ages, many technologies are 'double-edged swords,' on the one hand, they may enrich society and enrich the people, on the other hand, they may also be used by some people to harm the social interest and the interest of the masses."[123] Accordingly, Xi consolidated and strengthened the administrative center of information control (the CAC) and advanced new laws such as the 2017 Cybersecurity Law.[124]

The perverse effect is that civil society ends up in a relationship of dependency on the state for its own political communication. Reciprocally, the state becomes dependent on the citizenry to amplify its counterintelligence effectiveness. As the MSS's WeChat debut in July 2023 urged, "People's governments at all levels and relevant departments should organize anti-espionage security prevention publicity and education," and "television, cultural, and Internet information services should carry out targeted anti-espionage publicity and education for the entire society." This would enable "citizens and organizations to report behaviors that endanger national security."[125]

Global information infrastructure internationalizes China's domestic concerns. China becomes an exporter of information control as it ransacks the networks of Western media companies and China-focused nongovern-mental organizations. Another example of the internationalization of domestic information control is the controversy around TikTok based in part on fears of CCP influence via TikTok's algorithm.[126] But international influence of this sort lacks the coercive backstop of the PAP that makes domestic Chinese information operations so persuasive. As I discussed in chapter 5, the technological supply of influence cannot be evaluated sepa-rately from the international political demand for it.

The Contradictions of Cyber Power

The rise of China is the defining geopolitical event of the post–Cold War era, and the commercial internet grew dramatically during the same era. It would be surprising if these developments were not related. Indeed, the internet powered globalization, and globalization powered Chinese growth. The use of information technology, by fair means and foul, has helped China become a great power. Understanding Chinese cyber power thus helps us to understand the changing balance of power in general in the twenty-first century.

In the decades after the Cold War, Chinese grand strategy was character-ized by restraint and reform. But with the rise of Xi Jinping, China became more assertive and authoritarian. The fundamental political imperative for almost everything in Chinese policy is to bolster the rule of the CCP, and increasingly of Xi himself. The control imperative drives Chinese invest-ment in the digital economy, industrial espionage, cyber warfare, and infor-mation control. If the millennial dream of the internet was that democracy would follow technology, then China has shown how to unbundle eco-nomic and political liberalization. The Chinese appropriation of the digital infrastructure of liberal order (cyber superpower) aspires to capture the benefits of economic globalization while protecting the political sover-eignty of China, exploiting many different governments and nonstate actors in the process.

Cyber power in general is fraught with tensions because digital networks enable and link all other forms of power. Cyberspace constrains and enables economic power, intelligence power, military power, internal security, and almost everything else. As discussed above, internet standards and China's "Internet Plus" policies embody Beijing's quest for infrastructure power, a form of digitally enabled governance. Computer espionage conducted by the PLA and MSS, meanwhile, relies on Chinese intelligence power. Infor-matized warfare, centralized under the CMC in the Cyberspace Force (one of the successor organizations to the SSF), embodies the application of covert action strategies to augment military power. Information control, which includes the so-called Great Firewall of China, amplifies the CCP's bargaining power over the Chinese population. These different facets of cyber power can create synergy or interference. In the case of China, the inherent contradictions of cyber power loom large.

Everything about China is complicated, and cyber power is no exception. Chinese society is a complex mixture of capitalism and socialism in a shifting multipolar environment. China is deeply invested in the stability and functionality of shared global information infrastructure, where US actors still have disproportionate influence. The internet enables not only economic growth, which enhances CCP legitimacy, but also civil society, which threatens CCP control. Chinese intelligence and security agencies thus exploit the same infrastructure for economic and political advantage. The MSS infiltrates the US-dominated internet ecosystem to subvert US interests, while the PLA appropriates it to threaten the US military. As the information economy both empowers the CCP and contributes to its sense of insecurity, comprehensive censorship and surveillance bolster regime control. These contradictions shape the expression of Chinese cyber power, and even Marxist dialectics offer no easy path through them.

Different components of Chinese cyber power evolve with institutional changes at the international and domestic levels. These trends are moving in the opposite direction, with gradual decoupling internationally and increasing consolidation domestically. These two entwined institutional dynamics account for the unique character of Chinese cyber power.

First, economic liberalization abroad—reliance on collective institutions— is weakening. The weakening of the liberal peace at the international level makes *external* cyber conflict somewhat more complicated for China. With growing barriers to connectivity at the international level in the form of cybersecurity controls and economic sanctions, we should expect Chinese cyber operations to become more difficult, which in turn encourages greater investment in professional organization to overcome barriers.

Second, authoritarian consolidation at home—reliance on organic institutions—is strengthening. The strengthening of the authoritarian peace at the domestic level enables the Chinese government to enhance control in *internal* cyber conflict. With the strengthening of organic institutions at the domestic level, we should expect greater investment in information-control systems to discourage the expression of incompatible interests. Authoritarian consolidation should translate into more robust counterintelligence and internal security, which should improve influence over the domestic population.

The idiosyncrasy of Chinese cyber (super)power is itself instructive. I have stressed throughout this book that institutions shape cyber performance, so we should expect the unique institutional context of China to produce a particular expression of cyber power. It is different from US (or Russian, British, or Israeli) cyber power. This particularity underscores the general importance of institutional context.

Cyber power tends to mirror power in general. The Harvard Kennedy School compiled a "National Cyber Power Index," with cyber power defined as "the effective deployment of cyber capabilities by a state to achieve its national objectives."[127] The 2022 index roughly tracks the overall balance of power. By many measures of power, the United States remains ahead of China, even as China has pulled ahead of everyone else.[128] The United States and China likewise rank first and second in cyber power, while other countries cluster far behind.[129] The two leading powers in the world are as different from each other as they are from everyone else. This implies that the cyber power of the United States and China should have an outsized effect on global cybersecurity.

US-China relations are a complex pattern of cooperation and competition. These same conditions encourage secret statecraft. The unprecedented degree of economic interdependence between two rival power centers leads to an unprecedented potential for cyber conflict between them. Cybersecurity in the US-China relationship is thus a quarrel between "frenemies with benefits."[130] The mutual benefits of interconnectivity enable the unilateral benefits of cyber operations, and for the same reasons constrain their severity. Secret statecraft flourishes between peace and war, and increasingly between the infrastructure of liberal hegemony and the confrontation of geopolitical rivals. China's complicated experiment with networked authoritarianism is also perhaps a cautionary tale for the United States. The final chapter of this book will unpack the paradoxical implications of secret statecraft in cyberspace.

Conclusion

Good News and Bad News About Cyber Warfare

The cyberwar narrative is evergreen. "In 2023," warned an economist at the University of Chicago, "there will almost certainly be a major cyberattack. It could shut down Taiwan's airports and trains, paralyze British military computers, or swing a US election. This is terrifying, because each time this happens, there is a small risk that the aggrieved side will respond aggressively, maybe at the wrong party, and (worst of all) even if it carries the risk of nuclear escalation."[1]

Throughout 2023, there were reports of many cyber attacks, including the Volt Typhoon intrusions attributed to China and relentless Russian operations in Ukraine. But none of them prompted a dramatic counteraction. In 2024 there finally was a major cyber attack—the Salt Typhoon breach of US telecommunications—but the United States did not aggressively escalate. Meanwhile in Ukraine, Russian cyber operations reverted to an emphasis on espionage over sabotage.[2]

So long as society depends on computers, the possibility of cyber-enabled destruction and escalation can never be ruled out. Some vital systems remain vulnerable, and some threat actors are quite capable. But just because something is technically possible does not mean it is politically probable. In the historical record of cyber conflict, which is now decades long, we see far more cybercrime than cyber warfare, more espionage than sabotage, and more minor incidents than major disruptions. Most threat activity flies so far beneath the radar that it goes undetected or unreported altogether. This does *not* mean that cybersecurity is unimportant in politics. On the contrary, cybersecurity matters precisely *because* it is other than war.

I have argued throughout this book that cyber competition is a form of secret statecraft, or the use of organized deception for strategic advantage. Secret statecraft—which includes espionage, sabotage, subversion, and counterintelligence—can improve the efficiency of competition by quietly improving information or influencing behavior. Technology is increasing the scope, scale, speed, and general complexity of all kinds of secret state-craft. As a result, innovation in cyber conflict is filling out the bottom end of the conflict spectrum rather than the top. This perspective helps to explain the empirical pattern of cyber threat activity that we observe—a lot of little but little of a lot. This is cold comfort, because a lot more is always possible.

The Exception That Proves the Rule

This book opened with an account of a supply chain attack. Russian espionage via SolarWinds showed how the compromise of an obscure digital service could imperil the data of thousands of organizations, but this was an innovation in intelligence rather than warfare. As this book neared production, however, the world witnessed a far more devastating supply chain attack. At three thirty in the afternoon on September 17, 2024, Hezbollah operatives throughout Lebanon received messages on their pagers, ostensibly from Hezbollah leadership.[3] A few seconds later, the pagers exploded, killing at least 12 and injuring over 2,700. The next day, Hezbollah's two-way radios started exploding as well, killing 20 and injuring 450 more.[4] Several children were among the victims. Israel followed up with hundreds of air strikes on Hezbollah leadership, Hezbollah retaliated with rocket attacks, and Lebanon plunged into war again.

Does this mean that the cyberwar narrative has come to pass? Yes and no. A clever hack of a communication system did cause mass casualties, followed by military escalation. Whether this counts as a cyber attack depends on whether we limit the scope of the concept to digital hacking. Given that "cyber" comes from "cybernetics," I am inclined to entertain a broad definition encompassing all means of communication and control. As such, the pager attack looks like a remarkable outlier in the history of cyber operations. But even so, a key element of the cyberwar narrative is that logical code can create physical effects all by itself. Here, however, the Mossad physically intervened in a material supply chain to disguise real explosives and remote switches inside pagers, reportedly through a Hungarian front company that sold Taiwanese pagers to Hezbollah.[5] The Mossad created improvised explosive devices, not logic bombs.

The cyberwar narrative further stresses that the barriers to entry for catastrophic attack are low (and thus offense dominates defense). But this was a complicated operation, years in the making, supported by extensive reconnaissance and covert action. The attacker was a sophisticated state spy service with decades of experience in remote control assassination, including the employment of booby-trapped phones and robotic snipers. According to two former Mossad agents, Hezbollah first bought sixteen thousand sabotaged radios from a front company ten years earlier, and then later bought five thousand pagers from a different front replete with advertising and internet reviews; according to one agent, "We have an incredible array of possibilities of creating foreign companies that have no way of being traced back to Israel. . . . Shell companies over shell companies to affect the supply chain to our favor."[6] Israel exercised incredible strategic patience and disciplined discretion by carefully preparing an elaborate trap that could be used only once.

Military escalation did indeed follow the pager attack, but it was not initiated by the aggrieved party, and it was not unintended. The ultimate timing of Israel's offensive in Lebanon may have been triggered by indications that Hezbollah was getting suspicious about its communications, but Israel's campaign plan was already in place. The shock-and-awe offensive opened with the mass assassination of Hezbollah operatives and the sudden loss of communications. This surprise caused confusion and paranoia throughout the Hezbollah organization, which was then systematically decapitated by the Israeli Air Force and decimated by an Israeli ground invasion. Israel was able to eliminate many senior commanders in rapid succession, including Hezbollah leader Hassan Nasrallah, thanks to major improvements made in collection and analysis in the previous years.[7] Communications sabotage, therefore, was just one part of a major multidomain campaign that had been planned well in advance. This stands the cyberwar narrative on its head: Instead of cyber sabotage triggering an escalation to war, Israeli plans for war called for communication sabotage.

The framework of secret statecraft provides a more satisfying interpretation. We can dispense with a definitional debate about cyberwar and focus on the underlying political logic of deception. Israel ran a long con for a decade to fool Hezbollah into willingly but unwittingly sabotaging itself. One irony is that Hezbollah relied on radios and pagers because it was rightly worried about the security of its cell phones. Israeli intelligence both encouraged this paranoia and offered a treacherous alternative. Hezbollah's counterintelligence precaution thus drove its operatives into the crosshairs of Israeli assassins. As in the exploitations of SolarWinds and BeyondTrust, the victims trusted their security to an information system that became a vector for attack. But unlike those pure cyber operations, which only stole data at scale, the attack on Hezbollah was lethal, killing human beings at scale.

Deception is efficient because the victim does some of the work. Israel used organized deception to improve strategic efficiency by inflicting many enemy casualties with little friendly exposure. Indeed, the secret pager exploit promised such dramatic cost savings that it probably made war more attractive to Israel than diplomacy: Information asymmetry produced strategic instability.[8] This is a very different pattern than the US-Israel cyber campaign examined in chapter 5. Stuxnet provided a covert counterproliferation option in lieu of war, but the pager sabotage provided an option for starting a war by surprise. One kept the peace while the other ended it. One remained in the cyber domain while the other crossed domains. But both operations were intended to reduce the costs of war, either by avoiding it altogether or by fighting with a decisive advantage.

Indeed, Israel's failure to anticipate a devastating attack by Hamas on October 7, 2023, exactly fifty years after a massive surprise attack by Egypt, illustrates the disastrous costs of being deceived. While Jerusalem was distracted by domestic politics, thinning its defenses in Gaza and ignoring warning signs, Hamas launched a surprise assault that killed 1,200 Israeli civilians, precipitating a ghastly war that killed perhaps fifty times as many Palestinians.[9] There are many varieties of secret statecraft, but all aim to gain an unfair advantage over an unwitting opponent. Whether this improves or degrades strategic stability depends on the underlying political interests.

Israel was successful in sabotaging Hezbollah and gaining a strategic advantage, finally, because it met two hard-to-meet conditions for intelligence performance. Israeli intelligence was not only very good but also lucky enough to have obliging targets and a priceless opportunity. It remains to be seen whether Israel's technological advantages in efficiency can be converted into lasting political effectiveness. The history of chronic conflict in the region offers few reasons for optimism.

Empirical Findings

This book has developed a theory of intelligence performance, which is the operational foundation of secret statecraft. I have argued that persistent secret access to targets depends on vulnerable institutions and clandestine organization. These two institutional conditions change over time as intelligence competitors interact and react. Technological complexity complicates this interaction without providing lasting systematic advantage to either side. Put simply, institutional context determines intelligence performance.

I have used the theory to explain several important historical intelligence campaigns, summarizing the key variables in table C.1. Using the coding scheme from chapter 2, asterisks indicate more favorable conditions or better performance. Some coding is mixed because conditions varied within the case. Process tracing in these cases revealed strong support for the theory. I found that when both conditions were met, deception specialists were able to gain and maintain secret access to targets; when not, operations faltered. Additional support for the theory emerges from less detailed shadow cases that I have discussed throughout the book, including below, as listed chronologically in table C.2.

Table C.1 Intelligence performance in campaign studies

Case	Secret statecraft	Vulnerable institutions	Clandestine organization	Intelligence performance
Bletchley Park WWII (chap. 4)	Espionage (SIGINT)	Exposed (German cryptosystems)*	Sophisticated (British GC&CS)*	Persistent access (sustained success)*
Stuxnet / Op. Olympic Games 2000s (chap. 5)	Covert action (sabotage and diplomacy)	Disconnected (airgaps and vulnerable systems)‡	Sophisticated (advanced SIGINT agencies)*	Complex ops (mixed outcome of compromise and JCPOA)‡
Russian election interference 2016 (chap. 6)	Covert action (subversion)	Exposed (open digital media ecosystem)*	Dependent (US audiences reacting to noisy Russian messaging)‡	Loss of control (demand-driven political sorting)‡
SolarWinds Dec. 2020 (introduction)	Espionage (software supply chain)	Secure (but subtle vulnerability in development environment)‡	Sophisticated* → Noisy‡	Complex ops‡ → Infeasible†

* Best performance
‡ Reduced performance
† Worst performance

Table C.2 Intelligence performance in shadow cases

Case	Secret statecraft	Vulnerable institutions	Clandestine organization	Intelligence performance
German intel WWII (chap. 4)	Counterintel	Secure (disciplined security at GC&CS)‡	Incapable (poor security & coordination failures)†	Infeasible (systematic failure)†
Op. Bodyguard 1944 (chap. 4)	Subversion	Exposed (German bias and poor counterintel)*	Sophisticated (London Controlling Section)*	Successful military deception (Germany thins defenses before D-Day)*
Kim Philby 1940s–50s (introduction)	Espionage	Exposed* → Inaccessible†	Dependent‡ → Incapable†	Persistent access* → Infeasible†

(continued)

Case	Type	Exposed/Disconnected	Capability	Control/Outcome
Internet security 1970s–2010s (chap. 3)	Counterintel	Mixed (exposed ARPANET, secure PLI, maturing security industry)	Mixed (early hackers are barely capable, but later APTs are sophisticated)	Mixed (growing cybercrime, complex intel contests)
Great Firewall 2000s–2010s (chap. 7)	Counterintel	Disconnected (weak—censorship is selective)‡	Mixed (noisy Great Firewall vs. dependent netizens)	Mixed (friction, flooding, contested access)
PRC IP theft 2000s–2010s (chap. 7)	Espionage	Mixed (exposed "happy times" then increasingly secure or disconnected)	Mixed (early PLA is noisy; later MSS is more sophisticated)	Mixed (some persistence, with increasing operational complexity)
Op. Orchard (IAF) 2007 (chap. 5)	Sabotage (warfare)	Exposed (Syrian radars)*	Sophisticated (Israeli Air Force)*	Access (enabling deliberate disconnection to create a tactical window)*
Op. Nitro Zeus 2010? (chap. 5)	Sabotage (warfare)	Disconnected (airgaps and complex vulnerabilities)‡	Sophisticated (NSA and nascent US Cyber Command)*	Complex ops (unexecuted contingency plan)‡
NSOGroup 2016–23 (chap. 3)	Espionage (NSO) and Counterintelligence (clients)	Mixed (secure iOS and exposed civil society)	Mixed (sophisticated NSO with dependent and noisy clients)	Mixed (complex ops, loss of control, compromise and sanctions)
NotPetya 2017 (conclusion)	Sabotage (disruption)	Exposed*	Dependent‡	Loss of control (uncontrolled spread)‡
Russian election interference 2018–20 (chap. 6)	Subversion	Disconnected (US counterintel ops and platform controls)‡	Mixed (noisy Russian ops dependent on US audiences)	Infeasible (Russia is irrelevant to US disinfo and polarization)†
MS Exchange 2021 (chap. 7)	Espionage	Exposed*	Noisy (multiple PRC threat actors)‡	Loss of control‡
Colonial Pipeline 2021 (conclusion)	Sabotage (ransomware)	Exposed*	Noisy (must signal for extortion)‡	Loss of control (ransom paid then recovered)‡
Viasat hack 2022 (conclusion)	Sabotage (warfare)	Exposed*	Mixed (sophisticated GRU with noisy outcome)	Mixed (temporary denial, collateral damage)
Russia in Ukraine 2022–24 (conclusion)	Mixed (espionage, sabotage, subversion)	Mixed (disconnection due to war friction and secure/inaccessible due to capable defenders)	Mixed (sophisticated GRU with noisy and evolving tactics)	Mixed (temporary tactical successes yet chronic contestation)
Volt Typhoon 2023–24 (chap. 7)	Espionage (planning for sabotage)	Mixed (exposed infrastructure becoming more secure)	Mixed (once noisy PLA becoming more sophisticated)	Loss of control (compromised op with ambiguous signaling value)‡

Table C.2 (continued)

Case	Secret statecraft	Vulnerable institutions	Clandestine organization	Intelligence performance
Salt Typhoon 2024 (chap. 7)	Espionage	Exposed (telecoms providers with poor security)*	Mixed (sophisticated MSS-linked group with some noisiness)	Persistent access (maintained through discovery)*
CrowdStrike 2024 (chap. 2)	Counterintel	Mixed (Secure system becomes exposed after update)	Dependent (Reliance on Microsoft platform and Falcon service)‡	Loss of control (major outage)‡
Hezbollah pagers 2024 (conclusion)	Sabotage (warfare)	Exposed (via front companies providing connectivity to devices offering a false sense of security)*	Sophisticated (Mossad and Israeli military)*	Persistent access (waiting 10 years to coordinate assassinations with combat ops)*

* Best performance
‡ Reduced performance
† Worst performance

The case studies generally provide support for the theory, even as these cases are not perfectly comparable. The cases in table C.1 are all coherent intelligence campaigns sustained over time by an identifiable deception specialist, but they involve different technologies, operational concepts, and political purposes. There is even more heterogeneity in table C.2. All are intelligence contests, but some are discrete incidents (Orchard), while others are longer campaigns (Bodyguard) or mere plans (Nitro Zeus). Some focus on macro trends (internet security) and others on micro dynamics (Exchange). Nevertheless, I consider this heterogeneity to be a feature, not a bug. Showing that the theory applies to a broad repertoire of cases demonstrates its generality.

These case studies are not just single data points but complicated historical episodes. Many cases feature fine-grained variation in conditions, or changes over time. Tables C.1 and C.2 thus depict temporal variation in a few cases (SolarWinds, Philby) to show how changing conditions produce different outcomes. I have discussed other nuances in the text. The intrinsic complexity of intelligence results in a lot of mixed coding. Indeed, the ambiguity of cyber operations is the whole point of the theory, not a shortfall. I find that within-case variation is largely consistent with the expectations of the theory, which showcases its ability to handle complexity.

My primary focus in this book has been theory building, which is a task well served by qualitative comparison. The two conditions of the theory are perhaps best understood as heuristics that guide the assessment of inherently complex phenomena. They encourage attention to both "external" and "internal" institutional context in intelligence contests, which helps to avoid myopic fixation on technical tradecraft. Thick description of these conditions helps to clarify the workings of the theory in real-world circumstances, which are always complex and ambiguous. Future studies might devise quantitative identification strategies to further refine and test the theory.

Recall that the notion of intelligence performance is scoped narrowly to the operational level. Strategic success in secret statecraft is more indirect. This helps to explain why even the nominal successes in tables C.1 and C.2 are associated with ambiguous or minor political impacts. Bletchley Park is the most successful case in the book, and even its military contributions were indirect. Some commanders could use Ultra better than others, and all still had to win on the battlefield. If the dearth of asterisks in the tables suggests that intelligence performance cannot be taken for granted, the picture may be even less encouraging for its strategic impact.

Intelligence success is underrepresented in my cases. Indeed, intelligence failure gets much more attention in IR scholarship generally. The intelligence campaigns that we can study tend to be those that did not meet the conditions for intelligence performance, resulting in accidental compromise.

The empirical record of cyber conflict is thus a chronicle of offensive missteps. This is another reason why I included Bletchley Park, a richly documented case of intelligence success. There are almost certainly many successful US, Dutch, or Israeli campaigns that we will not hear about for a long time, if ever. But the missingness of cyber data is probably biased in support of secret statecraft and against the cyberwar narrative. A lot of threat activity is missing from public databases because deception specialists prefer to work in the shadows. Discretion, rather than escalation, produces a long tail of stealthy intrusions that we never detect. Destructive cyber warfare, by contrast, is unlikely to remain hidden. Indeed, coercive diplomacy depends on not hiding harm. Cyber operations are rarely black or white, but increasingly gray.

POTENTIAL CRITIQUES

Technology changes fast. Russia intervened to support Trump nearly a decade before this book was published. Stuxnet was conceived nearly two decades ago. This is an eternity in cyber time. But the argument in this book does not depend on the details of any given technology. I argue that cyberspace enables new versions of the old phenomena of secret statecraft. The nature of secret statecraft does not change, even though its conduct changes constantly.

Technology is complex. Accordingly, complexity is a major theme of this book. Much of the ostensible complexity of technology is really a reflection of complex interdependencies among numerous actors and social practices. The cases in table C.2 span over eighty years (from Bodyguard to the pager attack), a period in which intelligence practice became ever more complex. If the same theory can explain all these cases, then the theory will likely remain relevant as the technological state of the art becomes even more complex. Future studies can test this claim, of course.

Technology X is different. Perhaps artificial intelligence, quantum computing, or synthetic biology will transform cybersecurity. Many claims about emerging technologies tend to repeat familiar themes of the cyberwar narrative: Offense is dominant, catastrophe is imminent, and the United States lags behind. But there are many reasons—organizational, economic, strategic, rhetorical—to be skeptical of these claims. There is not space in this book to evaluate claims about specific emerging technologies, but I generally expect them to make institutional context even more important, not less.[10] Secret statecraft is primed to become both more complex and more frustrating, but this will not fundamentally transform politics.

Important cases are missing. I have not covered many of the "greatest hits" of cybersecurity, such as the Russian service-denial attacks in Estonia in 2007 and Georgia in 2008 or the North Korean attack on Sony in 2014 and WannaCry ransomware in 2017. Nor do I discuss anything after 2024, for obvious reasons. I have instead focused on well-known and well-documented cases that demonstrate both continuity and change in secret statecraft. My aim in this book has been to develop and substantiate an IR theory of intelligence performance that applies to cybersecurity, not to provide a comprehensive guide to cyber history and policy.[11]

These cases are state-centric. This may be unsurprising for an IR book on secret statecraft, but nonstate actors are ubiquitous in cybersecurity. Indeed, the civilianization of intelligence has been an important theme throughout this book. There have been prominent commercial (counter)intelligence actors in many cases (e.g., SolarWinds, CrowdStrike, NSOGroup). But the growing prominence of civilian actors does not mean that state actors are any less important. On the contrary, nation-state spy agencies have considerable capacity for deception, as well as the support of other coercive instruments of statecraft. Cyberspace tends to make powerful actors even more powerful. While there is indeed a state-centric bias in my cases, there is also a state-centric bias at the higher end of the spectrum of cyber conflict.

Cybercrime gets short shrift. Financially motivated theft and fraud account for the bulk of malicious activity in cyberspace. Criminal ransomware attacks create serious disruptions, such as degrading hospital services. Cybercrime can also have geopolitical consequences, as in North Korea's efforts to fund its nuclear program with ransomware attacks and cryptocurrency theft. This book has indeed focused mainly on national security cases; nonetheless, the theory of intelligence performance is general enough to interpret criminal cases as well. As a plausibility probe, consider the May 2021 attack on Colonial Pipeline. An Eastern European hacker group known as DarkSide conducted a ransomware attack against a major petroleum company in the eastern United States. It resulted in regional shortages of gasoline and jet fuel for five days and provoked a comprehensive government response.[12] I assess that Colonial's information systems were exposed (connected and vulnerable), but DarkSide had to be noisy (capable yet indiscreet) in order to extort Colonial. As the theory expects, DarkSide lost control after Colonial suspended operations out of an abundance of caution. Colonial did pay a ransom of $4.4 million in Bitcoin, but the Department of Justice recovered about 85 percent of it.[13] DarkSide achieved a narrow tactical victory (sabotage and compellence) but ultimately did not benefit from it and created a less permissive environment for future operations. Future research could explore more nonstate cybercrime.

You never know! Past performance does not ensure future results. Yet this is precisely why we need theory. The theory in this book highlights disincentives for escalation, including security imperatives and control problems. A basic point is that the constitutive role of institutions makes cyber operations unreliable in war, since war tends to degrade institutions. Cyberspace can indeed be useful in war, especially for intelligence support to operations in other domains (i.e., land, sea, air, space). But even then, fog and friction complicate cross-domain coordination. When institutional conditions are permissive, competitors can use cyber warfare to inflict friction on enemy organizations and societies, but the same friction makes it risky for them to expect too much of cyber warfare. Cyberspace is more useful for other things.

Cyber Warfare in Ukraine

One might expect cyber warfare to play a significant role in the war between Russia and Ukraine, which is still ongoing as of this writing. Both sides have been more than willing to inflict death and destruction on one another, so they should be willing to go for the jugular in cyberspace as well. Yet the war does not offer much support for the cyberwar narrative. On the contrary, the wartime cyber contest in Ukraine is more consistent with the secret statecraft framework of this book. While it is risky to speculate on an ongoing conflict, I will hazard a few observations that I expect will stand up.

The war in Ukraine is the most intense episode of land warfare in Europe since World War II, as well as the most dangerous nuclear crisis since the Cold War. At the lower end of the conflict spectrum, we see not only hacking and disinformation but also economic sanctions, food blockades, infrastructure sabotage, and contested commercial space operations. This all puts the marginal role of cybersecurity into perspective. Yet it is important to appreciate that no weapon, in any domain, has turned the tide. The war has lasted longer and cost more than all parties expected, and all have found new ways to frustrate one another. Cyberspace is an active domain of conflict and, for the same reasons, an indecisive one.

Secret statecraft, and not just in cyberspace, has been a continuous part of the war in Ukraine since it began in 2014. After the Maidan Revolution in Kyiv, Russia sent soldiers without insignia, or "little green men," to occupy Crimea. Moscow also intensified military support for Russian separatists in the Donbass. Ukraine soon became a test bed for Russian covert action and espionage in cyberspace, and it also catalyzed the improvement of Ukrainian counterintelligence.[14] Cyberspace was actively contested, but service-denial attacks remained uncoordinated with military operations.[15] The frozen conflict in Ukraine prior to 2022 recapitulated a familiar pattern in coercive diplomacy: Russian sabotage and subversion only stiffened Ukrainian resolve.[16] Ukraine gradually became better at countering Russian "gray zone" operations, thanks in part to Western assistance. As Russia's middle option between peace and war started to seem less promising, Vladimir Putin gambled on escalation.[17] Russia initiated a large-scale mobilization in 2021 and then invaded in February 2022.

The most active Russian threat actor in Ukraine has been the Main Intelligence Directorate of the General Staff (GRU). The GRU Information Operations Troops (Unit 55111) include the Eighty-Fifth Main Special Services Center (Unit 26165, a.k.a. APT28, Fancy Bear) and the Main Center for Special Technologies (Unit 74455, a.k.a. APT44, Sandworm).[18] Another GRU unit, specializing in assassinations and bombings, also has a small and rather immature cyber group (Unit 29155, a.k.a. Cadet Blizzard).[19] Coordination across GRU teams, much less with other hacking teams in the FSB or SVR, is limited, which is a liability for the condition of clandestine organization. APT28 (Fancy Bear) tends to focus more on espionage, including hacking the US Democratic National Committee in 2016. APT44 is Russia's premier cyber warfare unit, conducting the full spectrum of "information confrontation" operations, to use the Russian doctrinal term of art. APT44 attacked the Ukrainian electrical power grid twice, in 2015 and 2016; this demonstrated the feasibility of a classic cyberwar scenario, but Ukraine mitigated the outages within hours.[20]

One GRU campaign in Ukraine inadvertently created economic losses in Europe estimated in the billions of dollars.[21] In 2017, APT44 deployed NotPetya, a data wiper masquerading as ransomware that spilled beyond Ukraine's borders. NotPetya spread quickly because it combined the Mimikatz hacking tool with the NSA EternalBlue exploit (leaked by the Russian Shadow Brokers hacking group via a treacherous contractor with the NSA).[22] In terms of intelligence performance, the Ukrainian accounting software targeted by NotPetya (and, to a lesser extent, European commercial networks as well) can be coded as exposed. APT44 was somewhat dependent on third-party capabilities and was rather indiscreet. This combination of conditions resulted in the uncontrolled spread of NotPetya beyond its Ukrainian target. Russian subversion in Ukraine generally prioritized speed and scale over controllability, inflicting disruption without gaining any obvious strategic advantage.[23] The New Jersey Superior Court later ruled that NotPetya did not qualify for a "Hostile/Warlike Action" insurance exclusion.[24] Legally and conceptually, NotPetya was a peacetime sabotage operation, not an act of cyberwar.

Operations like NotPetya helped to create a reputation for the GRU as a ruthless cyber threat. But the opening phase of the Russian invasion disappointed those who had expected it to, as one journalist wrote, "give the world its first experience of a true cyber war."[25] Skeptics were quick to decry the absence of cyberwar in Ukraine.[26] Four factors help to explain this early nonstory. First, Russia probably did not plan to dismantle Ukraine's digital infrastructure, expecting instead to use it after a quick regime-change operation. Second, even if Russia did plan a cyber offensive, its intelligence agencies were as shambolic as the rest of the Russian effort. Russian spies succumbed to infighting and wishful thinking, failing to integrate operations with the rest of the Russian military.[27] Third, combat friction and dynamic network conditions undoubtedly undermined Russian cyber-planning assumptions.[28] The battle for Kyiv was fluid and confusing as Russian forces lunged on the capital and were repulsed by an improvised Ukrainian counteroffensive.[29] Self-organized civilian hacktivists on both sides further complicated the cyber operating environment.[30]

Fourth and most importantly, Ukraine and its allies put up a vigorous defense in cyberspace. Ukraine had ample strategic warning.[31] The Ukrainian intelligence service ran counterintelligence operations against FSB agent networks, and Ukraine's computer emergency response team (CERT-UA) countered GRU intrusions.[32] Kyiv also got by with a little help from its friends.[33] From December 2021 to March 2022, US Cyber Command deployed a "hunt forward team" from the Cyber National Mission Force "to identify and address any potential threats on [Ukrainian] networks and mitigate in order of severity."[34] *The New York Times* reported that the FBI acted on a secret court order "to go into domestic corporate networks and remove [Russian] malware, sometimes without the company's knowledge."[35] And the Biden administration publicly released intelligence on a number of occasions to "pre-bunk" Russian covert disinformation operations, undermining Russian pretexts for invasion and building coalition support for Ukraine.[36]

Throughout the war, US Cyber Command proactively countered Russian operations related to Ukraine,[37] and the US intelligence community also provided cyber-enabled intelligence support to the Ukrainian military.[38] Beginning in February 2022, Russian hackers conducted DDoS attacks, web defacements, and a spate of wiper campaigns targeting Ukrainian government systems and public infrastructure.[39] These disruptions were temporary and were mitigated shortly after detection. Commercial actors played a prominent role. Microsoft neutralized several Russian wipers and botnets, and its cloud infrastructure helped to defend Ukrainian government systems.[40] ESET partnered with CERT-UA to preempt a new version of the GRU Industroyer malware targeting the Ukrainian electricity grid.[41] Firms such as Amazon, ESET, Mandiant, Microsoft, and SpaceX (Starlink) improved Ukrainian cybersecurity and communications capacity.[42] Together these proactive, multilateral, broad-based defenses created a less permissive operating environment (i.e., less vulnerable institutions) for Russian hackers.

The Russian attack on Viasat is an interesting exception.[43] On the first day of the invasion, the GRU deployed a wiper (AcidRain) to target modems for a KA-SAT broadband communications network operated by a Eutelsat subsidiary of California-based Viasat.[44] This created collateral damage for "several thousand customers located in Ukraine and tens of thousands of other fixed broadband customers across Europe," according to Viasat,[45] including disrupting connections to 5,800 German wind turbines (but not the turbines themselves).[46] Russia's tactical synchronization of a cyber attack with military operations is reminiscent of Operation Orchard, in which Israel used cyber warfare to suppress Syrian radars during the 2007 air strike mentioned in chapter 5 (or the Israeli pager attack discussed above). Israel, however, was able to exploit the tactical window created by cyber operations to achieve a strategic effect, whereas Russia was not. The Ukrainian military was not exclusively reliant on satellite communications.[47] Russian electronic jamming on the battlefield was much more disruptive, but even then, Ukrainian ground commanders improvised alternatives through terrestrial circuits and informant networks.[48] In terms of intelligence performance, the GRU was a capable and discreet organization during the planning phase, while the KA-SAT network was an interconnected and vulnerable institution. This produced short-lived tactical success, albeit with uncontrolled collateral damage. Yet the noisy denial ensured an immediate counteraction: "Network stabilization and security mitigation actions began immediately," Viasat reported, "and the network was largely stabilized within hours and fully stabilized within several days."[49] The Viasat hack affected the cyber policy debate much more than it affected the war.

The GRU's emphasis on disruptive attacks in the first year of the war shifted to more emphasis on espionage in the second.[50] APT44 continued to carry out network infiltrations, wiper attacks, information operations, and tactical intelligence support. In at least one case, APT44 synchronized wiper attacks against electrical substations with Russian missile attacks.[51] But facing more robust Ukrainian cyber defenses, APT44 focused more on exploiting edge infrastructure (routers, VPN appliances) and "living off the land" to avoid detection. APT44 also prioritized wipers and cybercrime tools that were easier to deploy without detailed reconnaissance and careful preparation. Mandiant assessed that "APT44 is highly judicious about deploying its most advanced, and likely most costly to develop, tools. When custom malware is needed, APT44 typically deploys lightweight tools that are expendable and do not pose any significant attrition to the group's overall capabilities when used or exposed."[52] APT44 also relied on hacktivists to publicize some of its disruptions for propaganda purposes, which suggests that those attacks were not noticeable enough on their own.[53] The underlying performance conditions changed constantly. APT44 was usually capable but sometimes dependent and indiscreet. Wartime friction created barriers to access, and Ukrainian counterintelligence shored up vulnerabilities. Both sides adapted.

In the third year of the war, the GRU emphasis on disruption further waned. "What I think has changed," said the NSA's director of cybersecurity in October 2024, "is the Russians shifting back to more espionage."[54] The Ukrainian government likewise reported "an increase in the overall number of cyber incidents accompanied by a decrease in high and critical severity threats," with hackers focusing on maintaining discreet persistence rather than "just exploiting vulnerabilities wherever they can."[55] It is premature to draw any conclusions, but this shift is suggestive of a learning process whereby the Russians became disappointed with cyber warfare and reverted to a more promising focus on intelligence. Given the constitutive importance of collective institutions for any sort of cyber operations, this is exactly what I would expect.

The war in Ukraine is a cautionary tale for anyone who expects cyber warfare to be decisive in the opening phases of conflict or to have an outsized strategic effect. The intelligence contest in cyberspace was overshadowed by grueling battles of attrition and risks of nuclear escalation. At the same time, it would be a mistake to discount cyber warfare altogether. If the cyber conflict in Ukraine has been indecisive, this is partly because Ukrainian, NATO, and commercial actors have actively defended against sustained attacks from APT44 and others. The cyber domain in Ukraine remains actively contested, just like every other domain in this protracted war.[56]

The fundamental limiting factor for cyber warfare, in Ukraine or anywhere else, is the anarchic turbulence of combat. Common connections and predictable vulnerabilities are necessary conditions for intelligence exploitation, but institutions become unreliable in the fog and friction of war. One implication is that cyber operations may not work as planned, and only as planned, once the shooting begins. Another is that wartime cyber operations are more feasible during stable or static phases of war than during chaotic or mobile phases.[57] Cyber operations should be even more feasible on the margins of the conflict—for instance, to spy on or influence third parties not directly involved in combat. As such, cyber warfare is better understood as the espionage and subversion dimension of limited warfare in all other domains. Even this entails difficult cross-domain coordination problems. Not every state can solve them in every situation. As ever, cyber performance depends on contingent institutional context.

Net Assessment

National institutions shape the style of cyber operations. Russian hacking has a thuggish quality, combining technical sophistication and brazen intimidation to sow fear, uncertainty, and doubt. Chinese hacking, by contrast, is less about chaos than control: Beijing bolsters its overt legitimacy with covert espionage, subversion, and counterintelligence. North Korean operations are less mature than either of them, with a peculiar flair for cybercrime. US cyber campaigns, meanwhile, are notable for their exquisite overengineering, bureaucratic overhead, and legal caution.

The assessment of national cyber capabilities, therefore, must consider enabling institutional factors, not just technical tradecraft. National cyber operations also provide a lens through which to understand national political priorities. Chapter 7 thus used an institutional lens to understand Chinese cyber power. Because institutions affect intelligence, furthermore, cyber warfare with China may not be like cyber warfare with Russia. The good news is that cyber operations are still unlikely to determine the outcome of any war with China, but the bad news is that the adversaries may not appreciate what this implies.

General Timothy D. Haugh, commander of US Cyber Command and director of the NSA, in 2024, reported that he was "laser focused on the strategic and operational challenge the PRC presents in cyberspace."[58] Indeed, Chinese cyber campaigns have had a profound effect on the development of cybersecurity over the past three decades. The growing danger of war in the Pacific also entails a danger of cyber warfare more severe than anything seen in Ukraine. This possibility cannot be ignored, but it should not be exaggerated either. The Chinese and US militaries have both internalized the cyberwar narrative that digital attacks enable information dominance by paralyzing enemy forces or imposing costs on enemy leadership. Volt Typhoon activity associated with the PLA suggests that the Chinese military is willing and able to pre-position malicious code in US infrastructure. But these peacetime probes do not translate simply into wartime advantage, given that friction and turbulence will be intense in any war between the United States and China. Much depends on the capacity of clandestine organizations to control complex operations in these circumstances.

The biggest risk factor in this dyad is mutual ignorance about the art of the possible. Misrepresenting strengths and interests is a recipe for strategic instability.[59] The US and Chinese militaries each have cyber capabilities that are too sensitive or too provocative to reveal in advance. Since covert tools are difficult to use for overt signaling, each will have incentives to reserve their most potent cyber capabilities in the event of war. They will also have incentives to use them in the initial phases of war before they lose them as initial planning assumptions change.

In addition to misrepresenting their strength to others, militaries can also misperceive their own strengths by assuming that their information systems and cyber-warfare plans will work as expected. China probably has more unrealistic expectations in this regard than the United States. The PLA has bold doctrine for, but not much combat experience in, modern war. The US military, by contrast, has decades of practical experience with the nuances and frustrations of cyber operations on the battlefields of Iraq and Afghanistan. The PLA is also far more politicized, which hampers objective assessment and creative adaptation.

As a result, the cyber contribution to the balance of power and the costs of war is very hard to predict. This uncertainty raises the risks of flawed net assessments, false hopes for preemptive action, and mutual miscalculation. The worst possible outcome would be for both superpowers to stumble into a protracted war after commanders allow themselves to believe that automation or cyber warfare can provide a speedy solution to strategic problems. Friction and disappointment in the cyber domain are far more likely than paralysis and asymmetric advantage. In any shooting war between the United States and China, furthermore, cyberspace will be the least of anyone's problems. Dreams about information dominance will be eclipsed by risks of global economic depression and nuclear escalation.

Strategic planners, therefore, must seriously consider the possibility of a long and costly war with China, especially if plans for a short war depend on cyber warfare and automation. This means that cyber planning must plan to be disappointed. Cyber units, accordingly, must be prepared to adapt to unanticipated consequences. This may help to improve resilience in case of war with China. It may also reduce the chances of starting such a war in the first place, to the extent that realistic expectations for cyber warfare lead to more accurate self-assessments, or to the extent that resilient institutional capacity can be communicated to the adversary.[60]

Short of war, and even in a limited war, the United States and China still have enduring common interests in mutual connectivity and global trade. The same economic forces that enable cyber exploitation across the Pacific also condition the effects of security competition. Cyberspace may even provide a means of relieving pressure in a complicated political relationship. One lesson from Ukraine is the importance of maintaining a viable gray zone, lest a desperate adversary gamble on war. Intelligence contests do not necessarily undermine, and may even improve, long-term strategic competition. As demonstrated in the triangular relationship between the United States, Israel, and Iran in chapter 5, secret statecraft provides a way of mitigating the inevitable frictions and contradictions of international politics. Chronic intelligence competition—through cyberspace, human agents, satellites, and even spy balloons—may help the United States and China avoid something worse.

Cybersecurity Dilemmas

Cyber competition flourishes in the infrastructure of liberal order, such as it is. Therefore, there are two logical ways to eliminate cyber threats. Both are absurd. The first option is to start a large, destructive war that eliminates the conditions for the possibility of deception. In a state of absolute war in anarchy, there are no common institutions to enable deception. The second option is to establish a system of perfect control, with pervasive monitoring and ruthless enforcement. Hackers will find no place to hide in the nightmares of George Orwell and Hannah Arendt. A state of total peace is as inhospitable to intelligence as a state of total war.

Between these logical extremes, some degree of cyber insecurity is inevitable. Information systems cannot be perfectly defended without making them perfectly unusable. This means that organizations must make choices about where to prioritize protection and where to tolerate exploitation. Marginal improvements in cybersecurity in one area set the stage for new threats in another. Overt cooperation to improve cybersecurity invites covert operations to subvert it. But that's not necessarily a bad place to be, considering the alternatives.

There are upsides and downsides to every extreme, which means that there are a lot of trade-offs in the middle. Markets improve efficiency but threaten welfare, for instance, while governments improve coordination but create overhead. Most public or corporate policy in practice is concerned with evaluating and balancing such trade-offs, and then reevaluating and rebalancing them on an ongoing basis. The hardest problems, moreover, usually have to do with figuring out what matters, and where to compromise. Engineering outcomes is easier when goals and values are clear, which they rarely are in practice. This means that the dilemmas of cyber policy are as much about political philosophy as computer engineering. Those who know how must also ask why.

The basic policy implications of the theory of intelligence performance are easy to state, but value trade-offs make them hard to implement. The intelligence performance of an attacker depends on vulnerable institutions (connectivity and vulnerability) and clandestine organization (capacity and discretion). Therefore, to degrade the attacker's performance, a defender should try to make its own institutions less permissive (by reducing connectivity and limiting vulnerability) and the attacker's organization less proficient (by revealing discretion and countering capacity). But in an intelligence contest, defense also plays offense (i.e., counterintelligence collects intelligence and conducts covert action). To enhance its own intelligence performance, therefore, the defender also tries to make the attacker's institutions more exposed (by ensuring connectivity and encouraging vulnerability) and the defender's organization more sophisticated (by improving discretion and enhancing capacity). But this is a paradox. If the best defense is a good offense, then improving cybersecurity creates insecurity.

Table C.3 lists representative policy options for improving cybersecurity in each category. These may all be desirable, but it is not possible to have them all at the same time. These desiderata embody fundamental political trade-offs regarding institutions and intentions.[61] There are not enough pages to explore all the trade-offs implied by the table, but I will highlight a few to convey the intractable nature of cyber policy in practice.

The most obvious way to prevent cyber threats is to stop using cyberspace altogether, but this involves some obvious opportunity costs. Short of digital abstinence, threats may be limited by enterprise access controls such

Table C.3 Policy measures to improve cybersecurity based on the conditions for intelligence performance

	Improve defense		Improve offense	
Vulnerable institutions	*Reduce connectivity*	*Limit vulnerability*	*Ensure connectivity*	*Encourage vulnerability*
	Disconnection/ airgaps	Security protocols	Interoperability Multiple accesses	Manipulate architecture
	Access/privacy controls	Surveillance Counterintel-ligence	Open platforms	Stockpile exploits Social engineering
	Trade barriers			
Clandestine organization	*Reveal discretion*	*Counter capacity*	*Improve discretion*	*Enhance capacity*
	Threat hunting	Threat profiling	Operational security	Investment in spy services
	Incident response	Disable tooling		
	Public attribution	Sanction hostile entities	Careful planning Exercise restraint	Administration Recruit hackers

as classified information and public key infrastructure, or by national bans on foreign technologies (e.g., US restrictions on China's Huawei and TikTok). More rigorous security standards, workforce education, auditing practices, and safety certifications (e.g., a "software bill of materials") can also result in less vulnerable organizations and more reliable supply chains. But these measures increase compliance costs that undermine the efficiency of communication and coordination, which is the justification for using information systems in the first place.

Barriers are not the only way to improve security. A better way to deal with intelligence threats is to deceive the deceivers. Surreptitious surveillance, attribution investigations, undercover infiltration, botnet takedowns, and other forms of active counterintelligence help to reduce institutional vulnerability and disrupt organizational capacity. As defense plays offense, hostile assets become liabilities. Threat tooling can be disclosed and disabled, and hostile operators can be indicted and sanctioned. At the same time, counterintelligence invites controversy about privacy and civil liberties. Some parts of the US electorate, for instance, may see efforts to block Russian influence operations as an infringement on their freedom of speech. If openness is an exploitable feature of US democracy, then counterintelligence closure may seem undemocratic. The same paranoia that makes an attacker think twice before infiltrating a system also lends itself to political polarization.

If defense plays offense, then even the defender has an ironic interest in preserving a degree of institutional vulnerability. Counterintelligence agents become reticent about reporting threats when they want to protect their sensitive sources. Secret exploits that may be patched for the public good are hoarded for private advantage, which comes back to bite when threat actors use the same exploits (as with Conficker in chapter 5 and EternalBlue above). Intelligence agencies have even been known to manipulate encryption protocols or devices to create backdoors.[62] The tension between public security and private capacity is not limited to governments. Security companies such as NSOGroup and I-Soon become security threats to civil society. Global software platforms both provide the institutional environment for exploitation and are important intelligence actors themselves.

If offense plays defense, conversely, then the attacker has incentives to not exploit vulnerabilities too aggressively. Each side must make trade-offs—and keep making them. Operational security (discretion) is vital for protecting the fragile capabilities of a clandestine organization. Intelligence works best when it works in the shadows. More complex enterprises that are better defended raise the risk of compromise and mission failure. More politically sensitive entities carry additional risk of retaliation. Attackers considering such targets must carefully evaluate contingencies and plan accordingly.

Deception specialists also must make internal trade-offs. To improve clandestine organization, either for intelligence or counterintelligence, they must balance managerial coordination and unconstrained adaptation.[63] Too much of the former, and a bureaucracy struggles to keep up with its adversary. Too much of the latter, and cowboys start making mistakes. The unicorn of cybersecurity is a technically competent, unconventionally creative, organizationally loyal, and politically savvy hacker. But this beast is hard to discover, let alone recruit and retain. While it may be possible for bureaucracies to assimilate blue-haired hackers, operational cyber units must be prepared to cope with lost opportunities and embarrassing mistakes.

Nobody likes trade-offs. Cyber policy must compromise between efficiency and effectiveness, options and credibility, offense and defense, democracy and control, trust and temptation, and so forth. Classic policy trade-offs become more complex as economic interdependence and technological sophistication increase. Most policymakers prefer to avoid value trade-offs, of course, because public compromises make them vulnerable to political rivals and ideological constituents. This implies that cybersecurity will tend to become politicized as parochial interests emphasize private goods over public bads. A more constructive way to spin this is that cybersecurity depends on leadership: the ability to envision the future, set priorities and boundaries, align means with ends, and so on.

The overarching policy implication is that *cybersecurity is a process, not an outcome*. Intelligence practice is more about navigating endless minor crises and irritating challenges than about pulling off spectacular coups or decisive interventions. When intelligence works, it is often based on the accumulation of data and expertise over many years (as in Bletchley Park). When covert action works, it often just injects friction into an already complicated system, which may buy time for other policy options to emerge (as in Stuxnet). Defensive cybersecurity, likewise, requires an ongoing effort to identify and rebalance trade-offs, repair and reform institutions, improve the benefits of coordination, and mitigate the risks of deception. System confidentiality, data integrity, or authorized access can never be completely assured. But for similar reasons, offense does not systematically dominate defense. Intelligence performance emerges from sustained investment and ongoing adaptation. Organized deception is a long con. Cybersecurity, accordingly, is a long game.

How I Learned to Stop Worrying and Love the Gray Zone

Reframing cybersecurity as secret statecraft comes with good news and bad news. The good news is that the cyberwar narrative is not a useful guide to the future. The next war will not be decided in cyberspace. Hacking is not easy. Attribution is not impossible. Offense is not dominant. The same complexity that creates vulnerability for defense also creates friction for offense. Even the most skilled attackers may leave fingerprints, and less skilled attackers will leave more fingerprints. Combatants will look for opportunities for cyber warfare, but they are more likely to find frustration. Cyber attacks will rarely be escalatory, and they can even de-escalate crises. Cyber espionage will not be a simple shortcut to innovation, and it can even foster dependency. Cyber influence will not overthrow regimes, and it may even suggest weak resolve. These patterns are unlikely to change with artificial intelligence, quantum computing, or any other emerging technology. They are unlikely to change because technology did not create these patterns in the first place.

The bad news is that civil society is in the crosshairs. While cyberspace may not transform national security, it has ominous implications for human security. Cybersecurity is a high-tech intelligence contest that is conducted by, with, and through civilian systems. Commercial companies, nongovernmental organizations, academic laboratories, journalists, dissidents, and average citizens become intelligence actors, intermediaries, and targets. Repressive regimes use commercial spyware to expand the reach of internal security services. Autocracies and democracies alike impose information controls. Corporate surveillance and digital addiction encourage people to trade privacy for entertainment. Social media platforms roil with envy, resentment, and paranoia. Personal devices enable bullying, extortion, and intimate abuse. As ever, the weak suffer what they must, and there is no end in sight. At least there is job security in cybersecurity.

Institutions are the key to understanding both the good news and the bad news about cybersecurity. Institutions are the rules and tools that constrain and enable social interaction. Cyberspace is an institution in this sense, enabling communication and coordination at unprecedented scale. Overt cooperation at scale, in turn, enables covert competition at scale. The "good news" about cyber warfare, accordingly, is that secret statecraft is less feasible wherever institutions are weak or missing. Wars fought in anarchy tend to limit the viability of cyber warfare. This good news is still not great, since political actors may still decide to go to war for reasons that have nothing to do with cyberspace, and they may predicate their war plans on a sudden loss of connectivity via communications sabotage (as Hezbollah found out the hard way). The "bad news" about cyberspace and civil society, moreover, is that secret statecraft flourishes when institutions are robust or pervasive. Global economies and domestic regimes provide ideal conditions for cyber operations.

The upshot is that cyber warfare is less reliable *between* states, where institutions are thinner, while cyber exploitation is more relevant *within* societies, where institutions are denser. Intuitions about warfare, therefore, are not reliable guides to secret statecraft in cyberspace. Military combat, taken to the logical extreme, is a contest of strength between autonomous organizations in anarchy. Intelligence and cybersecurity, by contrast, are contests of wits within cooperatively entangled institutions. Warfare between states is the antithesis of cooperation, but cooperation is the condition for the possibility of deception. Deception and intelligence are still possible in war, of course, but only where there is some degree of institutionalization. It is no coincidence that intelligence plays such a large role in limited forms of war such as counterinsurgency and counterterrorism, where residual institutional constraints are still in force. Intelligence and counterintelligence are even more salient for internal security, which reinforces the institutions of state. It is also not surprising that intelligence is notoriously unreliable in major combat operations, where institutional constraints are weakest. Anarchy undermines intelligence.

Intuitions about deterrence are also misleading for cybersecurity. The deterrence revolution of the twentieth century was all about using the (nuclear) means of war in pursuit of the (negative) ends of peace. The deception revolution of the twenty-first century, by contrast, uses the (cyber) means of peace in pursuit of the (limited) ends of war. Deception and deterrence do not mix well, because bluffing undermines credibility, and secrecy undermines brandishing. As the eponymous analyst from the Bland Corporation in *Dr. Strangelove* observes, "The whole point of the doomsday machine is lost if you keep it a secret!" Yet the whole point of hacking the machine is lost if you *don't* keep it a secret! It is thus hardly surprising that US Cyber Command, in its first decade of existence, rejected deterrence as the cornerstone of cyber strategy.[64] (Later it awkwardly embraced the US National Security Strategy of "integrated deterrence."[65])

Some good news, perhaps, is that there is a growing community of expertise in cybersecurity, both in industry and in government. With decades of experience of cyber competition, we are finally moving beyond debates about the bogeyman of cyberwar to confront the actual security problems of cyberspace. The bad news is that these problems are really wicked.[66] Wicked problems in cybersecurity embody fundamental trade-offs across intentions and institutions at multiple scales. These problems both require integration and defy it. Ostensible solutions like "public-private partnership" and "whole-of-government effort" are really just descriptions of the intractability of integration.

There are at least three major integration problems in cybersecurity. The first tension is between military and intelligence affairs. This tension is embodied in the "dual hat" of General Haugh, who until recently was both commander of US Cyber Command and director of the NSA. This enabled him to employ the same technical capabilities under different legal authorities. Yet there is a serious tension between the culture of war and the culture of intelligence. Wars are episodic contests of strength between societies; intelligence is a chronic contest of wits within societies. Military cyber units can scale up espionage and covert action and rebrand them as technical reconnaissance and cyber warfare in order to be more consistent with military ideas and identities. But in the process, cyber units run afoul of classic intelligence controversies around privacy and counterintelligence. Efforts to combat foreign disinformation, for example, must walk a fine line in order to avoid becoming military interventions into democratic politics.[67]

The second important tension is between national security strategy and economic policy. The policy tools of law enforcement and regulation are different from the tools of the military intelligence community, and they are often more focused on domestic affairs than on international ones. While it is easy to focus on deception specialists and their campaigns, economic policy shapes the institutions that make deception possible in the first place. Before hackers can hack cyberspace, technologists and administrators must build it. Bureaucrats and engineers define technical standards and protocols, govern multistakeholder organizations, establish reporting requirements for breaches and cyber incidents, enforce cybercrime and privacy laws, implement health and safety regulations, impose economic sanctions and technical barriers to trade, and manage government procurement practices. These activities are generally not controlled by defense ministries or spy services, nor should they be, but rather economic agencies and the justice system. These constitutive activities shape the environment in which military and intelligence threat actors operate.

The third and trickiest tension is between the state and civil society. Cybersecurity is an intelligence contest that is more digitized, supersized, and civilianized than ever. Commercial firms and other civilian entities invent, own, and operate most of the infrastructure of cyberspace. The cybersecurity industry provides counterintelligence functionality for government and industry alike. Some commercial intelligence firms even rival the capabilities of nation-state spy agencies, and the lines between them are blurry. Mandiant, for example, was founded by a former US Air Force counterintelligence officer, employs many veteran intelligence personnel, and has unique access to its clients' data (telemetry), which US intelligence agencies are not allowed to directly collect. Other tech firms try to avoid appearing too close to the US government in order to maintain access to European and Asian markets. Perennial calls for better public-private information sharing just underscore the enduring tensions between commercial expertise and government authority.

There are no lasting solutions to any of these problems. Practitioners must chronically manage trade-offs in the liminal space between intelligence and warfare, security and economy, and government and industry. Along the way, military units will begin to look and act more like intelligence agencies, regulatory agencies will shape the operating environment for national security agencies, and civil society will be subverted in geopolitical competition. Cyber threats will flourish in the gray zone between peace and war, and cyber policy will flirt with countless shades of gray. The dilemmas of cybersecurity create an aporia of policy.

The study of secret statecraft also falls into a gray zone. The IR field long ignored phenomena of secrecy and intelligence in its focus on the big problems of war, peace, and deterrence. This is changing with a recent burgeoning of scholarship on deception theory, as discussed in chapter 1, thanks in no small part to the rising profile of cybersecurity in world politics. Most of the IR scholarship on deception theory to date has been in the subfield of security studies, with less in the subfield of international political economy. Yet the global liberal order (or what's left of it) creates a technological playground for realpolitik. Cyberspace is a product of transnational economic cooperation, and global security competition exploits it. Complex interactions between governments and markets, along with the domestic politics of entangled regimes, drive the dynamics of cybersecurity. The future of deception theory lies in the shadows between security and political economy.

That deception plays a role in war is well known. That deception is prevalent in peace is more unsettling. Rivals and predators may scheme to deceive, but friends and family wear masks as well. Yet while deception lays traps, it also saves face. Lurking in the search for truth is a paradox of self-deception.

Notes

Introduction

1. Kevin Mandia, "FireEye Shares Details of Recent Cyber Attack, Actions to Protect Community," FireEye, December 8, 2020. Note that the company's name has changed several times as Mandiant was acquired by FireEye, Inc., in 2013 and then by Google in 2022. These acquisitions have muddied the online record, but contemporary FireEye posts can be found at the Internet Archive's Wayback Machine at https://archive.org. For convenience I will just refer to this entity as Mandiant.

2. John Lambert, "Important Steps for Customers to Protect Themselves from Recent Nation-State Cyberattacks," Microsoft on the Issues, December 13, 2020, https://blogs.micro soft.com/on-the-issues/2020/12/13/customers-protect-nation-state-cyberattacks/; FireEye, "Highly Evasive Attacker Leverages SolarWinds Supply Chain to Compromise Multiple Global Victims With SUNBURST Backdoor," December 13, 2020, https://www.fireeye. com/blog/threat-research/2020/12/evasive-attacker-leverages-solarwinds-supply-chain-compromises-with-sunburst-backdoor.html.

3. SolarWinds Corporation, *Form 8-K: Current Report*, US Securities and Exchange Commission, December 14, 2020, https://www.sec.gov/Archives/edgar/data/0001739942/000162828 020017451/swi-20201214.htm.

4. "SolarWinds Hack Was 'Largest and Most Sophisticated Attack' Ever: Microsoft President," Reuters, February 15, 2021.

5. CISA Media Relations, "Joint Statement by the Federal Bureau of Investigation (FBI), the Cybersecurity and Infrastructure Security Agency (CISA), the Office of the Director of National Intelligence (ODNI), and the National Security Agency (NSA)," January 5, 2021, https://www. cisa.gov/news/2021/01/05/joint-statement-federal-bureau-investigation-fbi-cybersecurity-and-infrastructure.

6. David Smith, "US Scrambles to Understand Fallout of Suspected Russia Hack," *The Guardian*, December 18, 2020.

7. Jan Wolfe and Brendan Pierson, "Explainer—U.S. Government Hack: Espionage or Act of War?," Reuters, December 19, 2020.

8. David E. Sanger and Nicole Perlroth, "More Hacking Attacks Found as Officials Warn of 'Grave Risk' to U.S. Government," *New York Times*, December 17, 2020.

9. NSA Media Relations, "Russian SVR Targets U.S. and Allied Networks," NSA Cybersecurity Information, U/OO/132340-21, April 15, 2021, https://www.nsa.gov/News-Features/Feature-Stories/Article-View/Article/2573391/russian-foreign-intelligence-service-exploiting-five-publicly-known-vulnerabili/. Various commercial and government actors track the same threat actors or intrusion sets by different code names; standardized nomenclature remains elusive for both epistemological reasons (threats are uncertain and changing) and marketing imperatives (firms propose new names to distinguish themselves from competitors). APT is short for "advanced persistent threat."

10. White House, "FACT SHEET: Imposing Costs for Harmful Foreign Activities by the Russian Government," April 15, 2021, https://www.whitehouse.gov/briefing-room/statements-releases/2021/04/15/fact-sheet-imposing-costs-for-harmful-foreign-activities-by-the-russian-government/.

11. Dan Goodin, "US Government Strikes Back at Kremlin for SolarWinds Hack Campaign," *Ars Technica*, April 15, 2021, https://arstechnica.com/tech-policy/2021/04/us-government-strikes-back-at-kremlin-for-solarwinds-hack-campaign/.

12. Kim Philby, Anthony Blunt, Guy Burgess, John Cairncross, and Donald Maclean were recruited by Arnold Deutch, who had Western academic credentials yet worked for the OGPU, or Soviet secret police, the forerunner of the KGB. See Andrew and Mitrokhin 2000, 57. My account of this case draws heavily on Andrew 2009, 339–441.

13. Mandia, "FireEye Shares Details."

14. This also briefly raised questions about Philby's loyalty in the paranoid KGB, according to Andrew and Mitrokhin 2000, 125.

15. A virtual private network (VPN) provides secure remote access to a network. Hackers may have obtained VPN credentials by phishing a SolarWinds employee. On the hack and response, see Kim Zetter, "The Untold Story of the Boldest Supply-Chain Hack Ever," *Wired*, May 2, 2023, https://www.wired.com/story/the-untold-story-of-solarwinds-the-boldest-supply-chain-hack-ever/; Herr et al. 2021.

16. CrowdStrike Intelligence Team, "SUNSPOT Malware: A Technical Analysis," CrowdStrike, January 11, 2021, https://www.crowdstrike.com/blog/sunspot-malware-technical-analysis/.

17. Microsoft Threat Intelligence, "Deep Dive into the Solorigate Second-Stage Activation: From SUNBURST to TEARDROP and Raindrop," *Microsoft Security Blog*, January 20, 2021, https://www.microsoft.com/security/blog/2021/01/20/deep-dive-into-the-solorigate-second-stage-activation-from-sunburst-to-teardrop-and-raindrop/.

18. Andrew and Mitrokhin 2000, 154–56; Thurlow 2004.

19. The NSA was known as the Army Security Agency at the time. One-time pads are provably secure if and only if the key is the same length as the plaintext, truly random, and only used once. On Soviet mistakes and Western exploitation in this episode, see Andrew 2009, 420–24.

20. Andrew Higgins, "Even in Death, the Spy Kim Philby Serves the Kremlin's Purposes," *New York Times*, October 1, 2017.

21. Kim Zetter, "DOJ Detected SolarWinds Breach Months Before Public Disclosure," *Wired*, April 28, 2023, https://www.wired.com/story/solarwinds-hack-public-disclosure/.

22. Zetter, "Untold Story."

23. Microsoft Threat Intelligence, "Using Microsoft 365 Defender to Protect Against Solorigate," *Microsoft Security Blog*, December 28, 2020, https://www.microsoft.com/security/blog/2020/12/28/using-microsoft-365-defender-to-coordinate-protection-against-solorigate/.

24. "'Third Man' in Spy Case," *New York Times*, July 31, 1963.

25. FBI National Press Office, "Joint Statement by the Federal Bureau of Investigation (FBI), the Cybersecurity and Infrastructure Security Agency (CISA), and the Office of the Director of National Intelligence (ODNI)," Federal Bureau of Investigation, December 16, 2020, https://www.fbi.gov/news/pressrel/press-releases/joint-statement-by-the-federal-bureau-of-investigation-fbi-the-cybersecurity-and-infrastructure-security-agency-cisa-and-the-office-of-the-director-of-national-intelligence-odni.

26. Zetter, "Untold Story."

27. Andrew and Mitrokhin 2000, 155.

28. Cormac 2018, 50–53; Long and Cacciatore 2024.

29. Cram 1993.

30. For convenience I will refer to this agency as the GRU even though its official name changed in 2010 to the Main Directorate (GU) of the General Staff of the Armed Forces of the Russian Federation.

31. I explore this convergence in Lindsay 2020b, a book that did not have much to say about cybersecurity. This book fills the gap.

1. Defining Secret Statecraft

1. Or as one of Thomas Pynchon's characters puts it, "If you want the truth—I know I presume—you must look into the technology of these matters. . . . You must ask two questions. First, what is the real nature of synthesis? And then: What is the real nature of control?" Quoted in Mindell 2002, vii.

2. Pape 1996; T. Biddle 2002; Haun 2015.

3. These are not shown in figure 1.1, but compare figure 1.2.

4. For a review, see Dunn Cavelty et al. 2024.

5. For a review, see Carnegie 2021.

6. Winn Schwartau, "Computer Security," testimony to Committee on Science, Space, and Technology, US House of Representatives, 102nd Congress, June 27, 1991.

7. Keith Alexander, "Cyber Warfare in Ukraine Poses a Threat to Global System," *Financial Times,* February 15, 2022.

8. For example, Arquilla and Ronfeldt 1993; Campen et al. 1996; Rattray 2001; J. Adams 2001; McConnell 2009; Clarke and Knake 2010; Kello 2017; Buchanan and Imbrie 2022.

9. Branch 2021.

10. Valeriano and Maness 2015; Valeriano, Jensen, and Maness 2018; Kostyuk and Zhukov 2019; Kreps and Schneider 2019; Kaminska 2021; Schneider et al. 2022; Kostyuk and Gartzke 2023.

11. Amir et al. 2018; Bouwman et al 2020; Maschmeyer et al. 2021.

12. Inter alia, Libicki 2009; Liff 2012; Gartzke 2013; Lindsay 2015; Borghard and Lonergan 2017. For a counterpoint, notably highlighting the vulnerability of companies to nation-state punishment, see Sharp 2017.

13. Inter alia, Slayton 2017; Smeets 2022.

14. Inter alia, Hansen and Nissenbaum 2009; Brito and Watkins 2011; Dunn Cavelty 2013; T. Stevens 2016; Lawson 2020.

15. Kamiya et al. 2018; Eling and Wirfs 2019; He et al. 2020; Kamiya et al 2021; John Fell et al., "Towards a Framework for Assessing Systemic Cyber Risk," European Central Bank, November 15, 2022, https://www.ecb.europa.eu/press/financial-stability-publications/fsr/special/html/ecb.fsrart202211_03~9a8452e67a.en.html; Crosignani et al. 2023; Akoto 2025.

16. Slupska and Tanczer 2021; Egloff and Shires 2021; Shandler et al. 2023.

17. McGlave et al. 2024.

18. Kuerbis and Badiei 2017; Clarke and Knake 2019.

19. White 2019; Stevens and Devanny 2024.

20. Monte 2015, 15. On the role of intelligence in history generally, see Warner 2014; Andrew 2018; Rogg 2025.

21. Joshua Rovner, "Cyber War as an Intelligence Contest," War on the Rocks, September 16, 2019, https://warontherocks.com/2019/09/cyber-war-as-an-intelligence-contest/.

22. Gioe et al. 135; Rid 2023.

23. Lindsay and Cheung 2015; Rid 2016; Akoto 2021.

24. Rudner 2013; Brantly 2016.

25. Maurer 2018; Maschmeyer 2021; Canfil 2022; Whyte 2024; Deibert 2025.

26. Landau 2010; Deibert 2013; Roberts 2018.

27. Fitzgerald and Brantly 2017; Mandel 2019; Rid 2020.

28. Edwards et al. 2017; Egloff and Smeets 2023; Egloff and Dunn Cavelty 2021.

29. Warner 2019; Harknett and Smeets 2022; Chesney and Smeets 2023. For other analogies see Perkovich and Levite 2017.

30. Fischerkeller et al. 2022, 30, 34, 48, 40, 123.

31. Schneider et al. 2020.

32. On cumulative strategy before cyber, see J. Wylie 1989, 22–27. A classic example is intelligence support for antisubmarine warfare; see Ford and Rosenberg 2005.

33. In Lindsay 2020b, chap. 1, I describe this as the informational turn in military practice.

34. Lonergan 2024; Schneider 2025.

35. I discuss this in more detail in Lindsay 2021.

36. Jervis 1986. See also Andrew 2004; Ferris 1995. Jervis's own influential views on intelligence are compiled in Jervis 2011.

37. E.g., Gill and Phythian 2018; Bean 2018.

38. Carnegie 2021.

39. Carson 2018, 3.

40. Carson 2018; G. Smith 2019.

41. Downes and Lilley 2010; O'Rourke 2018; Poznansky 2020.

42. Levin 2020.

43. Carson and Yarhi-Milo 2017; Green and Long 2020.

44. Mearsheimer 2011; Schuessler 2015.

45. Petersen 2001; J. Scott 2008; Shapiro 2013.

46. This wonderful phrase was suggested by Joshua Rovner. Work on secret diplomacy includes L. Scott 2004; Yarhi-Milo 2013; Carnegie and Carson 2020; Haas and Yarhi-Milo 2021.

47. Kastner and Wohlforth 2024.

48. Lanoszka 2019; Rid 2020; Adler and Drieschova 2021.

49. King et al. 2013; Lee and Zhang 2017; Farrell and Newman 2019a.

50. Goldman 2013; Kindervater 2016; Wilke 2017.

51. Dahl 2013; Altman 2017; Matovski 2020.

52. Zegart 2000; Betts 2007; Rovner 2011; Yarhi-Milo 2014; Sims 2022.

53. For an extended review, see Freedman 2004.

54. On the complementarity of deterrence and deception, see Gartzke and Lindsay 2024.

55. M. Kaplan 1952, 548.

56. Baldwin 2020, 6–7. See Goddard et al. 2019.

57. Drawing on a classic typology from Harold Lasswell, see Baldwin 2020, 12. See also Goddard et al. 2019, 306–7.

58. Some append finance, intelligence, and law enforcement, to form the more unwieldy "DIMEFIL."

59. Baldwin 2020, 13.

60. Whaley 1982.

61. Machiavelli 1958, chap. 18.

62. Machiavelli 1958, chap. 18.

63. Machiavelli 1958, chap. 18.

64. E.g., "Strategy is the indispensable art of getting what we want, with what we have, in a world that seems set on denying us," in Brands 2023, 1.

65. For a fun introduction to IR paradigms, see Drezner 2014.

66. A third paradigm of constructivism focuses on social institutions such as communities of practice, intersubjective norms, and discursive arguments—e.g., Wendt 1999; Adler 2019. "Constructivism, however, represents an orthogonal dimension" to liberalism and realism, as noted by Kirshner 2022, 74. Pressed to locate constructivism on figure 1.2, I would thus highlight dynamic movement in this space as actors modify their ends (agency) and shape their means (structure) to enable and constrain other actors.

67. Glaser 1994; Musgrave 2019.

68. Goddard 2018; Farrell and Newman 2019b.

69. Many scholars advocate abandoning paradigms altogether—e.g., Lake 2011; Wight et al. 2013; Dunne et al. 2013; Bennett 2013. Yet the paradigmatic debate endures because institutional mobilization and power politics are enduring features of political reality, as discussed in

Goddard and Nexon 2016. Even among self-described postparadigmatic scholars, IR scholarship continues to cluster across the traditional realist-liberal divide: Kristensen 2018; Milner et al. 2023.

70. Schelling 2008, 4.
71. Schelling 2008, 8.
72. For extensive discussion, see Gartzke and Lindsay 2024. A similar typology appears in that book with different terminology, due to a different focus on grand strategy (there) rather than intelligence operations (here). The dimensions of institutions and competition in figure 1.2, and the strategies of warfare, deterrence, secret statecraft, and governance, can be mapped, respectively, onto the parameters of demand and cost and the strategies of defense, coercion, deception, and accommodation, in Gartzke and Lindsay 2024.
73. Gartzke and Lindsay 2017; Lindsay 2022; Schneider et al. 2023.
74. Thucydides 1996, 1.75.3, p. 43.
75. Dennett and Haugeland 1987; Mele 1992.
76. Rathbun 2012; Rosato 2021.
77. Rousseau 1920, pt. 2.
78. Ostrom 1990; Seabright 2010.
79. Elster 1989.
80. North 1990, 3.
81. Locke 1980, 66.
82. This is a central theme running throughout science and technology studies (STS)—inter alia, Bijker et al. 1987; Bowker and Star 1999; D. Nye 2006; Suchman 2007.
83. Law 1987.
84. Lawrence Lessig, "Code Is Law," *Harvard Magazine*, January 1, 2000, https://www.harvardmagazine.com/2000/01/code-is-law-html.
85. Winner 1977, 323–24.
86. Winner 1977, 323.
87. Lake 2009; Börzel and Risse 2021.
88. Sun Tzu 2020, 53.
89. Sims 2022.
90. Kahn 2001.
91. Herman 1996, 381.
92. Herman 1996, 385.
93. Locke 1980, 100.
94. North 1990, 31.
95. Rousseau 1920, pt. 2.
96. North 1990, 101.
97. North 1990, 134.
98. North 1990, 99.
99. DiMaggio and Powell 1991, 3–4.
100. Greg Miller, "The Intelligence Coup of the Century," *Washington Post*, February 11, 2020, https://www.washingtonpost.com/graphics/2020/world/national-security/cia-crypto-encryption-machines-espionage/.
101. Warner 2012b.
102. A classic cyber example is Mandiant, "APT1: Exposing One of China's Cyber Espionage Units," white paper, February 2013, https://www.mandiant.com/sites/default/files/2021-09/mandiant-apt1-report.pdf.
103. A good overview is Richelson 2018.
104. Zuboff 2019.
105. Rovner 2023, 139.
106. Clausewitz 1976, 119–21.
107. David A. Fulghum, Robert Wall, and Amy Butler, "Cyber-Combat's First Shot," *Aviation Week & Space Technology*, November 26, 2007.
108. This episode is discussed in more detail in this book's conclusion.
109. Moore 2022.

110. Poznansky 2022.
111. Buchanan and Cunningham 2020.
112. Buchanan 2017; Healey and Jervis 2020.
113. Valeriano et al. 2018; Lonergan and Lonergan 2023.
114. Gartzke and Lindsay 2018.
115. Green and Long 2020.
116. Jenny Jun, "The Political Economy of Ransomware," War on the Rocks, June 2, 2021, https://warontherocks.com/2021/06/the-political-economy-of-ransomware/.
117. Smeets 2022.
118. Gartzke 2013.
119. Borghard and Lonergan 2017.
120. Ellen Nakashima, "Trump Approved Cyber-Strikes Against Iranian Computer Database Used to Plan Attacks on Oil Tankers," *Washington Post*, June 22, 2019.
121. Lonergan and Lonergan 2022.
122. Maschmeyer 2022. See also Maschmeyer 2024.
123. Rid 2020.
124. Lee 2020; Adler and Drieschova 2021; Deibert 2022; Krieg 2023; Maschmeyer 2024; Whyte 2024; Kastner and Wohlforth 2024; Deibert 2025.
125. Carson 2016.
126. Cormac and Aldrich 2018.
127. Gannon et al. 2024.
128. Frankfurt 2005, 47–48.
129. Frankfurt 2005, 61. See also Kuran 1997.
130. Sartre 1992, 113.
131. Adler and Drieschova 2021.
132. Carnegie and Carson 2020.
133. L. Scott 2004; Yarhi-Milo 2013.
134. Goffman 1969; Shulman 2006.
135. Herman 1996, 177–78.
136. Andy Greenberg, "The Untold Story of the 2018 Olympics Cyberattack, the Most Deceptive Hack in History," *Wired*, October 17, 2019, https://www.wired.com/story/untold-story-2018-olympics-destroyer-cyberattack/.
137. Goffman 1969, 72.
138. Andi Wilson Thompson, "Assessing the Vulnerabilities Equities Process, Three Years After the VEP Charter," Lawfare, January 13, 2021, https://www.lawfaremedia.org/article/assessing-vulnerabilities-equities-process-three-years-after-vep-charter.

2. A Theory of Intelligence Performance

1. Sun Tzu 2020, 135.
2. Sun Tzu 2020, 134–35.
3. Du Mu, quoted in Sun Tzu 2002, 325.
4. Generally see Sims 2022.
5. Cf. "In security terms, persistence is a structural imperative," according to Fischerkeller et al. 2022, 34. As discussed in chapter 1, I view cyber persistence theory as a rediscovery of deception theory in a novel military context rather than as an alternative to understanding cybersecurity as an intelligence contest.
6. Brooks and Stanley 2007.
7. Cohen 2002; Talmadge 2015.
8. S. Biddle 2004.
9. Grauer 2016.
10. Hunzeker 2021.
11. Rovner 2011.
12. Zegart 2000; Yarhi-Milo 2014.

13. Jervis 2011; Dahl 2013.

14. Evera 1998; K. Adams 2003.

15. Jason Healey, "Understanding the Offense's Systemwide Advantage in Cyberspace," Lawfare, December 22, 2021, https://www.lawfaremedia.org/article/understanding-offenses-systemwide-advantage-cyberspace. See also Garfinkel and Dafoe 2019.

16. Glaser and Kaufmann 1998; S. Biddle 2001.

17. Gartzke and Lindsay 2015; Slayton 2017.

18. This is why warfare appears on the anarchic end of the institutional axis of the typology of strategies in figure 1.2.

19. An important lesson from the movie *The Princess Bride* is to never go up against a Sicilian when death is on the line, unless you are a masked pirate with a secret resistance to poison.

20. Lindsay 2020b, chap. 2. See also Latour 1990; J. Scott 1998; Bowker and Star 1999; Edwards 2010.

21. Discussing climate science, and the political controversies around it, Edwards (2019, 23) points out that "scientific memory requires truces: acceptance of common standards, suspending conflicts and disagreements to get on with routine data sharing, putting aside political and ideological differences to work together. Such truces—and the mature technological systems that embody them—endow knowledge infrastructures with considerable stability and inertia." Edwards's focus on memory implicitly recalls the Greek word for truth (*alethia*), which literally means "that which is not forgotten" or not obliviated by the infernal river Lethe, per Ahl and Roisman (1996, 94). Truth (*trewe*) is a political truce (*trewes*) that enables us to not forget (*alethia*). In information-theoretic terms, institutionally constrained channels are necessary for signals to reduce uncertainty about the spatially or temporally distant situation that generates them. The radical epistemological implication is that politics precedes the perfection of knowledge.

22. Clausewitz 1976, 117

23. Clausewitz 1976, 140.

24. Clausewitz 1976, 579–82.

25. E.g., Legro 2013; Morrow 2014. I am emphasizing the constraining aspect of institutions, defined as "the humanly devised constraints that shape human interaction," according to North (1990, 3).

26. Lake (2009) points out that the distinction between anarchy and hierarchy is continuous, not discrete. This same variability at the microscale conditions the possibility of information.

27. Echoes of the classic RMA debate resonate in current debates about AI, yet military AI performance remains dependent on collective institutions for data and judgment, as discussed in Goldfarb and Lindsay 2022; Lindsay 2023.

28. The hybrid model of figure 2.3 can also describe irregular forces that rely on intelligence and stealth to economize resources and limit exposure. Insurgents or commandos can gain efficient (asymmetric) advantages, but they typically perform poorly if lured into major combat operations without the support of regular forces, as discussed by S. Biddle (2021). Note that Biddle's "Napoleonic" model is more like figure 2.1, optimized for winning big battles, while his "Fabian" model is more like figure 2.3, relying on both secrecy and violence. Biddle stresses that Fabian strategies rely on coercion (e.g., murder and intimidation of civilians and ambush of government forces), which requires a modicum of military capacity. But pure intelligence threats in figure 2.2 are even more reliant on concealment and secrecy for their viability than Fabian forces, which severely limits the ability of spies to credibly communicate threats (see Green and Long 2020).

29. Sun Tzu 2020, 132.

30. The concepts of the "external information problem" and "internal information solution" that I used in Lindsay 2020b, chap. 2, can be mapped roughly onto "vulnerable institutions" and "clandestine organization" in this book, respectively.

31. On democratic peace theory, see Oneal and Russett 1997; Rosato 2003.

32. Poznansky 2020.

33. There are principled reasons for choosing these four particular components, but page constraints preclude a full discussion. The basic intuition may be gleaned from figure 1.2,

which is a scale-free trade-off space along the dimensions of institutionalization and coopera-tion, which recur in every sort of political setting. My two main explanatory factors (vulnera-ble institutions and clandestine organization) thus describe variation along the y-axis of institutionalization, from interdependence to anarchy, respectively. The two principal compo-nents of each of these factors describe variation along the x-axis of cooperation, from compat-ible to incompatible interests. *Connectivity* thus embodies the cooperative benefits of public institutions—the virtues of governance. *Vulnerability* refers to the potential for usurping the commonwealth—the enablers of espionage. *Capacity* refers to the private institutions that mobilize resources for competition—the organization of warfare. *Discretion*, finally, refers to strategic incentives to protect private resources from compromise—the restraint of deter-rence. The fact that these four components are spread across the four corners of figure 1.2 helps to explain why it is so hard to meet all these conditions at once. The conditions for intel-ligence performance embody fundamental political tensions.

34. Alexis Dorais-Joncas and Facundo Muñoz, "Jumping the Air Gap: 15 Years of Nation-State Effort," ESET, December 1, 2021, https://www.welivesecurity.com/2021/12/01/jumping-air-gap-15-years-nation-state-effort/.

35. I discuss several risk pathways for NC3 in Lindsay 2022.

36. Zegart 2000.

37. Anderson and Moore 2006.

38. The notion of "weird machines" describes surplus computational functionality in the deter-ministic machine that is logically possible but not intended. See Bratus et al. 2011; Dullien 2020.

39. In the XKCD comic "Exploits of a Mom" (https://xkcd.com/327/), a frustrated school administrator calls a parent and asks, "We're having some computer trouble. . . . Did you really name your son Robert');DROP TABLE Students;—?" Mom replies, "Oh. Yes. Little Bobby Tables, we call him." The administrator growls, "Well, we've lost this year's student records. I hope you're happy." This whimsical example of an SQL injection attack exploits the excess functionality embodied in a buffer overflow bug, which enables a nonstandard data input to hijack program control. It is also a blended counterintelligence operation that combines human agent operations, social engineering, and technical exploits to influence the target's behavior.

40. On vulnerability as affordance, see Rebecca Slayton, "Power and Vulnerability in Inter-national Relations: Whither Technology?," paper presented at the annual International Studies Association conference, San Francisco, April 4, 2024. On affordances in IR generally, see Adler-Nissen and Drieschova 2019.

41. Smeets 2022 catalogues this myriad of factors and more with the mnemonic "PETIO"—people, exploits, tooling, infrastructure, organization. See also Slayton 2017.

42. Lindsay 2020b, chap. 7.

43. Charles A. O'Reilly III and Michael L. Tushman, "The Ambidextrous Organization," *Harvard Business Review*, April 1, 2004.

44. Clausewitz 1976, 102, 153.

45. S. Biddle 2004.

46. On the significant institutional requirements for converting espionage into advantage, see Lindsay and Cheung 2015; Gilli and Gilli 2018.

47. Gartzke and Lindsay 2017; Green and Long 2020.

48. Schelling 2008, 81.

49. Technically this is a variant of deterrence by denial, the threat of successful defense. An important nuance here is that making coercive threats with secret capabilities is very hard (because of the cyber commitment problem), but using secret capabilities is tacitly constrained by deterrence. For detailed discussion see Lindsay 2015; Gartzke and Lindsay 2024. A similar mechanism is Foucault's panopticon, whereby the threat of surveillance by a watchman who cannot be seen compels social conformity with the rules.

50. Maschmeyer 2021; Pedersen and Jacobsen 2024.

51. Cram 1993.

52. Generally see Edwards et al. 2011; Lindsay 2017.

53. Rovner 2023.

54. Monte 2015, 92. Monte describes sources of friction for the attacker, including operator mistakes, technical complexity, flawed attack tools, system updates and upgrades in remote

systems, interference from other attackers, intervention of cybersecurity defenders, and bad luck. Sources of friction for the defender include administrator mistakes, flawed software, the inertia of legacy systems, coordination problems in the cybersecurity community, system complexity, user complacency, and bad luck.

55. Lindsay 2020b, 67–70. On the increasing complexity of sociotechnical systems generally, see Winner 1977; Demchak 1991.

56. Breznitz and Murphree 2011.

57. A CrowdStrike developer inadvertently created a null pointer in C++ and neglected to include a null check. When the compiled routine attempted to access an invalid address on host machines, it created a memory access violation that triggered the "blue screen of death." See CrowdStrike, "Falcon Content Update Remediation and Guidance Hub," Preliminary Post Incident Review, July 24, 2024, https://www.crowdstrike.com/falcon-content-update-remediation-and-guidance-hub/.

58. Ian Duncan, Daniel Gilbert, Lori Aratani, Shira Ovide, and Danny Nguyen, "Microsoft, CrowdStrike Outage Disrupts Travel and Business Worldwide," *Washington Post*, July 19, 2024.

59. Brian Fung and Sean Lyngaas, "Hackers Are Already Taking Advantage of the Crowd-Strike Outage Chaos," *CNN*, July 22, 2024.

60. This is a classic pattern in studies of complex industrial systems, such as Perrow 1999.

61. S. Biddle 2001; Grauer and Horowitz 2012.

62. On the growth of attack surfaces, see Garfinkel and Dafoe 2019. On measuring the US cyber attack surface, see Harry et al. 2025.

63. Bouwman et al. 2020; Maschmeyer et al. 2021; Parkinson 2024.

64. Bennett and Elman 2006.

65. Collier 2011; Mahoney 2015.

66. Torigian 2021.

67. From this perspective, it is misleading to describe qualitative case study as "small-n" research. Indeed, most "large-n" statistical analyses tend to ignore the rich contextual detail that improves confidence in theoretical explanations. The charge of "picking on the dependent variable" is also misleading, because the focus of process tracing is on understanding the mechanisms that link explanatory conditions to the outcome of interest. See McKeown 1999; Flyvbjerg 2006.

68. Eckstein 2000.

69. Warner 2012a; Fidler 2017.

70. Headrick 1991; Nickles 2003.

71. Law 2004.

72. Fairfield and Charman 2019.

73. On pragmatism and abduction in IR, see Friedrichs and Kratochwil 2009; Franke and Weber 2012.

74. For more detail, see Lindsay 2024, which itself is a step in this book's abduction. That article "abducts" four explanatory factors (connectivity, vulnerability, organization, discretion), but this book consolidates them into just two (vulnerable institutions and clandestine organization). The article also suggests a link between my brief discussion of IR paradigms in chapter 1 and the performance conditions in chapter 2: Liberal ideas motivate my focus on collective institutions, while realist ideas motivate my focus on autonomous organizations.

75. Bates et al. 1998.

3. Security in Cyberspace

1. E.g., Craig Timberg, "The Real Story of How the Internet Became So Vulnerable," *Washington Post*, May 30, 2015.

2. Isaacson 2014, 4. This genre might be described as nerd hagiography—e.g., Lyon and Hafner 1996. On the archetypes of internet history, see Rosenzweig 1998.

3. Barry M. Leiner et al., "Brief History of the Internet," Internet Society, 1997, https://www.internetsociety.org/internet/history-internet/brief-history-internet/.

4. Gibson 1984, 51. The word "cyberspace" first appeared in Gibson's earlier story "Burning Chrome," *Omni*, July 1982.

5. Shires 2020.

6. Joint Chiefs of Staff 2018, GL-4.

7. Haigh 2014; Branch 2021.

8. Schmidt and Cohen 2013, 222.

9. John Perry Barlow, "A Declaration of the Independence of Cyberspace," Electronic Frontier Foundation, February 8, 1996, https://www.eff.org/cyberspace-independence. See also Castells 2000.

10. Michael V. Hayden, "The Making of America's Cyberweapons," *Christian Science Monitor*, February 24, 2016.

11. Waltz 1979, 96.

12. David D. Clark, "Control Point Analysis," paper presented at the 40th Research Conference on Communication, Information and Internet Policy, TPRC, Fairfax, VA, September 22, 2012.

13. This metaphor is developed in Vaishnav 2010. There are similar many-to-many interfaces in biology; see Csete and Doyle 2004.

14. Downey 2001; S. Jackson 2014; DeNardis 2014; Mathew 2016; Slayton and Clarke 2020.

15. The notion of "interpretive flexibility" is developed in Kline and Pinch 1996.

16. North 1990, 4.

17. North 1990, 133.

18. North 1990, 113–17.

19. Brynjolfsson and Saunders 2010.

20. North himself routinely mixes examples of practice and equipment—e.g., "The development of standardized weights and measures, units of account, a medium of exchange, notaries, consuls, merchant law courts, and enclaves of foreign merchants protected by foreign princes in return for revenue were all part and parcel of the organizations, institutions, and instruments that made possible transacting and engaging in long-distance trade." North 1990, 121.

21. North 1990, 3.

22. On the extension of cognition into the cultural world, see Sterelny 2004; Clark 2007.

23. Technologies can also be described as "purposed systems" as different as "monetary systems, contracts, symphonies, and legal codes, as well as physical methods and devices," according to Arthur (2009, 55). Or in the idiom of science and technology studies (STS), humans engage in "heterogenous engineering" (Law 1987) to "co-produce" (Jasanoff 2004) the practices and artifacts of the "sociotechnical systems" (Hughes 2004) that constrain and enable them. Institutional interpretations of technology in IR include Herrera 2006, 7; McCarthy 2015, 4. Applications of STS ideas to cybersecurity include T. Stevens 2016; Balzacq and Dunn Cavelty 2016.

24. Winner 1977, 323.

25. Jepperson 1991, 146. I would add only that the OS not only "appears as an institution" but fundamentally is one.

26. Agar 2003.

27. Turing 1936, 251.

28. Mindell 2002.

29. Dupuy 2000; Kline 2015.

30. March and Simon 1958; Deutsch 1963; Steinbruner 1974.

31. Coined by N. Wiener 1948.

32. Yates 1989; Headrick 2000; Chandler and Cortada 2000.

33. Hughes 2004, 13.

34. Cortada 2012, 582.

35. Beniger 1986.

36. North 1990, 25.

37. Medina 2011.

38. DiMaggio and Powell 1991, 28.

39. Bowker and Star 1999, 135.
40. DeNardis 2014; M. Mueller 2017.
41. See generally Ostrom 1990; North 1990; Strange 1994.
42. Baran 1964, iii, v.
43. Lukasik 2011.
44. Abbate 1999, 5. Historians have long recognized the influence of national security on the development of computing in general: inter alia, Aspray 1990; Edwards 1996; Norberg and O'Neill 1996; Hughes 1998; Hugill 1999; Akera 2007; Slayton 2013.
45. Ware 1970, xi.
46. Note the attention to both technical and human "threat points" in Ware 1970, 6.
47. Bell and La Padula 1976, 8.
48. DuPont and Fidler 2016; Fidler 2017.
49. The idea of a civil-military partition was encouraged by an early director of ARPA, J. C. R. Licklider, in "Memorandum for Members and Affiliates of the Intergalactic Computer Network," Advanced Research Projects Agency, April 23, 1963.
50. Postel's function as the Internet Assigned Numbers Authority (IANA), which assigned IP and AS identifiers and managed DNS entries, later moved to the Internet Corporation for Assigned Names and Numbers (ICANN), initially under contract to the US Department of Commerce and made fully independent in 2016. See Fidler and Mundy 2020.
51. David D. Clark, "A Cloudy Crystal Ball: Visions of the Future," plenary presentation at the 24th meeting of the Internet Engineering Task Force, Cambridge, MA, July 17, 1992, 19.
52. R. Metcalfe, "The Stockings Were Hung by the Chimney with Care," RFC 602, December 1973, https://www.rfc-editor.org/info/rfc602.
53. Abbate 2010.
54. Cortada 2012.
55. For extended discussion of the IPv6 transition, see DeNardis 2009.
56. Traffic analysis made the NSA program a valuable trove of intelligence, even if the contents of datagrams remained encrypted. See Schneier 2014.
57. On digital retrenchment after Snowden, see Oppenheimer 2023. On the international politics of privacy, see Farrell and Newman 2019a.
58. Anderson and Moore 2006. See also the annual proceedings of the Workshop on the Economics of Information Security, at https://econinfosec.org/weis-archive/.
59. Shapiro and Varian 1999.
60. August and Tunca 2006.
61. Bauer and van Eeten 2009.
62. Anderson et al. 2013.
63. Generally, Akerlof 1970. For application to security, see Edelman 2011.
64. Generally, Olson 1965.
65. Clark, "Cloudy Crystal Ball," 8.
66. Clark, "Cloudy Crystal Ball," 9. Capitalization in the original.
67. The growing historiography of computer security includes Leeuw and Bergstra 2007; Yost 2015; Yost 2016; Fidler 2017; Slayton and Clarke 2020; Stewart 2021. With specific emphasis on informal or decentralized organization, see Sowell 2015; Mathew 2016; Kuerbis and Mueller 2017; Eeten 2017; Slayton and Clarke 2020.
68. For accessible accounts of the growing national security concerns about cyberspace in the 1990s, see Rid 2016; F. Kaplan 2016. On the bureaucratic evolution of US military cyber capacity and doctrine, see Warner 2012a; Hunt 2012; White 2019; Slayton 2021. On the development of US Cyber Command, see Schneider et al 2020; Lindsay 2021; Lonergan and Poznansky 2024.
69. Chaudhary et al. 2018.
70. Christina A. Cassidy, "US Cybersecurity Agency's Future Role in Elections Remains Murky Under the Trump Administration," Associated Press, January 30, 2025, https://apnews.com/article/cisa-dhs-cybersecurity-election-security-trump-d17f40ad31f85a7538a7904efbea6b49.
71. Sergei Klebnikov, "Apple, Microsoft, Amazon, Google and Facebook Make Up a Record Chunk of the S&P 500: Here's Why That Might Be Dangerous," *Forbes*, July 24, 2020; Naeem

Aslam, "What $322 Billion in Combined First Quarter Revenue from Alphabet, Apple, Facebook, Microsoft and Amazon Tells Us About Consumer Habits," *Forbes*, May 3, 2021; Zaw Thiha Tun, "Top 25 Stocks in the S&P 500 by Index Weight for January 2025," Investopedia, January 1, 2025, https://www.investopedia.com/the-best-25-sp500-stocks-8778635. The "magnificent 7" group of stocks adds chipmaker Nvidia and carmaker Tesla (AMAMANT?) to account for nearly 34 percent.

72. Gillespie 2018; Gorwa 2019a; Gorwa 2019b. More generally, see Abbott and Snidal 2010.

73. For an autobiographical account of Microsoft's contribution to cybersecurity, see Smith and Browne 2021. In contrast, a critical report from the US Cyber Safety Review Board, created in CISA in 2022 and modeled after the National Transportation Safety Board, found "that Microsoft's security culture was inadequate and requires an overhaul, particularly in light of the company's centrality in the technology ecosystem and the level of trust customers place in the company to protect their data and operations." Cyber Safety Review Board 2024, iii.

74. Atal 2021, 336. This is a new twist on the classic problem of regulatory capture analyzed by Stigler 1961.

75. DeNardis 2014, 242.

76. Kuerbis and Badiei 2017. Of the firms, 60 percent were American, recapitulating US dominance in the global arms market. Following at a distance were the United States' closest allies, the United Kingdom (7 percent) and Canada (4 percent).

77. Gartner Research, "Forecast: Information Security and Risk Management, Worldwide, 2022–2028, 1Q24 Update," press release, March 24, 2024.

78. For an optimistic industry perspective, see Clarke and Knake 2019. On professionalism and its perils, grounded in historical comparison to maritime privateering, see Egloff 2021.

79. Woods and Wolff 2025.

80. Maschmeyer et al. 2021.

81. Maurer 2018; Deibert 2020; Perlroth 2021.

82. Ronen Bergman and Mark Mazzetti, "The Battle for the World's Most Powerful Cyberweapon," *New York Times*, January 28, 2022.

83. For example, the "ForcedEntry" exploit implemented a computational architecture with the equivalent functionality of Javascript via a public protocol that iOS used to render graphical icons. ForcedEntry emulated arbitrary logic circuits that could be programmed to escape the iOS BlastDoor security perimeter through an integer overflow. ForcedEntry did not use any force; rather, it exploited a "weird machine" (see chapter 2) that was capable of more than iOS developers had intended. See Bill Marczak et al., "FORCEDENTRY: NSO Group iMessage Zero-Click Exploit Captured in the Wild," Citizen Lab, University of Toronto, September 13, 2021, https://citizenlab.ca/2021/09/forcedentry-nso-group-imessage-zero-click-exploit-captured-in-the-wild/; Ian Beer and Samuel Groß, "FORCEDENTRY: Sandbox Escape," Project Zero, March 31, 2022, https://googleprojectzero.blogspot.com/2022/03/forcedentry-sandbox-escape.html.

84. Dana Priest, "A UAE Agency Put Pegasus Spyware on Phone of Jamal Khashoggi's Wife Months Before His Murder, New Forensics Show," *Washington Post*, December 21, 2021.

85. John Scott-Railton et al., "Reckless VII: Wife of Journalist Slain in Cartel-Linked Killing Targeted with NSO Group's Spyware," Citizen Lab, University of Toronto, March 20, 2019, https://citizenlab.ca/2019/03/nso-spyware-slain-journalists-wife/; Natalie Kitroeff and Ronen Bergman, "How Mexico Became the Biggest User of the World's Most Notorious Spy Tool," *New York Times*, April 18, 2023.

86. Marczak et al., "FORCEDENTRY"; Bill Marczak et al., "Triple Threat: NSO Group's Pegasus Spyware Returns in 2022 with a Trio of iOS 15 and iOS 16 Zero-Click Exploit Chains," Citizen Lab, University of Toronto, April 18, 2023, https://citizenlab.ca/2023/04/nso-groups-pegasus-spyware-returns-in-2022/. For a gripping account of the intelligence contest between Citizen Lab and NSOGroup, see Deibert 2025.

87. Raphael Satter, "Undercover Spy Exposed in NYC Was 1 of Many," AP News, February 11, 2019.

88. Ronen Bergman and Patrick Kingsley, "Israeli Spyware Maker Is in Spotlight amid Reports of Wide Abuses," *New York Times*, July 18, 2021.

89. David E. Sanger, Nicole Perlroth, Ana Swanson, and Ronen Bergman, "U.S. Blacklists Israeli Firm NSO Group over Spyware," *New York Times*, November 3, 2021.

90. Drezner 2004; S. Brooks 2005; Starrs 2013.

91. M. Mueller 2010; DeNardis 2014.

92. Monteiro 2011; Cooley and Nexon 2020.

4. Espionage

1. Ultra also included intelligence derived from other Axis ciphers, but Enigma predominated.

2. Mahoney 2015.

3. Kennedy 2013, 359.

4. Mindell 2002.

5. Turing 1936; I. Good 2000.

6. Shannon 1945.

7. Soni and Goodman 2017, 104, 107.

8. Hinsley et al. 1979, 21n.

9. The Electronic Numerical Integrator and Computer (ENIAC), built in 1946 at the University of Pennsylvania, is usually described as the first digital, reprogrammable, electronic computer. Purpose-built Colossus was not designed to be reprogrammable, although its switches and circuits could be reconfigured, and indeed they were modified to perform new functions during the war. Colossus was one of the more remarkable, reliable, and practical machines to emerge in the "early digital" milieu of the 1940s, as discussed by Haigh and Priestley (2018). For a stronger claim about Colossus as computational precedent, see Copeland 2006.

10. Quoted in Grey 2012, 88.

11. Ellen Nakashima and Joby Warrick, "For NSA Chief, Terrorist Threat Drives Passion to 'Collect It All,'" *Washington Post*, July 14, 2013.

12. The vast literature on Bletchley Park includes the five-volume official history edited by F. H. Hinsley, declassified internal histories, practitioner memoirs, academic treatises, and countless documentaries and fictionalizations of mixed quality. An initial wave of histories based on this material includes Kahn 2012; Hinsley and Stripp 1993; Budiansky 2000; Smith and Erskine 2001. Reconsiderations of Bletchley Park with the benefit of open archives and nuanced interpretations include Ratcliff 2006; Grey 2012; Kenyon 2019; Haigh and Priestley 2020; Ferris 2020. My account draws mainly on these sources.

13. Howard 1990, 52.

14. Howard 1990, x.

15. Beyerchen 1996.

16. Kahn 2001, 86.

17. Ferris 2002.

18. Shannon 1945.

19. Shannon 1948.

20. For examples of traffic analysis by British intelligence during the war, see Thirsk 2001.

21. While cryptography today refers mainly to code making (defense), GC&CS also described its (offensive) codebreakers as cryptographers, and cryptanalytic techniques remain invaluable for verifying cryptographic security today; thus "cryptography" is sometimes used synonymously with "cryptology." For an accessible primer on classic cryptology, see Kahn 1996, 737–62. For developments in digital cryptography, see Aumasson 2018.

22. Kahn 1993, 239.

23. Arthur Sherbius, Ciphering Machine, US Patent Office 1657411, filed February 6, 1923, and issued January 24, 1928.

24. For a technical account of German cryptosystems by a GC&CS cryptographer, see J. Good 1993.

25. Ferris 2020, 173.

26. Shannon proved that it is possible to encode perfectly secure ciphertext using a so-called one-time pad. The practical problem with a one-time pad is producing enough truly random keys and getting them to all the communicators so they can use (and not reuse) them in the field. This problem led to the decryption of the KGB Venona documents that revealed the Cambridge Five, discussed in the introduction.

27. Cryptographers traditionally tried to protect everything, but Auguste Kerckhoffs argued in 1883 that only the key should be protected; this improved the "simplicity, reliability, rapidity, and so on" of practical encryption (efficiency) and ensured that "ordeal by cryptanalysis" provided a public guarantee of the system's security (effectiveness), as discussed in Kahn 1996, 233–35. Kerckhoffs's principle in effect separates the autonomous institution of the secret key (and the communications it protects) from the collective institution of the cryptosystem.

28. A. Miller 1995.

29. All encryption was symmetric before the internet era, so there was no need to qualify it. In the 1970s, British cryptographers and American academics independently discovered asymmetric encryption. As the name suggests, this uses different keys for encryption and decryption (or for digital signatures and authentication). For the technical details, see Aumasson 2018, 181–216. Asymmetric encryption enables secure communication over the internet with actors who never meet face to face, and it obviates the need to distribute symmetric keys (or enables actors to use slower asymmetric protocols to exchange symmetric keys for a faster session), which is vital for internet privacy and e-commerce. There is no free lunch in cryptography, however. Asymmetric encryption replaces the symmetric key distribution problem with the institutional complexity of public key infrastructure (PKI), which maps digital keys to real-world entities. Reliance on PKI introduces new risks, such as forged certificates and corrupted authorities. Even for advanced quantum protocols, institutional vulnerability remains a key factor conditioning the security of technical cryptosystems, as discussed in Lindsay 2020a.

30. Kahn 1993, 239.

31. Ratcliff 2006.

32. Kahn 1993, 239.

33. Erskine 2001b.

34. Erskine 2001a, 64.

35. Erskine 2001a, 69.

36. Erskine 2001c, 370.

37. Erskine 2001a, 62–64.

38. Bombes actually searched for all possible plugboard combinations that could *not* produce the menu, returning promising "stops" that could be fed back into an Enigma emulator. The other Enigma settings (rotor order, wheel settings, starting positions) were often cracked through manual cryptanalysis with the support of several ingenious paper aids. Bombes could be modified to perform different kinds of searches as well.

39. Kahn 2012, 269. Fingerprinting anticipates modern electronic intelligence (ELINT).

40. Ferris 2020, 219.

41. Ratcliff 2006, 95.

42. Kahn 2012, 168.

43. The Baudot code was a 5-bit public standard anticipating ASCII and Unicode. A stream cipher produces a continuous key the same length as the message.

44. Kenyon 2019, 26.

45. S. Wylie 2001, 323–24. Similarly, Marian Rejewski in Poland reconstructed Enigma rotor wiring patterns without ever seeing modifications adopted by Germany. Frank Rowlett and Genevieve Grotjan in the United States inferred Japanese Purple mechanisms without ever seeing an actual machine.

46. S. Wylie 2001, 323–24.

47. See also Hastings 2016, 449.

48. Ratcliff 2006, 231–32.

49. Howard 1990, 49–52.

50. Ferris 2020, 231.

51. Hastings 2016, 427, 495–96.

52. Lindsay 2020b, chap. 7.

53. Ferris 2020, 213.

54. Grey 2012, 214–15.

55. For a catalogue of Allied machinery, see Budiansky 2000, 359–62. The computer metaphor for GC&CS is developed further in Agar 2003, 203–9.

56. Erskine 2001a, 56.

57. Erskine 2001a, 73.

58. Kenyon 2019, 25.

59. Kenyon 2019, 24. In 1943, GC&CS relocated its cryptographic operations to a large two-story concrete building (Block D) with more space and better protection from aerial bombing, but the functional sections continued to be referred to as huts. Kenyon 2019, 21–22.

60. Brunt 2006.

61. Lewin 2008, 138–54.

62. Ferris 2020, 204.

63. Milner-Barry 1986.

64. Grey 2012, 55, 197.

65. Erskine 2001a, 58.

66. Turing 1936. Turing showed that a deterministic algorithm could not solve the "halting problem," the determination of whether any arbitrary program will come to completion or run on forever.

67. The design is described in characteristically inscrutable prose and scribbles in Turing 1939.

68. I. Good 2000.

69. Copeland 2006; Davis 2018, 153–70.

70. Turing 1950.

71. For the same reasons, Turing was not a very good manager. He chafed at the military regulations imposed on him. To cite but one example, "the authorities were irritated by Turing's apparently casual approach, insisting that since he signed up for Home Guard duties, he was under military law. Turing calmly pointed out that he was no such thing, and that he had stated as much on the form that he had signed. One of the questions on the form was: 'Do you understand that by enrolling in the Home Guard, you place yourself under military law?' Turing had written his answer: 'No.'" McKay 2010, 171. After the great reorganization of GC&CS, Turing was relieved of his supervisory duties in the Huts and used as a cryptanalytic free agent for the rest of the war. The standard biography is Hodges 2014.

72. Kenyon 2019, 149–51.

73. S. Wylie 2001, 339.

74. Ferris 2020, 187.

75. Haigh and Priestley 2018. Interestingly, the choice of Flowers to lead the engineering effort outside Bletchley Park helped to solve an internal disagreement among cryptographers on how best to proceed. Ferris 2020, 189.

76. Copeland 2001, 351.

77. Copeland 2001, 361. The pattern of "dots and crosses" (ones and zeros) on each of the rotor wheels was regularly changed by German operators according to a prearranged plan. Thus it was important to discover both the wheel patterns and the initial wheel settings in order to extract the key.

78. S. Wylie 2001, 340–41.

79. Hastings 2016, 414. For an account of the architecture of Colossus, see Haigh and Priestley 2018.

80. Quoted in Ferris 2020, 187.

81. Ratcliff 2006, chap. 4. "Ultra" was the code word for high-grade SIGINT from any source, Enigma as well as Lorentz.

82. Grey 2012, 122–23.

83. Ferris 2020, 260.

84. Hastings 2016, 218.

85. Kahn 2012, 247.
86. Ratcliff 2006, 33–55.
87. Hinsley et al. 1981, 636–37.
88. Ratcliff 2006, 159–79.
89. Grey 2012, 128.
90. Ratcliff 2006, 115–16.
91. Kahn 2012, 169.
92. Ferris 2020, 259.
93. Howard 1990, 4.
94. Howard 1990, 103–34.
95. M. Smith 2001.
96. This account draws from Howard 1990, 103–200.
97. Fearon 1997.
98. Howard 1990, 188.
99. Howard 1990, 199.
100. On the determinants of victory and the minor supporting role of intelligence—neither unimportant nor decisive—see Overy 1996; Keegan 2003; Kennedy 2013; O'Brien 2015; Hastings 2016.
101. Data from Hinsley et al. 1981; Hinsley et al. 1984, 483–87; Hinsley et al. 1988, 855–57.
102. Kahn 2012, 54.
103. Kahn 2012, 307. Kahn notes, "Perhaps not coincidentally, sinkings rose steadily from November 1944 to April 1945 in the North Atlantic and North Sea, although the absolute numbers remained small."
104. Kahn 2012, 252.
105. Kahn 2012, 264–66.
106. Grey 2012, 34–35. It is possible that Germany used some Enigma keys that GC&CS never identified, but this is unlikely given Y-branch coverage.
107. E.g., Fischerkeller et al. 2022.
108. J. Wylie 1989, 22–27.
109. Kahn 2012, 213.
110. Kennedy 2013, 59.
111. Quoted in Kahn 2012, 214.
112. Quoted in Ferris 2020, 266.
113. Hastings 2016, 84.
114. Hinsley et al. 1988, 897–99; Hastings 2016, 495.
115. Ferris 2020, 249.
116. Drea 1992; Andrew and Elkner 2003.
117. Quoted in Hastings 2016, 546.
118. Keegan 2003, 221–57.
119. Kennedy 2013, 61. For similar skepticism about Ultra in the Atlantic, see Keegan 2003, chap. 4.
120. Hastings 2016, 545.
121. Ferris 2020, 238.
122. Ferris 2020, 242.
123. Ferris 2020, 235.
124. Countless examples of operational impact can be found in the first three volumes of the official history *British Intelligence in the Second World War*, by Hinsley et al., which are subtitled *Its Influence on Strategy and Operations* and cover that subject in chronological order. The fourth and fifth volumes cover contributions to counterintelligence and deception operations, respectively.
125. Ehlers 2009, 339.
126. Ehlers 2009, 345–46.
127. Hastings 2016, 552.
128. Kenyon 2019, 243.
129. Kenyon 2019, 215.

5. Sabotage

1. Lindsay 2013.
2. Eugene Kaspersky, "The Man Who Found Stuxnet—Sergey Ulasen in the Spotlight," *Nota Bene*, November 2, 2011, https://eugene.kaspersky.com/2011/11/02/the-man-who-found-stuxnet-sergey-ulasen-in-the-spotlight/.
3. Alexander Gostev, "Myrtus and Guava, Episode 1," *Securelist*, Kaspersky Lab, July 15, 2010, https://securelist.com/myrtus-and-guava-episode-1/29614/; Nicolas Falliere, Liam O'Murchu, and Eric Chien, "W32.Stuxnet Dossier, Version 1.4," Symantec, February 4, 2011, https://docs.broadcom.com/doc/security-response-w32-stuxnet-dossier-11-en; Aleksandr Matrosov, Eugene Rodionov, David Harley, and Juraj Malcho, "Stuxnet Under the Microscope," ESET, January 20, 2011, https://www.welivesecurity.com/2010/11/02/stuxnet-paper-updated/; Langner 2011.
4. Albright et al. 2011.
5. David E. Sanger, "Obama Order Sped Up Wave of Cyberattacks Against Iran," *New York Times*, June 1, 2012; Zetter 2014.
6. Juan Andres Guerrero-Saade and Silas Cutler, "Who Is GOSSIPGIRL?," *Chronicle Blog*, April 9, 2019, https://medium.com/chronicle-blog/who-is-gossipgirl-3b4170f846c0.
7. E.g., Kerr et al. 2010; Farwell and Rohozinski 2011; J. Nye 2011; Denning 2012; Peterson 2013.
8. Quoted in Sanger, "Obama Order." Hayden's "somebody" is an interesting choice of words given that from 1999 to 2009, Hayden directed the NSA and then the CIA. During the same period of time, the United States developed and employed computer network operations against Iran.
9. See, inter alia, Barzashka 2013; Jenkins 2013; Lindsay 2013; Yannakogeorgos and Tikk 2016; C. Stevens 2020. Cf. Maher 2019.
10. Slayton 2017.
11. See figure 6 in Albright et al. 2015, 14.
12. Naturally occurring uranium ore consists mainly of the nonfissile isotope U-238 with a very low concentration of the fissile isotope U-235. The process of enrichment feeds uranium hexafluoride gas through a series of centrifuges (cascade) to separate and concentrate U-235. The Natanz facility operated multiple groups (modules) of centrifuge cascades of Pakistani design. LEU enriched to 3–5 percent U-235 requires hundreds of stages of enrichment and is suitable for light-water reactors. LEU refers to anything less than 20 percent and cannot be used directly to build a bomb, although it can be fed back into cascades to reach higher levels. Highly enriched uranium (HEU) refers to anything above 20 percent, which requires many hundreds or thousands more stages of enrichment and has some legitimate research applications. Weapons-grade HEU above 90 percent can serve as the fissile material for a bomb. A proliferator must be able to build a reliable weapon and delivery system to have a functional nuclear deterrent. For further discussion, see Office of the Deputy Assistant Secretary of Defense for Nuclear Matters 2020.
13. Volpe 2017.
14. Iranian president Mahmoud Ahmadinejad even called for Israel to be "wiped off the map," but interpretations of this are contested; see Glenn Kessler, "Did Ahmadinejad Really Say Israel Should Be 'Wiped Off the Map'?," *Washington Post*, October 5, 2011.
15. Bass 2015, 27–60.
16. David A. Fulghum, Robert Wall, and Amy Butler, "Cyber-Combat's First Shot," *Aviation Week & Space Technology*, November 16, 2007.
17. Amos Harel and Aluf Benn, "No Longer a Secret: How Israel Destroyed Syria's Nuclear Reactor," *Haaretz*, March 23, 2018, https://www.haaretz.com/world-news/MAGAZINE-no-longer-a-secret-how-israel-destroyed-syria-s-nuclear-reactor-1.5914407.
18. Raas and Long 2007.
19. Ronen Bergman and Mark Mazzetti, "The Secret History of the Push to Strike Iran," *New York Times*, September 4, 2019.
20. Rovner 2011, 137–84.
21. National Intelligence Council 2007.

22. Bergman and Mazzetti, "Secret History."

23. David E. Sanger, "U.S. Rejected Aid for Israeli Raid on Iranian Nuclear Site," *New York Times*, January 10, 2009; Katz and Hendel 2012, 185–86.

24. Bergman 2018, 622.

25. Bergman and Mazzetti, "Secret History." See also Katz and Hendel 2012, 178.

26. Kamel 2018.

27. Bergman and Mazzetti, "Secret History."

28. Falliere et al., "W32.Stuxnet Dossier."

29 Geoff McDonald, Liam O'Murchu, Stephen Doherty, and Eric Chien, "Stuxnet 0.5: The Missing Link," Symantec, February 26, 2013, https://docs.broadcom.com/doc/stuxnet-missing-link-13-en.

30. Ewen MacAskill, "Stuxnet Cyberworm Heads Off US Strike on Iran," *The Guardian*, January 16, 2011. Or perhaps the US appropriated as much as $400 million; see Seymour M. Hersh, "Preparing the Battlefield," *New Yorker*, June 29, 2008.

31. Zetter 2014, 310n4.

32. GReAT, "Equation Group: Questions and Answers," Kaspersky Lab, February 2015, https://media.kasperskycontenthub.com/wp-content/uploads/sites/43/2018/03/08064459/Equation_group_questions_and_answers.pdf.

33. GReAT, "A Fanny Equation: 'I Am Your Father, Stuxnet,'" *Securelist*, Kaspersky Lab, February 17, 2015, https://securelist.com/a-fanny-equation-i-am-your-father-stuxnet/68787/.

34. Juan Andres Guerrero-Saade and Silas Cutler, "Flame 2.0: Risen from the Ashes," Chronicle, April 9, 2019, available at https://silascutler.com/uploads/Flame_2.0_Risen_from_the_Ashes.pdf; GReAT, "The DuQu 2.0: Technical Details," Kaspersky Lab, June 11, 2015, https://media.kasperskycontenthub.com/wp-content/uploads/sites/43/2018/03/07205202/The_Mystery_of_Duqu_2_0_a_sophisticated_cyberespionage_actor_returns.pdf.

35. David E. Sanger and Mark Mazzetti, "U.S. Had Cyberattack Plan If Iran Nuclear Dispute Led to Conflict," *New York Times*, February 16, 2016; Gibney 2016.

36. Sanger and Mazzetti, "U.S. Had Cyberattack Plan."

37. On the emergence of offensive cyber operations behind closed doors in the NSA in the late 1990s and early 2000s, overcoming resistance from traditional SIGINT professionals, see C. Wiener 2016; Loleski 2019.

38. On the evolution of overt cyber strategy in the United States, see Goldman 2020, 31–46; Harknett and Smeets 2020; Lonergan and Poznansky 2024.

39. Walter Pincus, "Twisted View of CIA's Operation Merlin," *Washington Post*, January 26, 2015.

40. William J. Broad and David E. Sanger, "In Nuclear Net's Undoing, a Web of Shadowy Deals," *New York Times*, August 24, 2008.

41. Bergman 2018; Ben Hubbard, Farnaz Fassihi, and Ronen Bergman, "Iran Rattled as Israel Repeatedly Strikes Key Targets," *New York Times*, April 20, 2021.

42. David E. Sanger and Ronen Bergman, "How Israel, in Dark of Night, Torched Its Way to Iran's Nuclear Secrets," *New York Times*, July 15, 2018.

43. Bergman 2008; Crist 2012.

44. Zach Dorfman and Jenna McLaughlin, "The CIA's Communications Suffered a Catastrophic Compromise: It Started in Iran," *Yahoo News*, November 2, 2018, https://www.yahoo.com/news/cias-communications-suffered-catastrophic-compromise-started-iran-090018710.html.

45. Julian E. Barnes, Ronen Bergman, and Adam Goldman, "Israel's Spy Agency Snubbed the U.S.: Can Trust Be Restored?," *New York Times*, August 26, 2021.

46. Office of Public Affairs, "Seven Iranians Working for Islamic Revolutionary Guard Corps-Affiliated Entities Charged for Conducting Coordinated Campaign of Cyber Attacks Against U.S. Financial Sector," Department of Justice, March 24, 2016, https://www.justice.gov/opa/pr/seven-iranians-working-islamic-revolutionary-guard-corps-affiliated-entities-charged; J. D. Work, "Echoes of Ababil: Re-Examining Formative History of Cyber Conflict and Its Implications for Future Engagements," paper presented at the 86th Annual Meeting of the Society for Military History, Columbus, OH, May 11, 2019.

47. Bronk and Tikk-Ringas 2013; GReAT, "From Shamoon to Stonedrill: Wipers Attacking Saudi Organizations and Beyond," Kaspersky Lab, March 7, 2017, https://media.kaspersky contenthub.com/wp-content/uploads/sites/43/2018/03/07180722/Report_Shamoon_ StoneDrill_final.pdf.

48. US Attorney's Office, Northern District of Georgia, "Atlanta U.S. Attorney Charges Iranian Nationals for City of Atlanta Ransomware Attack," Department of Justice, December 5, 2018, https://www.justice.gov/usao-ndga/pr/atlanta-us-attorney-charges-iranian-nationals-city-atlanta-ransomware-attack.

49. Nicole Perlroth, "Without Nuclear Deal, U.S. Expects Resurgence in Iranian Cyberattacks," *New York Times*, May 11, 2018; Andrew Hanna, "The Invisible U.S.-Iran Cyber War," United States Institute of Peace, July 29, 2021, https://iranprimer.usip.org/blog/2019/oct/25/invisible-us-iran-cyber-war.

50. Conceptual overlap between cybersecurity and special operations is discussed in Fogarty and Nasi 2016.

51. Stuxnet 0.5 and 1.0, Fanny, Flame, miniFlame, and Gauss are discussed later in this chapter. Alexis Dorais-Joncas and Facundo Muñoz, "Jumping the Air Gap: 15 Years of Nation-State Effort," ESET, December 1, 2021, https://www.welivesecurity.com/2021/12/01/jumping-air-gap-15-years-nation-state-effort/.

52. Kim Zetter and Huib Modderkolk, "Revealed: How a Secret Dutch Mole Aided the U.S.-Israeli Stuxnet Cyberattack on Iran," *Yahoo News*, September 2, 2019, https://www.yahoo.com/news/revealed-how-a-secret-dutch-mole-aided-the-us-israeli-stuxnet-cyber-attack-on-iran-160026018.html.

53. Sanger 2018, 30.

54. GReAT, "Stuxnet: Zero Victims," *Securelist*, Kaspersky Lab, November 11, 2014, https://securelist.com/stuxnet-zero-victims/67483/.

55. Ron Rosenbaum, "Richard Clarke on Who Was Behind the Stuxnet Attack," *Smithsonian*, April 2012. The programmed stop date in later versions of Stuxnet was June 24, 2012, but an earlier November 2007 version had a July 4, 2009, stop date. This may suggest that there was some prior CIA operation, authorized separately, for US-only experiments before other partners were brought aboard with Olympic Games.

56. Falliere et al., "W32.Stuxnet Dossier."

57. McDonald et al., "Stuxnet 0.5."

58. Langner 2013.

59. White House 2011, 10.

60. Sanger, "Obama Order."

61. Foltz 2012; Yannakogeorgos and Tikk 2016.

62. Generally, Poznansky 2020.

63. Loleski 2019.

64. Andi Wilson Thompson, "Assessing the Vulnerabilities Equities Process, Three Years After the VEP Charter," *Lawfare*, January 13, 2021, https://www.lawfaremedia.org/article/assessing-vulnerabilities-equities-process-three-years-after-vep-charter.

65. Bowden 2011, 27–46.

66. Alexander Gostev, "Back to Stuxnet: The Missing Link," *Securelist*, Kaspersky Lab, June 11, 2012, https://securelist.com/back-to-stuxnet-the-missing-link/33174/; GReAT, "Fanny Equation."

67. Canonical accounts of Stuxnet mention four or five zero-days, or vulnerabilities that were unknown to vendors at the time that Stuxnet exploited them. But depending on how one counts, the four publicly reported samples of Stuxnet have collectively incorporated at least eight and perhaps fourteen zero-days (but never all of them at the same time). There is some ambiguity around the concept of a zero-day insofar as a technical exploit may incorporate multiple software vulnerabilities, the same vulnerability may be exploited in different ways, patches may close multiple vulnerabilities, or vulnerabilities may be known but not reported or patched for various reasons. The intuitive point is that Olympic Games knew many things that Microsoft and Siemens did not, and much more than was originally reported on Stuxnet.

68. Falliere et al., "W32.Stuxnet Dossier." Olympic Games targeted these firms presumably to increase the likelihood that a human agent would wittingly or unwittingly pass a copy of Stuxnet via a USB connection.

69. GReAT, "Stuxnet: Zero Victims."

70. The FBI assumed that Cartwright was a key source for David Sanger, but Sanger maintains that he met with Cartwright simply "to check that I had the history and implications right, and to get an independent view of whether any details I was reporting could jeopardize American national security." Sanger 2018, 32. Cartwright was convicted of the federal felony offense of lying, not leaking. Obama pardoned Cartwright in January 2017 prior to sentencing. Julia Harte, "Retired U.S. General Pleads Guilty to Lying to FBI in 'Stuxnet' Leak Case," Reuters, October 17, 2016.

71. Snowden has been described variously as a whistleblower, patriot, traitor, and Russian agent, and his motivation remains a mystery over a decade later. On the impact of Snowden, see Steven Levy, "How the NSA Almost Killed the Internet," Wired, January 7, 2014; Farrell and Newman 2019a.

72. Kim Zetter, "How a Russian Firm Helped Catch an Alleged NSA Data Thief," Politico, January 9, 2019, https://www.politico.com/story/2019/01/09/russia-kaspersky-lab-nsa-cybersecurity-1089131.

73. Among other suggestive technical artifacts, ASCII art in some code contained the caption "WON THE GOLD MEDAL," a possible reference to Olympic Games. Lorenzo Franceschi-Bicchierai, "The New Shadow Brokers Leak Connects the NSA to the Stuxnet Cyber Weapon Used on Iran," Vice, April 17, 2017, https://www.vice.com/en/article/shadow-brokers-nsa-stuxnet-iran/.

74. Southern District of New York, "Former CIA Officer Joshua Adam Schulte Sentenced to 40 Years in Prison for Espionage and Child Pornography Crimes," US Department of Justice, February 1, 2024, https://www.justice.gov/usao-sdny/pr/former-cia-officer-joshua-adam-schulte-sentenced-40-years-prison-espionage-and-child. The IOC was later renamed the Center for Cyber Intelligence.

75. Falliere et al., "W32.Stuxnet Dossier," 55.

76. This may be described as a "supra-threat actor." Juan Andrés Guerrero-Saade, "Draw Me Like One of Your French APTs—Expanding Our Descriptive Palette for Cyber Threat Actors," paper presented at annual Virus Bulletin conference, Montreal, October 3–5, 2018, https://www.virusbulletin.com/uploads/pdf/magazine/2018/VB2018-Guerrero-Saade.pdf.

77. GReAT, "Equation Group."

78. Central Intelligence Agency (via WikiLeaks, Vault 7: CIA Hacking Tools Revealed, February 2015, posted March 7, 2017, https://wikileaks.org/ciav7p1/cms/page_14588809.html), "What Did Equation Do Wrong, and How Can We Avoid Doing the Same?" The "Vault 7" CIA documents appear to be authentic, according to Ellen Nakashima and Shane Harris, "Elite CIA Unit That Developed Hacking Tools Failed to Secure Its Own Systems, Allowing Massive Leak, an Internal Report Found," Washington Post, June 16, 2020. The Vault 7 material has also been associated with yet another CNE platform, tracked as Longhorn (Symantec) and Lamberts (Kaspersky); see Runa Sandvik, "Made in America: Green Lambert for OS X," Objective-See, October 1, 2021, https://objective-see.com/blog/blog_0x68.html. On CIA IOC, see Ellen Nakashima, Greg Miller, and Julie Tate, "U.S., Israel Developed Flame Computer Virus to Slow Iranian Nuclear Efforts, Officials Say," Washington Post, June 19, 2012.

79. Central Intelligence Agency, "What Did Equation Do Wrong." There is some irony in the CIA critiquing NSA OPSEC in chats that were leaked through CIA OPSEC failures.

80. Franceschi-Bicchierai, "New Shadow Brokers"; Facundo Muñoz, "The Emerald Connection: EquationGroup Collaboration with Stuxnet," September 28, 2020, available at https://fmmresearch.wordpress.com/wp-content/uploads/2020/09/theemeraldconnectionreport_fmmr-2.pdf.

81. GReAT, "Fanny Equation."

82. Nakashima et al., "Flame Computer Virus."

83. Another such collaboration platform, apparently not related to Stuxnet, is the Regin tool linked to Five Eyes intelligence partners. See Symantec Security Response, "Regin: Top-Tier Espionage Tool Enables Stealthy Surveillance," Symantec, August 27, 2015, https://docs.broadcom.com/docs/regin-top-tier-espionage-tool-15-en.

84. McDonald et al., "Stuxnet 0.5."

85. GReAT, "Gauss: Abnormal Distribution," Kaspersky Lab, August 9, 2012, https://securelist.com/gauss-abnormal-distribution/36620/; GReAT, "miniFlame aka SPE: 'Elvis and His Friends,'" *Securelist*, Kaspersky Lab, October 15, 2012, https://securelist.com/miniflame-aka-spe-elvis-and-his-friends/68560/.

86. Boldizsár Bencsáth, Gábor Pék, Levente Buttyán, and Márk Félegyházi, "Duqu: A Stuxnet-Like Malware Found in the Wild," Laboratory of Cryptography and System Security (CrySyS Lab), Budapest University of Technology and Economics, with Ukatemi Technologies, October 14, 2011; Alexander Gostev, "Stuxnet/Duqu: The Evolution of Drivers," *Securelist*, Kaspersky Lab, December 28, 2011, https://securelist.com/stuxnetduqu-the-evolution-of-drivers/36462/.

87. The 8200 connection to Stuxnet was first reported in Sanger, "Obama Order." On 8200 generally, see John Reed, "Unit 8200: Israel's Cyber Spy Agency," *Financial Times*, July 10, 2015.

88. Boldizsár Bencsáth, "Territorial Dispute: NSA's Perspective on APT Landscape," Laboratory of Cryptography and System Security (CrySyS Lab), Budapest University of Technology and Economics, with Ukatemi Technologies, March 2018, 27, https://www.crysys.hu/publications/files/tedi/ukatemicrysys_territorialdispute.pdf; Juan Andres Guerrero-Saade and Silas Cutler, "Stuxshop: The Oldest Stuxnet Component Dials Up," Chronicle, April 9, 2019, available at https://silascutler.com/uploads/STUXSHOP_Stuxnet_Dials_In.pdf.

89. McDonald et al., "Stuxnet 0.5," 3.

90. Bergman and Mazzetti, "Secret History."

91. Alexander Gostev, "The Flame: Questions and Answers," *Securelist*, Kaspersky Lab, May 28, 2012, https://securelist.com/the-flame-questions-and-answers/34344/.

92. Guerrero-Saade and Cutler, "Flame 2.0."

93. GReAT, "DuQu 2.0," 42. Kaspersky reported several other forensic indicators suggestive of an Israeli source.

94. GReAT, "DuQu 2.0," 44.

95. The NSA allegedly used a toolkit called "territorial dispute" to detect simultaneous intrusions by other threat actors in its target networks. Bencsáth, "Territorial Dispute."

96. Amusingly, a Shadow Brokers file included a snippet of code with ASCII art of an Olympic medal; see Franceschi-Bicchierai, "New Shadow Brokers."

97. Zetter and Modderkolk, "Revealed." The participation of GCHQ is briefly discussed in *Zero Days* 2016.

98. Slayton 2017; Smeets 2022a.

99. Sanger, "Obama Order"; Sanger 2018, 9. On the covert-action oversight process in the US intelligence community, see Lowenthal 2020, 230–34.

100. On the origins of NSA cyber capacity, see C. Wiener 2016; Loleski 2019.

101. Nakashima et al., "Flame Computer Virus."

102. Zetter 2014, 317–18.

103. William J. Broad, John Markoff, and David E. Sanger, "Israeli Test on Worm Called Crucial in Iran Nuclear Delay," *New York Times*, January 15, 2011.

104. A leaked document from WikiLeaks states, "XXXXXXXXXXXX recommended that a policy of covert sabotage (unexplained explosions, accidents, computer hacking etc) would be more effective than a military strike whose effects in the region could be devastating." US Embassy Berlin, "German MFA Hope Iran Sanctions Target Leaders Not Masses," WikiLeaks, January 21, 2010, in "US Embassy Cables: Germany Ready to Support Iran Sanctions," *The Guardian*, January 18, 2011, https://www.theguardian.com/world/us-embassy-cables-documents/244617.

105. Broad et al., "Israeli Test on Worm."

106. Falliere et al., "W32.Stuxnet Dossier," 10.

107. Sanger, "Obama Order."

108. Yossi Melman, "Israel's Rash Behavior Blew Operation to Sabotage Iran's Computers," *Jerusalem Post*, February 16, 2016.

109. Freilich et al. 2023, 13.

110. Bergman and Mazzetti, "Secret History."

111. Bergman 2018, 623.

112. Bergman and Mazzetti, "Secret History."

113. Bergman and Mazzetti, "Secret History." See also Sanger and Mazzetti, "U.S. Had Cyberattack Plan."

114. Sanger and Mazzetti, "U.S. Had Cyberattack Plan." See also *Zero Days* 2016.

115. Sanger and Mazzetti, "U.S. Had Cyberattack Plan."

116. Albright et al. 2010.

117. From Albright et al. 2015.

118. See table 1 in Albright et al. 2011.

119. Albright et al. 2013, 3.

120. Albright and Burkhard 2020, 6.

121. Arshad Mohammed, "The Invisible Man: Bill Burns and the Secret Iran Talks," Reuters, January 2, 2014; Julian Borger, "Nuclear Talks Lead to Rare Meeting Between US and Iran," *The Guardian*, October 1, 2009.

122. Indira A. Lakshmanan, "'If You Can't Do This Deal . . . Go Back to Tehran,'" *Politico*, September 25, 2015, https://www.politico.com/magazine/story/2015/09/iran-deal-inside-story-213187.

123. Bergman and Mazzetti, "Secret History."

124. Bergman and Mazzetti, "Secret History."

125. Sanger and Mazzetti, "U.S. Had Cyberattack Plan."

126. JCPOA Annex III, para. 10.1, https://2009-2017.state.gov/documents/organization/245322.pdf. See also Maher 2019, 1029.

127. Maher 2019, 1027.

128. Cf., Valeriano et al. 2018.

129. Freilich et al. 2023, chap. 3; Anderson and Sadjadpour 2018; Work and Harknett 2020.

130. Bronk and Tikk-Ringas 2013.

131. Leon E. Panetta, "Remarks by Secretary Panetta on Cybersecurity," October 11, 2012, Homeland Security Digital Library, https://www.hsdl.org/?view&did=724128.

132. Dustin Volz and Jim Finkle, "U.S. Indicts Iranians for Hacking Dozens of Banks, New York Dam," Reuters, March 24, 2016; Joseph Berger, "A Dam, Small and Unsung, Is Caught Up in an Iranian Hacking Case," *New York Times*, March 25, 2016.

133. Julian E. Barnes, "U.S. Cyberattack Hurt Iran's Ability to Target Oil Tankers, Officials Say," *New York Times*, August 28, 2019.

134. Ellen Nakashima, "Trump Approved Cyber-Strikes Against Iranian Computer Database Used to Plan Attacks on Oil Tankers," *Washington Post*, June 22, 2019.

135. Lonergan and Lonergan 2022.

136. Sanger and Bergman, "How Israel."

137. Bergman 2018, 608, 622–25.

138. Ronen Bergman and Farnaz Fassihi, "The Scientist and the A.I.-Assisted, Remote-Control Killing Machine," *New York Times*, September 18, 2021.

139. Hubbard et al., "Iran Rattled."

140. Joe Tidy, "Predatory Sparrow: Who Are the Hackers Who Say They Started a Fire in Iran?," *BBC News*, July 10, 2022, https://www.bbc.com/news/technology-62072480.

141. Tom Bennett, "What We Know About Israel's Attack on Iran," *BBC News*, October 28, 2024, https://www.bbc.com/news/articles/cgr0yvrx4qpo.

142. Lindsay 2013, 365.

143. Fischerkeller et al. 2022.

144. Chesney and Smeets 2023; Dunn Cavelty et al. 2024.

6. Subversion

1. Sun Tzu 2020, 53.
2. I use "bullshit" in the technical sense of speech intended to persuade without regard to truth, per Frankfurt 2005, as discussed in chapter 1.
3. Inter alia, House Permanent Select Committee on Intelligence 2018; R. Mueller 2019; US Senate Select Committee on Intelligence 2020.
4. Inter alia, FireEye iSight Intelligence 2017; SecureWorks Counter Threat Unit, "IRON TWILIGHT Supports 'Active Measures,'" SecureWorks Threat Intelligence Research, March 30, 2017, https://www.secureworks.com/research/iron-twilight-supports-active-measures; CrowdStrike, "Our Work with the DNC: Setting the Record Straight," June 5, 2020, https://www.crowdstrike.com/blog/bears-midst-intrusion-democratic-national-committee/.
5. Office of the Director of National Intelligence 2017, i.
6. Office of the Director of National Intelligence 2017, ii.
7. Charles Maynes, "As US Reels from Capitol Violence, Russia Enjoys the Show," *Voice of America*, January 7, 2021, https://www.voanews.com/a/europe_us-reels-capitol-violence-russia-enjoys-show/6200451.html.
8. Chinese and Russian concepts of cybersecurity have always been more expansive in this regard, placing as much emphasis (or more) on content as on functionality. In this book I will use "IO" to refer to psychological influence operations, although the term is sometimes used more broadly to encompass cyber and electronic warfare.
9. E.g., Persily 2017; Whyte et al. 2020; Francois and Lin 2021; Vićić and Gartzke 2024.
10. Inter alia, O'Rourke 2018; Levin 2020; Lee 2020.
11. C. Jackson 2016.
12. Generally, Borden 1964; Constantinides 2006.
13. Chesney and Citron 2019; Lin and Kerr 2021; Whyte 2024.
14. Adler and Drieschova 2021.
15. Paul and Matthews 2016; Kragh and Åsberg 2017; Thomas 2019; Posard et al. 2020; Grisé et al. 2022.
16. Dmitri Alperovitch, "Bears in the Midst: Intrusion into the Democratic National Committee," CrowdStrike, June 15, 2016, https://www.crowdstrike.com/blog/bears-midst-intrusion-democratic-national-committee/; SecureWorks Counter Threat Unit, "Threat Group 4127 Targets Hillary Clinton Presidential Campaign," SecureWorks Threat Intelligence Research, June 16, 2016, https://www.secureworks.com/research/iron-twilight-supports-active-measures; FireEye iSight Intelligence, "APT28"; Nicole Gaouette, "FBI's Comey: Republicans Also Hacked by Russia," *CNN Politics*, January 10, 2017, http://cnn.com/2017/01/10/politics/comey-republicans-hacked-russia/index.html.
17. SecureWorks Counter Threat Unit, "Threat Group-4127 Targets Google Accounts," SecureWorks Threat Intelligence Research, June 26, 2016, https://www.secureworks.com/research/iron-twilight-supports-active-measures.
18. Will Oremus, "'Is This Something That's Going to Haunt Me the Rest of My Life?,'" *Slate*, December 14, 2016, http://slate.com/technology/2016/12/an-interview-with-charles-delavan-the-it-guy-whose-typo-led-to-the-podesta-email-hack.html.
19. CrowdStrike, "Our Work with the DNC"; R. Mueller 2019, 36–40.
20. Galeotti 2016.
21. CrowdStrike, "Our Work with the DNC"; Eric Lipton, David E. Sanger, and Scott Shane, "The Perfect Weapon: How Russian Cyberpower Invaded the U.S.," *New York Times*, December 13, 2016.
22. Huib Modderkolk, "Dutch Agencies Provide Crucial Intel About Russia's Interference in US-Elections," *De Volkskrant*, January 25, 2018, https://www.volkskrant.nl/gs-b4f8111b.
23. Alperovitch, "Bears in the Midst."
24. US Senate Select Committee on Intelligence 2020, 3:4.
25. R. Mueller 2019, 40–51.
26. Massimo Calabresi, "Inside Russia's Social Media War on America," *Time*, May 18, 2017.

27. Ellen Nakashima, "Cyber Researchers Confirm Russian Government Hack of Democratic National Committee," *Washington Post*, June 20, 2016; ThreatConnect Research Team, "Guccifer 2.0: All Roads Lead to Russia," ThreatConnect, July 26, 2016, https://threatconnect.com/blog/guccifer-2-all-roads-lead-russia/.

28. Ellen Nakashima, "Powerful NSA Hacking Tools Have Been Revealed Online," *Washington Post*, August 16, 2016.

29. Adrian Chen, "The Agency," *New York Times*, June 2, 2015.

30. Vićić and Gartzke 2024.

31. Etudo et al. 2023.

32. Jamieson 2018, 203.

33. Jamieson 2018, 203.

34. Weedon et al. 2017; Colin Crowell, "Our Approach to Bots and Misinformation," Twitter, June 14, 2017, https://blog.twitter.com/en_us/topics/company/2017/Our-Approach-Bots-Misinformation.

35. Rid 2020, 7.

36. Thrall 2007.

37. Thrall and Armstrong 2020, 74.

38. Benkler et al. 2018.

39. Benkler et al. 2018, 382.

40. Benkler et al. 2018, 267.

41. Garrett et al. 2020; Krafft and Donovan 2020.

42. Schelling argues that the flight of the most racist families from a mixed neighborhood eventually causes the least racist families to leave as well, resulting in the voluntary segregation of neighborhoods. Schelling 1960, 91.

43. See Bruns 2019; Driscoll and Steinert-Threlkeld 2020; Törnberg 2022.

44. Subsequent experiments suggest that Americans are motivated to condemn foreign involvement only when that involvement sides with the opposition rather than with their own party. Tomz and Weeks 2020.

45. Ashley Parker and David E. Sanger, "Donald Trump Calls on Russia to Find Hillary Clinton's Missing Emails," *New York Times*, July 27, 2016.

46. "Joint Statement from the Department of Homeland Security and Office of the Director of National Intelligence on Election Security," US Department of Homeland Security, October 7, 2016, https://www.dhs.gov/news/2016/10/07/joint-statement-department-homeland-security-and-office-director-national.

47. US Senate Select Committee on Intelligence 2020, 5:255.

48. US Senate Select Committee on Intelligence 2020, 5:vii.

49. "September 26, 2016 Debate Transcript," Commission on Presidential Debates, September 26, 2016, https://www.debates.org/voter-education/debate-transcripts/september-26-2016-debate-transcript/.

50. Andrew Roth, "Putin Denies That Russia Hacked the DNC but Says It Was for the Public Good," *Washington Post*, September 2, 2016.

51. Sun Tzu 2020, 134.

52. A leaked dossier of private intelligence reports, later discredited as shoddy opposition research, suggested that the Kremlin possessed salacious "kompromat" that might be used to blackmail Trump. See Paul Farhi, "The Washington Post Corrects, Removes Parts of Two Stories Regarding the Steele Dossier," *Washington Post*, November 12, 2021.

53. US Senate Select Committee on Intelligence 2020, 5:943. A perfunctory six paragraphs of "additional views from Republican senators" came to a different conclusion: "The Committee found no evidence that then-candidate Donald Trump or his campaign colluded with the Russian government in its efforts to meddle in the election" (5:941). The difference turns on the semantics of "cooperation" versus "collusion," but the evidence of knowing collaboration contained in the one-thousand-page report is overwhelming.

54. "Remarks by President Trump and President Putin of the Russian Federation in Joint Press Conference," White House, July 16, 2018, https://trumpwhitehouse.archives.gov/briefings-statements/remarks-president-trump-president-putin-russian-federation-joint-press-conference/.

55. Ellen Nakashima, "U.S. Cyber Command Operation Disrupted Internet Access of Russian Troll Factory on Day of 2018 Midterms," *Washington Post*, February 27, 2019; Allcott et al. 2019.

56. Russian influence doesn't merit a single mention (other than a passing reference to the Mueller investigation) in Sides et al. 2022, a comprehensive account of the 2020 election.

57. Paul M. Nakasone, "Statement of General Paul M. Nakasone, Commander, United States Cyber Command," US Senate Committee on Armed Services, February 14, 2019, 6, https://www.armed-services.senate.gov/imo/media/doc/Nakasone_02-14-19.pdf.

58. "Evaluation of the U.S. Department of Justice's Efforts to Coordinate Information Sharing About Foreign Malign Influence Threats to U.S. Elections," US Department of Justice, Office of the Inspector General, July 2024.

59. Sides et al. 2022, 23.

60. Sides et al. 2022, 267.

61. Arceneaux and Trues 2023.

62. Carrie Johnson, "Trump Offers Long-Promised Pardons to Some 1,500 January 6 Rioters," *National Public Radio*, January 20, 2025, https://www.npr.org/2025/01/20/g-s1-36809/trump-pardons-january-6-riot.

63. Lazer et al. 2018; Wilde 2024a.

64. Spangher et al. 2018; Zannettou et al. 2019; Ruck et al, 2019; Bail et al 2020; Helmus et al. 2020; Fisher 2020; Carter and Carter 2021; Lukito 2020. However, cf. Eady et al. 2023.

65. Etudo et al. 2023.

66. Vosoughi et al. 2018.

67. For extensive discussion, with surprisingly little mention of Russia, see Bernhard and O'Neill 2019a, 2019b, both special issues.

68. Sides et al. 2018.

69. Sides et al. 2018, 31.

70. Nate Silver, "The Real Story of 2016," FiveThirtyEight, January 19, 2017, https://fivethirtyeight.com/features/the-real-story-of-2016/.

71. Nate Silver, "How Much Did Russian Interference Affect the 2016 Election?," FiveThirtyEight, February 16, 2018, https://fivethirtyeight.com/features/how-much-did-russian-interference-affect-the-2016-election/.

72. Brennan Weiss, "A Russian Troll Factory Had a $1.25 Million Monthly Budget to Interfere in the 2016 US Election," *Business Insider*, February 16, 2018.

73. Alex Stamos, "An Update on Information Operations on Facebook," Facebook, September 6, 2017, https://about.fb.com/news/2017/09/information-operations-update/.

74. Sides et al. 2018, 191.

75. Hansen and Lim 2019; Jensen et al. 2019; Lucan Ahmad Way and Adam Casey, "Russia Has Been Meddling in Foreign Elections for Decades: Has It Made a Difference?," *Washington Post*, January 8, 2018.

76. Eady et al. 2023.

77. Sides et al. 2018, 191.

78. Kalla and Broockman 2018, 148. Cf. Campbell 2001.

79. Sides et al. 2018, 136, 191–92.

80. Comparative favorability ratings of each candidate are tracked in Sides et al. 2018, 137.

81. Nate Silver, "The Comey Letter Probably Cost Clinton the Election," FiveThirtyEight, May 3, 2017, https://fivethirtyeight.com/features/the-comey-letter-probably-cost-clinton-the-election/.

82. Jamieson 2018, 189–203.

83. Jamieson 2018. See also Jane Mayer, "How Russia Helped Swing the Election for Trump," *New Yorker*, September 24, 2018.

84. Jamieson 2018, 212.

85. Levin 2020.

86. Levin 2016, 186. US interventions, mostly earlier in the Cold War, account for 69 percent of Levin's total, while Russian interventions, mostly later in the Cold War and after it, account for only 31 percent. This runs counter to the conventional wisdom that authoritarians manipulate democracies more often.

87. Levin 2020, 230.

88. Levin 2020, 245.

89. Starbird et al. 2019, 15.

90. Julian E. Barnes, Glenn Thrush, and Steven Lee Myers, "U.S. Announces Plan to Counter Russian Influence Ahead of 2024 Election," *New York Times*, September 4, 2024.

91. Hannah Allam, Amy Gardner, and Yvonne Wingett Sanchez, "Panic Buttons, Drones, Snipers Among Plans to Guard a High-Risk Election," *Washington Post*, November 3, 2024.

92. "Amanpour Interviews Dave Chappelle and Jon Stewart," Royal Albert Hall, London, *CNN*, October 30, 2018, https://www.cnn.com/videos/world/2018/10/30/dave-chappelle-jon-stewart-amanpour.cnn.

7. Cyber Power

1. BeyondTrust, "BeyondTrust Reinforces Commitment to a Safer More Transparent Digital World by Signing CISA's Secure by Design Pledge," October 24, 2024, https://www.beyondtrust.com/press/cisa-secure-by-design. On the incident itself, see Ellen Nakashima and Jeff Stein, "Treasury's Sanctions Office Hacked by Chinese Government, Officials Say," *Washington Post*, January 1, 2025, https://www.washingtonpost.com/national-security/2025/01/01/treasury-hack-china/. Microsoft tracks Chinese threat actors under the name Typhoon (Salt, Flax, Silk, Twill, Volt, etc.). BeyondTrust was hacked by Silk Typhoon, according to Katrina Manson and Jake Bleiberg, "White House Rushes to Finish Cyber Order After China Hacks," *Bloomberg*, January 8, 2025, https://www.bloomberg.com/news/articles/2025-01-08/white-house-rushes-to-finish-cyber-order-after-china-hacks. Microsoft refers to other countries with different storms (Blizzard-Russia, Sandstorm-Iran, Tsunami-Israel, Sleet–North Korea, etc.). Different security companies often use different names to track the same groups, which is confusing but probably inevitable given the underlying epistemological problems of attribution and the market incentives of the threat intelligence industry.

2. Dustin Volz, "China's Salt Typhoon Hacking Campaign Hit Dozens of Countries, U.S. Official Says," *Wall Street Journal*, December 5, 2024, https://www.wsj.com/politics/national-security/dozens-of-countries-hit-in-chinese-telecom-hacking-campaign-top-u-s-official-says-2a3a5cca.

3. Andy Greenberg, "China's Salt Typhoon Spies Are Still Hacking Telecoms—Now by Exploiting Cisco Routers," *Wired*, February 13, 2025, https://www.wired.com/story/chinas-salt-typhoon-spies-are-still-hacking-telecoms-now-by-exploiting-cisco-routers/.

4. Office of the Director of National Intelligence, "Annual Threat Assessment of the U.S. Intelligence Community," February 2024, https://www.intelligence.gov/annual-threat-assessment.

5. US Department of the Treasury, "Treasury Sanctions Company Associated with Salt Typhoon and Hacker Associated with Treasury Compromise," January 17, 2025, https://home.treasury.gov/news/press-releases/jy2792.

6. Christopher A. Wray, "Director Wray's Opening Statement to the House Select Committee on the Strategic Competition Between the United States and the Chinese Communist Party," Federal Bureau of Investigation, January 31, 2024, https://www.fbi.gov/news/speeches/director-wrays-opening-statement-to-the-house-select-committee-on-the-chinese-communist-party. Cf. Arquilla and Ronfeldt 1993.

7. As reviewed in Lindsay 2015. See also Brooks and Wohlforth 2016; Gilli and Gilli 2018.

8. Betz and Stevens 2011, 44. Cf., Kuehl 2009; J. Nye 2010.

9. Mertha 2009.

10. Saha and Feng 2020.

11. Shirk 2007.

12. Naughton 2007.

13. Wuthnow and Fravel 2023, 1173. On PLA doctrine generally, see Fravel 2020.

14. Shirk 2022.
15. Qi 2015.
16. Cabestan 2021; Shirk 2022.
17. Zhang 2019.
18. Cf. Kang 2022.
19. deLisle and Goldstein 2021.
20. TikTok, a popular social media platform owned by the Beijing-based company Byte-Dance, became a political football in the United States. National security concerns emerged regarding the threat of espionage or surveillance over 170 million American TikTok users and the threat of subversion or influence of their content feeds through CCP manipulation of the TikTok algorithm. A ban on TikTok passed in both houses of Congress with strong bipartisan support in April 2024 and was unanimously upheld by the U.S. Supreme Court in January 2025 (see opinion nos. 24–656 and 24–657 on January 17, 2025). President Trump then issued an executive order on the first day of his second term that halted implementation of the ban.
21. CHIPS [Creating Helpful Incentives to Produce Semiconductors] and Science Act, H. R. 4346, Pub. L. No. 117–167, 117th Cong. (2022) (enacted); C. Miller 2022. In his first address to Congress on March 4, 2025, President Trump called for the repeal of the CHIPS Act, yet the Trump administration also levied new sanctions on China. Decoupling proceeds haltingly at best.
22. Hannas and Tatlow 2020; Cheung 2022.
23. Allison et al. 2021.
24. Kania 2021.
25. Segal 2020; Zaagman 2018.
26. DeNardis 2014; Hoffmann et al. 2020.
27. Zeng et al. 2017; M. Mueller 2017.
28. Steinfeld 2010.
29. Johnston 2019.
30. Xi Jinping, "Accelerate the Independent Innovation of Network Information Technology and Make Unremitting Efforts Towards the Goal of Building a Cyber Superpower," speech at the Thirty-Sixth Collective Study of the Politburo of the CCP, October 9, 2016, http://cpc.people.com.cn/n1/2016/1010/c64094-28763907.html.
31. "State Council Opinions Concerning Vigorously Moving Forward the 'Internet Plus' Plan," trans. Rogier Creemers, July 1, 2015, https://chinacopyrightandmedia.wordpress.com/2015/07/01/state-council-guiding-opinions-concerning-vigorously-moving-forward-the-internet-plus-plan/.
32. Xinhua News Agency, "The Small Leading Group for Cybersecurity and Informatization Held Its First Meeting," February 27, 2014, http://www.gov.cn/ldhd/2014-02/27/content_2625036.htm. On Chinese cybersecurity policy around the same time, see Lindsay 2015.
33. Doshi et al. 2021, 4–6.
34. Cyberspace Administration of China 2023. The phrases in this paragraph appear in the book's table of contents.
35. These represent my interpretation of the *shige jianchi* summarized in "General Secretary Xi Jinping's Important Thoughts on Cyber Superpower," CPC Learning Network, accessed August 8, 2023, https://www.12371.cn/special/xxzd/hxnr/wlqg/.
36. John Perry Barlow, "A Declaration of the Independence of Cyberspace," Electronic Frontier Foundation, February 8, 1996, https://www.eff.org/cyberspace-independence.
37. Cyberspace Administration of China 2023, chap. 8.
38. Herman 1996, 2.
39. Faligot 2019; Mattis and Brazil 2019.
40. Stout and Warner 2018.
41. Richard Bejtlich, "Testimony Before the U.S.-China Economic and Security Review Commission," Washington, DC, March 26, 2012. https://www.uscc.gov/sites/default/files/3.26.12bejtlich.pdf.

42. Hannas et al. 2013.

43. National Counterintelligence and Security Center 2018, 5.

44. Andy Greenberg, "The Full Story of the Stunning RSA Hack Can Finally Be Told," *Wired*, May 20, 2021.

45. Mandiant 2013.

46. A US State Department cable that leaked in 2011 states that US intelligence tracked Chinese cyber intrusions as Byzantine Hades going back at least to 2002. Brian Grow and Mark Hosenball, "Special Report: In Cyberspy, vs. Cyberspy, China Has the Edge," Reuters, April 14, 2011.

47. "Red Line Drawn: China Recalculates Its Use of Cyber Espionage," FireEye iSIGHT Intelligence, June 2016, https://www.fireeye.com/blog/threat-research/2016/06/red-line-drawn-china-espionage.html.

48. Kelli Vanderlee, "China's Capabilities for State-Sponsored Cyber Espionage," testimony before the US-China Economic and Security Review Commission, February 17, 2022, https://www.uscc.gov/sites/default/files/2022-02/Kelli_Vanderlee_Testimony.pdf.

49. Ellen Nakashima, "Following U.S. Indictments, China Shifts Commercial Hacking Away from Military to Civilian Agency," *Washington Post*, November 30, 2015.

50. Kania and Costello 2021.

51. Nicole Perlroth, David E. Sanger, and Scott Shane, "How Chinese Spies Got the N.S.A.'s Hacking Tools, and Used Them for Attacks," *New York Times*, May 6, 2019.

52. Ellen Nakashima and David J. Lynch, "U. S. Charges Chinese Hackers in Alleged Theft of Vast Trove of Confidential Data in 12 Countries," *Washington Post*, December 21, 2018.

53. Vanderlee, "China's Capabilities," 3.

54. Coline Chavane and TDR team, "A Three-Beat Waltz: The Ecosystem Behind Chinese State-Sponsored Cyber Threats," *Sekoia* (blog), November 2024, https://blog.sekoia.io/a-three-beats-waltz-the-ecosystem-behind-chinese-state-sponsored-cyber-threats/.

55. Microsoft Threat Intelligence Center, "HAFNIUM Targeting Exchange Servers with 0-Day Exploits," *Microsoft Security* (blog), March 16, 2021, https://www.microsoft.com/security/blog/2021/03/02/hafnium-targeting-exchange-servers/. I am grateful to Shachi Shah, Eric Martin, and Kangkyu Lee for research and insights contributing to this case.

56. Office of Public Affairs, "Four Chinese Nationals Working with the Ministry of State Security Charged with Global Computer Intrusion Campaign Targeting Intellectual Property and Confidential Business Information, Including Infectious Disease Research," US Department of Justice, July 18, 2021, https://www.justice.gov/opa/pr/four-chinese-nationals-working-ministry-state-security-charged-global-computer-intrusion.

57. Zach Dorfman, "Tech Giants Are Giving China a Vital Edge in Espionage," *Foreign Policy* (blog), December 23, 2020, https://foreignpolicy.com/2020/12/23/china-tech-giants-process-stolen-data-spy-agencies/.

58. Kim Zetter, "Unmasking China's State Hackers," *Zero Day* (newsletter), March 29, 2022, https://zetter.substack.com/p/unmasking-chinas-state-hackers.

59. Paul Mozur and Chris Buckley, "Spies for Hire: China's New Breed of Hackers Blends Espionage and Entrepreneurship," *New York Times*, August 26, 2021.

60. Chavane and TDR team, "Three-Beat Waltz," 25.

61. Edelstein 2017.

62. Ron Deibert, Arnav Manchanda, Rafal Rohozinski, Nart Villeneuve, and Greg Walton, "Tracking GhostNet: Investigating a Cyber Espionage Network," Citizen Lab, University of Toronto, and SecDev Group, March 29, 2009, https://citizenlab.ca/wp-content/uploads/2017/05/ghostnet.pdf.

63. "A New Approach to China," *Google* (blog), January 12, 2010, https://googleblog.blogspot.com/2010/01/new-approach-to-china.html.

64. Lindsay and Cheung 2015, 58–60.

65. E.g., Ross McKerchar, "Pacific Rim: Inside the Counter-Offensive—the TTPs Used to Neutralize China-Based Threats," Sophos X-Ops, October 31, 2024, https://news.sophos.com/en-us/2024/10/31/pacific-rim-neutralizing-china-based-threat/.

66. Insikt Group 2023, 12.

67. E.g., "The increased use of zero days over the last year from China-based actors likely reflects the first full year of China's vulnerability disclosure requirements for the Chinese security community and a major step in the use of zero-day exploits as a state priority." Microsoft 2022, 39. According to Sekoia, "At least 3530 'common' novel vulnerabilities, and 219 vulnerabilities considered as 'critical risk' would have been submitted to" CNITSEC in 2024 alone. Chavane and TDR team, "Three-Beat Waltz," 27.

68. Ellen Nakashima, Joseph Menn, and Shane Harris, "Chinese Hackers Breach Email of Commerce Secretary Raimondo and State Department Officials," *Washington Post*, July 14, 2023; Dustin Volz and Warren P. Strobel, "U.S. Ambassador to China Hacked in China-Linked Spying Operation," *Wall Street Journal*, July 20, 2023; Microsoft Security Response Center, "Microsoft Mitigates China-Based Threat Actor Storm-0558 Targeting of Customer Email," *Microsoft Security* (blog), July 11, 2023, https://msrc.microsoft.com/blog/2023/07/microsoft-mitigates-china-based-threat-actor-storm-0558-targeting-of-customer-email/.

69. Cyber Safety Review Board 2024, iii.

70. "Justice Department and FBI Conduct International Operation to Delete Malware Used by China-Backed Hackers," US Department of Justice, January 14, 2025, https://www.justice.gov/archives/opa/pr/justice-department-and-fbi-conduct-international-operation-delete-malware-used-china-backed.

71. Ellen Nakashima, "China Hacked Japan's Sensitive Defense Networks, Officials Say," *Washington Post*, August 17, 2023.

72. Xi Jinping, speech at the Joint Welcome Banquet of the Washington State Local Government and American Friendship Groups, Seattle, September 22, 2015, http://cpc.people.com.cn/n/2015/0924/c64094-27626923.html.

73. Poznansky 2020.

74. Krasner 1999.

75. Finklea et al. 2015.

76. Damian Paletta, "U.S. Intelligence Chief James Clapper Suggests China Behind OPM Breach," *Wall Street Journal*, June 25, 2015.

77. The Snowden leaks revealed an NSA program exploiting Google servers, and Olympic Games exploited Microsoft vulnerabilities.

78. IP Commission 2017.

79. Christopher Wray, "The Threat Posed by the Chinese Government and the Chinese Communist Party to the Economic and National Security of the United States," speech, Hudson Institute, Washington, DC, July 7, 2020, https://www.fbi.gov/news/speeches/the-threat-posed-by-the-chinese-government-and-the-chinese-communist-party-to-the-economic-and-national-security-of-the-united-states.

80. Josh Rogin, "NSA Chief: Cybercrime Constitutes the 'Greatest Transfer of Wealth in History,'" *Foreign Policy*, July 9, 2012.

81. Lindsay and Cheung 2015.

82. Saxenian 1994; Breznitz and Murphree 2011.

83. FBI Director Wray stated that "Chinese hackers . . . outnumber FBI Cyber personnel by at least 50 to 1." This totals at least 50,000 Chinese hackers if "the FBI has over 1,000 cyber personnel distributed throughout the United States." Respectively, Christopher Wray, "Director's Opening Statement to the House Committee on Appropriations Subcommittee on Commerce, Justice, Science, and Related Agencies, Federal Bureau of Investigation, April 27, 2023, https://www.fbi.gov/news/speeches/directors-opening-statement-to-the-house-committee-on-appropriations-subcommittee-on-commerice-justice-science-and-related-agencies; Bryan A. Vorndran, "Oversight of the FBI Cyber Division," Federal Bureau of Investigation, March 29, 2022, https://www.fbi.gov/news/testimony/oversight-of-the-fbi-cyber-division-032922.

84. Hannas et al. 2013; Hannas and Tatlow 2020.

85. Gilli and Gilli 2018.

86. Beckley 2018; Brooks and Wohlforth 2016.

87. S. Biddle 2004; Caverley 2007; R. Brooks 2008; Talmadge 2015; Grauer 2016; Long 2016.

88. For extensive discussion, see Lindsay 2020b, chap. 2.

89. Feigenbaum 2003.

90. Cunningham 2025, 191-97, 248-58.

91. McReynolds 2016; Burke et al. 2020.

92. Brooks and Wohlforth 2016; Beckley 2018.

93. Montgomery 2014; Heginbotham et al. 2015.

94. Yunxian Yu and Zongyi Yuan, "What Kind of Mobilization View Should the Information War Have?," *PLA Daily*, April 2, 2020, http://www.mod.gov.cn/jmsd/2020-04/02/content_4863000.htm.

95. Zilian Zhang and Daiwu Ma, "What Kind of Integration Concept Should Information Warfare Have?," *PLA Daily*, December 10, 2019, http://www.81.cn/jfjbmap/content/2019-12/10/content_249559.htm.

96. Costello and McReynolds 2018; Kania and Costello 2021.

97. Cunningham 2025, 208-33.

98. Zhuo Chen, "Defense Ministry Spokesperson's Remarks on Recent Media Queries Concerning the PLA Information Support Force," Ministry of National Defense of the People's Republic of China, April 22, 2024, http://eng.mod.gov.cn/xb/News_213114/NewsRelease/16302635.html.

99. Lonergan and Poznansky 2024.

100. Talmadge 2015, chap. 1.

101. Australian Cyber Security Centre, "People's Republic of China State-Sponsored Cyber Actor Living off the Land to Evade Detection," Australian Signals Directorate, May 25, 2023, https://www.cyber.gov.au/about-us/advisories/prc-state-sponsored-cyber-actor-living-off-the-land-to-evade-detection.

102. Microsoft Threat Intelligence, "Volt Typhoon Targets US Critical Infrastructure with Living-off-the-Land Techniques," *Microsoft Security* (blog), May 24, 2023, https://www.microsoft.com/en-us/security/blog/2023/05/24/volt-typhoon-targets-us-critical-infrastructure-with-living-off-the-land-techniques/.

103. Cybersecurity and Infrastructure Security Agency, "PRC State-Sponsored Actors Compromise and Maintain Persistent Access to U.S. Critical Infrastructure," Cybersecurity Advisory AA24–038A, February 7, 2024, https://www.cisa.gov/news-events/cybersecurity-advisories/aa24-038a.

104. Buchanan and Cunningham 2020.

105. Joshua Rovner, "Everything, Everywhere, All at Once? Cyberspace Operations and Chinese Strategy," War on the Rocks, March 25, 2024, https://warontherocks.com/2024/03/everything-everywhere-all-at-once-cyberspace-operations-and-chinese-strategy/.

106. Chase et al. 2015; Cozad 2016.

107. Chavane and TDR team, "Three-Beat Waltz," 25.

108. Chavane and TDR team, "Three-Beat Waltz," 16.

109. Tsai 2016.

110. Kania 2020.

111. McKune 2015.

112. "Xi Jinping Issued Important Instructions for the National Cyber Security Publicity Week," *Xinhua*, September 16, 2019, http://www.xinhuanet.com/politics/leaders/2019-09/16/c_1125000571.htm.

113. Borden 1964.

114. Ruan et al. 2021.

115. King et al. 2013; Gallagher and Miller 2021.

116. Deibert et al. 2012; Roberts 2018.

117. Marczak et al. 2015.

118. Eva Dou, "Documents Link Huawei to China's Surveillance Programs," *Washington Post*, December 14, 2021.

119. This project marks a reversal for Google, which in 2010 left China due to rising concerns about censorship and the hacking of Google systems. See Sarah McKune and Ronald Deibert, "Google's Dragonfly: A Bellwether for Human Rights in the Digital Age," *Just Security*, August 2, 2018, https://www.justsecurity.org/59941/googles-dragonfly-bellwether-human-rights-digital-age/.

120. Roberts 2018.
121. Compare Carson 2016; Cormac and Aldrich 2018.
122. Fedasiuk 2021.
123. Xi Jinping, speech at the Work Conference for Cybersecurity and Informatization, April 19, 2016, translated by Rogier Creemers, *China Copyright and Media*, April 26, 2016, https://chinacopyrightandmedia.wordpress.com/2016/04/19/speech-at-the-work-conference-for-cybersecurity-and-informatization/.
124. Creemers 2017.
125. Ministry of State Security, "Anti-Espionage Requires the Mobilization of the Whole Society!," *WeChat* (blog), July 31, 2023, https://mp.weixin.qq.com/s/KHGKLZ2q98giMAa JTIVJ3g.
126. See supra note 20.
127. Voo et al. 2022, 7. The index includes a variety of indicators for strengthening national cyber defenses, improving commercial technology competence, defining cyber norms and standards, electronically surveilling domestic groups, manipulating the information environment, and engaging in foreign intelligence collection, infrastructure disruption, and cyber-crime. Given the heterogeneity of all these indicators, one could be excused for questioning the coherence of the concept of cyber power.
128. Brooks and Wohlforth 2016; Beckley 2018.
129. Voo et al. 2022, 10.
130. Clara Ferreira Marques, "China and Russia Are Frenemies with Benefits," *Bloomberg*, February 3, 2022, https://www.bloomberg.com/opinion/articles/2022-02-04/vladimir-putin-and-xi-jinping-meet-as-frenemies-with-benefits. See also Kania and Segal 2021.

Conclusion

1. Chris Blattman, "Cyber Warfare Is Getting Real," *Wired*, December 17, 2022. See also Jason Healey, "Is Cyber Revolutionary or Barely Relevant in Modern Warfare?," War on the Rocks, February 28, 2025, https://warontherocks.com/2025/02/is-cyber-revolutionary-or-barely-relevant-in-modern-warfare.
2. Adam Janofsky, "NSA Cyber Chief: Espionage Is Now Russia's Focus for Cyberattacks on Ukraine," *Recorded Future News*, October 10, 2024, https://therecord.media/russia-ukraine-espionage-luber-nsa.
3. Sheera Frenkel and Ronen Bergman. "Israel Planted Explosives in Pagers Sold to Hezbollah, Officials Say," *New York Times*, September 17, 2024.
4. Christiaan Triebert and Aric Toler, "Walkie-Talkies in Lebanon May Have Held More Explosives Than Pagers, a Times Analysis Finds," *New York Times*, September 18, 2024.
5. Sheera Frenkel, Ronen Bergman, and Hwaida Saad, "How Israel Built a Modern-Day Trojan Horse: Exploding Pagers," *New York Times*, September 18, 2024.
6. Raffi Berg, "Ex-Israeli Agents Reveal How Hezbollah Pager Attacks Were Carried Out," *BBC News*, December 23, 2024, https://www.bbc.com/news/articles/cwy3l02wxqdo.
7. Journalists describe Israeli targeting processes: "Once a Hezbollah operative is identified, his daily patterns of movements are fed into a vast database of information, siphoned off from devices that could include his wife's cell phone, his smart car's odometer, or his location. These can be identified from sources as disparate as a drone flying overhead, from a hacked CCTV camera feed that he happens to pass by, and even from his voice captured on the microphone of a modern TV's remote control, according to several Israeli officials." Mehul Srivastava, James Shotter, and Raya Jalabi, "How Israeli Spies Penetrated Hezbollah," *Financial Review*, September 30, 2024, https://www.afr.com/world/middle-east/how-israeli-spies-penetrated-hezbollah-20240930-p5keha.
8. Generally, Fearon 1995; Matovski 2020.
9. Stein 2024.
10. I discuss quantum computing and AI, respectively, in Lindsay 2020a; Lindsay 2023.

11. More synoptic coverage can be found in Stevens and Devanny 2024; Puyvelde and Brantly 2025.

12. Kimberly Wood, "Cybersecurity Policy Responses to the Colonial Pipeline Ransomware Attack," *Georgetown Environmental Law Review*, March 7, 2023, https://www.law.georgetown.edu/environmental-law-review/blog/cybersecurity-policy-responses-to-the-colonial-pipeline-ransomware-attack/.

13. Brett Wolf, "Recovery of Colonial Pipeline Ransom Funds Highlights Traceability of Cryptocurrency, Experts Say," Reuters, June 23, 2021.

14. Brantly et al. 2017.

15. Kostyuk and Zhukov 2019.

16. Wilde 2024b.

17. This argument is discussed in more detail in Gannon et al. 2024.

18. Roncone et al. 2024.

19. Andy Greenberg, "Russia's Most Notorious Special Forces Unit Now Has Its Own Cyber Warfare Team," *Wired*, September 5, 2024.

20. Kim Zetter, "Inside the Cunning, Unprecedented Hack of Ukraine's Power Grid," *Wired*, March 3, 2016.

21. Crosignani et al. 2023.

22. Kim Zetter, "How a Russian Firm Helped Catch an Alleged NSA Data Thief," *Politico*, January 9, 2019, https://www.politico.com/story/2019/01/09/russia-kaspersky-lab-nsa-cybersecurity-1089131.

23. Maschmeyer 2021.

24. Merck & Co. Inc. and International Indemnity Ltd. v. Ace American Insurance Company et al., Superior Court of New Jersey, Appellate Division, Docket No. A-1879–21, May 1, 2023, https://www.njcourts.gov/system/files/court-opinions/2023/a1879-21a1882-21.pdf.

25. Maggie Miller, "Russian Invasion of Ukraine Could Redefine Cyber Warfare," *Politico*, January 28, 2022, https://www.politico.com/news/2022/01/28/russia-cyber-army-ukraine-00003051. See also Keith Alexander, "Cyber Warfare in Ukraine Poses a Threat to Global System," *Financial Times*, February 15, 2022.

26. Erica D. Lonergan, Shawn W. Lonergan, Brandon Valeriano, and Benjamin Jensen, "Putin's Invasion of Ukraine Didn't Rely on Cyberwarfare: Here's Why," *Washington Post*, March 7, 2022; Kostyuk and Gartzke 2022.

27. Greg Miller and Catherine Belton, "Russia's Spies Misread Ukraine and Misled Kremlin as War Loomed," *Washington Post*, August 19, 2022.

28. Pedersen and Jacobsen 2024.

29. Paul Sonne, Isabelle Khurshudyan, Serhiy Morgunov, and Kostiantyn Khudov, "Battle for Kyiv: Ukrainian Valor, Russian Blunders Combined to Save the Capital," *Washington Post*, August 24, 2022.

30. Kate Conger and Adam Satariano, "Volunteer Hackers Converge on Ukraine Conflict with No One in Charge," *New York Times*, March 4, 2022; Anh V. Vu, Daniel R. Thomas, Ben Collier, Alice Hutchings, Richard Clayton, and Ross Anderson, "Getting Bored of Cyberwar: Exploring the Role of the Cybercrime Underground in the Russia-Ukraine Conflict," arXiv, August 24, 2022, https://doi.org/10.48550/arXiv.2208.10629.

31. Gustafson et al. 2024.

32. Valerie Hopkins, "A Hack of the Defense Ministry, Army and State Banks Was the Largest of Its Kind in Ukraine's History," *New York Times*, February 15, 2022; Miller and Belton, "Russia's Spies Misread Ukraine."

33. Mehul Srivastava, Madhumita Murgia, and Hannah Murphy, "The Secret US Mission to Bolster Ukraine's Cyber Defences Ahead of Russia's Invasion," *Financial Times*, March 9, 2022.

34. Cyber National Mission Force Public Affairs, "Before the Invasion: Hunt Forward Operations in Ukraine," US Cyber Command, November 28, 2022, National Security Archive, https://nsarchive.gwu.edu/sites/default/files/documents/rmsj3h-751x3/2022-11-28-CNMF-Before-the-Invasion-Hunt-Forward-Operations-in-Ukraine.pdf.

35. Kate Conger and David E. Sanger, "U.S. Says It Secretly Removed Malware Worldwide, Pre-empting Russian Cyberattacks," *New York Times,* April 6, 2022.

36. Julian E. Barnes and Adam Entous, "How the U.S. Adopted a New Intelligence Playbook to Expose Russia's War Plans," *New York Times,* February 24, 2023.

37. Julian E. Barnes, "The Pentagon Says It Has Helped Ukraine Thwart Russian Cyberattacks," *New York Times,* December 19, 2022.

38. Julian E. Barnes and Helene Cooper, "Ukrainian Officials Drew on U.S. Intelligence to Plan Counteroffensive," *New York Times,* September 10, 2022.

39. These wiper campaigns were known by names such as WhisperGate, HermeticWiper, IsaacWiper, CaddyWiper, DesertBlade, and DoubleZero, per ESET Research, "A Year of Wiper Attacks in Ukraine," *WeLiveSecurity* (blog), February 24, 2023, https://www.welivesecurity.com/2023/02/24/year-wiper-attacks-ukraine/.

40. David E. Sanger, Julian E. Barnes, and Kate Conger, "As Tanks Rolled into Ukraine, So Did Malware: Then Microsoft Entered the War," *New York Times,* March 1, 2022; Tom Burt, "Disrupting Cyberattacks Targeting Ukraine," *Microsoft on the Issues,* April 7, 2022, https://blogs.microsoft.com/on-the-issues/2022/04/07/cyberattacks-ukraine-strontium-russia/.

41. ESET Research, "Industroyer2: Industroyer Reloaded," *WeLiveSecurity* (blog), April 12, 2022, https://www.welivesecurity.com/2022/04/12/industroyer2-industroyer-reloaded/.

42. Susan Landau, "Cyberwar in Ukraine: What You See Is Not What's Really There," Lawfare, September 30, 2022, https://www.lawfaremedia.org/article/cyberwar-ukraine-what-you-see-not-whats-really-there.

43. Poirier 2022.

44. Juan Andrés Guerrero-Saade, "AcidRain: A Modem Wiper Rains Down on Europe," SentinelOne, March 31, 2022, https://www.sentinelone.com/labs/acidrain-a-modem-wiper-rains-down-on-europe/.

45. Viasat, "KA-SAT Network Cyber Attack Overview," *Viasat* (blog), March 30, 2022, https://news.viasat.com/blog/corporate/ka-sat-network-cyber-attack-overview.

46. "Satellite Outage Knocks Out Thousands of Enercon's Wind Turbines," Reuters, February 28, 2022.

47. Kim Zetter, "Viasat Hack 'Did Not' Have Huge Impact on Ukrainian Military Communications, Official Says," *Zero Day* (newsletter), September 26, 2022, https://www.zetterzeroday.com/viasat-hack-did-not-have-huge-impact/.

48. "Military communications were completely paralyzed," according to a Ukrainian commander. "We had to work through informants. I'm not going to put all the cards on the table, but we knew with 95 percent accuracy even [the Russians'] smallest movements through other means. This was all locals." Quoted in Sonne et al., "Battle for Kyiv."

49. Viasat, "KA-SAT Network Cyber Attack Overview."

50. Roncone et al. 2024, 10.

51. Ken Proska, John Wolfram, Jared Wilson, et al., "Sandworm Disrupts Power in Ukraine Using a Novel Attack Against Operational Technology," *Mandiant* (blog), April 4, 2024, https://www.mandiant.com/resources/blog/sandworm-disrupts-power-ukraine-operational-technology.

52. Roncone et al. 2024, 6.

53. Dan Black and Gabby Roncone, "The GRU's Disruptive Playbook," *Mandiant* (blog), July 12, 2023, https://www.mandiant.com/resources/blog/gru-disruptive-playbook.

54. Janofsky, "NSA Cyber Chief."

55. "Russian Cyber Operations: APT Activity Report H1 2024," State Service of Special Communications and Information Protection of Ukraine, September 22, 2024, https://cip.gov.ua/en/news/cyber-operations-rf-h1-2024-report, pp. 24, 5.

56. Brantly and Brantly 2024; Pedersen and Jacobsen 2024.

57. Kostyuk et al. 2024.

58. Timothy D. Haugh, "Posture Statement of General Timothy D. Haugh, Commander, United States Cyber Command, Before the 118th Congress Senate Committee on Armed Services," US Cyber Command, April 10, 2024, 3.

59. These dynamics are discussed extensively in Gartzke and Lindsay 2024.

60. Green and Long 2020.

61. Each of the main columns of table C.3 (improve defense and offense) recapitulates the trade-off space across political logics described in figure 1.2. The rows of table C.3 (vulnerable institutions and clandestine organization) reflect trade-offs in institutionalization along the y-axis. The minor columns reflect trade-offs in cooperation along the x-axis. This means that connectivity reflects the benefits of governance, vulnerability the risks of espionage, capacity the organization for warfare, and discretion the restraint of deterrence. There are inherent tensions across all of these on each side of the intelligence contest, which makes it difficult to do all of them at the same time without some creative institutional design and infrastructural partition. Compounding the tension, both sides of the intelligence contest play defense and offense, but defense and offense make opposite trade-offs in this space. For some practical advice on navigating cybersecurity policy, see Puyvelde & Brantly 2025.

62. Nicole Perlroth, Jeff Larson, and Scott Shane, "N.S.A. Able to Foil Basic Safeguards of Privacy on Web," *New York Times*, September 5, 2013; Greg Miller, "The Intelligence Coup of the Century," *Washington Post*, February 11, 2020.

63. On "adaptive management," see Lindsay 2020b, 220–27.

64. Goldman 2020, 31–46.

65. For more on this tension, see Erik Gartzke and Jon R. Lindsay, "The U.S. Department of Deterrence," *War on the Rocks* (blog), July 22, 2024, https://warontherocks.com/2024/07/the-u-s-department-of-deterrence/.

66. "Wicked," in this sense, means hard to definitively define, much less solve, per Rittel and Webber 1973.

67. I discuss this tension in more detail in Lindsay 2021. See also Schneider 2025.

References

Abbate, Janet. 1999. *Inventing the Internet*. MIT Press.

Abbate, Janet. 2010. "Privatizing the Internet: Competing Visions and Chaotic Events, 1987–1995." *IEEE Annals of the History of Computing* 32 (1): 10–22.

Abbott, Kenneth W., and Duncan Snidal. 2010. "International Regulation Without International Government: Improving IO Performance Through Orchestration." *Review of International Organizations* 5 (3): 315–44.

Adams, James. 2001. *The Next World War: Computers Are the Weapons and the Front Line Is Everywhere*. Simon & Schuster.

Adams, Karen Ruth. 2003. "Attack and Conquer? International Anarchy and the Offense-Defense-Deterrence Balance." *International Security* 28 (3): 45–83.

Adler, Emanuel. 2019. *World Ordering: A Social Theory of Cognitive Evolution*. Cambridge University Press.

Adler, Emanuel, and Alena Drieschova. 2021. "The Epistemological Challenge of Truth Subversion to the Liberal International Order." *International Organization* 75 (2): 359–86.

Adler-Nissen, Rebecca, and Alena Drieschova. 2019. "Track-Change Diplomacy: Technology, Affordances, and the Practice of International Negotiations." *International Studies Quarterly* 63 (3): 531–45.

Agar, Jon. 2003. *The Government Machine: A Revolutionary History of the Computer*. MIT Press.

Ahl, Frederick, and Hanna M. Roisman. 1996. *The Odyssey Re-Formed*. Cornell University Press.

Akera, Atsushi. 2007. *Calculating a Natural World: Scientists, Engineers, and Computers During the Rise of U.S. Cold War Research*. MIT Press.

Akerlof, George A. 1970. "The Market for 'Lemons': Quality Uncertainty and the Market Mechanism." *Quarterly Journal of Economics* 84 (3): 488–500.

Akoto, William. 2021. "International Trade and Cyber Conflict: Decomposing the Effect of Trade on State-Sponsored Cyber Attacks." *Journal of Peace Research* 58 (5): 1083–97.

Akoto, William. 2025. "State-Sponsored Cyber Attacks and Co-Movements in Stock Market Returns: Evidence from US Cybersecurity Defense Contractors." *Business and Politics* 27 (1): 95–113.

Albright, David, Paul Brannan, and Christina Walrond. 2010. *Did Stuxnet Take Out 1,000 Centrifuges at the Natanz Enrichment Plant?* Institute for Science and International Security. https://isis-online.org/isis-reports/detail/did-stuxnet-take-out-1000-centrifuges-at-the-natanz-enrichment-plant/.

Albright, David, Paul Brannan, and Christina Walrond. 2011. *Stuxnet Malware and Natanz: Update of ISIS December 22, 2010 Report.* Institute for Science and International Security.

Albright, David, and Sarah Burkhard. 2020. *Iranian Breakout Estimates and Enriched Uranium Stocks.* Institute for Science and International Security.

Albright, David, Christina Walrond, and Andrea Stricker. 2013. *ISIS Analysis of IAEA Iran Safeguards Report.* Institute for Science and International Security.

Albright, David, Serena Kelleher-Vergantini, Andrea Stricker, and Daniel Schnur. 2015. *Analysis of IAEA Iran Safeguards Report.* Institute for Science and International Security.

Allcott, Hunt, Matthew Gentzkow, and Chuan Yu. 2019. "Trends in the Diffusion of Misinformation on Social Media." *Research & Politics* 6 (2). https://doi.org/10.1177/2053168019848554.

Allison, Graham T., Kevin Klyman, Karina Barbesino, and Hugo Yen. 2021. *The Great Tech Rivalry: China vs. the U.S.* Belfer Center for Science and International Affairs, Harvard Kennedy School.

Altman, Dan. 2017. "By Fait Accompli, Not Coercion: How States Wrest Territory from Their Adversaries." *International Studies Quarterly* 61 (4): 881–91.

Amir, Eli, Shai Levi, and Tsafrir Livne. 2018. "Do Firms Underreport Information on Cyber-Attacks? Evidence from Capital Markets." *Review of Accounting Studies* 23 (3): 1177–206.

Anderson, Collin, and Karim Sadjadpour. 2018. *Iran's Cyber Threat: Espionage, Sabotage, and Revenge.* Carnegie Endowment for International Peace. https://carnegieendowment.org/2018/01/04/iran-s-cyber-threat-espionage-sabotage-and-revenge-pub-75134.

Anderson, Ross, Chris Barton, Rainer Böhme, et al. 2013. "Measuring the Cost of Cybercrime." In *The Economics of Information Security and Privacy*, edited by Rainer Böhme. Springer-Verlag.

Anderson, Ross, and Tyler Moore. 2006. "The Economics of Information Security." *Science* 314 (5799): 610–13.

Andrew, Christopher. 2004. "Intelligence, International Relations and 'Under-Theorisation.'" *Intelligence and National Security* 19 (2): 170–84.

Andrew, Christopher. 2009. *Defend the Realm: The Authorized History of MI5.* Knopf Doubleday.

Andrew, Christopher. 2018. *The Secret World: A History of Intelligence.* Yale University Press.

Andrew, Christopher, and Julie Elkner. 2003. "Stalin and Foreign Intelligence." *Totalitarian Movements and Political Religions* 4 (1): 69–94.

Andrew, Christopher, and Vasili Mitrokhin. 2000. *The Sword and the Shield: The Mitrokhin Archive and the Secret History of the KGB*. Basic Books.

Arceneaux, Kevin, and Rory Truex. 2023. "Donald Trump and the Lie." *Perspectives on Politics* 21 (3): 863–79.

Arquilla, John, and David Ronfeldt. 1993. "Cyberwar Is Coming!" *Comparative Strategy* 12 (2): 141–65.

Arthur, W. Brian. 2009. *The Nature of Technology: What It Is and How It Evolves*. Simon & Schuster.

Aspray, William. 1990. *John von Neumann and the Origins of Modern Computing*. Edited by Thomas J. Misa. MIT Press.

Atal, Maha Rafi. 2021. "The Janus Faces of Silicon Valley." *Review of International Political Economy* 28 (2): 336–50.

August, Terrence, and Tunay I. Tunca. 2006. "Network Software Security and User Incentives." *Management Science* 52 (11): 1703–20.

Aumasson, Jean-Philippe. 2018. *Serious Cryptography: A Practical Introduction to Modern Encryption*. No Starch.

Bail, Christopher A., Brian Guay, Emily Maloney, et al. 2020. "Assessing the Russian Internet Research Agency's Impact on the Political Attitudes and Behaviors of American Twitter Users in Late 2017." *Proceedings of the National Academy of Sciences* 117 (1): 243–50.

Baldwin, David A. 2020. *Economic Statecraft*. New ed. Princeton University Press.

Balzacq, Thierry, and Myriam Dunn Cavelty. 2016. "A Theory of Actor-Network for Cyber-Security." *European Journal of International Security* 1 (2): 176–98.

Baran, Paul. 1964. *On Distributed Communications: I. Introduction to Distributed Communications Networks*. RAND Corporation. https://www.rand.org/pubs/research_memoranda/RM3765.html.

Barzashka, Ivanka. 2013. "Are Cyber-Weapons Effective? Assessing Stuxnet's Impact on the Iranian Enrichment Programme." *RUSI Journal* 158 (2): 48–56.

Bass, Warren. 2015. *A Surprise Out of Zion? Case Studies in Israel's Decisions on Whether to Alert the United States to Preemptive and Preventive Strikes, from Suez to the Syrian Nuclear Reactor*. RAND Corporation.

Bates, Robert H., Avner Greif, Margaret Levi, Jean-Laurent Rosenthal, and Barry R. Weingast. 1998. *Analytic Narratives*. Princeton University Press.

Bauer, Johannes M., and Michel J. G. van Eeten. 2009. "Cybersecurity: Stakeholder Incentives, Externalities, and Policy Options." *Telecommunications Policy* 33 (10–11): 706–19.

Bean, Hamilton. 2018. "Intelligence Theory from the Margins: Questions Ignored and Debates Not Had." *Intelligence and National Security* 33 (4): 527–40.

Beckley, Michael. 2018. "The Power of Nations: Measuring What Matters." *International Security* 43 (2): 7–44.

Bell, D. Elliott, and Leonard J. La Padula. 1976. *Secure Computer System: Unified Exposition and Multics Interpretation*. MITRE Corporation.

Beniger, James R. 1986. *The Control Revolution: Technological and Economic Origins of the Information Society*. Harvard University Press.

Benkler, Yochai, Robert Faris, and Harold Roberts. 2018. *Network Propaganda: Manipulation, Disinformation, and Radicalization in American Politics*. Oxford University Press.

Bennett, Andrew. 2013. "The Mother of All Isms: Causal Mechanisms and Structured Pluralism in International Relations Theory." *European Journal of International Relations* 19 (3): 459–81.

Bennett, Andrew, and Colin Elman. 2006. "Complex Causal Relations and Case Study Methods: The Example of Path Dependence." *Political Analysis* 14 (3): 250–67.

Bergman, Ronen. 2008. *The Secret War with Iran: The 30-Year Clandestine Struggle Against the World's Most Dangerous Terrorist Power*. Free Press.

Bergman, Ronen. 2018. *Rise and Kill First: The Secret History of Israel's Targeted Assassinations*. Random House.

Bernhard, Michael, and Daniel O'Neill. 2019a. "Trump: Causes and Consequences." *Perspectives on Politics* 17 (2): 317–24.

Bernhard, Michael, and Daniel O'Neill. 2019b. "Trump: Causes and Consequences (the Sequel)." *Perspectives on Politics* 17 (3): 643–44.

Betts, Richard K. 2007. *Enemies of Intelligence: Knowledge and Power in American National Security*. Columbia University Press.

Betz, David J., and Tim Stevens. 2011. *Cyberspace and the State: Towards a Strategy for Cyberpower*. Routledge.

Beyerchen, Alan. 1996. "From Radio to Radar: Interwar Military Adaptation to Technological Change in Germany, the United Kingdom, and the United States." In *Military Innovation in the Interwar Period*, edited by Williamson Murray and Allan Reed Millett. Cambridge University Press.

Biddle, Stephen. 2001. "Rebuilding the Foundations of Offense-Defense Theory." *Journal of Politics* 63 (3): 741–74.

Biddle, Stephen. 2004. *Military Power: Explaining Victory and Defeat in Modern Battle*. Princeton, NJ: Princeton University Press.

Biddle, Stephen. 2021. *Nonstate Warfare: The Military Methods of Guerillas, Warlords, and Militias*. Princeton University Press.

Biddle, Tami Davis. 2002. *Rhetoric and Reality in Air Warfare: The Evolution of British and American Ideas About Strategic Bombing, 1914–1945*. Princeton University Press.

Bijker, Wiebe E., Thomas P. Hughes, and Trevor Pinch, eds. 1987. *The Social Construction of Technological Systems: New Directions in the Sociology and History of Technology*. MIT Press.

Borden, Neil H. 1964. "The Concept of the Marketing Mix." *Journal of Advertising Research* 4 (2): 2–7.

Borghard, Erica D., and Shawn W. Lonergan. 2017. "The Logic of Coercion in Cyberspace." *Security Studies* 26 (3): 452–81.

Börzel, Tanja A., and Thomas Risse. 2021. *Effective Governance Under Anarchy*. Cambridge University Press.

Bouwman, Xander, Harm Griffioen, Jelle Egbers, Christian Doerr, Bram Klievink, and Michel van Eeten. 2020. "A Different Cup of TI? The Added Value of Commercial Threat Intelligence." *29th USENIX Security Symposium (USENIX Security 20)*, 433–50.

Bowden, Mark. 2011. *Worm: The First Digital World War*. Atlantic Monthly Press.

Bowker, Geoffrey C., and Susan Leigh Star. 1999. *Sorting Things Out: Classification and Its Consequences*. MIT Press.

Branch, Jordan. 2021. "What's in a Name? Metaphors and Cybersecurity." *International Organization* 75 (1): 39–70.

Brands, Hal. 2023. Introduction to *New Makers of Modern Strategy: From the Ancient World to the Digital Age*, edited by Hal Brands. Princeton University Press.

Brantly, Aaron F., and Nataliya D. Brantly. 2024. "The Bitskrieg That Was and Wasn't: The Military and Intelligence Implications of Cyber Operations During Russia's War on Ukraine." *Intelligence and National Security* 39 (3): 1–21.

Brantly, Aaron Franklin. 2016. *The Decision to Attack: Military and Intelligence Cyber Decision-Making*. University of Georgia Press.

Brantly, Aaron F., Nerea M. Cal, and Devlin P. Winkelstein. 2017. *Defending the Borderland: Ukrainian Military Experiences with IO, Cyber, and EW*. Army Cyber Institute.

Bratus, Sergey, Michael E. Locasto, Meredith L. Patterson, Len Sassaman, and Anna Shubina. 2011. "Exploit Programming: From Buffer Overflows to 'Weird Machines' and Theory of Computation." *USENIX ;Login:* 36 (6). https://www.usenix.org/publications/login/december-2011-volume-36-number-6/exploit-programming-buffer-overflows-weird.

Breznitz, Dan, and Michael Murphree. 2011. *Run of the Red Queen: Government, Innovation, Globalization, and Economic Growth in China*. Yale University Press.

Brito, Jerry, and Tate Watkins. 2011. "Loving the Cyber Bomb: The Dangers of Threat Inflation in Cybersecurity Policy." *Harvard National Security Journal* 3 (1): 39–84.

Bronk, Christopher, and Eneken Tikk-Ringas. 2013. "The Cyber Attack on Saudi Aramco." *Survival* 55 (2): 81–96.

Brooks, Risa. 2008. *Shaping Strategy: The Civil-Military Politics of Strategic Assessment*. Princeton University Press.

Brooks, Risa A., and Elizabeth A. Stanley, eds. 2007. *Creating Military Power: The Sources of Military Effectiveness*. Stanford University Press.

Brooks, Stephen G. 2005. *Producing Security: Multinational Corporations, Globalization, and the Changing Calculus of Conflict*. Princeton University Press.

Brooks, Stephen G., and William C. Wohlforth. 2016. "The Rise and Fall of the Great Powers in the Twenty-First Century: China's Rise and the Fate of America's Global Position." *International Security* 40 (3): 7–53.

Bruns, Axel. 2019. *Are Filter Bubbles Real?* Polity.

Brunt, Rodney M. 2006. "Special Documentation Systems at the Government Code and Cypher School, Bletchley Park, During the Second World War." *Intelligence and National Security* 21 (1): 129–48.

Brynjolfsson, Erik, and Adam Saunders. 2010. *Wired for Innovation: How Information Technology Is Reshaping the Economy*. MIT Press.

Buchanan, Ben. 2017. *The Cybersecurity Dilemma: Hacking, Trust and Fear Between Nations*. Oxford University Press.

Buchanan, Ben, and Fiona S. Cunningham. 2020. "Preparing the Cyber Battlefield: Assessing a Novel Escalation Risk in a Sino-American Crisis." *Texas National Security Review* 3 (4): 54–81.

Buchanan, Ben, and Andrew Imbrie. 2022. *The New Fire: War, Peace, and Democracy in the Age of AI*. MIT Press.

Budiansky, Stephen. 2000. *Battle of Wits: The Complete Story of Codebreaking in World War II*. Free Press.

Burke, Edmund J., Kristen Gunness, Cortez A. Cooper III, and Mark Cozad. 2020. *People's Liberation Army Operational Concepts*. RAND Corporation. https:// www.rand.org/pubs/research_reports/RRA394-1.html.

Cabestan, Jean-Pierre. 2021. "China's Foreign and Security Policy Institutions and Decision-Making Under Xi Jinping." *British Journal of Politics and International Relations* 23 (2): 319–36.

Campbell, James E. 2001. "When Have Presidential Campaigns Decided Election Outcomes?" *American Politics Research* 29 (5): 437–60.

Campen, Alan D., Douglas H. Dearth, and R. Thomas Goodden, eds. 1996. *Cyberwar: Security, Strategy, and Conflict in the Information Age*. AFCEA.

Canfil, Justin Key. 2022. "The Illogic of Plausible Deniability: Why Proxy Conflict in Cyberspace May No Longer Pay." *Journal of Cybersecurity* 8 (1). https://doi. org/10.1093/cybsec/tyac007.

Carnegie, Allison. 2021. "Secrecy in International Relations and Foreign Policy." *Annual Review of Political Science* 24 (1): 213–33.

Carnegie, Allison, and Austin Carson. 2020. *Secrets in Global Governance: Disclosure Dilemmas and the Challenge of International Cooperation*. Cambridge University Press.

Carson, Austin. 2016. "Facing Off and Saving Face: Covert Intervention and Escalation Management in the Korean War." *International Organization* 70 (1): 103–31.

Carson, Austin. 2018. *Secret Wars: Covert Conflict in International Politics*. Princeton University Press.

Carson, Austin, and Keren Yarhi-Milo. 2017. "Covert Communication: The Intelligibility and Credibility of Signaling in Secret." *Security Studies* 26 (1): 124–56.

Carter, Erin Baggott, and Brett L. Carter. 2021. "Questioning More: RT, Outward-Facing Propaganda, and the Post-West World Order." *Security Studies* 30 (1): 49–78.

Castells, Manuel. 2000. *The Rise of the Network Society: The Information Age; Economy, Society and Culture*. Wiley.

Caverley, Jonathan D. 2007. "United States Hegemony and the New Economics of Defense." *Security Studies* 16 (4): 598–614.

Chandler, Alfred D., Jr., and James W. Cortada, eds. 2000. *A Nation Transformed by Information: How Information Has Shaped the United States from Colonial Times to the Present*. Oxford University Press.

Chase, Michael S., Jeffrey Engstrom, Tai Ming Cheung, et al. 2015. *China's Incomplete Military Transformation*. RAND Corporation.

Chaudhary, Tarun, Jenna Jordan, Michael Salomone, and Phil Baxter. 2018. "Patchwork of Confusion: The Cybersecurity Coordination Problem." *Journal of Cybersecurity* 4 (1). https://doi.org/10.1093/cybsec/tyy005.

Chesney, Robert, and Danielle Citron. 2019. "Deepfakes and the New Disinformation War: The Coming Age of Post-Truth Geopolitics." *Foreign Affairs* 98 (1): 147–55.

Chesney, Robert, and Max Smeets, eds. 2023. *Deter, Disrupt, or Deceive: Assessing Cyber Conflict as an Intelligence Contest*. Georgetown University Press.

Cheung, Tai Ming. 2022. *Innovate to Dominate: The Rise of the Chinese Techno-Security State*. Cornell University Press.

Clark, Andy. 2007. "Curing Cognitive Hiccups: A Defense of the Extended Mind." *Journal of Philosophy* 104 (4): 163–92.

Clarke, Richard A., and Robert K. Knake. 2010. *Cyber War: The Next Threat to National Security and What to Do About It*. Ecco.

Clarke, Richard A., and Robert K. Knake. 2019. *The Fifth Domain: Defending Our Country, Our Companies, and Ourselves in the Age of Cyber Threats*. Penguin.

Clausewitz, Carl von. 1976. *On War*. Translated by Michael Howard and Peter Paret. Princeton University Press.

Cohen, Eliot A. 2002. *Supreme Command: Soldiers, Statesmen and Leadership in Wartime*. Simon & Schuster.

Collier, David. 2011. "Understanding Process Tracing." *PS: Political Science & Politics* 44 (4): 823–30.

Constantinides, E. 2006. "The Marketing Mix Revisited: Towards the 21st Century Marketing." *Journal of Marketing Management* 22 (3–4): 407–38.

Cooley, Alexander, and Daniel Nexon. 2020. *Exit from Hegemony: The Unraveling of the American Global Order*. Oxford University Press.

Copeland, B. Jack. 2001. "Colossus and the Dawning of the Computer Age." In *Action This Day: Bletchley Park from the Breaking of the Enigma Code to the Birth of the Modern Computer*, edited by Michael Smith and Ralph Erskine. Bantam.

Copeland, B. Jack. 2006. "Colossus and the Rise of the Modern Computer." In *Colossus: The Secrets of Bletchley Park's Codebreaking Computers*, edited by B. Jack Copeland. Oxford University Press.

Cormac, Rory. 2018. *Disrupt and Deny: Spies, Special Forces, and the Secret Pursuit of British Foreign Policy*. Oxford University Press.

Cormac, Rory, and Richard J. Aldrich. 2018. "Grey Is the New Black: Covert Action and Implausible Deniability." *International Affairs* 94 (3): 477–94.

Cortada, James W. 2012. *The Digital Flood: Diffusion of Information Technology Across the United States, Europe, and Asia*. Oxford University Press.

Costello, John, and Joe McReynolds. 2018. "China's Strategic Support Force: A Force for a New Era." China Strategic Perspectives. National Defense University, Institute for National Strategic Studies.

Cozad, Mark. 2016. *PLA Joint Training and Implications for Future Expeditionary Capabilities*. RAND Corporation. https://www.rand.org/pubs/testimonies/CT451.html.

Cram, Cleveland. 1993. *Of Moles and Molehunters: A Review of Counterintelligence Literature, 1977–92*. Center for the Study of Intelligence.

Creemers, Rogier. 2017. "Cyber China: Upgrading Propaganda, Public Opinion Work and Social Management for the Twenty-First Century." *Journal of Contemporary China* 26 (103): 85–100.

Crist, David. 2012. *The Twilight War: The Secret History of America's Thirty-Year Conflict with Iran*. Penguin.

Crosignani, Matteo, Marco Macchiavelli, and André F. Silva. 2023. "Pirates Without Borders: The Propagation of Cyberattacks Through Firms' Supply Chains." *Journal of Financial Economics* 147 (2): 432–48.

Csete, Marie, and John Doyle. 2004. "Bow Ties, Metabolism and Disease." *Trends in Biotechnology* 22 (9): 446–50.

Cunningham, Fiona S. *Under the Nuclear Shadow: China's Information-Age Weapons in International Security*. Princeton University Press, 2025.

Cyber Safety Review Board. 2024. *Review of the Summer 2023 Microsoft Exchange Online Intrusion*. Cybersecurity and Infrastructure Security Agency.

Cyberspace Administration of China. 2023. *Introduction to General Secretary Xi Jinping's Important Thoughts on Cyber Superpower*. People's Press.

Dahl, Erik J. 2013. *Intelligence and Surprise Attack: Failure and Success from Pearl Harbor to 9/11 and Beyond*. Georgetown University Press.

Davis, Martin. 2018. *The Universal Computer: The Road from Leibniz to Turing*. 3rd ed. CRC Press.

Deibert, Ronald J. 2013. *Black Code: Inside the Battle for Cyberspace*. McClelland & Stewart.

Deibert, Ronald J. 2020. *Reset: Reclaiming the Internet for Civil Society (The CBC Massey Lectures)*. House of Anansi.

Deibert, Ronald J. 2022. "Subversion Inc: The Age of Private Espionage." *Journal of Democracy* 33 (2): 28–44.

Deibert, Ronald J. 2025. *Chasing Shadows: Cyber Espionage, Subversion, and the Global Fight for Democracy*. Simon & Schuster.

Deibert, Ronald, John Palfrey, Rafal Rohozinski, and Jonathan Zittrain, eds. 2012. *Access Contested: Security, Identity, and Resistance in Asian Cyberspace*. MIT Press.

deLisle, Jacques, and Avery Goldstein, eds. 2021. *After Engagement: Dilemmas in U.S.-China Security Relations*. Brookings Institution Press.

Demchak, Chris C. 1991. *Military Organizations, Complex Machines: Modernization in the U.S. Armed Services*. Cornell University Press.

DeNardis, Laura. 2009. *Protocol Politics: The Globalization of Internet Governance*. MIT Press.

DeNardis, Laura. 2014. *The Global War for Internet Governance*. Yale University Press.

Dennett, Daniel C., and John Haugeland. 1987. "Intentionality." In *The Oxford Companion to the Mind*, edited by Richard L. Gregory. Oxford University Press.

Denning, Dorothy E. 2012. "Stuxnet: What Has Changed?" *Future Internet* 4 (3): 672–87.

Deutsch, Karl Wolfgang. 1963. *Nerves of Government: Models of Political Communication*. Free Press.

DiMaggio, Paul, and Walter W. Powell. 1991. Introduction to *The New Institutionalism in Organizational Analysis*, edited by Paul DiMaggio and Walter W. Powell. University of Chicago Press.

Doshi, Rush, Emily de La Bruyère, Nathan Picarsic, and John Ferguson. 2021. *China as a "Cyber Great Power": Beijing's Two Voices in Telecommunications*. Brookings Institution. https://www.brookings.edu/wp-content/uploads/2021/04/FP_20210405_china_cyber_power.pdf.

Downes, Alexander B., and Mary Lauren Lilley. 2010. "Overt Peace, Covert War? Covert Intervention and the Democratic Peace." *Security Studies* 19 (2): 266–306.

Downey, Greg. 2001. "Virtual Webs, Physical Technologies, and Hidden Workers: The Spaces of Labor in Information Internetworks." *Technology and Culture* 42 (2): 209–35.

Drea, Edward J. 1992. *MacArthur's ULTRA: Codebreaking and the War Against Japan, 1942–1945*. University Press of Kansas.

Drezner, Daniel W. 2004. "The Global Governance of the Internet: Bringing the State Back In." *Political Science Quarterly* 119 (3): 477–98.

Drezner, Daniel W. 2014. *Theories of International Politics and Zombies: Revived Edition*. Princeton University Press.

Driscoll, Jesse, and Zachary C. Steinert-Threlkeld. 2020. "Social Media and Russian Territorial Irredentism: Some Facts and a Conjecture." *Post-Soviet Affairs* 36 (2): 101–21.

Dullien, Thomas. 2020. "Weird Machines, Exploitability, and Provable Unexploitability." *IEEE Transactions on Emerging Topics in Computing* 8 (2): 391–403.

Dunn Cavelty, Myriam. 2013. "From Cyber-Bombs to Political Fallout: Threat Representations with an Impact in the Cyber-Security Discourse." *International Studies Review* 15 (1): 105–22.

Dunn Cavelty, Myriam, Tobias Pulver, and Max Smeets. 2024. "The Evolution of Cyberconflict Studies." *International Affairs* 100 (6): 2317–39.

Dunne, Tim, Lene Hansen, and Colin Wight. 2013. "The End of International Relations Theory?" *European Journal of International Relations* 19 (3): 405–25.

DuPont, Quinn, and Bradley Fidler. 2016. "Edge Cryptography and the Codevelopment of Computer Networks and Cybersecurity." *IEEE Annals of the History of Computing* 38 (4): 55–73.

Dupuy, Jean-Pierre. 2000. *The Mechanization of the Mind: On the Origins of Cognitive Science*. Princeton University Press.

Eady, Gregory, Tom Paskhalis, Jan Zilinsky, Richard Bonneau, Jonathan Nagler, and Joshua A. Tucker. 2023. "Exposure to the Russian Internet Research Agency Foreign Influence Campaign on Twitter in the 2016 US Election and Its Relationship to Attitudes and Voting Behavior." *Nature Communications* 14 (1). https://doi.org/10.1038/s41467-022-35576-9.

Eckstein, Harry. 2000. "Case Study and Theory in Political Science." In *Case Study Method*, edited by Roger Gomm, Martyn Hammersley, and Peter Foster. Sage.

Edelman, Benjamin. 2011. "Adverse Selection in Online 'Trust' Certifications and Search Results." *Electronic Commerce Research and Applications* 10 (1): 17–25.

Edelstein, David M. 2017. *Over the Horizon: Time, Uncertainty, and the Rise of Great Powers*. Cornell University Press.

Edwards, Benjamin, Alexander Furnas, Stephanie Forrest, and Robert Axelrod. 2017. "Strategic Aspects of Cyberattack, Attribution, and Blame." *Proceedings of the National Academy of Sciences* 114 (11): 2825–30.

Edwards, Paul N. 1996. *The Closed World: Computers and the Politics of Discourse in Cold War America*. MIT Press.

Edwards, Paul N. 2010. *A Vast Machine: Computer Models, Climate Data, and the Politics of Global Warming*. MIT Press.

Edwards, Paul N. 2019. "Knowledge Infrastructures Under Siege: Climate Data as Memory, Truce, and Target." In *Data Politics: Worlds, Subjects, Rights*, edited by Didier Bigo, Engin Isin, and Evelyn Ruppert. Routledge.

Edwards, Paul N., Matthew S. Mayernik, Archer Batcheller, Geoffrey Bowker, and Christine Borgman. 2011. "Science Friction: Data, Metadata, and Collaboration." *Social Studies of Science* 4 (6): 667–90.

Eeten, Michel van. 2017. "Patching Security Governance: An Empirical View of Emergent Governance Mechanisms for Cybersecurity." *Digital Policy, Regulation and Governance* 19 (6): 429–48.

Egloff, Florian J. 2021. *Semi-State Actors in Cybersecurity.* Oxford University Press.

Egloff, Florian J., and Myriam Dunn Cavelty. 2021. "Attribution and Knowledge Creation Assemblages in Cybersecurity Politics." *Journal of Cybersecurity* 7:tyab002.

Egloff, Florian J., and James Shires. 2021. "The Better Angels of Our Digital Nature? Offensive Cyber Capabilities and State Violence." *European Journal of International Security* 8:130–49.

Egloff, Florian J., and Max Smeets. 2023. "Publicly Attributing Cyber Attacks: A Framework." *Journal of Strategic Studies* 46 (3): 502–33.

Ehlers, Robert S. 2009. *Targeting the Third Reich: Air Intelligence and the Allied Bombing Campaigns.* University Press of Kansas.

Eling, Martin, and Jan Wirfs. 2019. "What Are the Actual Costs of Cyber Risk Events?" *European Journal of Operational Research* 272 (3): 1109–19.

Elster, Jon. 1989. *The Cement of Society: A Survey of Social Order.* Cambridge University Press.

Erskine, Ralph. 2001a. "Breaking Air Force and Army Enigma." In *Action This Day: Bletchley Park from the Breaking of the Enigma Code to the Birth of the Modern Computer*, edited by Michael Smith and Ralph Erskine. Bantam.

Erskine, Ralph. 2001b. "Cillies." In *Action This Day: Bletchley Park from the Breaking of the Enigma Code to the Birth of the Modern Computer*, edited by Michael Smith and Ralph Erskine. Bantam.

Erskine, Ralph. 2001c. "Enigma's Security: What the Germans Really Knew." In *Action This Day: Bletchley Park from the Breaking of the Enigma Code to the Birth of the Modern Computer*, edited by Michael Smith and Ralph Erskine. Bantam.

Etudo, Ugochukwu, Christopher Whyte, Victoria Yoon, and Niam Yaraghi. 2023. "From Russia with Fear: Fear Appeals and the Patterns of Cyber-Enabled Influence Operations." *Journal of Cybersecurity* 9 (1). https://doi.org/10.1093/cybsec/tyad016.

Evera, Stephen van. 1998. "Offense, Defense, and the Causes of War." *International Security* 22 (4): 5–43.

Fairfield, Tasha, and Andrew Charman. 2019. "A Dialogue with the Data: The Bayesian Foundations of Iterative Research in Qualitative Social Science." *Perspectives on Politics* 17 (1): 154–67.

Faligot, Roger. 2019. *Chinese Spies: From Chairman Mao to Xi Jinping.* Translated by Natasha Lehrer. Hurst.

Farrell, Henry, and Abraham L. Newman. 2019a. *Of Privacy and Power: The Transatlantic Struggle over Freedom and Security.* Princeton University Press.

Farrell, Henry, and Abraham L. Newman. 2019b. "Weaponized Interdependence: How Global Economic Networks Shape State Coercion." *International Security* 44 (1): 42–79.

Farwell, James P., and Rafal Rohozinski. 2011. "Stuxnet and the Future of Cyber War." *Survival* 53:23–40.

Fearon, James D. 1995. "Rationalist Explanations for War." *International Organization* 49 (3): 379–414.

Fearon, James D. 1997. "Signaling Foreign Policy Interests: Tying Hands Versus Sinking Costs." *Journal of Conflict Resolution* 41 (1): 68–90.

Fedasiuk, Ryan. 2021. "A Different Kind of Army: The Militarization of China's Internet Trolls." *China Brief* 21 (7). https://jamestown.org/program/a-different-kind-of-army-the-militarization-of-chinas-internet-trolls/.

Feigenbaum, Evan. 2003. *China's Techno-Warriors: National Security and Strategic Competition from the Nuclear to the Information Age.* Stanford University Press.

Ferris, John. 1995. "Coming In from the Cold War: The Historiography of American Intelligence, 1945–1990." *Diplomatic History* 19 (1): 87–115.

Ferris, John. 2002. "The Road to Bletchley Park: The British Experience with Signals Intelligence, 1892–1945." *Intelligence and National Security* 17 (1): 53–84.

Ferris, John. 2020. *Behind the Enigma: The Authorized History of GCHQ, Britain's Secret Cyber-Intelligence Agency.* Bloomsbury.

Fidler, Bradley. 2017. "Cybersecurity Governance: A Prehistory and Its Implications." *Digital Policy, Regulation and Governance* 19 (6): 449–65.

Fidler, Bradley, and Russ Mundy. 2020. *The Creation and Administration of Unique Identifiers, 1967–2017.* ICANN.

Finklea, Kristin, Michelle D. Christensen, Eric A. Fischer, Susan V. Lawrence, and Catherine A. Theohary. 2015. *Cyber Intrusion into U.S. Office of Personnel Management: In Brief.* Congressional Research Service.

FireEye iSight Intelligence. 2017. *APT28: At the Center of the Storm.* FireEye [Mandiant]. https://www.mandiant.com/sites/default/files/2021-09/APT28-Center-of-Storm-2017.pdf.

Fischerkeller, Michael P., Emily O. Goldman, and Richard J. Harknett. 2022. *Cyber Persistence Theory: Redefining National Security in Cyberspace.* Oxford University Press.

Fisher, Aleksandr. 2020. "Demonizing the Enemy: The Influence of Russian State-Sponsored Media on American Audiences." *Post-Soviet Affairs* 36 (4): 281–96.

Fitzgerald, Chad W., and Aaron F. Brantly. 2017. "Subverting Reality: The Role of Propaganda in 21st Century Intelligence." *International Journal of Intelligence and CounterIntelligence* 30 (2): 215–40.

Flyvbjerg, Bent. 2006. "Five Misunderstandings About Case-Study Research." *Qualitative Inquiry* 12 (2): 219–45.

Fogarty, Stephen G., and Jamie O. Nasi. 2016. "Special Operations Forces Truths—Cyber Truths." *Cyber Defense Review* 1 (2): 19–28.

Foltz, Andrew C. 2012. "Stuxnet, Schmitt Analysis, and the Cyber 'Use-of-Force' Debate." *Joint Force Quarterly*, no. 67: 40–48.

Ford, Christopher, and David Rosenberg. 2005. *The Admirals' Advantage: U.S. Navy Operational Intelligence in World War II and the Cold War.* Naval Institute Press.

Francois, Camille, and Herb Lin. 2021. "The Strategic Surprise of Russian Information Operations on Social Media in 2016 in the United States: Mapping a Blind Spot." *Journal of Cyber Policy* 6 (1): 9–30.

Franke, Ulrich, and Ralph Weber. 2012. "At the Papini Hotel: On Pragmatism in the Study of International Relations." *European Journal of International Relations* 18 (4): 669–91.

Frankfurt, Harry G. 2005. *On Bullshit*. Princeton University Press.

Fravel, M. Taylor. 2020. *Active Defense: China's Military Strategy Since 1949*. Princeton University Press.

Freedman, Lawrence. 2004. *Deterrence*. Polity.

Freilich, Charles D., Matthew S. Cohen, and Gabi Siboni. 2023. *Israel and the Cyber Threat: How the Startup Nation Became a Global Cyber Power*. Oxford University Press.

Friedrichs, Jörg, and Friedrich Kratochwil. 2009. "On Acting and Knowing: How Pragmatism Can Advance International Relations Research and Methodology." *International Organization* 63 (4): 701–31.

Galeotti, Mark. 2016. *Putin's Hydra: Inside Russia's Intelligence Services*. Policy brief. European Council on Foreign Relations.

Gallagher, Mary, and Blake Miller. 2021. "Who Not What: The Logic of China's Information Control Strategy." *China Quarterly* 248 (1): 1011–36.

Gannon, J. Andrés, Erik Gartzke, Jon R. Lindsay, and Peter Schram. 2024. "The Shadow of Deterrence: Why Capable Actors Engage in Contests Short of War." *Journal of Conflict Resolution* 68 (2–3): 230–68.

Garfinkel, Ben, and Allan Dafoe. 2019. "How Does the Offense-Defense Balance Scale?" *Journal of Strategic Studies* 42 (6): 736–63.

Garrett, R. Kelly, Daniel Sude, and Paolo Riva. 2020. "Toeing the Party Lie: Ostracism Promotes Endorsement of Partisan Election Falsehoods." *Political Communication* 37 (2): 157–72.

Gartzke, Erik. 2013. "The Myth of Cyberwar: Bringing War in Cyberspace Back Down to Earth." *International Security* 38 (2): 41–73.

Gartzke, Erik, and Jon R. Lindsay. 2015. "Weaving Tangled Webs: Offense, Defense, and Deception in Cyberspace." *Security Studies* 24 (2): 316–48.

Gartzke, Erik, and Jon R. Lindsay. 2017. "Thermonuclear Cyberwar." *Journal of Cybersecurity* 3 (1): 37–48.

Gartzke, Erik, and Jon R. Lindsay. 2018. "The Cyber Commitment Problem and the Destabilization of Nuclear Deterrence." In *Bytes, Bombs, and Spies: The Strategic Dimensions of Offensive Cyber Operations*, edited by Herbert S. Lin and Amy B. Zegart. Brookings Institution Press.

Gartzke, Erik, and Jon R. Lindsay. 2024. *Elements of Deterrence: Strategy, Technology, and Complexity in Global Politics*. Oxford University Press.

Gibney, Alex, dir. 2016. *Zero Days*. YouTube. https://www.youtube.com/watch?v=SoRoMykmibE.

Gibson, William. 1984. *Neuromancer*. Ace Books.

Gill, Peter, and Mark Phythian. 2018. "Developing Intelligence Theory." *Intelligence and National Security* 33 (4): 467–71.

Gillespie, Tarleton. 2018. *Custodians of the Internet: Platforms, Content Moderation, and the Hidden Decisions That Shape Social Media*. Yale University Press.

Gilli, Andrea, and Mauro Gilli. 2018. "Why China Hasn't Caught Up Yet: Military-Technological Superiority and the Limits of Imitation, Reverse Engineering, and Cyber-Espionage." *International Security* 43 (3): 141–89.

Gioe, David V., Michael S. Goodman, and Tim Stevens. 2020. "Intelligence in the Cyber Era: Evolution or Revolution?" *Political Science Quarterly* 135 (2): 191–224.

Glaser, Charles L. 1994. "Realists as Optimists: Cooperation as Self-Help." *International Security* 19 (3): 50–90.

Glaser, Charles L., and Chaim Kaufmann. 1998. "What Is the Offense-Defense Balance and Can We Measure It?" *International Security* 22 (4): 44–82.

Goddard, Stacie E. 2018. "Embedded Revisionism: Networks, Institutions, and Challenges to World Order." *International Organization* 72 (4): 763–97.

Goddard, Stacie E., Paul K. MacDonald, and Daniel H. Nexon. 2019. "Repertoires of Statecraft: Instruments and Logics of Power Politics." *International Relations* 33 (2): 304–21.

Goddard, Stacie E., and Daniel H. Nexon. 2016. "The Dynamics of Global Power Politics: A Framework for Analysis." *Journal of Global Security Studies* 1 (1): 4–18.

Goffman, Erving. 1969. *Strategic Interaction*. University of Pennsylvania Press.

Goldfarb, Avi, and Jon R. Lindsay. 2022. "Prediction and Judgment: Why Artificial Intelligence Increases the Importance of Humans in War." *International Security* 46 (3): 7–50.

Goldman, Emily O., ed. 2013. *Information and Revolutions in Military Affairs*. Routledge.

Goldman, Emily O. 2020. "The Cyber Paradigm Shift." In *Ten Years In: Implementing Strategic Approaches to Cyberspace*, edited by Jacquelyn G. Schneider, Emily O. Goldman, and Michael Warner. Newport Papers 45. US Naval War College.

Good, I. J. 2000. "Turing's Anticipation of Empirical Bayes in Connection with the Cryptanalysis of the Naval Enigma." *Journal of Statistical Computation and Simulation* 66 (2): 101–11.

Good, Jack. 1993. "Enigma and Fish." In *Codebreakers: The Inside Story of Bletchley Park*, edited by F. H. Hinsley and Alan Stripp. Oxford University Press.

Gorwa, Robert. 2019a. "The Platform Governance Triangle: Conceptualising the Informal Regulation of Online Content." *Internet Policy Review* 8 (2): 1–22.

Gorwa, Robert. 2019b. "What Is Platform Governance?" *Information, Communication & Society* 22 (6): 854–71.

Grauer, Ryan. 2016. *Commanding Military Power: Organizing for Victory and Defeat on the Battlefield*. Cambridge University Press.

Grauer, Ryan, and Michael C. Horowitz. 2012. "What Determines Military Victory? Testing the Modern System." *Security Studies* 21 (1): 83–112.

Green, Brendan Rittenhouse, and Austin Long. 2020. "Conceal or Reveal? Managing Clandestine Military Capabilities in Peacetime Competition." *International Security* 44 (3): 48–83.

Grey, Christopher. 2012. *Decoding Organization: Bletchley Park, Codebreaking and Organization Studies*. Cambridge University Press.

Grisé, Michelle, Alyssa Demus, Yuliya Shokh, Marta Kepe, Jonathan W. Welburn, and Khrystyna Holynska. 2022. *Rivalry in the Information Sphere: Russian Conceptions of Information Confrontation*. RAND Corporation. https://www.rand.org/pubs/research_reports/RRA198-8.html.

Gustafson, Kristian, Dan Lomas, and Steven Wagner. 2024. "Intelligence Warning in the Ukraine War, Autumn 2021–Summer 2022." *Intelligence and National Security* 39 (3): 400–419.

Haas, Melinda, and Keren Yarhi-Milo. 2021. "To Disclose or Deceive? Sharing Secret Information Between Aligned States." *International Security* 45 (3): 122–61.

Haigh, Thomas. 2014. "We Have Never Been Digital." *Communications of the ACM* 57 (9): 24–28.

Haigh, Thomas, and Mark Priestley. 2018. "Colossus and Programmability." *IEEE Annals of the History of Computing* 40 (4): 5–27.

Haigh, Thomas, and Mark Priestley. 2020. "Contextualizing Colossus: Codebreaking Technology and Institutional Capabilities." *Technology and Culture* 61 (3): 871–900.

Hannas, William C., James C. Mulvenon, and Anna B. Puglisi. 2013. *Chinese Industrial Espionage: Technology Acquisition and Military Modernization*. Routledge.

Hannas, William C., and Didi Kirsten Tatlow, eds. 2020. *China's Quest for Foreign Technology: Beyond Espionage*. Routledge.

Hansen, Isabella, and Darren J. Lim. 2019. "Doxing Democracy: Influencing Elections via Cyber Voter Interference." *Contemporary Politics* 25 (2): 150–71.

Hansen, Lene, and Helen Nissenbaum. 2009. "Digital Disaster, Cyber Security, and the Copenhagen School." *International Studies Quarterly* 53 (4): 1155–75.

Harknett, Richard J., and Max Smeets. 2022. "Cyber Campaigns and Strategic Outcomes." *Journal of Strategic Studies* 45 (4): 534–67.

Harry, Charles, Ido Sivan-Sevilla, and Mark McDermott. 2025. "Measuring the Size and Severity of the Integrated Cyber Attack Surface Across US County Governments." *Journal of Cybersecurity* 11 (1). https://doi.org/10.1093/cybsec/tyae032.

Hastings, Max. 2016. *The Secret War: Spies, Ciphers, and Guerrillas, 1939–1945*. HarperCollins.

Haun, Phil M. 2015. *Coercion, Survival, and War: Why Weak States Resist the United States*. Stanford University Press.

He, Chris Zhijian, Tracie Frost, and Robert E. Pinsker. 2020. "The Impact of Reported Cybersecurity Breaches on Firm Innovation." *Journal of Information Systems* 34 (2): 187–209.

Headrick, Daniel R. 1991. *The Invisible Weapon: Telecommunications and International Politics, 1851–1945*. Oxford University Press.

Headrick, Daniel R. 2000. *When Information Came of Age: Technologies of Knowledge in the Age of Reason and Revolution, 1700–1850*. Oxford University Press.

Healey, Jason, and Robert Jervis. 2020. "The Escalation Inversion and Other Oddities of Situational Cyber Stability." *Texas National Security Review* 3 (4): 30–53.

Heginbotham, Eric, Michael Nixon, Forrest E. Morgan, et al. 2015. *The U.S.-China Military Scorecard*. RAND Corporation.

Helmus, Todd C., James V. Marrone, Marek N. Posard, and Danielle Schlang. 2020. *Russian Propaganda Hits Its Mark: Experimentally Testing the Impact of Russian Propaganda and Counter-Interventions*. RAND Corporation. https://www.rand.org/pubs/research_reports/RRA704-3.html.

Herman, Michael. 1996. *Intelligence Power in Peace and War*. Cambridge University Press.

Herr, Trey, Will Loomis, Emma Schroeder, Stewart Scott, Simon Handler, and Tianjiu Zuo. 2021. *Broken Trust: Lessons from Sunburst*. Atlantic Council. https://www.atlanticcouncil.org/wp-content/uploads/2021/03/BROKEN-TRUST.pdf.

Herrera, Geoffrey L. 2006. *Technology and International Transformation: The Railroad, the Atom Bomb, and the Politics of Technological Change*. State University of New York Press.

Hinsley, F. H., and Alan Stripp, eds. 1993. *Codebreakers: The Inside Story of Bletchley Park*. Oxford University Press.

Hinsley, F. H., E. E. Thomas, C. F. G. Ransom, and R. C. Knight. 1979. *British Intelligence in the Second World War: Its Influence on Strategy and Operations*. Vol. 1. Her Majesty's Stationery Office.

Hinsley, F. H., E. E. Thomas, C. F. G. Ransom, and R. C. Knight. 1981. *British Intelligence in the Second World War: Its Influence on Strategy and Operations*. Vol. 2. Her Majesty's Stationery Office.

Hinsley, F. H., E. E. Thomas, C. F. G. Ransom, and R. C. Knight. 1984. *British Intelligence in the Second World War: Its Influence on Strategy and Operations*. Vol. 3.1. Her Majesty's Stationery Office.

Hinsley, F. H., E. E. Thomas, C. A. G. Simkins, and C. F. G. Ransom. 1988. *British Intelligence in the Second World War: Its Influence on Strategy and Operations*. Vol. 3.2. Her Majesty's Stationery Office.

Hodges, Andrew. 2014. *Alan Turing: The Enigma*. Rev. ed. Princeton University Press.

Hoffmann, Stacie, Dominique Lazanski, and Emily Taylor. 2020. "Standardising the Splinternet: How China's Technical Standards Could Fragment the Internet." *Journal of Cyber Policy* 5 (2): 239–64.

House Permanent Select Committee on Intelligence. 2018. *Report on Russian Active Measures*. 115th Congress, House of Representatives. https://docs.house.gov/meetings/IG/IG00/20180322/108023/HRPT-115-1_1-p1-U3.pdf.

Howard, Michael. 1990. *British Intelligence in the Second World War: Strategic Deception*. Vol. 5. Cambridge University Press.

Hughes, Thomas P. 1998. *Rescuing Prometheus: Four Monumental Projects That Changed the Modern World*. Random House.

Hughes, Thomas P. 2004. *Human-Built World: How to Think About Technology and Culture*. University of Chicago Press.

Hugill, Peter J. 1999. *Global Communications Since 1844: Geopolitics and Technology*. Johns Hopkins University Press.

Hunt, Edward. 2012. "US Government Computer Penetration Programs and the Implications for Cyberwar." *IEEE Annals of the History of Computing* 34 (3): 4–21.

Hunzeker, Michael A. 2021. *Dying to Learn: Wartime Lessons from the Western Front*. Cornell University Press.

Insikt Group. 2023. *Charting China's Climb as a Leading Global Cyber Power*. Recorded Future. https://go.recordedfuture.com/hubfs/reports/cta-2023-1107.pdf.

IP Commission. 2017. *Update to the IP Commission Report, The Theft of American Intellectual Property: Reassessments of the Challenge and United States Policy*. Commission on the Theft of American Intellectual Property and the National Bureau of Asian Research.

Isaacson, Walter. 2014. *The Innovators: How a Group of Hackers, Geniuses, and Geeks Created the Digital Revolution*. Simon & Schuster.

Jackson, Colin F. 2016. "Information Is Not a Weapons System." *Journal of Strategic Studies* 39 (5–6): 820–46.

Jackson, Steven J. 2014. "Rethinking Repair." In *Media Technologies*, edited by Tarleton Gillespie, Pablo J. Boczkowski, and Kirsten A. Foot. MIT Press.

Jamieson, Kathleen Hall. 2018. *Cyberwar: How Russian Hackers and Trolls Helped Elect a President: What We Don't, Can't, and Do Know*. Oxford University Press.

Jasanoff, Sheila, ed. 2004. *States of Knowledge: The Co-Production of Science and the Social Order*. Routledge.

Jenkins, Ryan. 2013. "Is Stuxnet Physical? Does It Matter?" *Journal of Military Ethics* 12 (1): 68–79.

Jensen, Benjamin, Brandon Valeriano, and Ryan Maness. 2019. "Fancy Bears and Digital Trolls: Cyber Strategy with a Russian Twist." *Journal of Strategic Studies* 42 (2): 212–34.

Jepperson, Ronald L. 1991. "Institutions, Institutional Effects, and Institutionalism." In *The New Institutionalism in Organizational Analysis*, edited by Paul DiMaggio and Walter W. Powell. University of Chicago Press.

Jervis, Robert. 1986. "Intelligence and Foreign Policy: A Review Essay." Edited by Christopher Andrew, David Dilks, and Ernest R. May. *International Security* 11 (3): 141–61.

Jervis, Robert. 2011. *Why Intelligence Fails: Lessons from the Iranian Revolution and the Iraq War*. Cornell University Press.

Johnston, Alastair Iain. 2019. "China in a World of Orders: Rethinking Compliance and Challenge in Beijing's International Relations." *International Security* 44 (2): 9–60.

Joint Chiefs of Staff. 2018. *Cyberspace Operations*. Joint Publication 3–12.

Kahn, David. 1993. "An Enigma Chronology." *Cryptologia* 17 (3): 237–46.

Kahn, David. 1996. *The Codebreakers: The Comprehensive History of Secret Communication from Ancient Times to the Internet*. Rev. ed. Simon & Schuster.

Kahn, David. 2001. "An Historical Theory of Intelligence." *Intelligence and National Security* 16 (3): 79–92.

Kahn, David. 2012. *Seizing the Enigma: The Race to Break the German U-Boat Codes, 1933–1945*. Rev. ed. Naval Institute Press.

Kalla, Joshua L., and David E. Broockman. 2018. "The Minimal Persuasive Effects of Campaign Contact in General Elections: Evidence from 49 Field Experiments." *American Political Science Review* 112 (1): 148–66.

Kamel, Amir Magdy. 2018. "The JCPOA: How Iran's Grand Strategy Stifled the US." *Middle Eastern Studies* 54 (4): 706–22.

Kaminska, Monica. 2021. "Restraint Under Conditions of Uncertainty: Why the United States Tolerates Cyberattacks." *Journal of Cybersecurity* 7 (1): 1–15.

Kamiya, Shinichi, Jun-Koo Kang, Jungmin Kim, Andreas Milidonis, and René M. Stulz. 2018. "What Is the Impact of Successful Cyberattacks on Target Firms?" National Bureau of Economic Research, Working Paper Series. https://doi.org/10.3386/w24409.

Kamiya, Shinichi, Jun-Koo Kang, Jungmin Kim, Andreas Milidonis, and René M. Stulz. 2021. "Risk Management, Firm Reputation, and the Impact of Successful Cyberattacks on Target Firms." *Journal of Financial Economics* 139 (3): 719–49.

Kang, David C. 2022. "Still Getting Asia Wrong: No 'Contain China' Coalition Exists." *Washington Quarterly* 45 (4): 79–98.

Kania, Elsa B. 2020. "The Ideological Battlefield: China's Approach to Political Warfare and Propaganda in an Age of Cyber Conflict." In *Information Warfare in the Age of Cyber Conflict*, edited by Christopher Whyte, A. Trevor Thrall, and Brian M. Mazanec. Routledge.

Kania, Elsa B. 2021. "China's Drive for Innovation Within a World of Profound Changes." *Asia Policy* 28 (2): 17–31.

Kania, Elsa B., and John Costello. 2021. "Seizing the Commanding Heights: The PLA Strategic Support Force in Chinese Military Power." *Journal of Strategic Studies* 44 (2): 218–64.

Kania, Elsa B., and Adam Segal. 2021. "Globalized Innovation and Great Power Competition." In *After Engagement: Dilemmas in U.S.-China Security Relations*, edited by Jacques deLisle and Avery Goldstein. Brookings Institution Press.

Kaplan, Fred. 2016. *Dark Territory: The Secret History of Cyber War*. New York: Simon & Schuster.

Kaplan, Morton A. 1952. "An Introduction to the Strategy of Statecraft." *World Politics* 4 (4): 548–76.

Kastner, Jill, and William C. Wohlforth. 2024. *A Measure Short of War: A Brief History of Great Power Subversion*. Oxford University Press.

Katz, Yaakov, and Yoaz Hendel. 2012. *Israel vs. Iran: The Shadow War*. Potomac Books.

Keegan, John. 2003. *Intelligence in War: Knowledge of the Enemy from Napoleon to Al-Qaeda*. Knopf.

Kello, Lucas. 2017. *The Virtual Weapon and International Order*. Yale University Press.

Kennedy, Paul. 2013. *Engineers of Victory: The Problem Solvers Who Turned the Tide in the Second World War*. Random House.

Kenyon, David. 2019. *Bletchley Park and D-Day: The Untold Story of How the Battle for Normandy Was Won*. Yale University Press.

Kerr, Paul K., John Rollins, and Catherine A. Theohary. 2010. *The Stuxnet Computer Worm: Harbinger of an Emerging Warfare Capability*. Congressional Research Service.

Kindervater, Katharine Hall. 2016. "The Emergence of Lethal Surveillance: Watching and Killing in the History of Drone Technology." *Security Dialogue* 47 (3): 223–38.

King, Gary, Jennifer Pan, and Margaret E. Roberts. 2013. "How Censorship in China Allows Government Criticism but Silences Collective Expression." *American Political Science Review* 107 (2): 326–43.

Kirshner, Jonathan. 2022. *An Unwritten Future: Realism and Uncertainty in World Politics*. Princeton University Press.

Kline, Ronald R. 2015. *The Cybernetics Moment: Or Why We Call Our Age the Information Age*. Johns Hopkins University Press.

Kline, Ronald R., and Trevor Pinch. 1996. "Users as Agents of Technological Change: The Social Construction of the Automobile in the Rural United States." *Technology and Culture* 37 (4): 763–95.

Kostyuk, Nadiya, and Erik Gartzke. 2022. "Why Cyber Dogs Have Yet to Bark Loudly in Russia's Invasion of Ukraine (Summer 2022)." *Texas National Security Review* 5 (3): 113–26.

Kostyuk, Nadiya, and Erik Gartzke. 2023. "Fighting in Cyberspace: Internet Access and the Substitutability of Cyber and Military Operations." *Journal of Conflict Resolution* 68 (1): 80–107.

Kostyuk, Nadiya, Jon R. Lindsay, Emily Kim, et al. 2024. "Combat and Connectivity: Explaining Internet Outages in the Russo-Ukrainian War." Working paper, August 9.

Kostyuk, Nadiya, and Yuri M. Zhukov. 2019. "Invisible Digital Front: Can Cyber Attacks Shape Battlefield Events?" *Journal of Conflict Resolution* 63 (2): 317–47.

Krafft, P. M., and Joan Donovan. 2020. "Disinformation by Design: The Use of Evidence Collages and Platform Filtering in a Media Manipulation Campaign." *Political Communication* 37 (2): 194–214.

Kragh, Martin, and Sebastian Åsberg. 2017. "Russia's Strategy for Influence Through Public Diplomacy and Active Measures: The Swedish Case." *Journal of Strategic Studies* 40 (6): 773–816.

Krasner, Stephen D. 1999. *Sovereignty: Organized Hypocrisy*. Princeton University Press.

Kreps, Sarah, and Jacquelyn Schneider. 2019. "Escalation Firebreaks in the Cyber, Conventional, and Nuclear Domains: Moving Beyond Effects-Based Logics." *Journal of Cybersecurity* 5 (1). https://doi.org/10.1093/cybsec/tyz007.

Krieg, Andreas. 2023. *Subversion: The Strategic Weaponization of Narratives*. Georgetown University Press.

Kristensen, Peter Marcus. 2018. "International Relations at the End: A Sociological Autopsy." *International Studies Quarterly* 62 (2): 245–59.

Kuehl, Daniel T. 2009. "From Cyberspace to Cyberpower: Defining the Problem." In *Cyberpower and National Security*, edited by Franklin D Kramer, Stuart H Starr, and Larry K Wentz. National Defense University Press.

Kuerbis, Brenden, and Farzaneh Badiei. 2017. "Mapping the Cybersecurity Institutional Landscape." *Digital Policy, Regulation and Governance* 19 (6): 466–92.

Kuerbis, Brenden, and Milton Mueller. 2017. "Internet Routing Registries, Data Governance, and Security." *Journal of Cyber Policy* 2 (1): 64–81.

Kuran, Timur. 1997. *Private Truths, Public Lies: The Social Consequences of Preference Falsification*. Harvard University Press.

Lake, David A. 2009. *Hierarchy in International Relations*. Cornell University Press.

Lake, David A. 2011. "Why 'Isms' Are Evil: Theory, Epistemology, and Academic Sects as Impediments to Understanding and Progress." *International Studies Quarterly* 55 (2): 465–80.

Landau, Susan Eva. 2010. *Surveillance or Security? The Risks Posed by New Wiretapping Technologies*. MIT Press.

Langner, Ralph. 2011. "Stuxnet: Dissecting a Cyberwarfare Weapon." *IEEE Security Privacy* 9 (3): 49–51.

Langner, Ralph. 2013. *To Kill a Centrifuge: A Technical Analysis of What Stuxnet's Creators Tried to Achieve*. Langner Group.

Lanoszka, Alexander. 2019. "Disinformation in International Politics." *European Journal of International Security* 4 (2): 227–48.

Latour, Bruno. 1990. "Drawing Things Together." In *Representation in Scientific Practice*, edited by Michael Lynch and Steve Woolgar. MIT Press.

Law, John. 1987. "Technology and Heterogeneous Engineering: The Case of Portuguese Expansion." In *The Social Construction of Technological Systems: New*

Directions in the Sociology and History of Technology, edited by Wiebe E. Bijker, Thomas P. Hughes, and Trevor J. Pinch. Anniversary ed. MIT Press.

Law, John. 2004. *After Method: Mess in Social Science Research*. Routledge.

Lawson, Sean T. 2020. *Cybersecurity Discourse in the United States: Cyber-Doom Rhetoric and Beyond*. Routledge.

Lazer, David M. J., Matthew A. Baum, Yochai Benkler, et al. 2018. "The Science of Fake News." *Science* 359 (6380): 1094–96.

Lee, Melissa M. 2020. *Crippling Leviathan: How Foreign Subversion Weakens the State*. Cornell University Press.

Lee, Melissa M., and Nan Zhang. 2017. "Legibility and the Informational Foundations of State Capacity." *Journal of Politics* 79 (1): 118–32.

Leeuw, Karl Maria Michael de, and Jan Bergstra, eds. 2007. *The History of Information Security: A Comprehensive Handbook*. Elsevier Science.

Legro, Jeffrey W. 2013. *Cooperation Under Fire: Anglo-German Restraint During World War II*. Cornell University Press.

Levin, Dov H. 2016. "When the Great Power Gets a Vote: The Effects of Great Power Electoral Interventions on Election Results." *International Studies Quarterly* 60 (2): 189–202.

Levin, Dov H. 2020. *Meddling in the Ballot Box: The Causes and Effects of Partisan Electoral Interventions*. Oxford University Press.

Lewin, Ronald. 2008. *Ultra Goes to War*. Reissue. Pen and Sword Military.

Libicki, Martin C. 2009. *Cyberdeterrence and Cyberwar*. RAND Corporation.

Liff, Adam P. 2012. "Cyberwar: A New 'Absolute Weapon'? The Proliferation of Cyberwarfare Capabilities and Interstate War." *Journal of Strategic Studies* 35 (3): 401–28.

Lin, Herbert, and Jaclyn Kerr. 2021. "On Cyber-Enabled Information Warfare and Information Operations." In *The Oxford Handbook of Cyber Security*, edited by Paul Cornish. Oxford University Press.

Lindsay, Jon R. 2013. "Stuxnet and the Limits of Cyber Warfare." *Security Studies* 22 (3): 365–404.

Lindsay, Jon R. 2015. "China and Cybersecurity: Controversy and Context." In *China and Cybersecurity: Espionage, Strategy, and Politics in the Digital Domain*, edited by Jon R. Lindsay, Tai Ming Cheung, and Derek S. Reveron. Oxford University Press.

Lindsay, Jon R. 2016. "Tipping the Scales: The Attribution Problem and the Feasibility of Deterrence Against Cyber Attack." *Journal of Cybersecurity* 1 (1): 53–67.

Lindsay, Jon R. 2017. "Target Practice: Counterterrorism and the Amplification of Data Friction." *Science, Technology, & Human Values* 42 (6): 1061–99.

Lindsay, Jon R. 2020a. "Demystifying the Quantum Threat: Infrastructure, Implementation, and Intelligence Advantage." *Security Studies* 29 (2): 335–61.

Lindsay, Jon R. 2020b. *Information Technology and Military Power*. Cornell University Press.

Lindsay, Jon R. 2021. "Cyber Conflict vs. Cyber Command: Hidden Dangers in the American Military Solution to a Large-Scale Intelligence Problem." *Intelligence and National Security* 36 (2): 260–78.

Lindsay, Jon R. 2022. "Cyber Operations and Nuclear Escalation: A Dangerous Gamble." In *Nuclear Command, Control, and Communications: A Primer on US*

Systems and Future Challenges, edited by James J. Wirtz and Jeffrey A. Larsen. Georgetown University Press.

Lindsay, Jon R. 2023. "War Is from Mars, AI Is from Venus: Rediscovering the Institutional Context of Military Automation." *Texas National Security Review* 7 (1): 29–47.

Lindsay, Jon R. 2024. "Abducted by Hackers: Using the Case of Bletchley Park to Construct a Theory of Intelligence Performance That Generalizes to Cybersecurity." *Journal of Peace Research* 61 (1): 87–102.

Lindsay, Jon R., and Tai Ming Cheung. 2015. "From Exploitation to Innovation: Acquisition, Absorption, and Application." In *China and Cybersecurity: Espionage, Strategy, and Politics in the Digital Domain,* edited by Jon R. Lindsay, Tai Ming Cheung, and Derek S. Reveron. Oxford University Press.

Locke, John. 1980. *Second Treatise of Government.* Edited by C. B. Macpherson. Hackett.

Loleski, Steven. 2019. "From Cold to Cyber Warriors: The Origins and Expansion of NSA's Tailored Access Operations (TAO) to Shadow Brokers." *Intelligence and National Security* 34 (1): 112–28.

Lonergan, Erica D. 2024. "Emerging Technology and the Cult of the Offensive." *Contemporary Security Policy* 45 (3): 459–93.

Lonergan, Erica D., and Shawn W. Lonergan. 2022. "Cyber Operations, Accommodative Signaling, and the De-Escalation of International Crises." *Security Studies* 31 (1): 32–64.

Lonergan, Erica D., and Shawn W. Lonergan. 2023. *Escalation Dynamics in Cyberspace.* Oxford University Press.

Lonergan, Erica D., and Michael Poznansky. 2024. "Competing Visions for US Grand Strategy in Cyberspace." *Security Studies* 33 (4): 607–39.

Long, Austin. 2016. *The Soul of Armies: Counterinsurgency Doctrine and Military Culture in the US and UK.* Cornell Studies in Security Affairs. Cornell University Press.

Long, Stephen, and Francesco Cacciatore. 2024. "One Size Does Not Fit All: Rollback Orthodoxy and Anglo-American Covert Action in Albania and Ukraine in the Early Cold War." *Intelligence and National Security* 39 (4): 599–619.

Lowenthal, Mark M. 2020. *Intelligence: From Secrets to Policy.* 8th ed. CQ Press.

Lukasik, S. 2011. "Why the Arpanet Was Built." *IEEE Annals of the History of Computing* 33 (3): 4–21.

Lukito, Josephine. 2020. "Coordinating a Multi-Platform Disinformation Campaign: Internet Research Agency Activity on Three U.S. Social Media Platforms, 2015 to 2017." *Political Communication* 37 (2): 238–55.

Lyon, Matthew, and Katie Hafner. 1996. *Where Wizards Stay Up Late: The Origins of the Internet.* Simon & Schuster.

Machiavelli, Nicolo. 1958. *The Prince.* Translated by William K. Marriott. J. M. Dent & Sons.

Maher, Richard. 2019. "The Covert Campaign Against Iran's Nuclear Program: Implications for the Theory and Practice of Counterproliferation." *Journal of Strategic Studies* 44 (7): 1014-1040.

Mahoney, James. 2015. "Process Tracing and Historical Explanation." *Security Studies* 24 (2): 200–218.

Mandel, Robert. 2019. *Global Data Shock: Strategic Ambiguity, Deception, and Surprise in an Age of Information Overload*. Stanford University Press.

Mandiant. 2013. *APT1: Exposing One of China's Cyber Espionage Units*. https://www.mandiant.com/sites/default/files/2021-09/mandiant-apt1-report.pdf.

March, James G., and Herbert A. Simon. 1958. *Organizations*. New York: John Wiley and Sons.

Marczak, Bill, Nicholas Weaver, Jakub Dalek, et al. 2015. *China's Great Cannon*. Research brief. Citizen Lab, Munk School of Global Affairs, University of Toronto. https://citizenlab.org/2015/04/chinas-great-cannon/.

Maschmeyer, Lennart. 2021. "The Subversive Trilemma: Why Cyber Operations Fall Short of Expectations." *International Security* 46 (2): 51–90.

Maschmeyer, Lennart. 2022. "Subversion, Cyber Operations and Reverse Structural Power in World Politics." *European Journal of International Relations* 29 (1): 79–103.

Maschmeyer, Lennart. 2024. *Subversion: From Covert Operations to Cyber Conflict*. Oxford University Press.

Maschmeyer, Lennart, Ronald Deibert, and Jon R. Lindsay. 2021. "A Tale of Two Cybers: How Threat Reporting by Cybersecurity Firms Systematically Underrepresents Threats to Civil Society." *Journal of Information Technology & Politics* 18 (1): 1–20.

Mathew, Ashwin J. 2016. "The Myth of the Decentralised Internet." *Internet Policy Review* 5 (3). https://doi.org/10.14763/2016.3.425.

Matovski, Aleksandar. 2020. "Strategic Intelligence and International Crisis Behavior." *Security Studies* 29 (5): 964–90.

Mattis, Peter, and Matthew Brazil. 2019. *Chinese Communist Espionage: An Intelligence Primer*. Naval Institute Press.

Maurer, Tim. 2018. *Cyber Mercenaries: The State, Hackers, and Power*. Cambridge University Press.

McCarthy, Daniel R. 2015. *Power, Information Technology, and International Relations Theory: The Power and Politics of US Foreign Policy and the Internet*. Palgrave Macmillan.

McConnell, Mike. 2009. "Cyberwar Is the New Atomic Age." *New Perspectives Quarterly* 26 (3): 72–77.

McGlave, Claire C., Hannah Neprash, and Sayeh Nikpay. "Hacked to Pieces? The Effects of Ransomware Attacks on Hospitals and Patients." Social Science Research Network, August 19, 2024. https://doi.org/10.2139/ssrn.4579292.

McKay, Sinclair. 2010. *The Secret Life of Bletchley Park: The WWII Codebreaking Centre and the Men and Women Who Worked There*. Aurum.

McKeown, Timothy J. 1999. "Case Studies and the Statistical Worldview: Review of King, Keohane, and Verba's *Designing Social Inquiry: Scientific Inference in Qualitative Research*." *International Organization* 53 (1): 161–90.

McKune, Sarah. 2015. "'Foreign Hostile Forces': The Human Rights Dimension of China's Cyber Campaigns." In *China and Cybersecurity: Espionage, Strategy, and Politics in the Digital Domain*, edited by Jon R. Lindsay, Tai Ming Cheung, and Derek S. Reveron. Oxford University Press.

McReynolds, Joe. 2016. "China's Military Strategy for Network Warfare." In *China's Evolving Military Strategy*, edited by Joe McReynolds. Brookings Institution Press.

Mearsheimer, John J. 2011. *Why Leaders Lie: The Truth About Lying in International Politics*. Oxford University Press.

Medina, Eden. 2011. *Cybernetic Revolutionaries: Technology and Politics in Allende's Chile*. MIT Press.

Mele, Alfred R. 1992. *Springs of Action: Understanding Intentional Behavior*. Oxford University Press.

Mertha, Andrew. 2009. "'Fragmented Authoritarianism 2.0': Political Pluralization in the Chinese Policy Process." *China Quarterly* 200 (December): 995–1012.

Microsoft. 2022. *Microsoft Digital Defense Report 2022*. https://www.microsoft.com/en-us/security/business/microsoft-digital-defense-report-2022.

Miller, A. Ray. 1995. "The Cryptographic Mathematics of Enigma." *Cryptologia* 19 (1): 65–80.

Miller, Chris. 2022. *Chip War: The Fight for the World's Most Critical Technology*. Simon & Schuster.

Milner, Helen V., Ryan Powers, and Erik Voeten. 2023. "The Myth of the Eclectic IR Scholar?" *International Studies Perspectives* 24 (3): 308–35.

Milner-Barry, P. S. 1986. "'Action This Day': The Letter from Bletchley Park Cryptanalysts to the Prime Minister, 21 October 1941." *Intelligence and National Security* 1 (2): 272–76.

Mindell, David A. 2002. *Between Human and Machine: Feedback, Control, and Computing Before Cybernetics*. Johns Hopkins University Press.

Monte, Matthew. 2015. *Network Attacks and Exploitation: A Framework*. Wiley.

Monteiro, Nuno P. 2011. "Unrest Assured: Why Unipolarity Is Not Peaceful." *International Security* 36 (3): 9–40.

Montgomery, Evan Braden. 2014. "Contested Primacy in the Western Pacific: China's Rise and the Future of U.S. Power Projection." *International Security* 38 (4): 115–49.

Moore, Daniel. 2022. *Offensive Cyber Operations: Understanding Intangible Warfare*. Hurst.

Morrow, James D. 2014. *Order Within Anarchy: The Laws of War as an International Institution*. Cambridge University Press.

Mueller, Milton L. 2010. *Networks and States: The Global Politics of Internet Governance*. MIT Press.

Mueller, Milton L. 2017. *Will the Internet Fragment? Sovereignty, Globalization and Cyberspace*. Polity.

Mueller, Robert S., III. 2019. *Report on the Investigation unto Russian Interference in the 2016 Presidential Election*. US Department of Justice.

Musgrave, Paul. 2019. "International Hegemony Meets Domestic Politics: Why Liberals Can Be Pessimists." *Security Studies* 28 (3): 451–78.

National Counterintelligence and Security Center. 2018. *Foreign Economic Espionage in Cyberspace*. Office of the Director of National Intelligence. https://www.dni.gov/files/NCSC/documents/news/20180724-economic-espionage-pub.pdf.

National Intelligence Council. 2007. *Iran: Nuclear Intentions and Capabilities*. National Intelligence Estimate. Office of the Director of National Intelligence.

Naughton, Barry. 2007. *The Chinese Economy: Transitions and Growth*. MIT Press.

Nickles, David Paull. 2003. *Under the Wire: How the Telegraph Changed Diplomacy*. Harvard University Press.

Norberg, Arthur L., and Judy E. O'Neill. 1996. *Transforming Computer Technology: Information Processing for the Pentagon, 1962–1986*. Johns Hopkins University Press.

North, Douglass C. 1990. *Institutions, Institutional Change, and Economic Performance*. Cambridge University Press.

Nye, David E. 2006. *Technology Matters: Questions to Live With*. MIT Press.

Nye, Joseph S., Jr. 2010. *Cyber Power*. Belfer Center for Science and International Affairs, Harvard Kennedy School. https://apps.dtic.mil/sti/citations/ADA522626.

Nye, Joseph S., Jr. 2011. "Nuclear Lessons for Cyber Security?" *Strategic Studies Quarterly* 5 (4): 18–38.

O'Brien, Phillips Payson. 2015. *How the War Was Won*. Cambridge University Press.

Office of the Deputy Assistant Secretary of Defense for Nuclear Matters. 2020. "Nuclear Fuel Cycle and Proliferation." In *Nuclear Matters Handbook 2020*. US Government Printing Office.

Office of the Director of National Intelligence. 2017. *Assessing Russian Activities and Intentions in Recent US Elections*. Intelligence Community Assessment. National Intelligence Council. https://www.dni.gov/files/documents/ICA_2017_01.pdf.

Olson, Mancur. 1965. *The Logic of Collective Action*. Harvard University Press.

Oneal, John R., and Bruce M. Russett. 1997. "The Classical Liberals Were Right: Democracy, Interdependence, and Conflict, 1950–1985." *International Studies Quarterly* 41 (2): 267–94.

Oppenheimer, Harry. 2023. "Essays on Digital Interdependence and Globalization." PhD diss., Harvard University. https://dash.harvard.edu/handle/1/37375738.

O'Rourke, Lindsey A. 2018. *Covert Regime Change: America's Secret Cold War*. Cornell University Press.

Ostrom, Elinor. 1990. *Governing the Commons: The Evolution of Institutions for Collective Action*. Cambridge University Press.

Overy, Richard. 1996. *Why the Allies Won*. New York: W. W. Norton.

Pape, Robert Anthony. 1996. *Bombing to Win: Air Power and Coercion in War*. Cornell University Press.

Parkinson, Sarah E. 2024. "Unreported Realities: The Political Economy of Media-Sourced Data." *American Political Science Review* 118 (3): 1527–32.

Paul, Christopher, and Miriam Matthews. 2016. *The Russian 'Firehose of Falsehood' Propaganda Model*. RAND Corporation. http://www.rand.org/pubs/perspectives/PE198.html.

Pedersen, Frederik A. H., and Jeppe T. Jacobsen. 2024. "Narrow Windows of Opportunity: The Limited Utility of Cyber Operations in War." *Journal of Cybersecurity* 10 (1). https://doi.org/10.1093/cybsec/tyae014.

Perkovich, George, and Ariel E. Levite, eds. 2017. *Understanding Cyber Conflict: 14 Analogies*. Georgetown University Press.

Perlroth, Nicole. 2021. *This Is How They Tell Me the World Ends: The Cyberweapons Arms Race*. Bloomsbury.

Perrow, Charles. 1999. *Normal Accidents: Living with High-Risk Technologies*. 2nd ed. Princeton University Press.

Persily, Nathaniel. 2017. "The 2016 U.S. Election: Can Democracy Survive the Internet?" *Journal of Democracy* 28 (2): 63–76. https://doi.org/10.1353/jod.2017.0025.

Petersen, Roger. 2001. *Resistance and Rebellion: Lessons from Eastern Europe*. Cambridge University Press.

Peterson, Dale. 2013. "Offensive Cyber Weapons: Construction, Development, and Employment." *Journal of Strategic Studies* 36 (1): 120–24.

Poirier, Clémence. 2022. *The War in Ukraine from a Space Cybersecurity Perspective*. European Space Policy Institute. https://www.espi.or.at/wp-content/uploads/2022/10/ESPI-Short-1-Final-Report.pdf.

Posard, Marek N., Marta Kepe, Hilary Reininger, James V. Marrone, Todd C. Helmus, and Jordan R. Reimer. 2020. *From Consensus to Conflict: Understanding Foreign Measures Targeting U.S. Elections*. RAND Corporation. https://www.rand.org/pubs/research_reports/RRA704-1.html.

Poznansky, Michael. 2020. *In the Shadow of International Law: Covert Intervention in the Postwar World*. Oxford University Press.

Poznansky, Michael. 2022. "Revisiting Plausible Deniability." *Journal of Strategic Studies* 45 (4): 511–33.

Puyvelde, Damien Van, and Aaron F. Brantly. 2025. *Cybersecurity: Politics, Governance and Conflict in Cyberspace*. 2nd ed. Polity.

Qi, Hao. 2015. "China Debates the 'New Type of Great Power Relations.'" *Chinese Journal of International Politics* 8 (4): 349–70.

Raas, Whitney, and Austin Long. 2007. "Osirak Redux? Assessing Israeli Capabilities to Destroy Iranian Nuclear Facilities." *International Security* 31 (4): 7–33.

Ratcliff, R. A. 2006. *Delusions of Intelligence: Enigma, Ultra, and the End of Secure Ciphers*. Cambridge University Press.

Rathbun, Brian C. 2012. *Trust in International Cooperation: International Security Institutions, Domestic Politics and American Multilateralism*. Cambridge University Press.

Rattray, Gregory J. 2001. *Strategic Warfare in Cyberspace*. MIT Press.

Richelson, Jeffrey T. 2018. *The U.S. Intelligence Community*. 7th ed. Routledge.

Rid, Thomas. 2016. *Rise of the Machines: A Cybernetic History*. W. W. Norton.

Rid, Thomas. 2020. *Active Measures: The Secret History of Disinformation and Political Warfare*. Farrar, Straus and Giroux.

Rid, Thomas. 2023. "A Revolution in Intelligence." In *The New Makers of Modern Strategy: From the Ancient World to the Digital Age*, edited by Hal Brands, 1092–118. Princeton University Press.

Rittel, Horst W. J., and Melvin M. Webber. 1973. "Dilemmas in a General Theory of Planning." *Policy Sciences* 4 (2): 155–69.

Roberts, Margaret E. 2018. *Censored: Distraction and Diversion Inside China's Great Firewall*. Princeton University Press.

Rogg, Jeff. 2025. *The Spy and the State: The Story of American Intelligence*. Oxford University Press.

Roland, Alex, and Philip Shiman. 2002. *Strategic Computing: DARPA and the Quest for Machine Intelligence, 1983–1993*. MIT Press.

Roncone, Gabby, Dan Black, John Wolfram, et al. 2024. *APT44: Unearthing Sandworm*. Mandiant. https://services.google.com/fh/files/misc/apt44-unearthing-sandworm.pdf.

Rosato, Sebastian. 2003. "The Flawed Logic of Democratic Peace Theory." *American Political Science Review* 97 (4): 585–602.

Rosato, Sebastian. 2021. *Intentions in Great Power Politics: Uncertainty and the Roots of Conflict*. Yale University Press.

Rosenzweig, Roy. 1998. "Wizards, Bureaucrats, Warriors, and Hackers: Writing the History of the Internet." *American Historical Review* 103 (5): 1530–52.

Rousseau, Jean-Jacques. 1920. "A Dissertation on the Origin and Foundation of the Inequality of Mankind." In *The Social Contract & Discourses*, translated by George Douglas Howard Cole. J. M. Dent & Sons. https://www.gutenberg.org/ebooks/46333.

Rovner, Joshua. 2011. *Fixing the Facts: National Security and the Politics of Intelligence*. Cornell University Press.

Rovner, Joshua. 2023. "Theory of Sabotage." *Études françaises de renseignement et de cyber* 1 (1): 139–53.

Ruan, Lotus, Jeffrey Knockel, and Masashi Crete-Nishihata. 2021. "Information Control by Public Punishment: The Logic of Signalling Repression in China." *China Information* 35 (2): 133–57.

Ruck, Damian J., Natalie M. Rice, Joshua Borycz, and R. Alexander Bentley. 2019. "Internet Research Agency Twitter Activity Predicted 2016 U.S. Election Polls." *First Monday* 7 (1). https://doi.org/10.5210/fm.v24i7.10107.

Rudner, Martin. 2013. "Cyber-Threats to Critical National Infrastructure: An Intelligence Challenge." *International Journal of Intelligence and CounterIntelligence* 26 (3): 453–81.

Saha, Sagatom, and Ashley Feng. 2020. "Global Supply Chains, Economic Decoupling, and U.S.-China Relations, Part 1: The View from the United States." *China Brief* 20 (6). https://jamestown.org/program/global-supply-chains-economic-decoupling-and-u-s-china-relations-part-1-the-view-from-the-united-states/.

Sanger, David E. 2018. *The Perfect Weapon: War, Sabotage, and Fear in the Cyber Age*. Crown.

Sartre, Jean-Paul. 1992. *Being and Nothingness*. Translated by Hazel E. Barnes. Simon & Schuster.

Saxenian, AnnaLee. 1994. *Regional Advantage: Culture and Competition in Silicon Valley and Route 128*. Harvard University Press.

Schelling, Thomas C. 1960. *The Strategy of Conflict*. Harvard University Press.

Schelling, Thomas C. 2008. *Arms and Influence*. Yale University Press.

Schmidt, Eric, and Jared Cohen. 2013. *The New Digital Age: Reshaping the Future of People, Nations and Business*. Alfred A. Knopf.

Schneider, Jacquelyn G. 2025. "The Digital Cult of the Offensive and the US Military." *Journal of Strategic Studies* 48 (1): 36–59.

Schneider, Jacquelyn G., Emily O. Goldman, and Michael Warner, eds. 2020. *Ten Years In: Implementing Strategic Approaches to Cyberspace*. Newport Papers 45. US Naval War College.

Schneider, Jacquelyn G., Benjamin Schechter, and Rachael Shaffer. 2022. "A Lot of Cyber Fizzle but Not a Lot of Bang: Evidence About the Use of Cyber Operations from Wargames." *Journal of Global Security Studies* 7 (2). https://doi.org/10.1093/jogss/ogac005.

Schneider, Jacquelyn G., Benjamin Schechter, and Rachael Shaffer. 2023. "Hacking Nuclear Stability: Wargaming Technology, Uncertainty, and Escalation." *International Organization* 77 (3): 633–67.

Schneier, Bruce. 2014. "Metadata = Surveillance." *IEEE Security & Privacy* 12 (2): 88.

Schuessler, John M. 2015. *Deceit on the Road to War: Presidents, Politics, and American Democracy*. Cornell University Press.

Scott, James C. 1998. *Seeing like a State: How Certain Schemes to Improve the Human Condition Have Failed*. Yale University Press.

Scott, James C. 2008. *Weapons of the Weak: Everyday Forms of Peasant Resistance*. Yale University Press.

Scott, Len. 2004. "Secret Intelligence, Covert Action and Clandestine Diplomacy." *Intelligence and National Security* 19 (2): 322–41.

Seabright, Paul. 2010. *The Company of Strangers: A Natural History of Economic Life*. Rev. ed. Princeton University Press.

Segal, Adam. 2020. "China's Vision for Cyber Sovereignty and the Global Governance of Cyberspace." In *An Emerging China-Centric Order: China's Vision for a New World Order in Practice*, edited by Nadège Rolland. National Bureau of Asian Research.

Shandler, Ryan, Michael L. Gross, and Daphna Canetti. 2023. "Cyberattacks, Psychological Distress, and Military Escalation: An Internal Meta-Analysis." *Journal of Global Security Studies* 8 (1). https://doi.org/10.1093/jogss/ogac042.

Shannon, Claude E. 1945. *A Mathematical Theory of Cryptography*. Technical Report. Bell Labs.

Shannon, Claude E. 1948. "A Mathematical Theory of Communication." *Bell System Technical Journal* 27:379–423, 623–56.

Shapiro, Carl, and Hal R. Varian. 1999. *Information Rules: A Strategic Guide to the Network Economy*. Harvard Business School Press.

Shapiro, Jacob N. 2013. *The Terrorist's Dilemma: Managing Violent Covert Organizations*. Princeton University Press.

Sharp, Travis. 2017. "Theorizing Cyber Coercion: The 2014 North Korean Operation Against Sony." *Journal of Strategic Studies* 40 (7): 898–926.

Shires, James. 2020. "Cyber-Noir: Cybersecurity and Popular Culture." *Contemporary Security Policy* 41 (1): 82–107.

Shirk, Susan L. 2007. *China: Fragile Superpower*. Oxford University Press.

Shirk, Susan L. 2022. *Overreach: How China Derailed Its Peaceful Rise*. Oxford University Press.

Shulman, David. 2006. *From Hire to Liar: The Role of Deception in the Workplace*. Cornell University Press.

Sides, John, Chris Tausanovitch, and Lynn Vavreck. 2022. *The Bitter End: The 2020 Presidential Campaign and the Challenge to American Democracy*. Princeton University Press.

Sides, John, Michael Tesler, and Lynn Vavreck. 2018. *Identity Crisis: The 2016 Presidential Campaign and the Battle for the Meaning of America*. Princeton University Press.

Sims, Jennifer E. 2022. *Decision Advantage: Intelligence in International Politics from the Spanish Armada to Cyberwar*. Oxford University Press.

Slayton, Rebecca. 2013. *Arguments That Count: Physics, Computing, and Missile Defense, 1949–2012*. MIT Press.

Slayton, Rebecca. 2017. "What Is the Cyber Offense-Defense Balance? Conceptions, Causes, and Assessment." *International Security* 41 (3): 72–109.

Slayton, Rebecca. 2021. "What Is a Cyber Warrior? The Emergence of U.S. Military Cyber Expertise, 1967–2018." *Texas National Security Review* 4 (1): 61–96.

Slayton, Rebecca, and Brian Clarke. 2020. "Trusting Infrastructure: The Emergence of Computer Security Incident Response, 1989–2005." *Technology and Culture* 61 (1): 173–206.

Slupska, Julia, and Leonie Maria Tanczer. 2021. "Threat Modeling Intimate Partner Violence: Tech Abuse as a Cybersecurity Challenge in the Internet of Things." In *The Emerald International Handbook of Technology-Facilitated Violence and Abuse*, edited by Jane Bailey, Asher Flynn, and Nicola Henry. Emerald Studies in Digital Crime, Technology and Social Harms. Emerald.

Smeets, Max. 2022a. "Cyber Arms Transfer: Meaning, Limits and Implications." *Security Studies* 31 (1): 65–91.

Smeets, Max. 2022b. *No Shortcuts: Why States Struggle to Develop a Military Cyber-Force*. Hurst.

Smith, Brad, and Carol Ann Browne. 2021. *Tools and Weapons: The Promise and the Peril of the Digital Age*. Rev. ed. Penguin.

Smith, Gregory L. 2019. "Secret but Constrained: The Impact of Elite Opposition on Covert Operations." *International Organization* 73 (3): 685–707.

Smith, Michael. 2001. "Bletchley Park, Double Cross and D-Day." In *Action This Day: Bletchley Park from the Breaking of the Enigma Code to the Birth of the Modern Computer*, edited by Michael Smith and Ralph Erskine. Bantam.

Smith, Michael, and Ralph Erskine, eds. 2001. *Action This Day: Bletchley Park from the Breaking of the Enigma Code to the Birth of the Modern Computer*. Bantam.

Soni, Jimmy, and Rob Goodman. 2017. *A Mind at Play: How Claude Shannon Invented the Information Age*. Simon & Schuster.

Sowell, Jesse Horton. 2015. "Finding Order in a Contentious Internet." PhD diss., Engineering Systems Division, Massachusetts Institute of Technology.

Spangher, Alexander, Gireeja Ranade, Besmira Nushi, Adam Fourney, and Eric Horvitz. 2018. "Analysis of Strategy and Spread of Russia-Sponsored Content in the US in 2017." arXiv, October 23. https://doi.org/10.48550/arXiv.1810.10033.

Starbird, Kate, Ahmer Arif, and Tom Wilson. 2019. "Disinformation as Collaborative Work: Surfacing the Participatory Nature of Strategic Information Operations." *Proceedings of the ACM on Human-Computer Interaction* 3 (127): 1–26.

Starrs, Sean. 2013. "American Economic Power Hasn't Declined—It Globalized! Summoning the Data and Taking Globalization Seriously." *International Studies Quarterly* 57 (4): 817–30.

Stein, Janice Gross. 2024. "Bringing Politics Back In: The Neglected Explanation of the Oct. 7 Surprise Attack." *Texas National Security Review* 7 (4): 73–93.

Steinbruner, John. 1974. *The Cybernetic Theory of Decision: New Dimensions of Political Analysis*. Princeton University Press.

Steinfeld, Edward S. 2010. *Playing Our Game: Why China's Economic Rise Doesn't Threaten the West*. Oxford University Press.

Sterelny, Kim. 2004. "Externalism, Epistemic Artefacts and the Extended Mind." In *The Externalist Challenge: New Studies on Cognition and Intentionality*, edited by Richard Schantz. De Gruyter.

Stevens, Clare. 2020. "Assembling Cybersecurity: The Politics and Materiality of Technical Malware Reports and the Case of Stuxnet." *Contemporary Security Policy* 41 (1): 129–52.

Stevens, Tim. 2016. *Cyber Security and the Politics of Time*. Cambridge University Press.

Stevens, Tim, and Joe Devanny. 2024. *Research Handbook on Cyberwarfare*. Edward Elgar.

Stewart, Andrew J. 2021. *A Vulnerable System: The History of Information Security in the Computer Age*. Cornell University Press.

Stigler, George J. 1961. "The Economics of Information." *Journal of Political Economy* 69 (3): 213–25.

Stout, Mark, and Michael Warner. 2018. "Intelligence Is as Intelligence Does." *Intelligence and National Security* 33 (4): 517–26.

Strange, Susan. 1994. *States and Markets*. 2nd ed. Continuum.

Suchman, Lucy A. 2007. *Human-Machine Reconfigurations: Plans and Situated Actions*. 2nd ed. Cambridge University Press.

Sun Tzu. 2002. *The Art of War: The Essential Translation of the Classic Book of Life*. Translated by John Minford. Penguin Books.

Sun Tzu. 2020. *The Art of War*. Translated by Michael Nylan. W. W. Norton.

Talmadge, Caitlin. 2015. *The Dictator's Army: Battlefield Effectiveness in Authoritarian Regimes*. Cornell University Press.

Thirsk, James W. 2001. "Traffic Analysis: A Log-Reader's Tale." In *Action This Day: Bletchley Park from the Breaking of the Enigma Code to the Birth of the Modern Computer*, edited by Michael Smith and Ralph Erskine. Bantam.

Thomas, Timothy L. 2019. *Russian Military Thought: Concepts and Elements*. MITRE Corporation.

Thrall, A. Trevor. 2007. "A Bear in the Woods? Threat Framing and the Marketplace of Values." *Security Studies* 16 (3): 452–88.

Thrall, A. Trevor, and Andrew Armstrong. 2020. "Bear Market? Grizzly Steppe and the American Marketplace of Ideas." In *Information Warfare in the Age of Cyber Conflict*, edited by Christopher Whyte, A. Trevor Thrall, and Brian M. Mazanec. Routledge.

Thucydides. 1996. *The Landmark Thucydides: A Comprehensive Guide to The Peloponnesian War*. Edited by Robert B. Strassler. Translated by Richard Crawley. Free Press.

Thurlow, Richard. 2004. "Soviet Spies and British Counter-Intelligence in the 1930s: Espionage in the Woolwich Arsenal and the Foreign Office Communications Department." *Intelligence and National Security* 19 (4): 610–31.

Tomz, Michael, and Jessica L. P. Weeks. 2020. "Public Opinion and Foreign Electoral Intervention." *American Political Science Review* 114 (3): 856–73.

Torigian, Joseph. 2021. "A New Case for the Study of Individual Events in Political Science." *Global Studies Quarterly* 1 (4). https://doi.org/10.1093/isagsq/ksab035.

Törnberg, Petter. 2022. "How Digital Media Drive Affective Polarization Through Partisan Sorting." *Proceedings of the National Academy of Sciences* 119 (42). https://doi.org/10.1073/pnas.2207159119.

Tsai, Wen-Hsuan. 2016. "How 'Networked Authoritarianism' Was Operationalized in China: Methods and Procedures of Public Opinion Control." *Journal of Contemporary China* 25 (101): 731–44.

Turing, Alan M. 1936. "On Computable Numbers, with an Application to the Entscheidungsproblem." *Proceedings of the London Mathematical Society* s2–42 (1): 230–65.

Turing, Alan M. 1939. *Treatise on the Enigma*. Government Code & Cipher School.

Turing, Alan M. 1950. "I.—Computing Machinery and Intelligence." *Mind* 59 (236): 433–60.

US Senate Select Committee on Intelligence. 2020. *Russian Active Measures Campaigns and Interference in the 2016 U.S. Election.* Vols. 1–5. 116th Congress, Senate. https://www.intelligence.senate.gov/publications/report-select-committee-intelligence-united-states-senate-russian-active-measures.

Vaishnav, Chintan. 2010. "The End of Core: Should Disruptive Innovation in Telecommunication Invoke Discontinuous Regulation?" PhD diss., Engineering Systems Division, Massachusetts Institute of Technology.

Valeriano, Brandon, Benjamin M. Jensen, and Ryan C. Maness. 2018. *Cyber Strategy: The Evolving Character of Power and Coercion.* Oxford University Press.

Valeriano, Brandon, and Ryan C. Maness. 2015. *Cyber War Versus Cyber Realities: Cyber Conflict in the International System.* Oxford University Press.

Vićić, Jelena, and Erik Gartzke. 2024. "Cyber-Enabled Influence Operations as a 'Center of Gravity' in Cyberconflict: The Example of Russian Foreign Interference in the 2016 US Federal Election." *Journal of Peace Research* 61 (1): 10–27.

Vićić, Jelena, and Richard Harknett. 2024. "Identification-Imitation-Amplification: Understanding Divisive Influence Campaigns Through Cyberspace." *Intelligence and National Security* 39 (5): 897–914.

Volpe, Tristan A. 2017. "Atomic Leverage: Compellence with Nuclear Latency." *Security Studies* 26 (3): 517–44.

Voo, Julia, Irfan Hemani, and Daniel Cassidy. 2022. *National Cyber Power Index 2022.* Belfer Center for Science and International Affairs, Harvard Kennedy School. https://www.belfercenter.org/publication/national-cyber-power-index-2022

Vosoughi, Soroush, Deb Roy, and Sinan Aral. 2018. "The Spread of True and False News Online." *Science* 359 (6380): 1146–51.

Waltz, Kenneth N. 1979. *Theory of International Politics.* Addison-Wesley.

Ware, Willis H. 1970. *Security Controls for Computer Systems: Report of Defense Science Board Task Force on Computer Security.* Office of the Director of Defense Research and Engineering. https://www.rand.org/pubs/reports/R609-1.html.

Warner, Michael. 2012a. "Cybersecurity: A Pre-History." *Intelligence and National Security* 27 (5): 781–99.

Warner, Michael. 2012b. "Fragile and Provocative: Notes on Secrecy and Intelligence." *Intelligence and National Security* 27 (2): 223–40.

Warner, Michael. 2014. *The Rise and Fall of Intelligence: An International Security History.* Georgetown University Press.

Warner, Michael. 2019. "A Matter of Trust: Covert Action Reconsidered." *Studies in Intelligence* 63 (4): 33–41.

Weedon, Jen, William Nuland, and Alex Stamos. 2017. *Information Operations and Facebook.* Facebook.

Wendt, Alexander. 1999. *Social Theory of International Politics.* Cambridge University Press.

Whaley, Barton. 1982. "Toward a General Theory of Deception." *Journal of Strategic Studies* 5 (1): 178–92.

White, Sarah P. 2019. "Subcultural Influence on Military Innovation: The Development of U.S. Military Cyber Doctrine." PhD diss., Harvard University. https://dash.harvard.edu/handle/1/42013038.

White House. 2011. *International Strategy for Cyberspace: Prosperity, Security, and Openness in a Networked World*. Executive Office of the President of the United States.

Whyte, Christopher. 2024. *Subversion 2.0: Leaderlessness, the Internet, and the Fringes of Global Society*. Oxford University Press.

Whyte, Christopher, A. Trevor Thrall, and Brian M. Mazanec, eds. 2020. *Information Warfare in the Age of Cyber Conflict*. Routledge.

Wiener, Craig. 2016. "Penetrate, Exploit, Disrupt, Destroy: The Rise of Computer Network Operations as a Major Military Innovation." PhD diss., George Mason University.

Wiener, Norbert. 1948. *Cybernetics, or Control and Communication in the Animal and in the Machine*. Wiley.

Wight, Colin, Lene Hansen, Tim Dunne, Patrick Thaddeus Jackson, and Daniel H. Nexon. 2013. "International Theory in a Post-Paradigmatic Era: From Substantive Wagers to Scientific Ontologies." *European Journal of International Relations* 19 (3): 543–65.

Wilde, Gavin. 2024a. "From Panic to Policy: The Limits of Foreign Propaganda and the Foundations of an Effective Response." *Texas National Security Review* 7 (2): 42–55.

Wilde, Gavin. 2024b. *Russia's Countervalue Cyber Approach: Utility or Futility?* Carnegie Endowment for International Peace. https://carnegieendowment.org/2024/02/05/russia-s-countervalue-cyber-approach-utility-or-futility-pub-91534.

Wilke, Christiane. 2017. "Seeing and Unmaking Civilians in Afghanistan: Visual Technologies and Contested Professional Visions." *Science, Technology, & Human Values* 42 (6): 1031–60.

Winner, Langdon. 1977. *Autonomous Technology: Technics-Out-of-Control as a Theme in Political Thought*. MIT Press.

Woods, Daniel W., and Josephine Wolff. 2025. "A History of Cyber Risk Transfer." *Journal of Cybersecurity* 11 (1). https://doi.org/10.1093/cybsec/tyae028.

Work, J. D., and Richard J. Harknett. 2020. *Troubled Vision: Understanding Recent Israeli-Iranian Offensive Cyber Exchanges*. Atlantic Council. https://www.atlanticcouncil.org/in-depth-research-reports/issue-brief/troubled-vision-understanding-israeli-iranian-offensive-cyber-exchanges/.

Wuthnow, Joel, and M. Taylor Fravel. 2023. "China's Military Strategy for a 'New Era': Some Change, More Continuity, and Tantalizing Hints." *Journal of Strategic Studies* 46 (6–7): 1149–84.

Wylie, J. C. 1989. *Military Strategy: A General Theory of Power Control*. Edited by John B. Hattendorf. Naval Institute Press.

Wylie, Shaun. 2001. "Breaking Tunny and the Birth of Colossus." In *Action This Day: Bletchley Park from the Breaking of the Enigma Code to the Birth of the Modern Computer*, edited by Michael Smith and Ralph Erskine. Bantam.

Yannakogeorgos, Panayotis A., and Eneken Tikk. 2016. "Stuxnet as Cyber-Enabled Sanctions Enforcement." Eighth International Conference on Cyber Conflict, October 2016. https://doi.org/10.1109/CYCONUS.2016.7836630.

Yarhi-Milo, Keren. 2013. "Tying Hands Behind Closed Doors: The Logic and Practice of Secret Reassurance." *Security Studies* 22 (3): 405–35.

Yarhi-Milo, Keren. 2014. *Knowing the Adversary: Leaders, Intelligence, and Assessment of Intentions in International Relations.* Princeton University Press.

Yates, JoAnne. 1989. *Control Through Communication: The Rise of System in American Management.* Johns Hopkins University Press.

Yost, Jeffrey R. 2015. "Computer Security." *IEEE Annals of the History of Computing* 37 (2): 6–7.

Yost, Jeffrey R. 2016. "Computer Security, Part 2." *IEEE Annals of the History of Computing* 38 (4): 10–11.

Zaagman, Elliot. 2018. "Cyber Sovereignty and the PRC's Vision for Global Internet Governance." *China Brief* 18 (10). https://jamestown.org/program/cyber-sovereignty-and-the-prcs-vision-for-global-internet-governance/.

Zannettou, Savvas, Michael Sirivianos, Jeremy Blackburn, and Nicolas Kourtellis. 2019. "The Web of False Information: Rumors, Fake News, Hoaxes, Clickbait, and Various Other Shenanigans." *Journal of Data and Information Quality* 11 (3): 1–37.

Zegart, Amy B. 2000. *Flawed by Design: The Evolution of the CIA, JCS, and NSC.* Stanford University Press.

Zeng, Jinghan, Tim Stevens, and Yaru Chen. 2017. "China's Solution to Global Cyber Governance: Unpacking the Domestic Discourse of 'Internet Sovereignty.'" *Politics & Policy* 45 (3): 432–64.

Zetter, Kim. 2014. *Countdown to Zero Day: Stuxnet and the Launch of the World's First Digital Weapon.* Crown.

Zhang, Ketian. 2019. "Cautious Bully: Reputation, Resolve, and Beijing's Use of Coercion in the South China Sea." *International Security* 44 (1): 117–59.

Zuboff, Shoshana. 2019. *The Age of Surveillance Capitalism: The Fight for a Human Future at the New Frontier of Power.* PublicAffairs.

Index

Figures and tables are indicated by "f" and "t" following page numbers.

state, 230–31; theft of intellectual property from, 184; US and freedom of speech, 162

clandestine organizations, 4–5; capacity and, 59–60, 65, 225, 226*t*, 240n33; China's development of, 188–96; discretion and, 59, 61, 65, 94, 225, 226*t*, 227, 240n33; improving cybersecurity based on conditions for, 225–28, 226*t*; increasing complexity of, 66, 216; intelligence performance requiring, 7–8, 25, 50, 53, 59–62, 182, 211, 225; sophistication and capability levels, 10, 59–60, 60*t*

Clapper, James, 194

Clark, David, 84, 86

Clausewitz, Carl von, 15, 53–54, 60

Clinton, Hillary R., 155, 157, 164, 175. *See also* presidential election and Russian disinformation

CNAs (computer network attacks), 41

CNE (computer network exploitation), 40

CNITSEC (China Information Technology Security Evaluation Center), 193

Coats, Dan, 171

Cobalt Strike (penetration testing tool), 6, 8

codebreaking. *See* Bletchley Park; cryptanalysis

COIS (Community Online Intelligence Service), 83, 84

Cold War: access barriers in, 57; CIA's role, 28, 38; resilient communications in, 90; subversion in, 13, 159

Colonial Pipeline (2021), 213*t*, 217

combined-arms warfare doctrine, 60

Comey, James, 175

COMINT (communications intelligence), 39

command-and-control servers/systems. *See* C2; C4ISR

Commerce Department, US, 1, 87

Commission on the Theft of American Intellectual Property (US), 195

comparison of case studies, 125, 128, 159–60, 180–81, 210–17, 212–14*t*. *See also* Bletchley Park; China; presidential election and Russian disinformation; Stuxnet

competition, 34–35; agreed competition, 152; cyberspace, 27; economic, 14, 33, 195; intelligence collaborators as competitors, 142; intelligence contests, 64–67, 90, 98, 189, 193, 200, 215, 224, 225, 228, 230; secret statecraft seeking competitive gain, 4, 34–35, 208; strategic, 14–15; war as competition between societies, 36

Conficker internet worm, 136, 137*t*, 227

connectivity: authoritarian regimes and, 18; benefits of, 207; Bletchley Park and,

101–2, 108–9, 111, 116–18; common interests of China and US in, 224; complexity of cyberspace and, 93–94; defined, 101; geographical, 108–9; improving cybersecurity based on, 225–28, 226*t*; limiting, 85, 110; presidential election (US, 2016) and Russian access, 159, 166–67; public, 103; Stuxnet and, 133, 139, 146; subversion and, 159; vulnerable institutions and, 55–57, 63–65, 94, 111, 116, 166, 225, 240n33. *See also* access barriers; airgaps

conspiracy theorists, 177

contingency of advantage, 15–16, 50, 81, 222

corporate networks, 9, 17, 37, 60, 80–81, 88, 91–92, 98, 123, 138–39, 184, 228

Cortada, James, 80

counterintelligence, 8–10, 16–17, 44–45; acting below threshold of armed conflict, 28; Bletchley Park and, 100; case studies, 70; Chinese internal use of, 201–5; cybersecurity and, 17, 86–88; defined, 44; Germany in WWII, 107, 110–11, 212*t*; Hezbollah and, 210; intelligence contests and, 65; intelligence performance and, 47, 53; malware and, 41, 45, 140, 150; Microsoft and, 88; outcomes of, 63, 64; rise of global industry in, 88–89, 230; as secret statecraft, 32*f*, 38, 39*t*; Ukraine and, 220

counterterrorism, 89, 229

covert action, 11–12; Bletchley Park and, 100; intelligence performance and, 47; Israeli assassination of Iranian nuclear scientists, 131, 144, 151; outcomes of, 63; political developments affecting, 49; Stuxnet and, 126, 129, 131, 150–52; US and Chinese facade of promises not to engage in, 193–95; US-China capabilities and, 223; in US-Iranian ongoing relations, 151. *See also* sabotage; subversion

CrowdStrike, 6, 9, 66–67, 162–64, 214*t*, 217, 241n57

cryptanalysis, 104–8, 112, 245n21. *See also* Bletchley Park

cryptography, 102–4, 102*f*, 245n21. *See also* encryption

Cunningham, Fionna, 198

cybercrime, 2, 23, 27, 62, 66, 86, 208, 217, 221

cybernetics, 79–80, 98, 209

cyber persistence theory, 28, 29, 238n5

cyber power: Chinese case study, 14–15, 19, 72, 180–207; defined, 182; innovation and, 195–96, 209; institutional context's importance in shaping, 206–7, 222; linking all other forms of power, 205; military power and cyber capabilities, 181–82, 196–201. *See also* China

www.ingramcontent.com/pod-product-compliance
Lightning Source LLC
Chambersburg PA
CBHW020826270326
41928CB00006B/452